A-Z BRAD

C000228688

CONTENTS

REFERENCE

Motorway	M606
A Road	A647
B Road	B6147
Dual Carriageway	
One-way Street — Traffic flow on A Roads is indicated by a heavy line on the driver's left.	➡
Large Scale Pages only	⇒
Restricted Access	
Pedestrianized Road	
Track / Footpath	
Residential Walkway	
Cycleway (selected)	
Railway	Station Heritage Sta. Level Crossing Tunnel
Built-up Area	DRAKE ST
Local Authority Boundary	—··—··—
Posttown Boundary	
Postcode Boundary within Posttown	— — —

Map Continuation	42 Large Scale Centres 4
Car Park (selected)	P
Church or Chapel	†
Fire Station	■
Hospital	H
House Numbers (A & B Roads only)	13 8
Information Centre	i
National Grid Reference	431
Police Station	▲
Post Office	★
Toilet: without facilities for the Disabled	▽
with facilities for the Disabled	▽
for exclusive use by the Disabled	▽
Educational Establishment	
Hospital or Hospice	
Industrial Building	
Leisure or Recreational Facility	
Place of Interest	
Public Building	
Shopping Centre or Market	
Other Selected Buildings	

SCALE

Map Pages 6-61   1:15,840

0 ... ¼ ... ½ Mile
0 ... 250 ... 500 ... 750 Metres
4 inches (10.16cm) to 1 mile   6.31cm to 1km

Map Pages 4-5 & 62   1:7,920

0 ... ⅛ ... ¼ Mile
0 ... 100 ... 200 ... 300 ... 400 Metres
8 inches (20.32cm) to 1 mile   12.63cm to 1km

Copyright of Geographers' A-Z Map Company Ltd.

Head Office:
Fairfield Road, Borough Green, Sevenoaks, Kent TN15 8PP
Telephone: 01732 781000
www.a-zmaps.co.uk

Copyright © Geographers' A-Z Map Co. Ltd.   Edition 2 2004

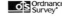 Ordnance Survey® This product includes mapping data licensed from Ordnance Survey® with the permission of the Controller of Her Majesty's Stationery Office.

© Crown Copyright 2004. Licence number 100017302

2 KEY TO MAP PAGES

Laneshaw Bridge

Water Sheddles Reservoir

Ponden Reservoir

Widdop Reservoir

Gorple Reservoirs

Walshaw Dean Reservoirs

Hebden Water

Hebden Bridge

Todmorden

Withens Clough Reservoir

Walsden

Warland Reservoir

SCALE

| 0 | 1 | 2 Miles |
| 0 | 1 | 2 | 3 Kilometres |

Beechcliffe
Stockbridge

Riddlesden

6 Braithwaite

7 Thwaites

8

KEIGHLEY

Ingrow

Oakworth

10 **11**

12 **13**

14
Harden

Stanbury

Lees

Haworth

Cullingworth

Wilsden

20 **21**
Oxenhope

22 **23**

24

Denholme

Denholme Clough

Thornton

30 **31** **32**

Denholme Gate

LARGE SCALE **62** HALIFAX TOWN CENTRE

Pecket Well

38

39
Mixenden

40
Ambler Thorn

Wainstalls

Illingworth

Booth

Midgley

Ovenden

46 **47** **48**

Mytholmroyd

Luddenden

HALIFAX

SOWERBY BRIDGE

Savile Park

54 **55**

56

Sowerby

Norland Town

Ripponden

Barkisland

Greetland

60
Holywell Green

Stainland

23

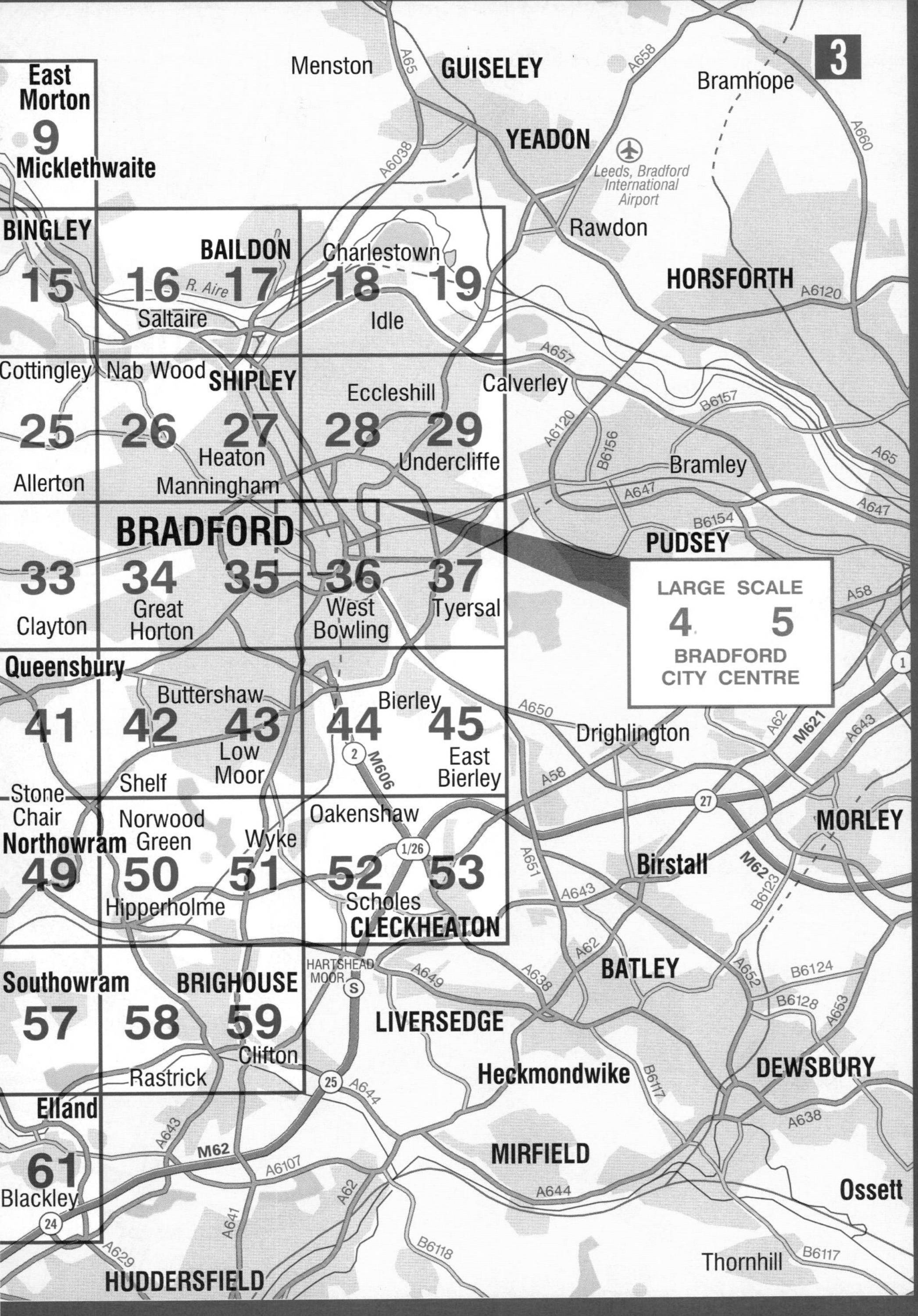

East Morton
9
Micklethwaite
Menston
GUISELEY
YEADON
Bramhope
Leeds, Bradford International Airport
Rawdon
BINGLEY
15
BAILDON
16
17
R. Aire
Saltaire
Charlestown
18
19
Idle
HORSFORTH
Cottingley
Nab Wood
SHIPLEY
Eccleshill
Calverley
25
26
27
28
29
Heaton
Undercliffe
Allerton
Manningham
Bramley
BRADFORD
PUDSEY
33
34
35
36
37
Clayton
Great Horton
West Bowling
Tyersal
LARGE SCALE
4
5
BRADFORD CITY CENTRE
Queensbury
Buttershaw
41
42
43
44
45
Bierley
Low Moor
Shelf
East Bierley
Drighlington
Stone Chair
Northowram
Norwood Green
Wyke
Oakenshaw
49
50
51
52
53
Hipperholme
Scholes
CLECKHEATON
MORLEY
Birstall
BATLEY
Southowram
BRIGHOUSE
HARTSHEAD MOOR
57
58
59
Clifton
Rastrick
LIVERSEDGE
Heckmondwike
DEWSBURY
Elland
61
Blackley
MIRFIELD
Ossett
Thornhill
HUDDERSFIELD
A65
A658
A660
A6038
A6120
A657
B6157
B6156
A647
B6154
A58
A650
A62
M621
A643
M606
M62
A651
B6123
A638
A649
A652
B6124
B6128
A653
B6117
A644
A6107
A641
A629
B6118
1
2
1/26
24
25
27
S

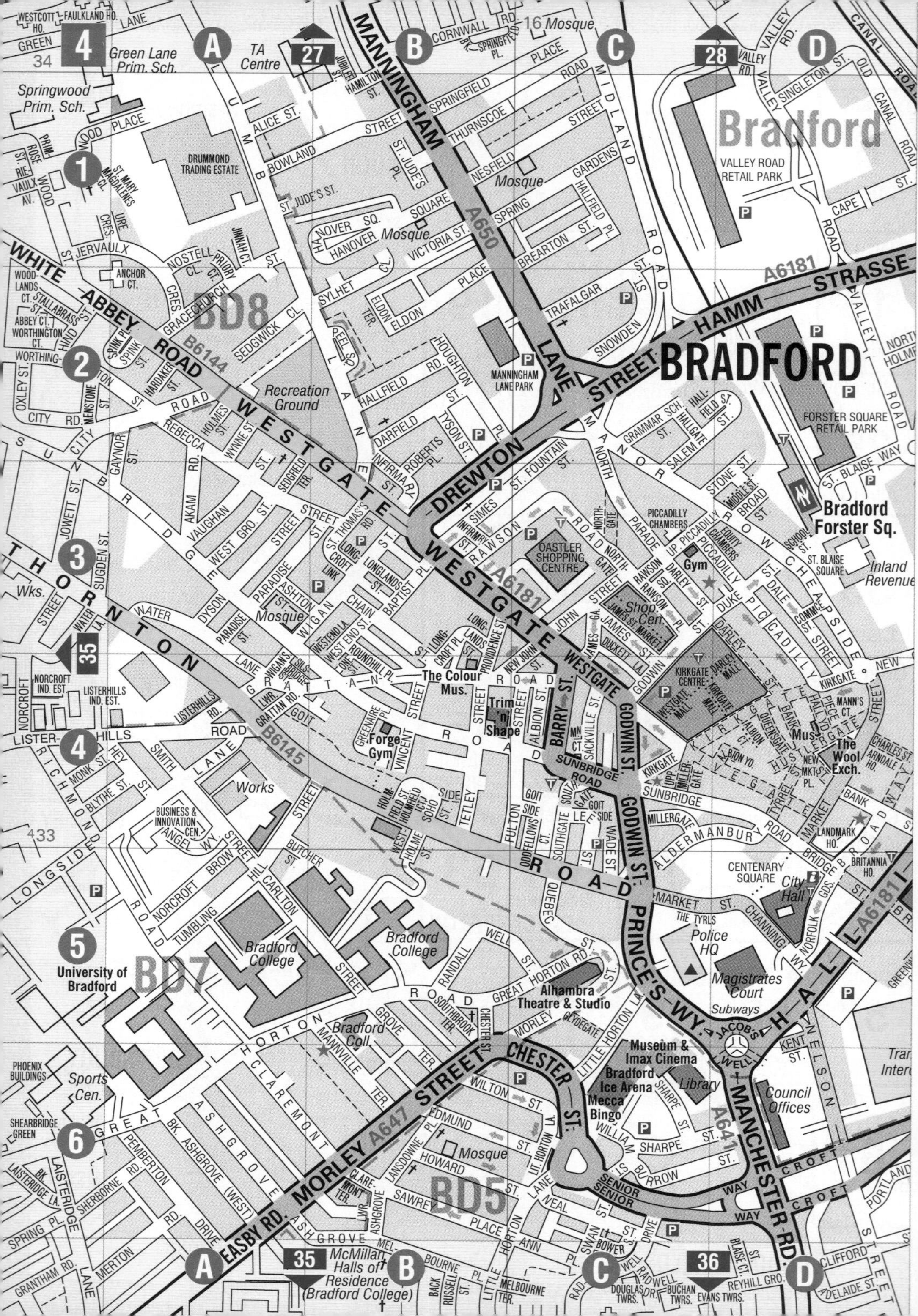
4
27
28
35
36
Bradford
BRADFORD
BD8
BD7
BD5
MANNINGHAM LANE
WESTGATE
DREWTON STREET
HAMM STRASSE
WHITE ABBEY ROAD
THORNTON ROAD
SUNBRIDGE ROAD
GREAT HORTON RD.
MORLEY STREET
PRINCE'S WY.
MANCHESTER RD.
GODWIN ST.
CHESTER ST.
DRUMMOND TRADING ESTATE
VALLEY ROAD RETAIL PARK
FORSTER SQUARE RETAIL PARK
Bradford Forster Sq.
OASTLER SHOPPING CENTRE
KIRKGATE CENTRE
Recreation Ground
MANNINGHAM LANE PARK
University of Bradford
Bradford College
Alhambra Theatre & Studio
Museum & Imax Cinema
Bradford Ice Arena
Mecca Bingo
Library
Council Offices
Police HQ
Magistrates Court
City Hall
CENTENARY SQUARE
The Wool Exch.
The Colour Mus.
Inland Revenue
Green Lane Prim. Sch.
Springwood Prim. Sch.
TA Centre
Sports Cen.
McMillan Halls of Residence (Bradford College)

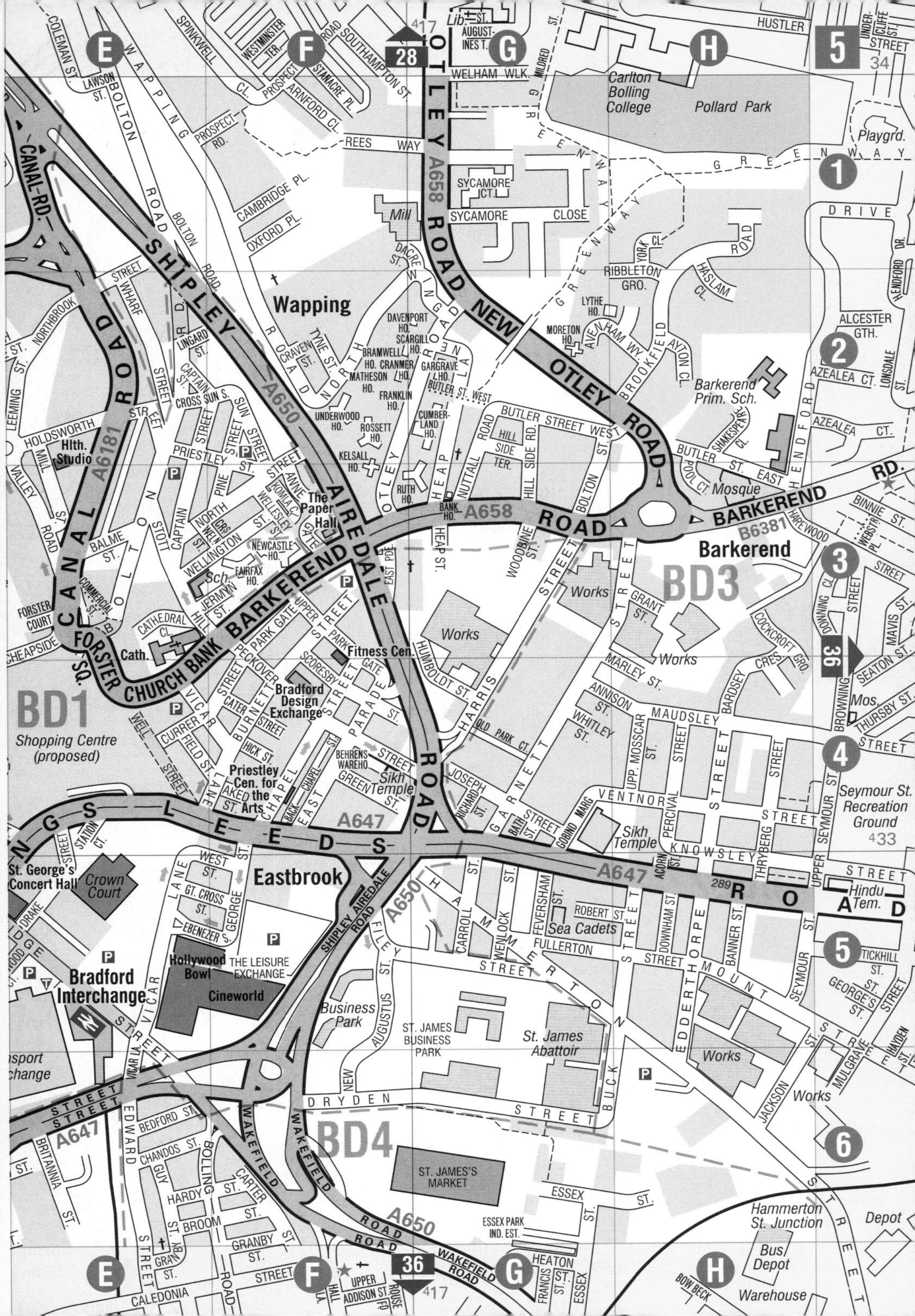

5
E
F
G
H
28
417
34
Carlton Bolling College
Pollard Park
Playgrd.
GREENWAY
1
OTLEY ROAD
A658
REES WAY
SYCAMORE CT.
SYCAMORE CLOSE
Mill
Wapping
CANAL RD.
SHIPLEY
A650
CANAL ROAD
A6181
NEW OTLEY ROAD
Barkerend Prim. Sch.
2
AZEALEA CT.
ALCESTER GTH.
HENDFORD DR.
LONSDALE ST.
BUTLER STREET WEST
BUTLER ST. EAST
Mosque
BARKEREND RD.
B6381
Barkerend
3
BD3
ROAD
AIREDALE
The Paper Hall
BARKEREND
CHURCH BANK
Cath.
Hlth. Studio
Fitness Cen.
Bradford Design Exchange
Works
36
BD1
Shopping Centre (proposed)
Priestley Cen. for the Arts
Sikh Temple
4
Seymour St. Recreation Ground
433
LEEDS
A647
ROAD
Hindu Tem.
St. George's Concert Hall
Crown Court
Eastbrook
Hollywood Bowl
THE LEISURE EXCHANGE
Cineworld
Bradford Interchange
Sea Cadets
5
Business Park
ST. JAMES BUSINESS PARK
St. James Abattoir
Works
6
BD4
ST. JAMES'S MARKET
DRYDEN STREET
WAKEFIELD ROAD
A650
ESSEX PARK IND. EST.
Hammerton St. Junction
Depot
Bus Depot
Warehouse
36
417
E
F
G
H

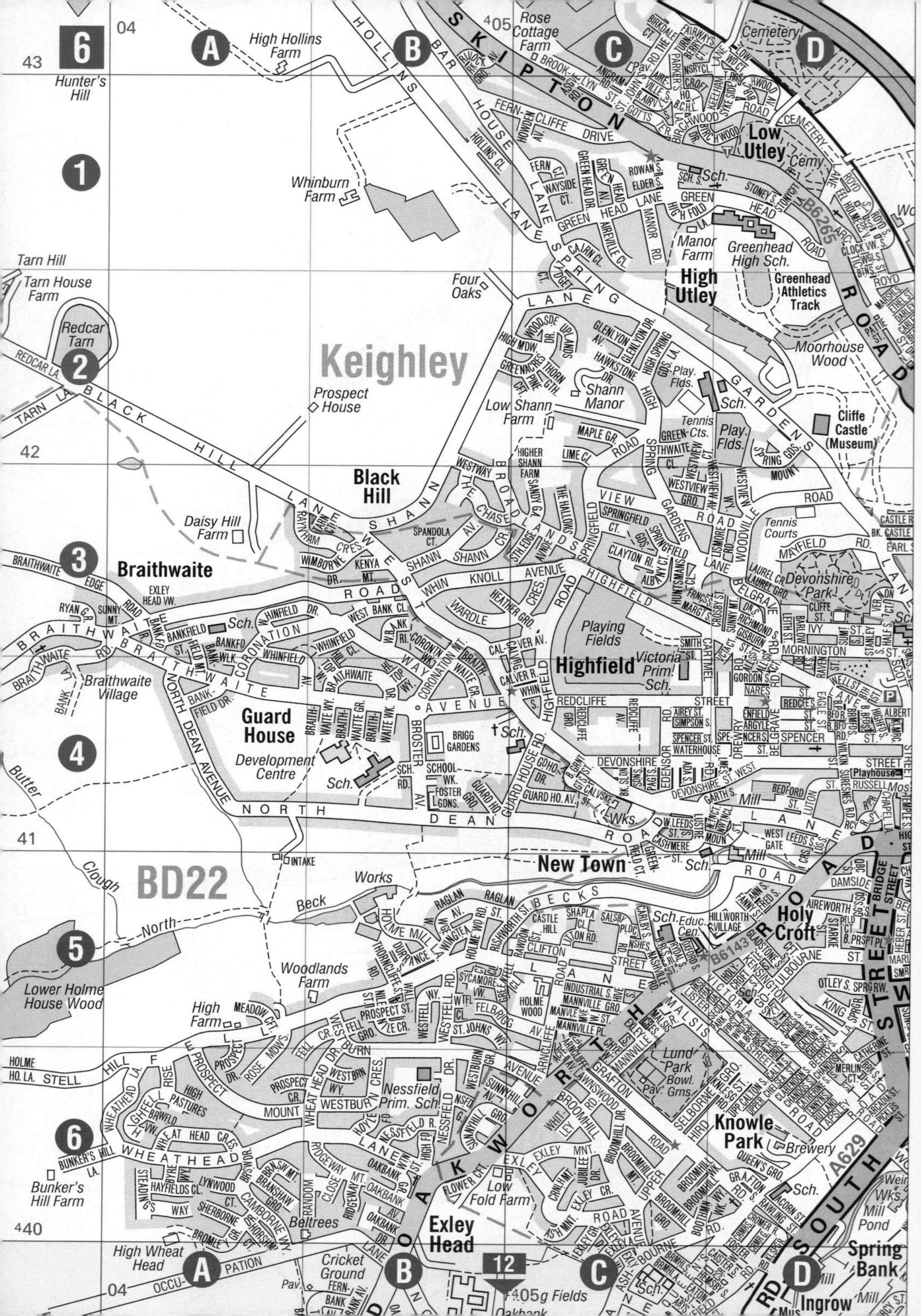
04
A
B
C
D
405
43
42
41
440
1
2
3
4
5
6
12
Keighley
BD22
Hunter's Hill
High Hollins Farm
Rose Cottage Farm
Cemetery
Whinburn Farm
Low Utley
High Utley
Manor Farm
Greenhead High Sch.
Greenhead Athletics Track
Tarn Hill
Tarn House Farm
Redcar Tarn
Four Oaks
Prospect House
Moorhouse Wood
Shann Manor
Low Shann Farm
Cliffe Castle (Museum)
Black Hill
Daisy Hill Farm
Braithwaite
Braithwaite Village
Guard House
Development Centre
Highfield
Playing Fields
Victoria Prim. Sch.
Devonshire Park
Tennis Courts
Playhouse
New Town
Works
Beck
North Beck
Clough
Butter
Woodlands Farm
Lower Holme House Wood
High Farm
Holy Croft
Lund Park Bowl. Grns.
Knowle Park
Brewery
Nessfield Prim. Sch.
Low Fold Farm
Exley Head
Beltrees
Bunker's Hill Farm
High Wheat Head
Cricket Ground
Spring Bank
Ingrow
Mill Pond
SKIPTON ROAD
SKIPTON ROAD
HOLLINS LANE
BAR HOUSE LANE
FERNCLIFFE DRIVE
GREEN HEAD LANE
SPRING GARDENS LANE
BLACK HILL LANE
SHANN LANE
WEST LANE
WHIN KNOLL AVENUE
HIGHFIELD LANE
BRAITHWAITE ROAD
CORONATION WAY
NORTH DEAN AVENUE
NORTH DEAN ROAD
BECKS ROAD
DEVONSHIRE STREET
SPENCER STREET
MORNINGTON ST.
MAYFIELD RD.
OAKWORTH ROAD
HOLME MILL LANE
STELL HILL
WHEATHEAD LANE
PROSPECT MOUNT
NESSFIELD DR.
EXLEY ROAD
SOUTH STREET
A629
B6143
B6265

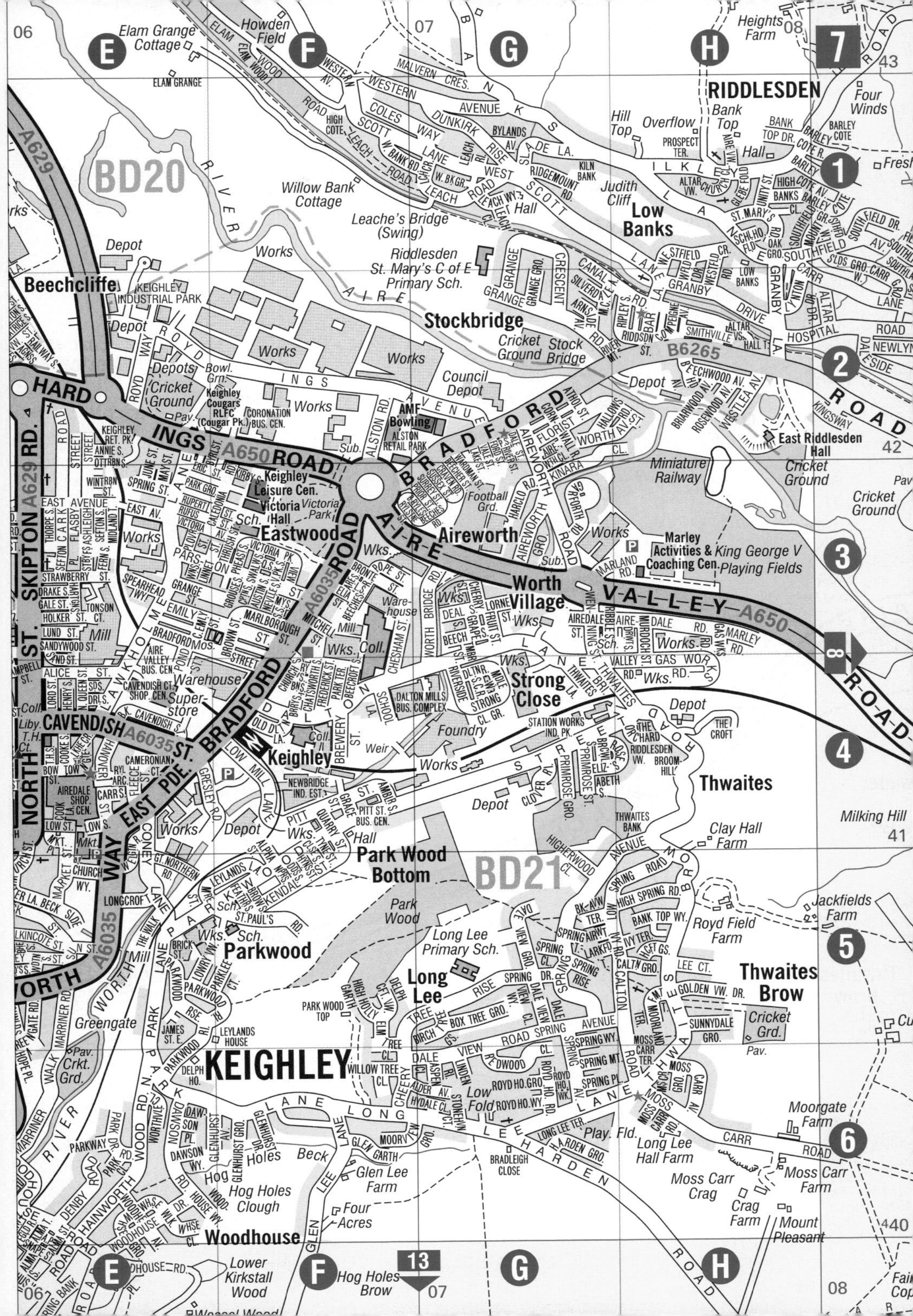
RIDDLESDEN
Low Banks
Stockbridge
Aireworth
Eastwood
Worth Village
Strong Close
Thwaites
Keighley
Park Wood Bottom
Parkwood
Long Lee
Thwaites Brow
KEIGHLEY
Woodhouse
Beechcliffe
BD20
BD21
A629
A650
A6035
B6265
HARD INGS ROAD
BRADFORD ROAD
AIRE VALLEY ROAD
SKIPTON RD.
NORTH ST.
CAVENDISH ST.
EAST PDE.
WORTH WAY
ILKLEY ROAD
HOSPITAL ROAD
WESTERN AV.
SCOTT LANE
LEACH ROAD
HOLLINS LANE
PARK LANE
LONG LEE LANE
HARDEN ROAD
CARR ROAD
MOSS CARR RD.
DALTON LANE
STATION WORKS IND. PK.
DALTON MILLS BUS. COMPLEX
NEWBRIDGE IND. EST.
KEIGHLEY INDUSTRIAL PARK
AIREDALE SHOP. CEN.
Keighley Leisure Cen.
Victoria Hall
Keighley Cougars RLFC (Cougar Pk.)
AMF Bowling
ALSTON RETAIL PARK
Marley Activities & Coaching Cen.
King George V Playing Fields
Miniature Railway
East Riddlesden Hall
Riddlesden St. Mary's C of E Primary Sch.
Long Lee Primary Sch.
Leache's Bridge (Swing)
Willow Bank Cottage
Elam Grange Cottage
Howden Field
Heights Farm
Four Winds
Milking Hill
Clay Hall Farm
Jackfields Farm
Royd Field Farm
Moorgate Farm
Moss Carr Farm
Moss Carr Crag
Long Lee Hall Farm
Crag Farm
Mount Pleasant
Glen Lee Farm
Four Acres
Hog Holes Clough
Lower Kirkstall Wood
Hog Holes Brow
Park Wood
Greengate
Cricket Ground
Football Grd.
Depot
Works
13

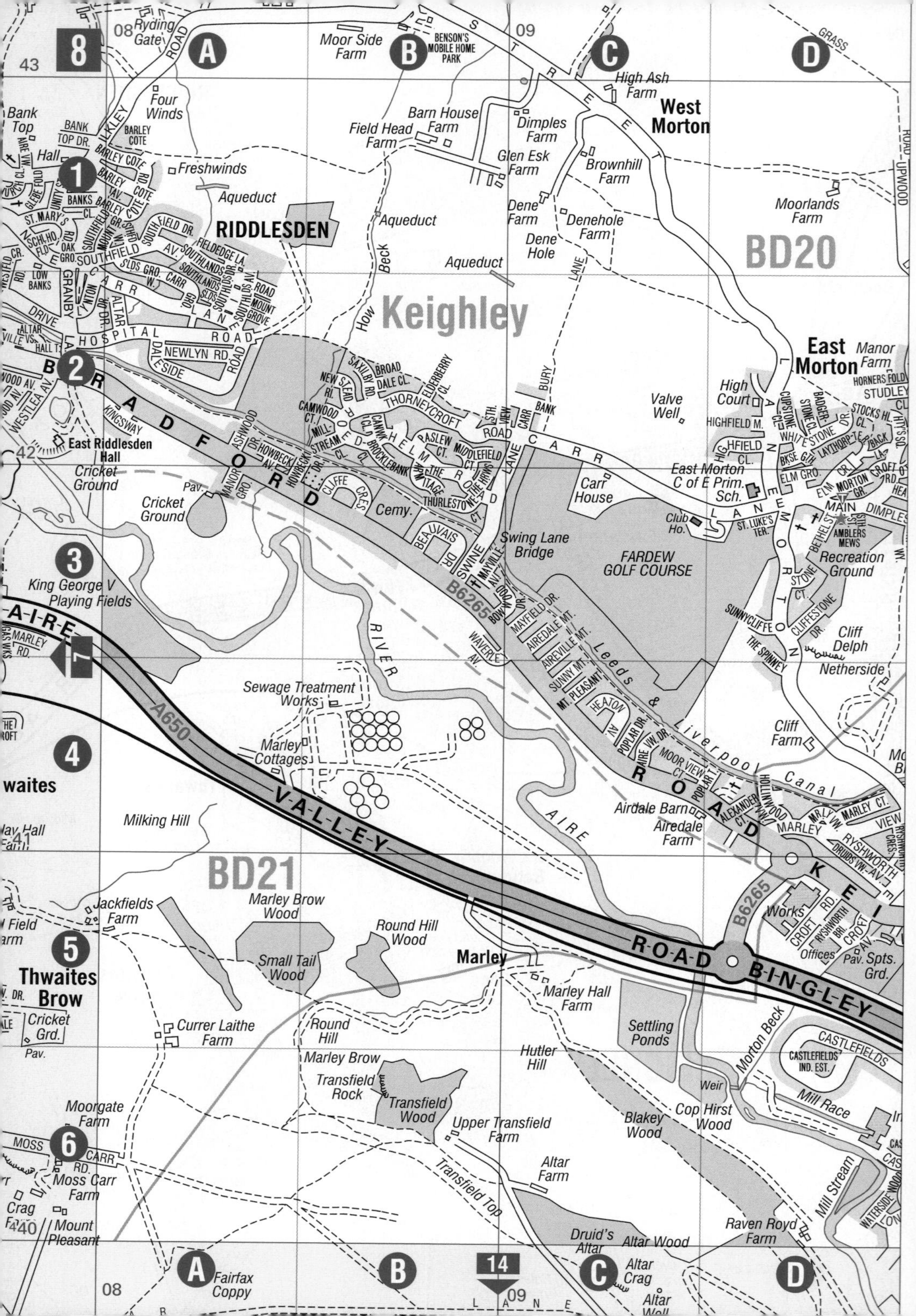

Ryding Gate
Moor Side Farm
BENSON'S MOBILE HOME PARK
High Ash Farm
West Morton
Four Winds
Bank Top
Barn House Farm
Field Head Farm
Dimples Farm
Glen Esk Farm
Brownhill Farm
Freshwinds
Aqueduct
Dene Farm
Denehole Farm
Dene Hole
Moorlands Farm
RIDDLESDEN
BD20
Keighley
How Beck
East Morton
Manor Farm
High Court
Valve Well
East Riddlesden Hall
Cricket Ground
Carr House
East Morton C of E Prim. Sch.
Club Ho.
Cemy.
Swing Lane Bridge
FARDEW GOLF COURSE
Recreation Ground
King George V Playing Fields
Cliff Delph
Netherside
Leeds & Liverpool Canal
Sewage Treatment Works
Cliff Farm
Marley Cottages
Milking Hill
Airdale Barn
Airedale Farm
BD21
Jackfields Farm
Marley Brow Wood
Round Hill Wood
Small Tail Wood
Marley
Marley Hall Farm
Thwaites Brow
Cricket Grd.
Currer Laithe Farm
Round Hill
Settling Ponds
Works
Offices
Spts. Grd.
CASTLEFIELDS IND. EST.
Marley Brow
Hutler Hill
Transfield Rock
Transfield Wood
Weir
Cop Hirst Wood
Blakey Wood
Mill Race
Moorgate Farm
Upper Transfield Farm
Moss Carr Farm
Altar Farm
Transfield Top
Mill Stream
Crag Farm
Mount Pleasant
Druid's Altar
Altar Wood
Raven Royd Farm
Altar Crag
Fairfax Coppy
Altar Well
BRADFORD ROAD
AIRE VALLEY ROAD
A650
B6265
BINGLEY ROAD
KEIGHLEY ROAD
RIVER AIRE
Morton Beck
HOSPITAL ROAD
CARR LANE
MORTON LANE
STREET LANE
14
7

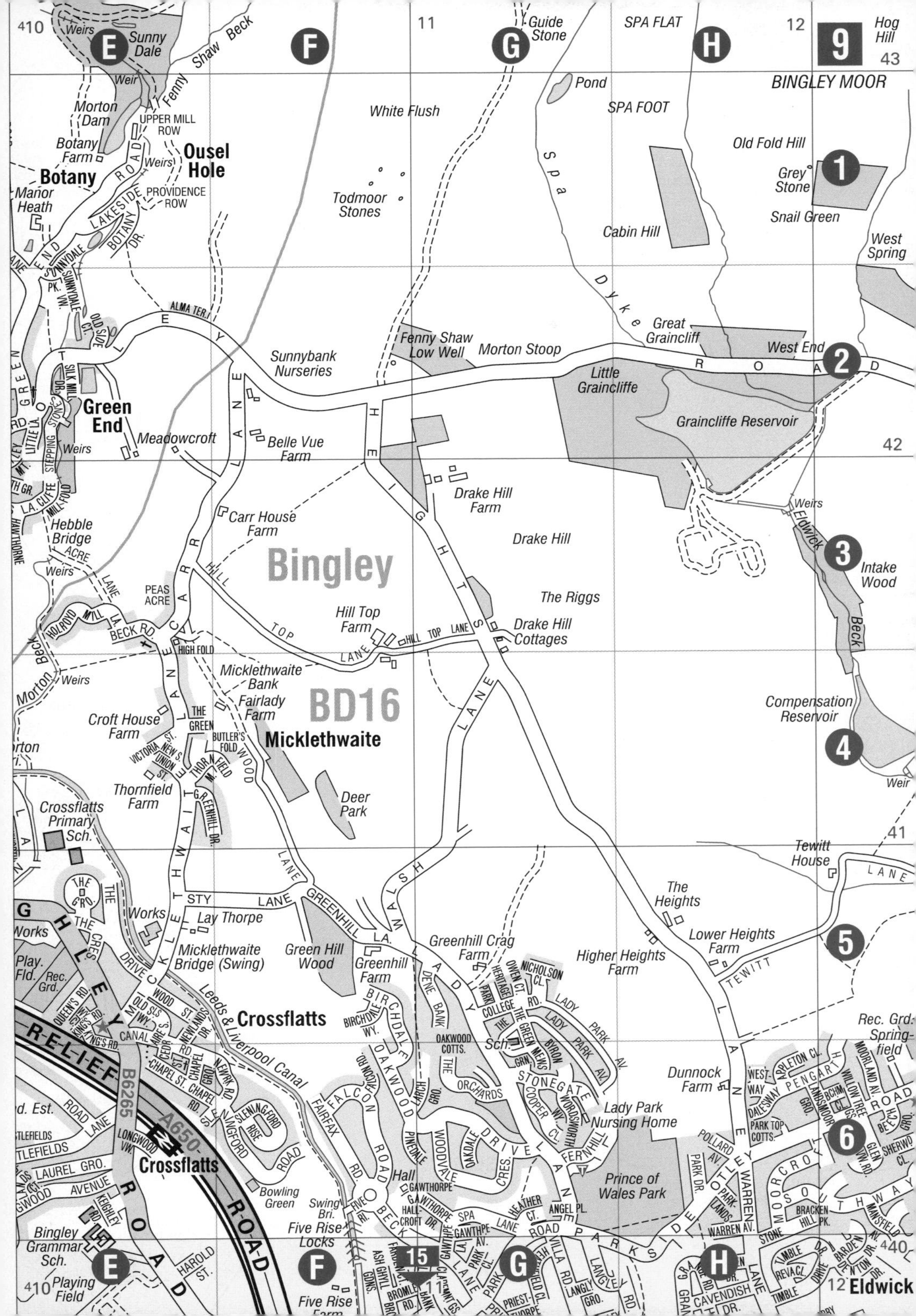
Bingley
BD16
Botany
Ousel Hole
Green End
Micklethwaite
Crossflatts
Eldwick
BINGLEY MOOR
Graincliffe Reservoir
Compensation Reservoir
Prince of Wales Park
Leeds & Liverpool Canal
Five Rise Locks
Morton Dam
Sunny Dale
Todmoor Stones
White Flush
Drake Hill
The Riggs
Deer Park
Green Hill Wood
Intake Wood
Crossflatts Primary Sch.
Bingley Grammar Sch.
Lady Park Nursing Home
RELIEF ROAD
A650
B6265
15

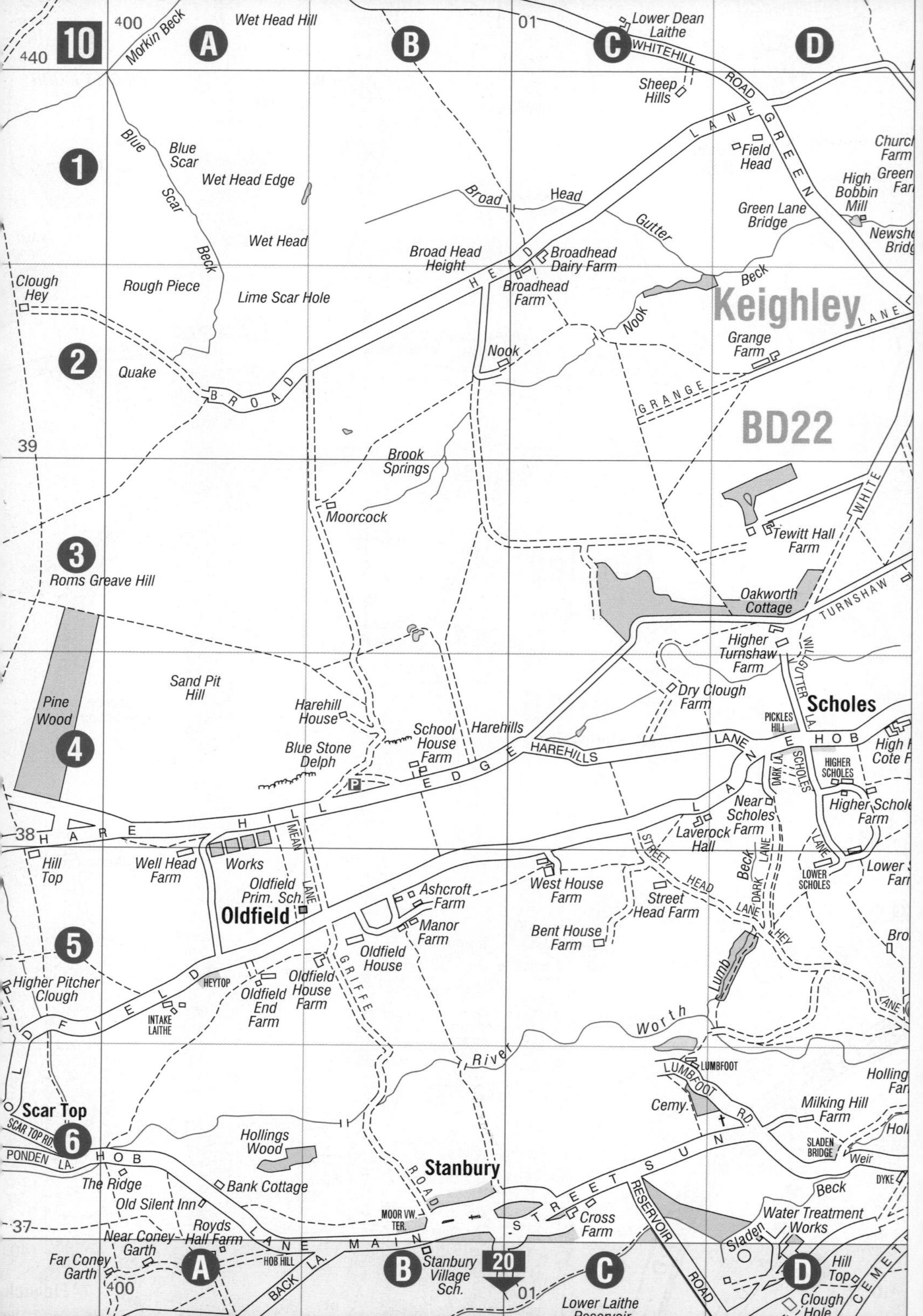

Wet Head Hill
Morkin Beck
Lower Dean Laithe
Whitehill Road
Sheep Hills
Green Lane
Field Head
Church Farm
Blue Scar
Blue Scar Beck
Wet Head Edge
Broad Head
Gutter
Green Lane Bridge
High Bobbin Mill
Wet Head
Broad Head Height
Broadhead Dairy Farm
Broadhead Farm
Beck
Clough Hey
Rough Piece
Lime Scar Hole
Keighley
Nook
Grange Farm
Quake
Broad Head Lane
Grange
BD22
Brook Springs
Moorcock
Tewitt Hall Farm
White Lane
Roms Greave Hill
Oakworth Cottage
Turnshaw
Higher Turnshaw Farm
Sand Pit Hill
Pine Wood
Harehill House
Blue Stone Delph
School House Farm
Harehills
Dry Clough Farm
Will Gutter La.
Scholes
Pickles Hill
Harehills Lane
Hob Lane
Higher Scholes
Scholes La.
Dark La.
Hare Hill Edge
Near Scholes Farm
Laverock Hall
Higher Scholes Farm
Hill Top
Well Head Farm
Works
Mean Lane
Oldfield Prim. Sch.
Oldfield
Street Head Lane
West House Farm
Street Head Farm
Ashcroft Farm
Manor Farm
Bent House Farm
Lower Scholes
Dark Lane
Hey Lane
Lumb Beck
Oldfield House
Oldfield Lane
Higher Pitcher Clough
Heytop
Oldfield End Farm
Oldfield House Farm
Griffe
Intake Laithe
River Worth
Lumbfoot
Lumbfoot Rd.
Cemy.
Scar Top
Scar Top Rd.
Milking Hill Farm
Ponden La.
Hob Hill
Hollings Wood
Sladen Bridge
Weir
Stanbury
Road
The Ridge
Bank Cottage
Sun Street
Reservoir Road
Beck
Dyke
Old Silent Inn
Moor Vw. Ter.
Water Treatment Works
Royds Hall Farm
Near Coney Garth
Main Lane
Cross Farm
Sladen
Far Coney Garth
Back La.
Stanbury Village Sch.
Hill Top
Clough Hole
Lower Laithe Reservoir
Cemetery
20
400
440
39
38
37
01

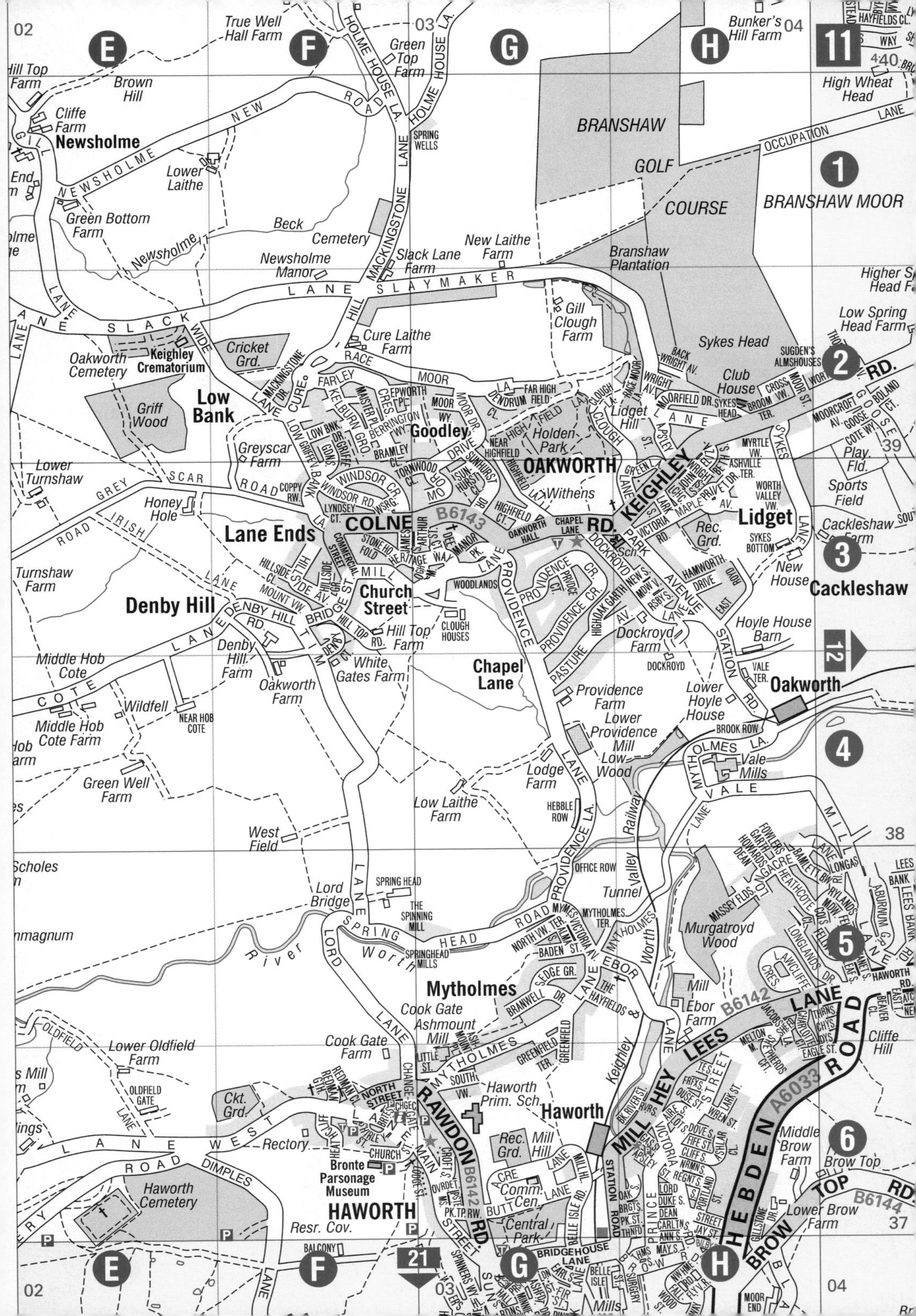

11
02
03
04
E
F
G
H
1
2
3
4
5
6
12
21
37
38
39
40
True Well Hall Farm
Bunker's Hill Farm
Green Top Farm
High Wheat Head
Hill Top Farm
Brown Hill
Cliffe Farm
Newsholme
BRANSHAW
GOLF
COURSE
OCCUPATION LANE
BRANSHAW MOOR
Lower Laithe
Green Bottom Farm
Beck
Cemetery
Newsholme Manor
Slack Lane Farm
New Laithe Farm
Branshaw Plantation
Higher Spring Head Farm
Low Spring Head Farm
SLAYMAKER LANE
SLACK LANE
Gill Clough Farm
Sykes Head
Cure Laithe Farm
Keighley Crematorium
Cricket Grd.
Oakworth Cemetery
Club House
Low Bank
Griff Wood
Goodley
OAKWORTH
Holden Park
Lidget Hill
Lidget
Greyscar Farm
Lower Turnshaw
GREY SCAR ROAD
Honey Hole
Play Fld.
Sports Field
COLNE RD.
KEIGHLEY RD.
B6143
Lane Ends
Cackleshaw Farm
Rec. Grd.
Withens
Church Street
Denby Hill
Turnshaw Farm
New House
Cackleshaw
Hill Top Farm
Denby Hill Farm
Chapel Lane
Dockroyd Farm
Hoyle House Barn
Middle Hob Cote
White Gates Farm
Oakworth Farm
Providence Farm
Lower Hoyle House
Oakworth
Wildfell
Middle Hob Cote Farm
Lower Providence Mill
Low Wood
Vale Mills
Green Well Farm
Lodge Farm
Low Laithe Farm
West Field
Railway
Scholes
Lord Bridge
Tunnel
Valley
Murgatroyd Wood
River Worth
SPRING HEAD ROAD
Mytholmes
Mill Ebor Farm
Cook Gate Ashmount Mill
Lower Oldfield Farm
Cook Gate Farm
Cliffe Hill
Haworth Prim. Sch.
Haworth
Ckt. Grd.
Rec. Grd.
Mill Hill
Rectory
Bronte Parsonage Museum
Haworth Cemetery
Comm. Cen.
Central Park
HAWORTH
Resr. Cov.
Middle Brow Farm
Brow Top
Lower Brow Farm
B6142
A6033
B6144
HEBDEN ROAD
MILL HEY
LEES LANE
RAWDON RD.
WEST LANE
BROW TOP RD.

Bunker's Hill Farm
A
B
C
D
Exley Head
6
Low Fold
High Wheat Head
Beltrees
Cricket Ground
Playing Fields
Oakbank School
Spring Bank
Ingrow West
Mill Pond
Mus.
OCCUPATION
1
BRANSHAW MOOR
Ingrow
Bogthorn
Higher Spring Head Farm
Low Spring Head Farm
Bracken Bank
Greystones Farm
Sykes Head
2
Club House
KEIGHLEY ROAD
B6143
Hainworth Wood
Cricket Grd.
Red Holt
Lodge
Hainworth
Almshouses
Weir Sluices
Worth Valley Prim. Sch.
Damems
Hermit Hole
Hill Top
Play. Fld.
Sports Field
Lidget
3
Cackleshaw
Cackleshaw Farm
Harewood Hill
Harewood Hill Farm
BD22
A629
Whins Wood Park
Hainworth Farm
Hoyle House Barn
11
Railway
Valley
Keighley and Worth
Oakworth
Ashgrove Farm
Keighley
4
Vale Mills
Lower Pierce Close Farm
Upper Pierce Close Farm
HALIFAX ROAD
Reservoir
Lees Moor
Crag View Farm
Quarry House
Lees Moor Farm
Myrtle Farm
Lees
Bocking
Cross Roads Pk.
LEES
Highfield House
5
HAWORTH RD.
Barcroft
B6142
LEES LANE
Cliffe Hill
Cross Roads
Green Head Farm
Sugden Reservoir
A6033
Cliffe View
Cliffe House
Ellar
Saw Mills
Wicking Crag
Staples Brow
6
Brow Top Farm
Sugden Wood
HEBDEN BROW
TOP ROAD B6144
Sugden Brow
Springfield Farm
Lower Brow Farm
Stump Cross
Stump Cross Farm
Cullingworth Fields
22
Field Head
Bank Bottom Laithe

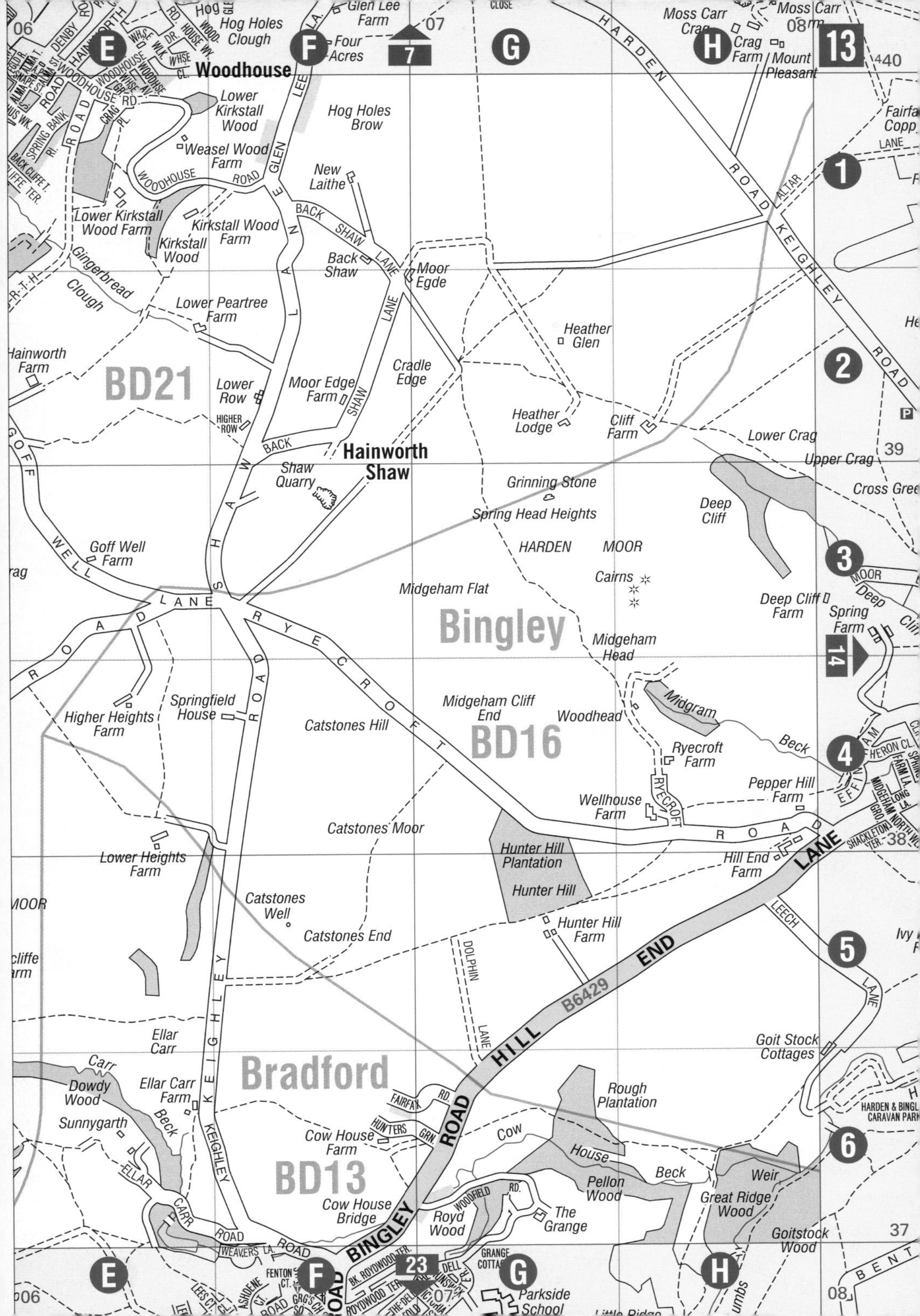
Woodhouse
Hog Holes Clough
Glen Lee Farm
Four Acres
7
Moss Carr Crag
Moss Carr
Crag Farm
Mount Pleasant
Lower Kirkstall Wood
Weasel Wood Farm
Hog Holes Brow
New Laithe
Lower Kirkstall Wood Farm
Kirkstall Wood Farm
Kirkstall Wood
Back Shaw
Moor Egde
Gingerbread Clough
Lower Peartree Farm
Heather Glen
Hainworth Farm
BD21
Lower Row
Higher Row
Moor Edge Farm
Cradle Edge
Heather Lodge
Cliff Farm
Lower Crag
Upper Crag
Hainworth Shaw
Shaw Quarry
Grinning Stone
Spring Head Heights
Deep Cliff
Cross Gree
Harden Moor
Goff Well Farm
Cairns
Midgeham Flat
Deep Cliff Farm
Spring Farm
Bingley
Midgeham Head
14
Springfield House
Higher Heights Farm
Midgeham Cliff End
Woodhead
Midgram Beck
Catstones Hill
BD16
Ryecroft Farm
Pepper Hill Farm
Wellhouse Farm
Catstones Moor
Hunter Hill Plantation
Hunter Hill
Hill End Farm
Lower Heights Farm
Catstones Well
Catstones End
Hunter Hill Farm
B6429
Ellar Carr
Goit Stock Cottages
Carr
Dowdy Wood
Ellar Carr Farm
Bradford
Rough Plantation
Sunnygarth
Cow House Farm
Cow House Beck
Pellon Wood
Weir
Great Ridge Wood
BD13
Cow House Bridge
Royd Wood
The Grange
Goitstock Wood
Harden & Bingley Caravan Park
23
Parkside School
Harden Road
Altar Lane
Keighley Road
Back Shaw Lane
Glen Lee Lane
Woodhouse Road
Goff Well Lane
Ryecroft Road
Keighley Road
Hill End Lane
Leech Lane
Dolphin Lane
Bingley Road
Ellar Carr Road
Weavers La.
Fairfax Rd.
Hunters Grn.
Woodfield Rd.
Heron Cl.
Shackleton Ter.
Midgeham Gro.
Lees Ct.
Ashdene Ct.
Fenton Ct.
Bk. Roydwood Ter.
Roydwood Ter.
Dell
Grange Cotts.

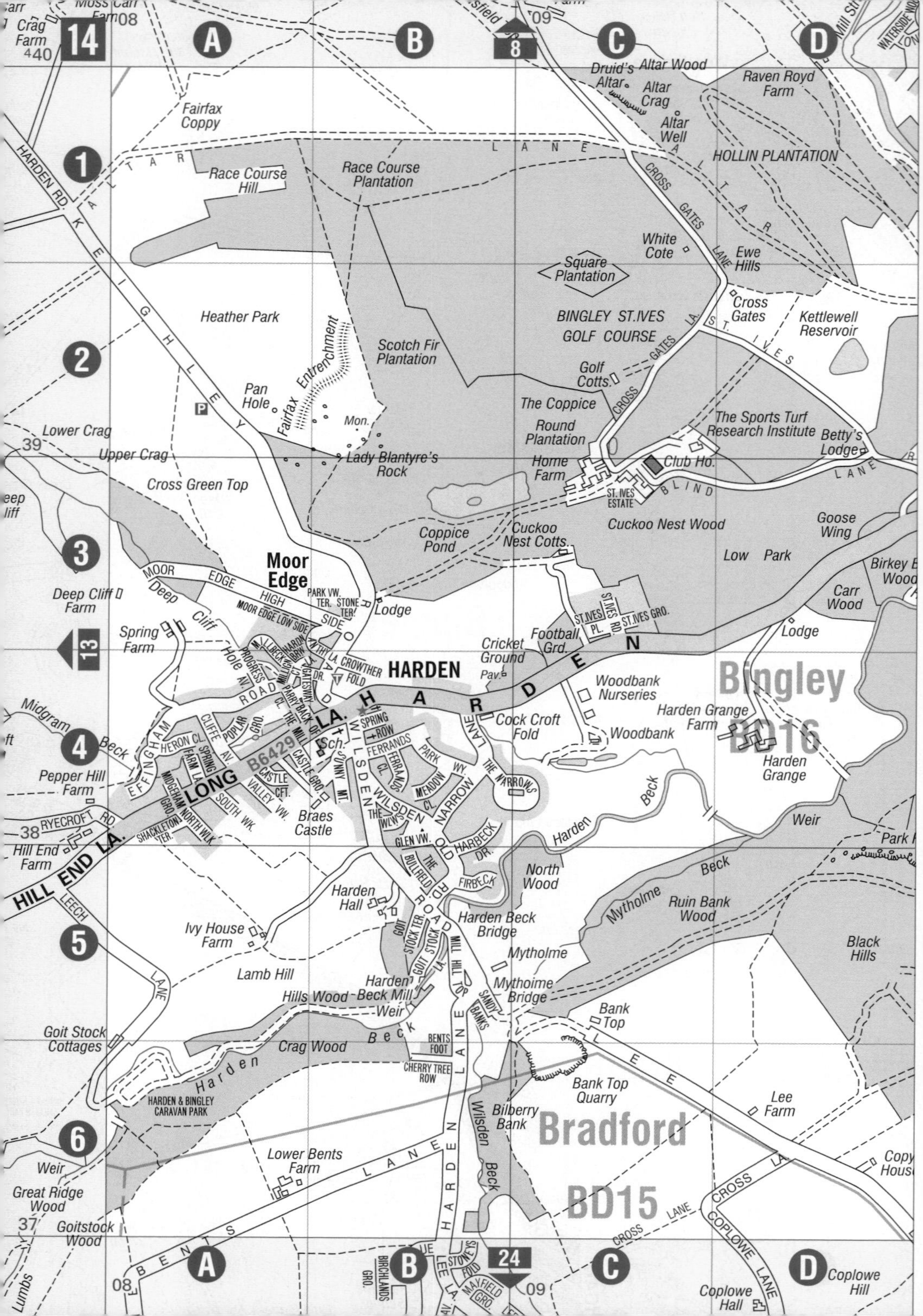

14
A
B
C
D
8
13
24
1
2
3
4
5
6
Crag Farm
Moss Carr Farm
Fairfax Coppy
Race Course Hill
Race Course Plantation
Druid's Altar
Altar Wood
Altar Crag
Altar Well
Raven Royd Farm
HOLLIN PLANTATION
ALTAR LANE
HARDEN RD
KEIGHLEY ROAD
CROSS GATES LANE
White Cote
Ewe Hills
Square Plantation
Heather Park
Fairfax Entrenchment
Scotch Fir Plantation
BINGLEY ST.IVES GOLF COURSE
Cross Gates
Kettlewell Reservoir
ST. IVES
Golf Cotts.
Pan Hole
Mon.
The Coppice
Round Plantation
The Sports Turf Research Institute
Betty's Lodge
Lower Crag
Upper Crag
Lady Blantyre's Rock
Home Farm
Club Ho.
ST. IVES ESTATE
BLIND LANE
Cross Green Top
Deep Cliff
Coppice Pond
Cuckoo Nest Cotts.
Cuckoo Nest Wood
Goose Wing
Low Park
Moor Edge
MOOR EDGE HIGH SIDE
MOOR EDGE LOW SIDE
PARK VW. TER.
STONE TER.
Lodge
Deep Cliff Farm
Carr Wood
Birkey Bank Wood
ST.IVES PL.
ST.IVES RD.
ST.IVES GRO.
Spring Farm
Deep Cliff Hole
Cricket Ground
Football Grd.
Pav.
HARDEN
HARDEN LA.
Bingley
BD16
CROWTHER FOLD
PROGRESS AV.
ROAD
Woodbank Nurseries
Harden Grange Farm
Midgram Beck
EFFINGHAM
HERON CL.
CLIFFE AV.
POPLAR
SPRING FARM LA.
LONG LA.
B6429
SPRING ROW
FERRANDS
PARK WY.
Cock Croft Fold
Woodbank
Harden Grange
Pepper Hill Farm
MIDGEHAM GRO.
SOUTH WK.
NORTH WLK.
CASTLE CFT.
VALLEY VW.
SUNNY MT.
WILSDEN RD.
MEADOW CL.
NARROW LANE
THE NARROWS
Harden Beck
Weir
Park
RYECROFT RD
SHACKLETONS TER.
Braes Castle
THE WLWS
GLEN VW.
HARBECK DR.
Hill End Farm
HILL END LA.
LEECH LANE
THE BULLFIELD
FIRBECK
North Wood
Mytholme Beck
Ruin Bank Wood
Harden Hall
Harden Beck Bridge
Mytholme
Ivy House Farm
GOIT STOCK TER.
GOIT STOCK LA.
MILL HILL TOP
Black Hills
Lamb Hill
Harden Beck Mill
Hills Wood
Weir
Mytholme Bridge
SANDY BANKS
Bank Top
Goit Stock Cottages
Crag Wood
BENTS FOOT
CHERRY TREE ROW
LEE LANE
HARDEN & BINGLEY CARAVAN PARK
Bank Top Quarry
Lee Farm
Bilberry Bank
Bradford
Wilsden Beck
Weir
Lower Bents Farm
BENTS LANE
HARDEN LANE
BD15
CROSS LANE
COPLOWE LANE
Copy House
Great Ridge Wood
Goitstock Wood
Lumbs
BIRCHLANDS GRO.
STONEYS FOLD
MAYFIELD GRO.
Coplowe Hall
Coplowe Hill
08
09
440
39
38
37

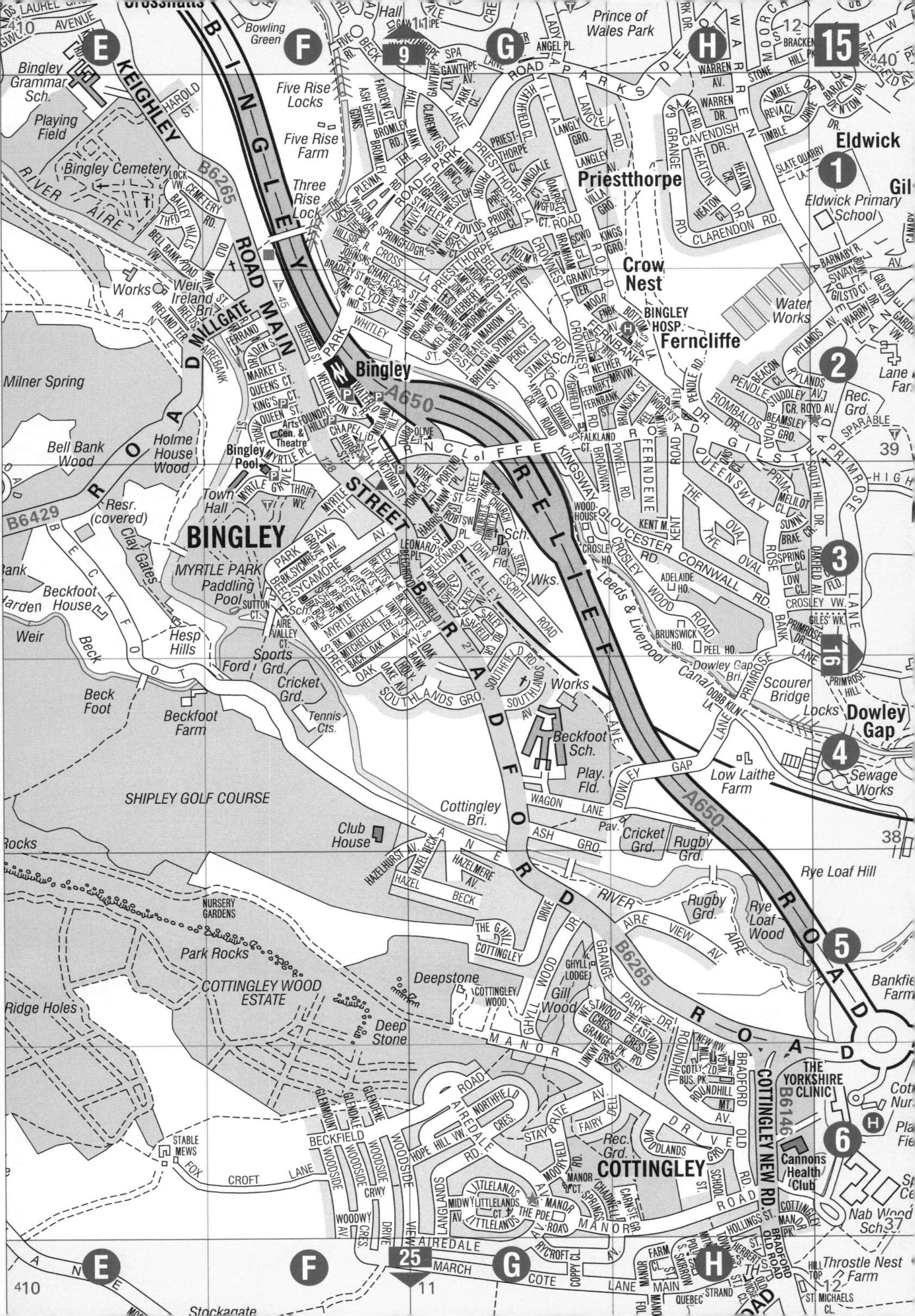
15
BINGLEY
Bingley
Priestthorpe
Crow Nest
Ferncliffe
Eldwick
Dowley Gap
COTTINGLEY
SHIPLEY GOLF COURSE
COTTINGLEY WOOD ESTATE
Prince of Wales Park
Bingley Cemetery
Five Rise Locks
Three Rise Lock
Bingley Grammar Sch.
Bingley Pool
Town Hall
MYRTLE PARK Paddling Pool
Beckfoot Sch.
Low Laithe Farm
Sewage Works
Rye Loaf Hill
THE YORKSHIRE CLINIC
Cannons Health Club
Deepstone
Park Rocks
Ridge Holes
Milner Spring
Bell Bank Wood
Holme House Wood
Beckfoot House
Beckfoot Farm
Beck Foot
Hesp Hills
Cottingley Bri.
Gill Wood
Rye Loaf Wood
Scourer Bridge Locks
Leeds & Liverpool Canal
BINGLEY HOSP.
Eldwick Primary School
Water Works
Throstle Nest Farm
A650
B6265
B6429
B6146
9
16
25
410
440
11
12
37
38
39
E
F
G
H
1
2
3
4
5
6

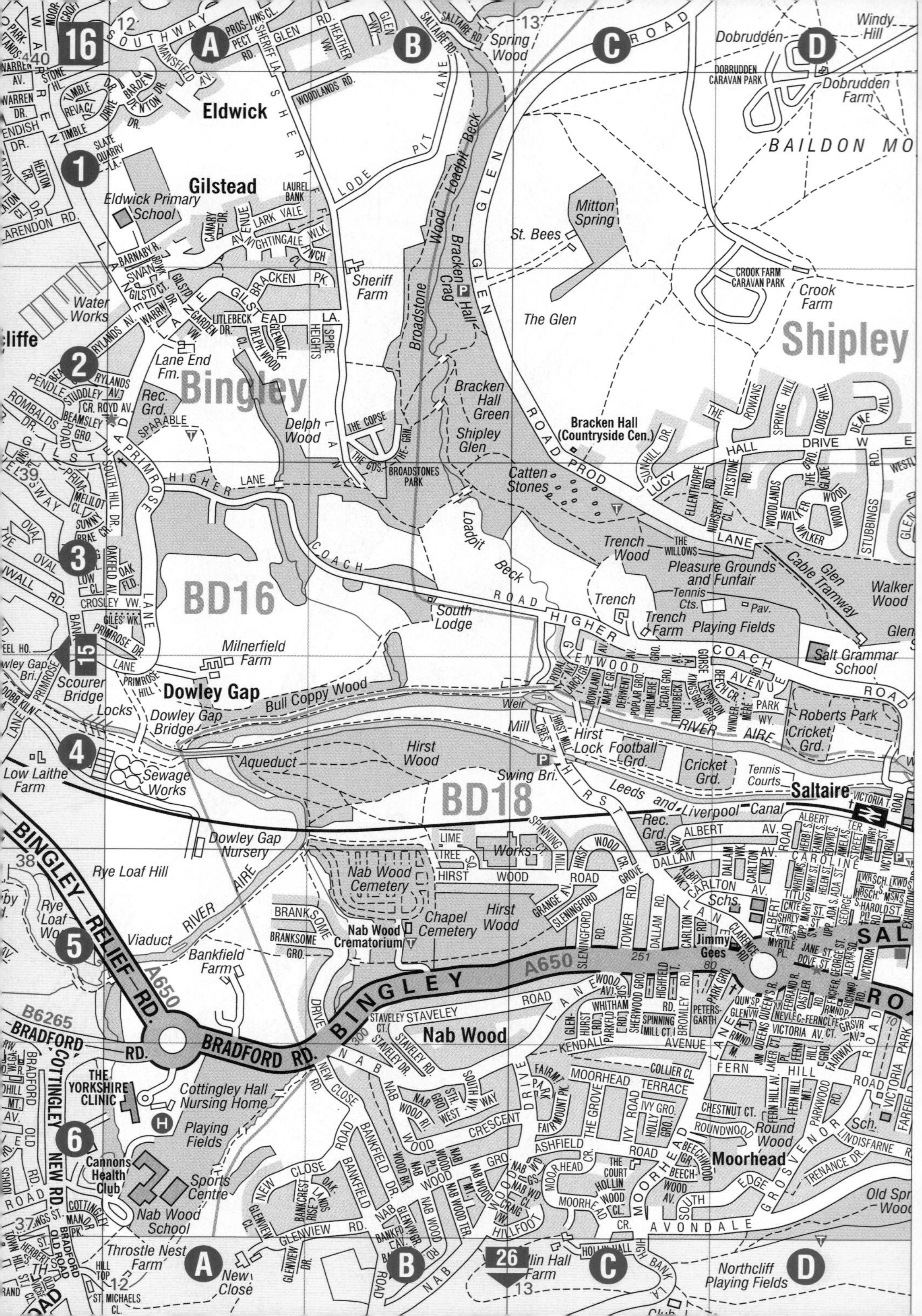

Eldwick
Gilstead
Eldwick Primary School
Water Works
Bingley
Lane End Fm.
Rec. Grd.
Delph Wood
Sheriff Farm
Broadstone Wood
Loadpit Beck
Bracken Hall Crag
Bracken Hall Green
Shipley Glen
The Glen
Mitton Spring
St. Bees
Spring Wood
Dobrudden
Windy Hill
Dobrudden Caravan Park
Dobrudden Farm
BAILDON MO
Crook Farm Caravan Park
Crook Farm
Shipley
Bracken Hall (Countryside Cen.)
Catten Stones
Trench Wood
Pleasure Grounds and Funfair
Glen Cable Tramway
Walker Wood
Trench
Trench Farm
Playing Fields
Salt Grammar School
Roberts Park
Cricket Grd.
BD16
South Lodge
Milnerfield Farm
Dowley Gap
Bull Coppy Wood
Scourer Bridge
Locks
Dowley Gap Bridge
Weir
Mill
Hirst Lock
Football Grd.
Cricket Grd.
Tennis Courts
Low Laithe Farm
Sewage Works
Aqueduct
Hirst Wood
Swing Bri.
BD18
Saltaire
Leeds and Liverpool Canal
Rec. Grd.
Dowley Gap Nursery
Rye Loaf Hill
River Aire
Works
Nab Wood Cemetery
Chapel Cemetery
Hirst Wood
Nab Wood Crematorium
Viaduct
Bankfield Farm
Bingley Relief Rd.
A650
B6265
Bradford Rd.
Nab Wood
Jimmy Gees
The Yorkshire Clinic
Cottingley Hall Nursing Home
Playing Fields
Cannons Health Club
Sports Centre
Nab Wood School
Throstle Nest Farm
New Close
Moorhead
Round Wood
Old Spring Wood
Northcliff Playing Fields
Hollin Hall Farm

15
26

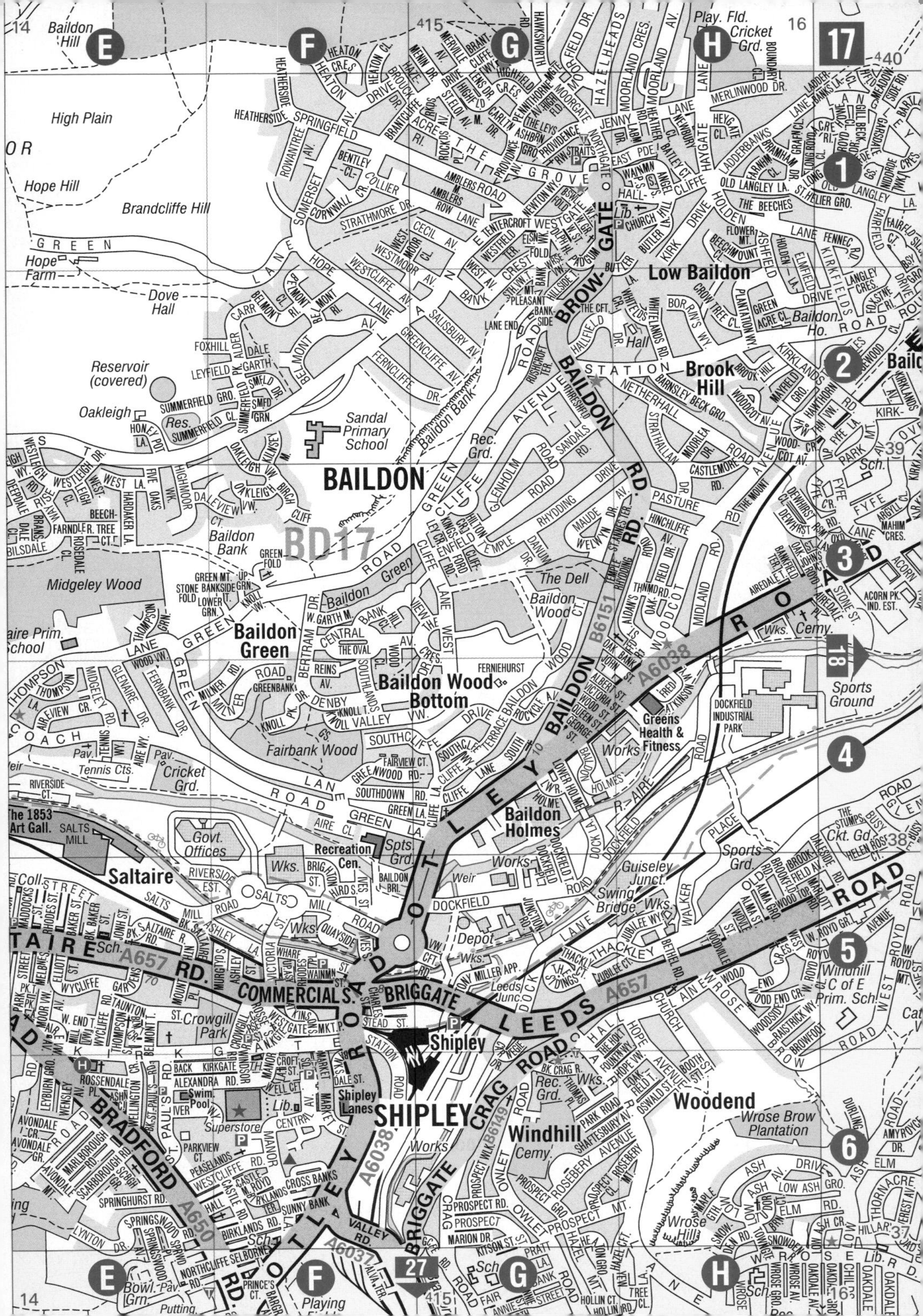
17
14
415
16
440
E
F
G
H
1
2
3
4
5
6
Baildon Hill
High Plain
Hope Hill
Brandcliffe Hill
Hope Farm
Dove Hall
Reservoir (covered)
Oakleigh
Res.
Sandal Primary School
BAILDON
BD17
Baildon Bank
Midgeley Wood
Baildon Green
Rec. Grd.
Low Baildon
Brook Hill
Hall
The Dell
Baildon Wood
Baildon Wood Bottom
Ferniehurst
Fairbank Wood
Tennis Cts.
Cricket Grd.
Pav.
The 1853 Art Gall.
Salts Mill
Govt. Offices
Recreation Cen.
Spts. Grd.
Saltaire
Wks.
Baildon Holmes
Works
Greens Health & Fitness
Dockfield Industrial Park
Sports Ground
Sports Grd.
Guiseley Junct.
Swing Bridge
Weir
Depot
Leeds Junc.
Crowgill Park
Shipley
SHIPLEY
Shipley Lanes
Swim. Pool
Superstore
Lib.
Windhill
Cemy.
Rec. Grd.
Woodend
Wrose Brow Plantation
Wrose Hill
Windhill C of E Prim. Sch.
Ckt. Gd.
Sch.
Bowl. Grn.
Putting
Playing
Play. Fld.
Cricket Grd.
Acorn Pk. Ind. Est.
Baildon Ho.
Baildon Rd.
Bradford Road
Otley Road
Leeds Road
Commercial St.
Briggate
Saltaire Rd.
Crag Road
Green Lane
Hope Lane
Station Road
Brow Gate
The Grove
A657
A6038
A6037
A650
B6151
B6149
18
27
39
38
37

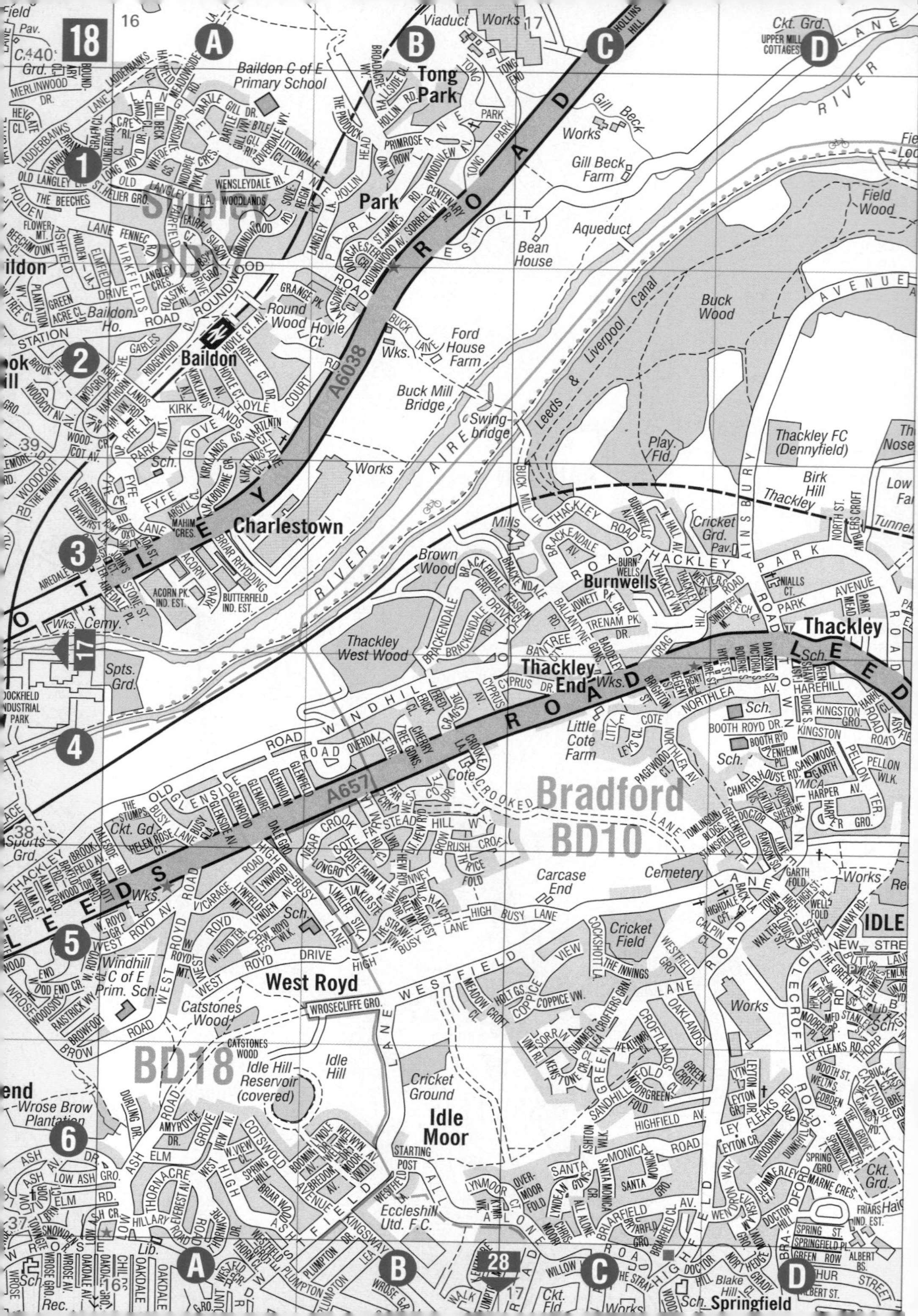
A
B
C
D
1
2
3
4
5
6
16
17
Viaduct
Works
Baildon C of E Primary School
Tong Park
Park
Gill Beck
Works
Gill Beck Farm
Field Wood
Aqueduct
Bean House
ESHOLT
RIVER
Buck Wood
AVENUE
Leeds & Liverpool Canal
Round Wood
Hoyle Ct.
Ford House Farm
Wks.
Baildon
A6038
ROAD
Buck Mill Bridge
Swing-bridge
Play. Fld.
Thackley FC (Dennyfield)
Birk Hill
Thackley Tunnel
Works
AIRE
Charlestown
Cricket Grd.
Burnwells
Brown Wood
THACKLEY ROAD
Thackley
Thackley West Wood
Thackley End
Wks.
Spts. Grd.
Cemy.
ACORN PK. IND. EST.
BUTTERFIELD IND. EST.
WINDHILL
LEEDS ROAD
A657
Little Cote Farm
Cote
CROOKED LANE
Bradford
BD10
Sch.
YMCA
Carcase End
Cemetery
Works
IDLE
Wks.
Sch.
Windhill C of E Prim. Sch.
West Royd
WESTFIELD LANE
Catstones Wood
BD18
Idle Hill Reservoir (covered)
Idle Hill
Cricket Ground
Idle Moor
Cricket Field
Works
Wrose Brow Plantation
Eccleshill Utd. F.C.
Springfield
Blake Hill
Ckt. Grd.
28
Lib.
Sch

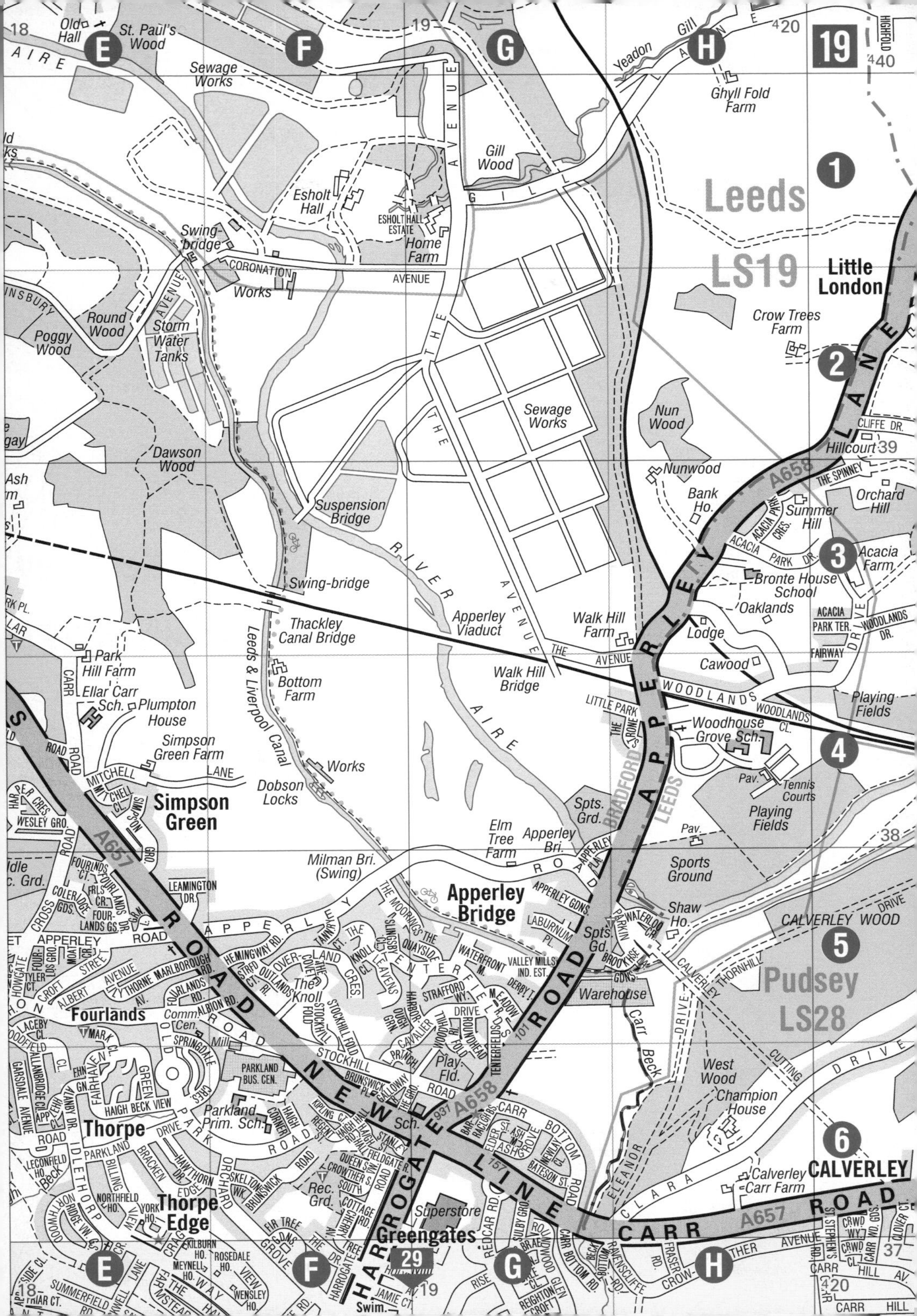
Leeds
LS19
Little London
Pudsey
LS28
Apperley Bridge
Simpson Green
Fourlands
Thorpe
Thorpe Edge
Greengates
CALVERLEY
Sewage Works
Esholt Hall
ESHOLT HALL ESTATE
Home Farm
Gill Wood
Ghyll Fold Farm
Yeadon Gill
Crow Trees Farm
Nun Wood
Nunwood
Bank Ho.
Summer Hill
Orchard Hill
Hillcourt
Acacia Farm
Bronte House School
Oaklands
Lodge
Cawood
Walk Hill Farm
Walk Hill Bridge
Apperley Viaduct
Suspension Bridge
Swing-bridge
Thackley Canal Bridge
Leeds & Liverpool Canal
Bottom Farm
Works
Dobson Locks
Park Hill Farm
Ellar Carr Sch.
Plumpton House
Simpson Green Farm
Dawson Wood
Round Wood
Poggy Wood
Storm Water Tanks
Coronation Works
St. Paul's Wood
Old Hall
Woodhouse Grove Sch.
Playing Fields
Tennis Courts
Sports Ground
Spts. Grd.
Elm Tree Farm
Apperley Bri.
Milman Bri. (Swing)
Shaw Ho.
Warehouse
Valley Mills Ind. Est.
Carr Beck
West Wood
Champion House
Calverley Carr Farm
Parkland Bus. Cen.
Parkland Prim. Sch.
Superstore
Rec. Grd.
Play. Fld.
APPERLEY ROAD
HARROGATE ROAD
NEW LINE
CARR ROAD
A657
A658
CALVERLEY WOOD DRIVE
CALVERLEY CUTTING
CLARA DRIVE
WOODLANDS DR.
THE AVENUE
RIVER AIRE
BRADFORD
LEEDS

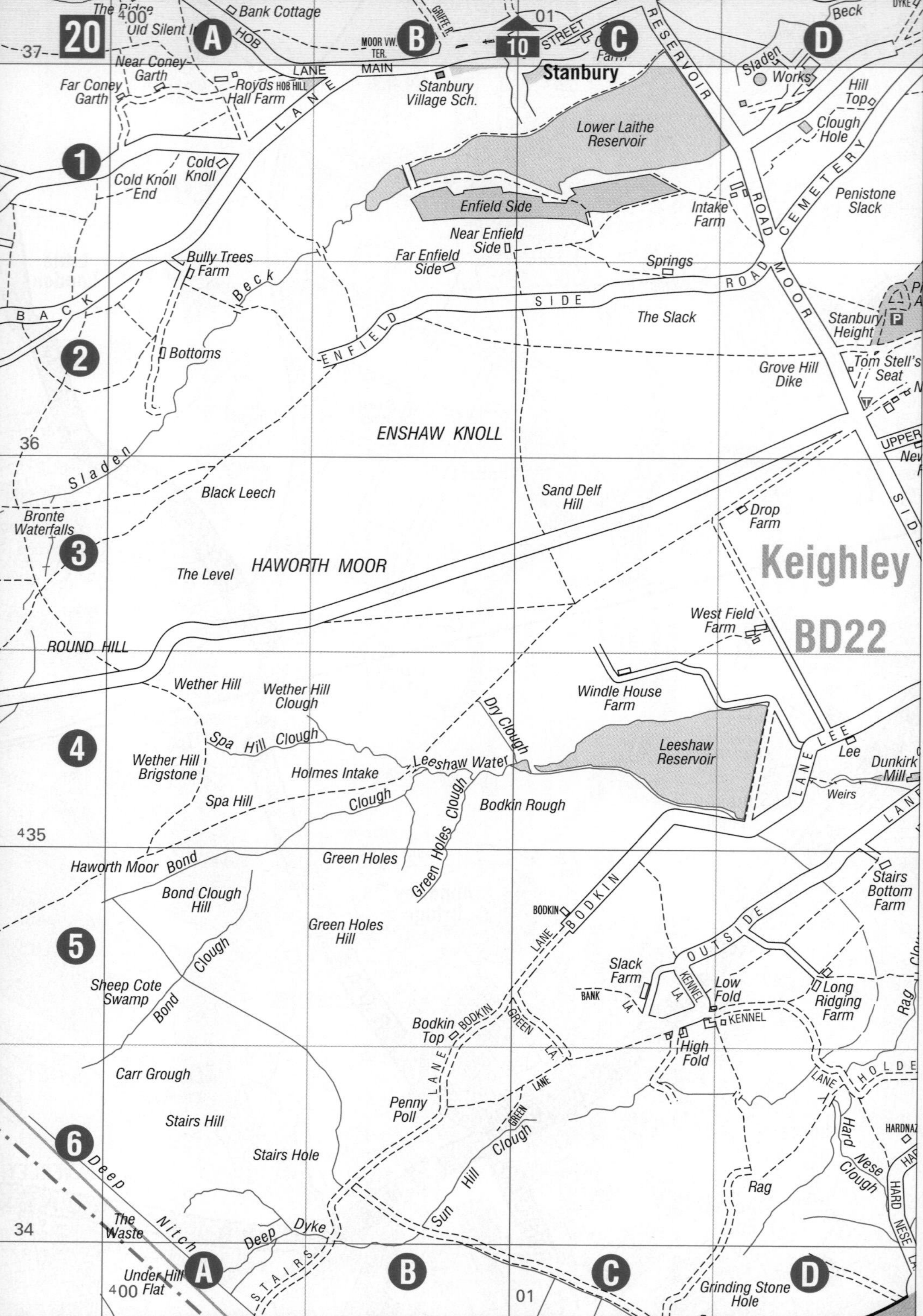

20

The Ridge
Old Silent I.
Bank Cottage
A
HOB
MOOR VW. TER.
B
GRUFFI
01
STREET
10
C
RESERVOIR
Beck
DYKE
D

37
400
Sladen
Works
Hill Top

Near Coney Garth
HOB HILL
LANE
MAIN
Stanbury Village Sch.
Stanbury
Farm
Clough Hole

Far Coney Garth
Royds Hall Farm
1
LANE
Penistone Slack

Cold Knoll End
Cold Knoll
Enfield Side
Intake Farm

Bully Trees Farm
Near Enfield Side
Springs

Far Enfield Side
ROAD
The Slack
MOOR
Stanbury Heights
P
P

BACK
Beck
ENFIELD
SIDE
ROAD
Tom Stell's Seat

Bottoms
Grove Hill Dike
UPPER
Nev

2

36
Sladen
ENSHAW KNOLL
SIDE

Black Leech
Sand Delf Hill
Drop Farm

Bronte Waterfalls
3
HAWORTH MOOR
Keighley

The Level
West Field Farm
BD22

ROUND HILL
Wether Hill
Wether Hill Clough
Dry Clough
Windle House Farm

4
Spa Hill Clough
Leeshaw Water
Leeshaw Reservoir
LANE
LEE
Lee
Dunkirk Mill

Wether Hill Brigstone
Holmes Intake
Weirs

435
Spa Hill
Clough
Bodkin Rough

Haworth Moor Bond
Green Holes
Green Holes Clough
Stairs Bottom Farm

Bond Clough Hill
Green Holes Hill
BODKIN
BODKIN
OUTSIDE
Long Ridging Farm

5
Clough
Slack Farm
Low Fold
KENNEL
Rag

Sheep Cote Swamp
Bond
Bodkin Top
LANE
BANK
LA.
High Fold
KENNEL

Carr Grough
LANE
GREEN
HOLDE

Stairs Hill
Penny Poll
LA.
Hard
HARDNAZ
HAR

6
Deep
Nitch
Stairs Hole
Sun Hill Clough
GREEN Clough
Rag
Nese Clough
HARD
NESE

34
The Waste
STAIRS
Deep
Dyke
A
B
C
Grinding Stone Hole
D

Under Hill
400 Flat
01

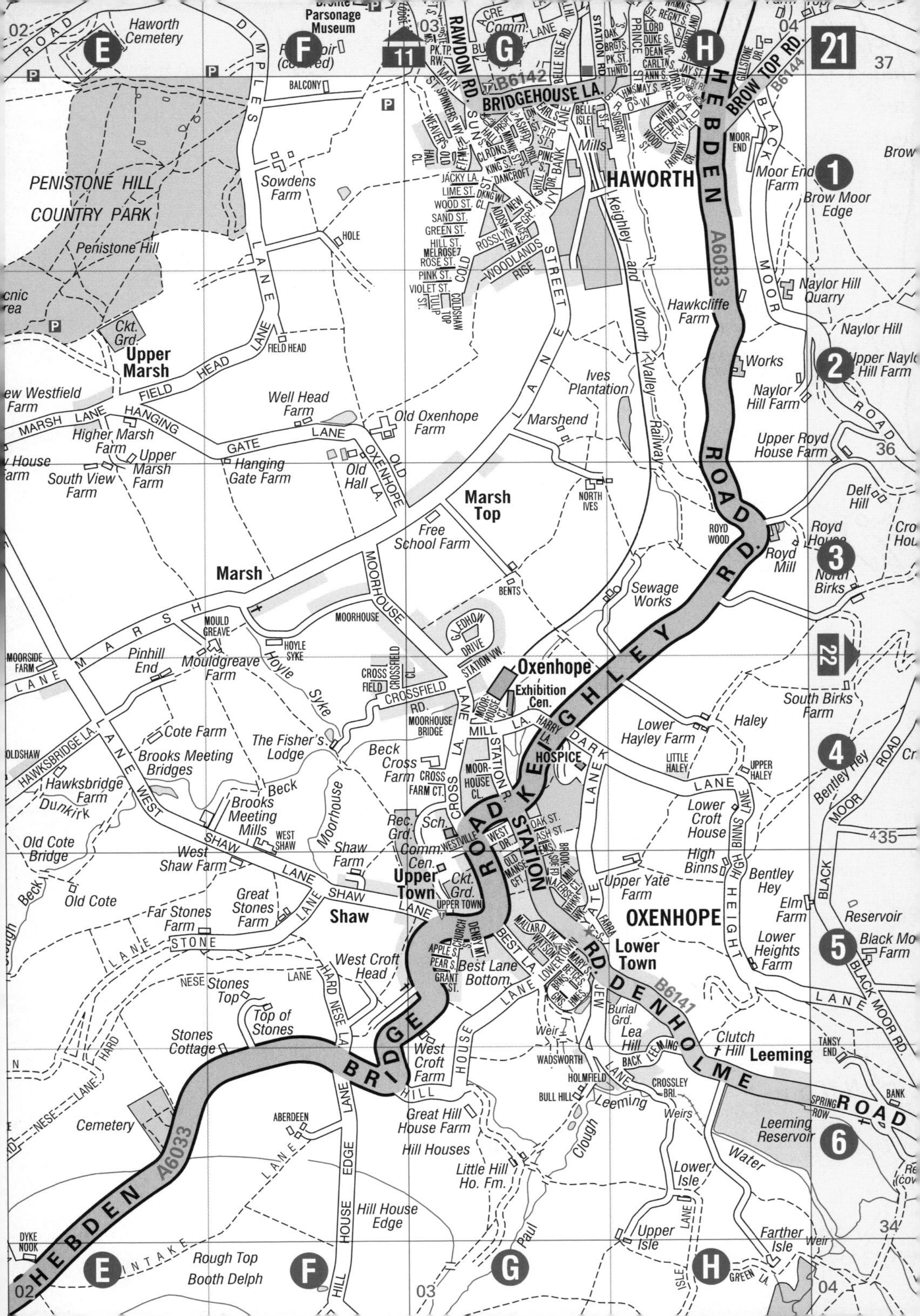

Haworth Cemetery
Brontë Parsonage Museum
Reservoir (covered)
11
HAWORTH
PENISTONE HILL COUNTRY PARK
Penistone Hill
Upper Marsh
Sowdens Farm
Well Head Farm
Old Oxenhope Farm
Higher Marsh Farm
Upper Marsh Farm
South View Farm
Hanging Gate Farm
Old Hall
Marshend
Ives Plantation
Marsh Top
Free School Farm
Marsh
Hawkcliffe Farm
Moor End Farm
Brow Moor Edge
Naylor Hill Quarry
Naylor Hill
Upper Naylor Hill Farm
Naylor Hill Farm
Upper Royd House Farm
Delf Hill
Royd Mill
North Birks
Sewage Works
Oxenhope
Exhibition Cen.
HOSPICE
Mouldgreave Farm
Pinhill End
Cote Farm
The Fisher's Lodge
Beck Cross Farm
Brooks Meeting Bridges
Hawksbridge Farm
Dunkirk
Brooks Meeting Mills
Old Cote Bridge
West Shaw Farm
Shaw Farm
Upper Town
Old Cote
Great Stones Farm
Far Stones Farm
Shaw
South Birks Farm
Haley
Lower Hayley Farm
Lower Croft House
High Binns
Upper Yate Farm
Bentley Hey
Elm Farm
Reservoir
OXENHOPE
Lower Heights Farm
Black Moor Farm
Lower Town
West Croft Head
Best Lane Bottom
Stones Top
Top of Stones
Stones Cottage
West Croft Farm
Burial Grd.
Lea Hill
Clutch Hill
Leeming
Leeming Reservoir
Cemetery
Great Hill House Farm
Hill Houses
Little Hill Ho. Fm.
Lower Isle
Upper Isle
Farther Isle
Hill House Edge
Rough Top
Booth Delph
HEBDEN BRIDGE ROAD
A6033
KEIGHLEY ROAD
STATION RD.
DENHOLME ROAD
B6141
B6142
B6144
BRIDGEHOUSE LA.
BROW TOP RD.
22
E F G H
1 2 3 4 5 6
02 03 04
34 35 36 37

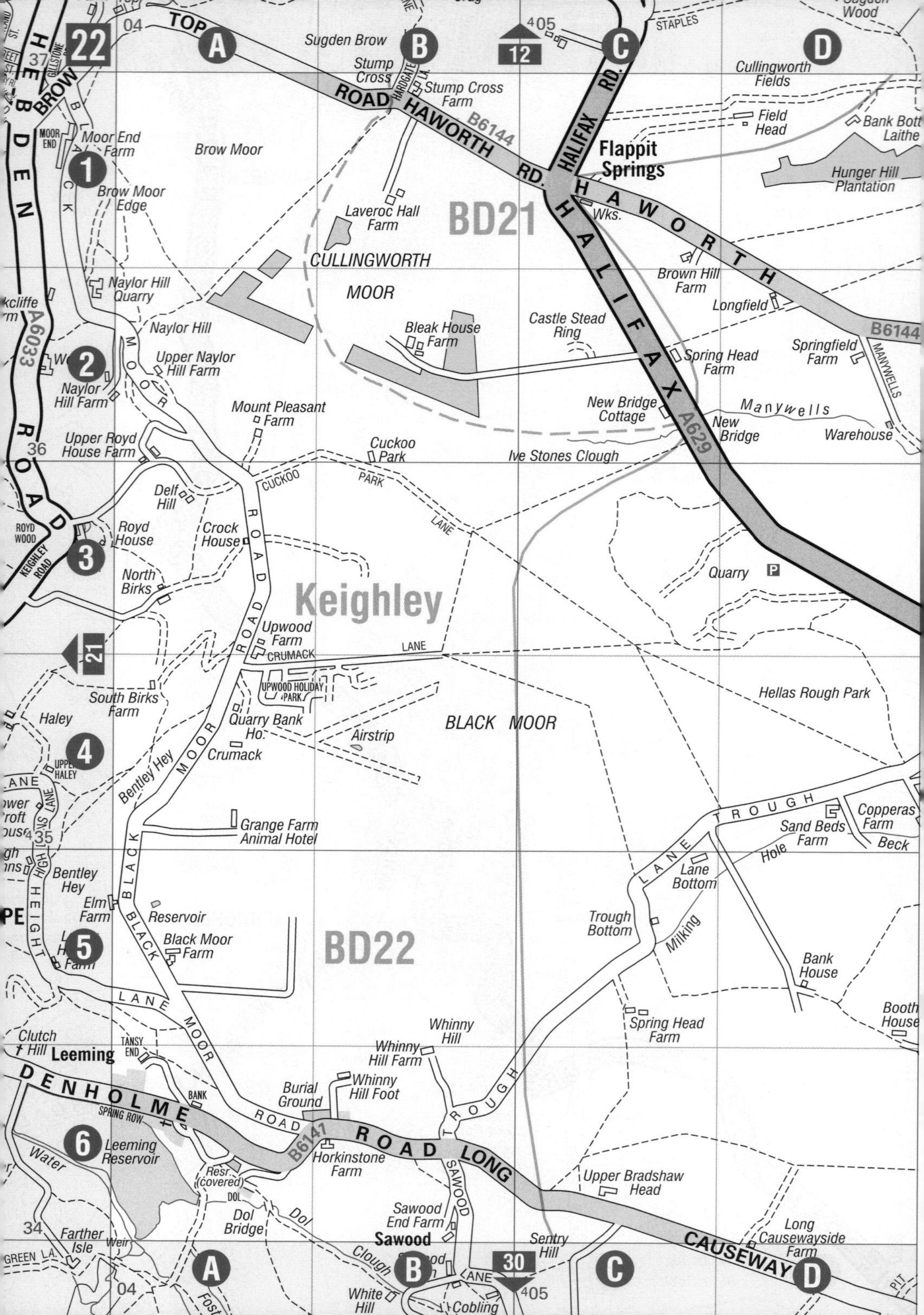

TOP ROAD
HAWORTH RD.
B6144
HALIFAX RD.
Flappit Springs
HAWORTH
HALIFAX
A629
BD21
CULLINGWORTH MOOR
Sugden Brow
Stump Cross
Stump Cross Farm
HARDGATE LA.
STAPLES
Sugden Wood
Cullingworth Fields
Field Head
Bank Bottom Laithe
Hunger Hill Plantation
Wks.
Brow Moor
Moor End Farm
Brow Moor Edge
Laveroc Hall Farm
Naylor Hill Quarry
Naylor Hill
Upper Naylor Hill Farm
Naylor Hill Farm
Bleak House Farm
Castle Stead Ring
Brown Hill Farm
Longfield
Spring Head Farm
Springfield Farm
MANYWELLS
Manywells
New Bridge Cottage
New Bridge
Warehouse
Mount Pleasant Farm
Cuckoo Park
CUCKOO PARK LANE
Ive Stones Clough
HEBDEN BROW
HEBDEN ROAD
A6033
BLACK MOOR ROAD
Upper Royd House Farm
Delf Hill
Royd House
ROYD WOOD
KEIGHLEY ROAD
Crock House
North Birks
Keighley
Quarry
Upwood Farm
CRUMACK LANE
UPWOOD HOLIDAY PARK
South Birks Farm
Haley
UPPER HALEY
Quarry Bank Ho.
Crumack
Airstrip
BLACK MOOR
Hellas Rough Park
Bentley Hey
Grange Farm Animal Hotel
TROUGH LANE
Copperas Farm
Sand Beds Farm
Hole Beck
Lane Bottom
HIGH FIELD LANE
HIGH HEIGHT
Bentley Hey
Elm Farm
Reservoir
Trough Bottom
Milking
BD22
Black Moor Farm
Bank House
Booth House
LANE
Spring Head Farm
Whinny Hill
Whinny Hill Farm
Clutch Hill
Leeming
TANSY END
DENHOLME ROAD
B6147
BANK
SPRING ROW
Burial Ground
Whinny Hill Foot
TROUGH
LONG CAUSEWAY
Leeming Reservoir
Water
Horkinstone Farm
SAWOOD
Resr. (covered)
DOL
Dol Bridge
Dol Clough
Upper Bradshaw Head
Sawood End Farm
Sawood
Farther Isle
Weir
GREEN LA.
Sentry Hill
Long Causewayside Farm
White Hill
Cobling
PIT
405
04
37
36
35
34

12
21
30

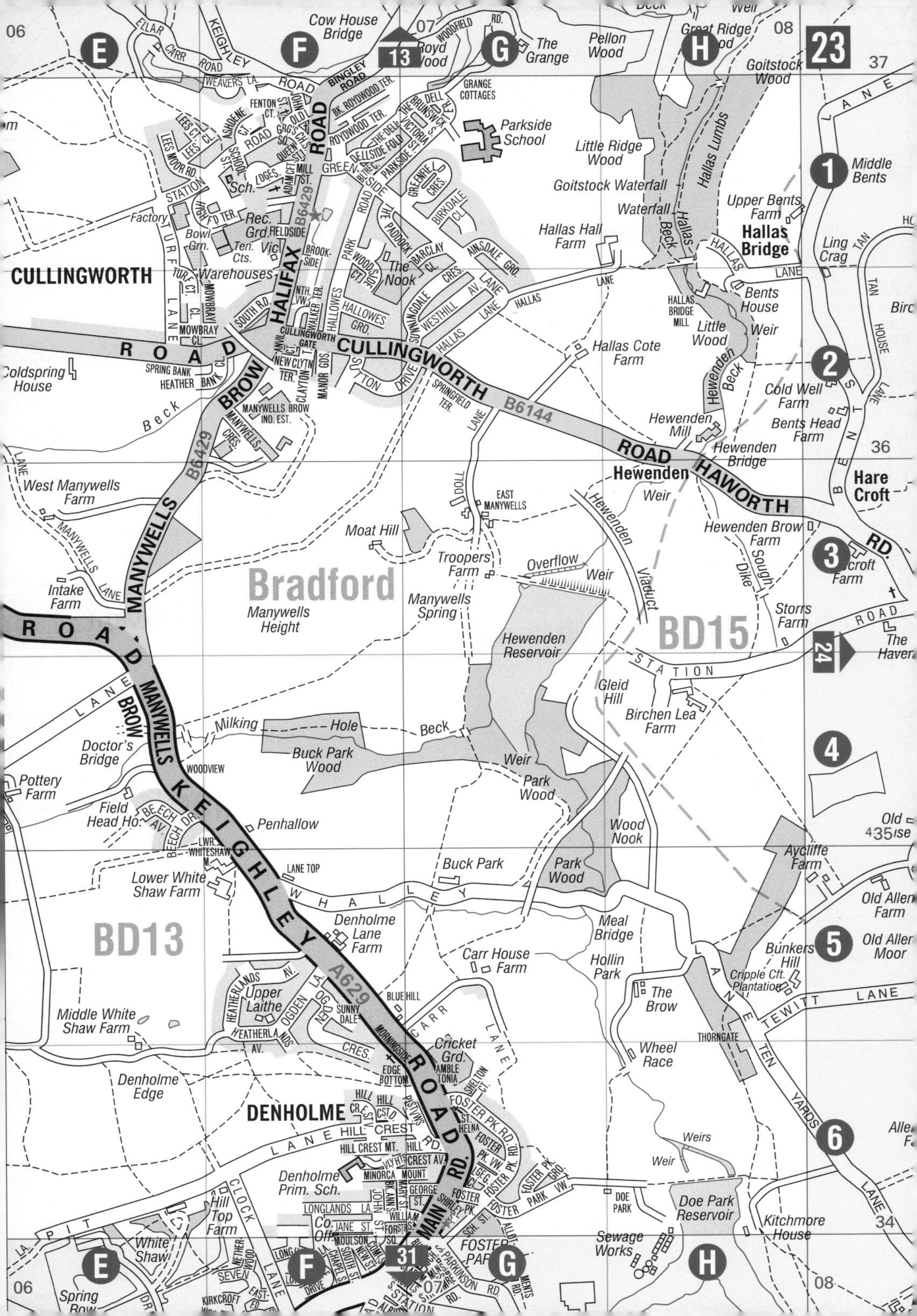

23
13
24
31
E
F
G
H
1
2
3
4
5
6
06
07
08
37
36
35
34
CULLINGWORTH
DENHOLME
Bradford
BD15
BD13
Hewenden
Hallas Bridge
Hare Croft
Cow House Bridge
Royd Wood
The Grange
Pellon Wood
Great Ridge Wood
Goitstock Wood
Parkside School
Little Ridge Wood
Goitstock Waterfall
Waterfall
Hallas Lumbs
Middle Bents
Upper Bents Farm
Ling Crag
Hallas Hall Farm
Bents House
Hallas Bridge Mill
Little Wood
Weir
Hallas Cote Farm
Cold Well Farm
Bents Head Farm
Hewenden Mill
Hewenden Bridge
Hewenden Brow Farm
Storrs Farm
The Haven
Moat Hill
Troopers Farm
Overflow
Manywells Spring
Manywells Height
Hewenden Reservoir
Gleid Hill
Birchen Lea Farm
West Manywells Farm
Intake Farm
Coldspring House
Doctor's Bridge
Pottery Farm
Field Head Ho.
Penhallow
Buck Park Wood
Park Wood
Wood Nook
Buck Park
Lower White Shaw Farm
Denholme Lane Farm
Carr House Farm
Meal Bridge
Hollin Park
The Brow
Wheel Race
Aycliffe Farm
Old Allen Farm
Old Allen Moor
Bunkers Hill
Cripple Cft. Plantation
Thorngate
Middle White Shaw Farm
Upper Laithe
Cricket Grd.
Denholme Edge
Denholme Prim. Sch.
Hill Top Farm
White Shaw
Spring Row
Doe Park
Doe Park Reservoir
Sewage Works
Kitchmore House
Weirs
Factory
Bowl Grn.
Ten. Cts.
Rec. Grd.
Warehouses
Sch.
The Nook
Manywells Brow Ind. Est.
Milking Hole Beck
Beck
Viaduct
Hewenden Beck
Sough Dike
HALIFAX ROAD
B6429
B6144
A629
CULLINGWORTH ROAD
HAWORTH ROAD
MANYWELLS BROW
KEIGHLEY ROAD
MANYWELLS BROW
STATION ROAD
WHALLEY LANE
TEN YARDS LANE
TEWITT LANE
CARR LANE
PIT LANE
CLOCK LANE
MAIN RD.
BENTS LANE
TAN HOUSE LANE
BINGLEY ROAD
HALLAS LANE
DOLL LANE
SPRINGFIELD TER.
SUTTON DRIVE
HALLOWES PARK ROAD
MOWBRAY CL.
TURF LANE
FOSTER PARK VW.
LONGLANDS LA.
HILL CREST

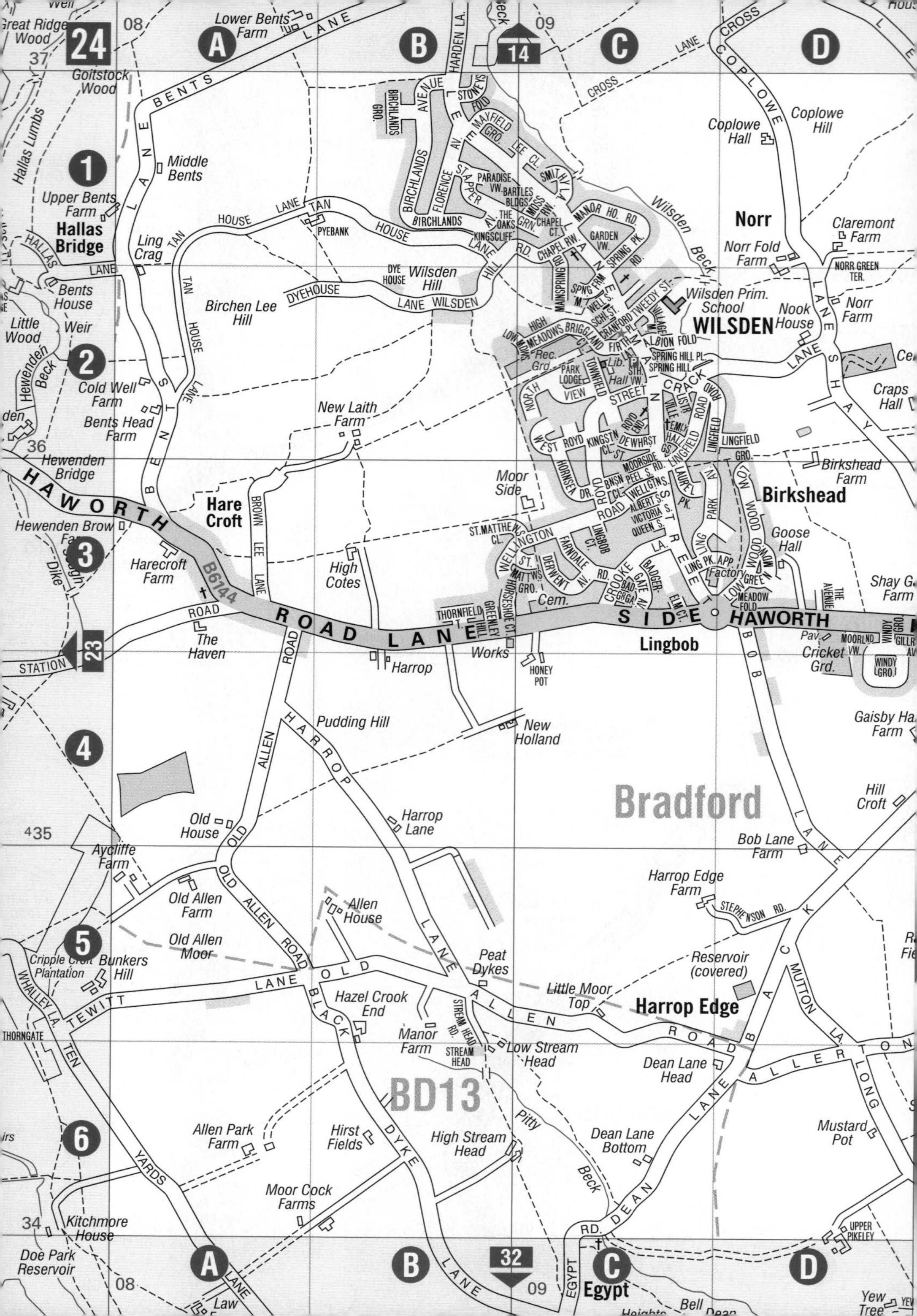
A
B
C
D
1
2
3
4
5
6
08
09
37
36
35
34
14
23
32
Great Ridge Wood
Goitstock Wood
Hallas Lumbs
Lower Bents Farm
BENTS LANE
HARDEN LA.
CROSS LANE
COPLOWE LANE
Middle Bents
Upper Bents Farm
Hallas Bridge
HALLAS LANE
Bents House
Little Wood
Weir
Hewenden Beck
Ling Crag
TAN HOUSE LANE
PYEBANK
Birchen Lee Hill
DYEHOUSE LANE
DYE HOUSE
Wilsden Hill
WILSDEN HILL RD.
Cold Well Farm
Bents Head Farm
New Laith Farm
Hewenden Bridge
HAWORTH ROAD
Hewenden Brow Farm
Harecroft Farm
Hare Croft
BROWN LEE LANE
High Cotes
B6144
ROAD LANE SIDE
The Haven
STATION ROAD
Harrop
Works
HONEY POT
Lingbob
Moor Side
BIRCHLANDS GRO.
BIRCHLANDS AVENUE
STONEYS FOLD
MAYFIELD GRO.
LEE CL.
SMITHY LA.
FLORENCE AV.
STAPPER AV.
PARADISE VW.
BARTLES BLDGS.
MOSS RW.
THE OAKS
KINGSCLIFF
CHAPEL CT.
MANOR HO. RD.
GARDEN VW.
SPRING PK. RD.
CHAPEL RW.
MAINSPRING RD.
Wilsden Beck
Wilsden Prim. School
WILSDEN
TWEEDY ST.
HIGH MEADOWS
BRIGGLAND CT.
ALBION FOLD
SPRING HILL PL.
SPRING HILL
Rec. Grd.
PARK LODGE
TOWNFIELD
Lib.
STH. Hall VW.
CRACK
NORTH VIEW STREET
WEST ROYD
KINGSTN CL.
DEWHRST ST.
LINGFIELD
MOORSIDE RD.
PEEL S.
LAUREL PK.
ALBERT S.
VICTORIA S.
QUEEN S.
HORNSEA DR.
ROYD ROAD
LINGBOB CT.
WELLINGTON
ST. MATTHEWS CL.
FARNDALE RD.
DERWENT AV.
CROOKE LA.
BADGER GATE
ELM CT.
LING PARK AV.
LING PK. APP
Factory
LOW WOOD
MEADOW FOLD
GREEN
Birkshead
Birkshead Farm
Goose Hall
Norr
Coplowe Hall
Coplowe Hill
Claremont Farm
Norr Fold Farm
NORR GREEN TER.
Norr Farm
Nook House
SHAY LANE
Craps Hall
THE AVENUE
Shay Gate Farm
HAWORTH
Pav.
MOORLND VW.
WINDY GRO.
Cricket Grd.
Cem.
THORNFIELD
GREENLEY HILL
HORSESHOE CT.
Pudding Hill
New Holland
HARROP LANE
ALLEN ROAD
OLD ALLEN ROAD
Old House
Harrop Lane
Bradford
Gaisby Hall Farm
Hill Croft
BOB LANE
Bob Lane Farm
Harrop Edge Farm
STEPHENSON RD.
BACK LANE
Reservoir (covered)
Harrop Edge
MUTTON LA.
Aycliffe Farm
Old Allen Farm
Allen House
Old Allen Moor
Peat Dykes
Little Moor Top
ALLEN ROAD
Cripple Croft Plantation
Bunkers Hill
TEWITT LANE
WHALLEY LA.
THORNGATE
TEN YARDS LANE
BLACK DYKE LANE
Hazel Crook End
Manor Farm
STREAM HEAD RD.
STREAM HEAD
Low Stream Head
Dean Lane Head
ALLERTON LA.
LONG LA.
BD13
Allen Park Farm
Hirst Fields
High Stream Head
Pitty Beck
Dean Lane Bottom
Mustard Pot
Moor Cock Farms
Kitchmore House
Doe Park Reservoir
DEAN LANE
DEAN RD.
EGYPT RD.
Egypt
UPPER PIKELEY
Yew Tree
Law
Bell Dean

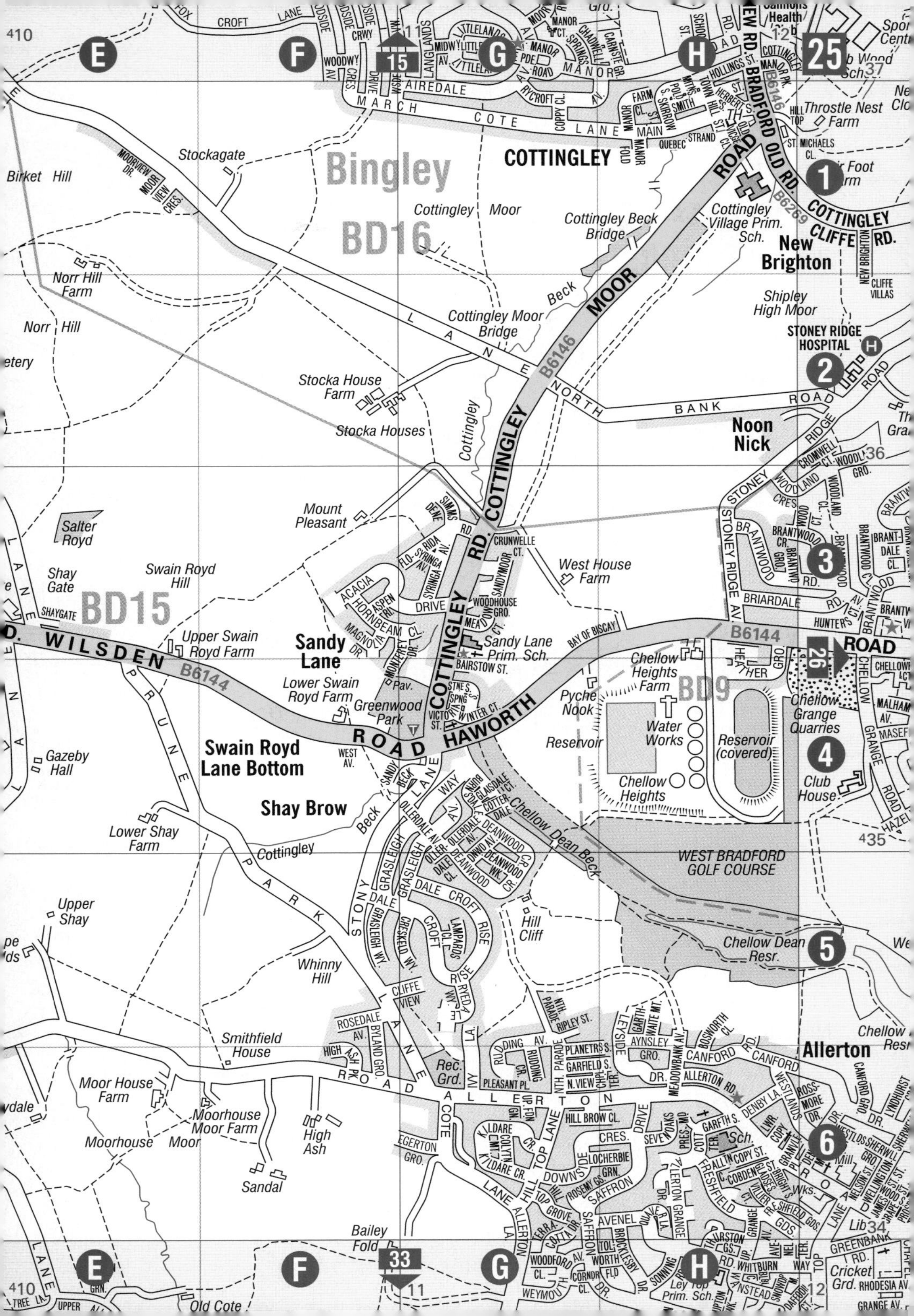

25
15
33
26
E
F
G
H
1
2
3
4
5
6
Bingley
BD16
BD15
BD9
COTTINGLEY
New Brighton
Noon Nick
Sandy Lane
Swain Royd Lane Bottom
Shay Brow
Allerton
Birket Hill
Stockagate
Cottingley Moor
Cottingley Beck Bridge
Cottingley Village Prim. Sch.
Shipley High Moor
STONEY RIDGE HOSPITAL
Norr Hill Farm
Norr Hill
Cottingley Moor Bridge
Stocka House Farm
Stocka Houses
Mount Pleasant
Salter Royd
Shay Gate
Swain Royd Hill
West House Farm
Upper Swain Royd Farm
Sandy Lane Prim. Sch.
Lower Swain Royd Farm
Greenwood Park
Chellow Heights Farm
Pyche Nook
Water Works
Reservoir
Reservoir (covered)
Chellow Heights
Chellow Grange Quarries
Club House
Gazeby Hall
Lower Shay Farm
WEST BRADFORD GOLF COURSE
Chellow Dean Beck
Upper Shay
Hill Cliff
Chellow Dean Resr.
Whinny Hill
Smithfield House
Moor House Farm
Moorhouse Moor Farm
Moorhouse Moor
High Ash
Sandal
Bailey Fold
Ley Top Prim. Sch.
Cricket Grd.
Rec. Grd.
Throstle Nest Farm
MARCH COTE LANE
AIREDALE
BRADFORD OLD RD.
NEW RD.
COTTINGLEY MOOR ROAD
COTTINGLEY RD.
COTTINGLEY CLIFFE RD.
NORTH BANK ROAD
STONEY RIDGE ROAD
WILSDEN ROAD
HAWORTH ROAD
PRUNE PARK LANE
STONY LANE
ALLERTON ROAD
ALLERTON LANE
COTE LANE
B6146
B6269
B6144
410
435

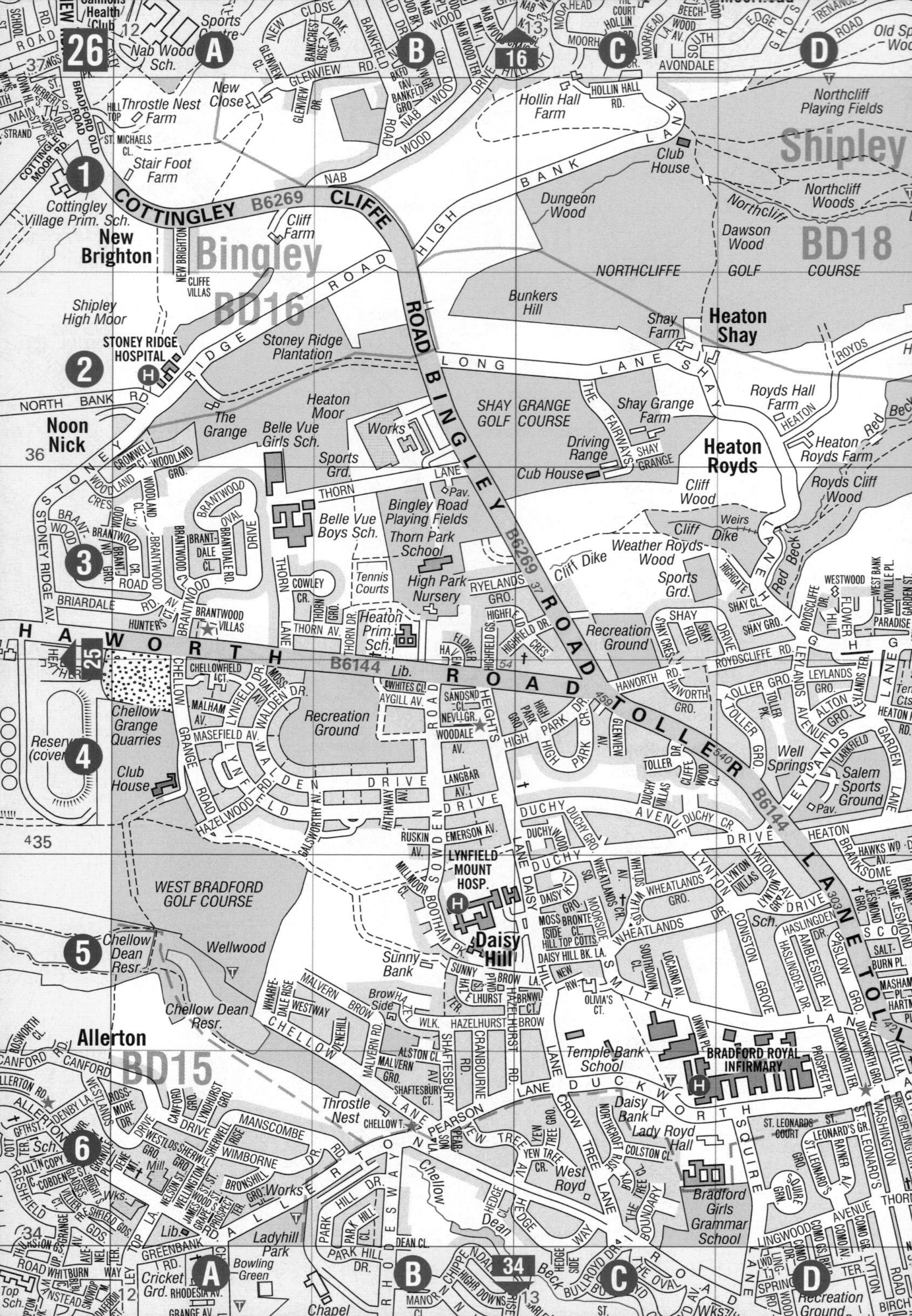

26
A
B
C
D
16
Nab Wood Sch.
Sports Centre
New Close
Throstle Nest Farm
Stair Foot Farm
Hollin Hall Farm
Northcliff Playing Fields
Shipley
Club House
Northcliff Woods
Dungeon Wood
Dawson Wood
BD18
NORTHCLIFFE GOLF COURSE
Cottingley Village Prim. Sch.
New Brighton
COTTINGLEY CLIFFE
B6269
Cliff Farm
Bingley
BD16
Shipley High Moor
Bunkers Hill
Heaton Shay
Shay Farm
STONEY RIDGE HOSPITAL
Stoney Ridge Plantation
LONG LANE
NORTH BANK RD.
Noon Nick
Heaton Moor
The Grange
Belle Vue Girls Sch.
Works
SHAY GRANGE GOLF COURSE
Shay Grange Farm
Royds Hall Farm
Heaton Royds
Heaton Royds Farm
Driving Range
Cub House
Sports Grd.
Cliff Wood
Royds Cliff Wood
Bingley Road Playing Fields
Belle Vue Boys Sch.
Thorn Park School
Weirs
Cliff Dike
Weather Royds Wood
High Park Nursery
Tennis Courts
Sports Grd.
Heaton Prim. Sch.
Recreation Ground
BINGLEY ROAD
HAWORTH ROAD
B6144
25
Lib.
Chellow Grange Quarries
Reservoir (covered)
Club House
Recreation Ground
TOLLER LANE
Well Springs
Salem Sports Ground
Pav.
WEST BRADFORD GOLF COURSE
LYNFIELD MOUNT HOSP.
Daisy Hill
Chellow Dean Resr.
Wellwood
Sunny Bank
Temple Bank School
BRADFORD ROYAL INFIRMARY
Allerton
BD15
Throstle Nest
Daisy Bank
Lady Royd Hall
West Royd
Bradford Girls Grammar School
Ladyhill Park
Bowling Green
Cricket Grd.
Chellow Dean
Top Sch.
Chapel
34
Recreation Ground
1
2
3
4
5
6

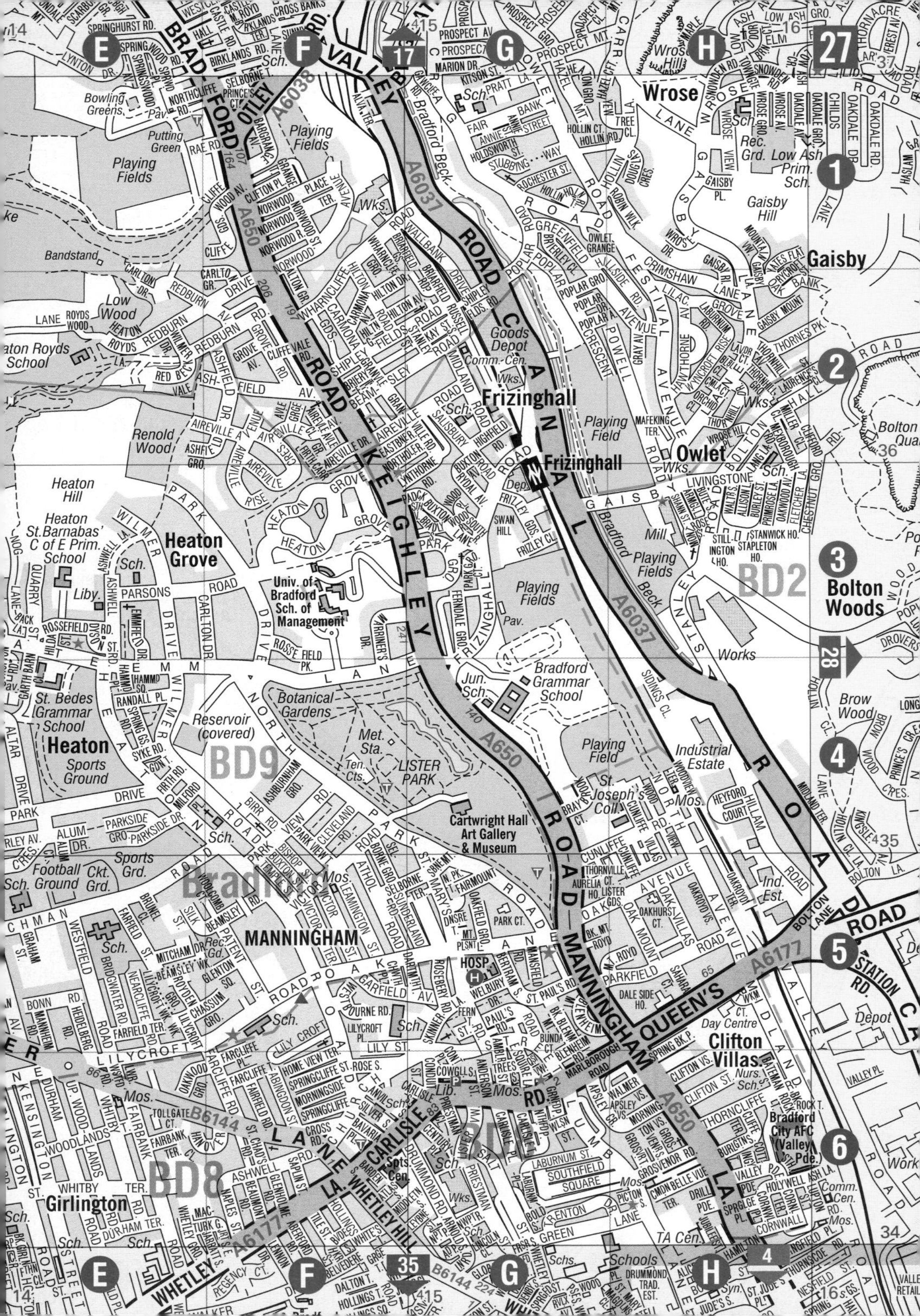

27
17
28
35
4
E
F
G
H
1
2
3
4
5
6
Wrose
Gaisby
Owlet
Frizinghall
Bolton Woods
BD2
BD9
BD8
Heaton Grove
Heaton
Low Wood
Heaton Royds School
Heaton Hill
Renold Wood
Gaisby Hill
Brow Wood
MANNINGHAM
Girlington
Clifton Villas
Bradford
Goods Depot
Playing Fields
Univ. of Bradford Sch. of Management
Bradford Grammar School
Botanical Gardens
LISTER PARK
Cartwright Hall Art Gallery & Museum
Reservoir (covered)
Heaton Sports Ground
St. Bedes Grammar School
Heaton St.Barnabas' C of E Prim. School
Industrial Estate
St. Joseph's Coll.
Bradford City AFC (Valley Pde.)
Football Ground
Low Ash Prim. Sch.
Bradford Beck
A650
A6037
A6038
A6177
B6144
KEIGHLEY ROAD
MANNINGHAM LANE
CANAL ROAD
BRADFORD ROAD
OTLEY ROAD
VALLEY ROAD
QUEEN'S ROAD
CARLISLE ROAD
WHETLEY LANE
LUMB LANE
EMM LANE
HEATON ROAD

28
A
B
C
D
18
17
16
1
2
3
4
5
6
27
36
4
5
Eccleshill Utd. F.C.
Wrose
Gaisby
Gaisby Hill
Low Ash Prim. Sch.
Rec. Grd.
Shipley
BD18
Owlet
Bolton Wood Quarries
Bolton Old Hall
Playing Field
Bolton Woods
Poplars Farm Prim. Sch.
Brow Wood
Bolton
Swain House
Hanson School
Feversham Coll.
Swain House Prim. Sch.
Sports Centre
Grove House Prim. Sch.
Bradford
BD2
Bolton Outlanes
ECCLESHILL
Moor End
Springfield
Five Lane Ends
Superstore
Enterprise 5 Lane Ends
Abbey Ct. Leis.
Ckt. Fld.
Works
Shop. Cen.
Wellington Prim. Sch.
UNDERCLIFFE
Bolton House
PEEL PARK
THE TERRACE
Bowling Greens
Tennis Courts
Statue
Sikh Temp.
Undercliffe Cemetery
Play. Flds.
College
Pollard Park
Bradford Moor
Wapping
Clifton Villas
Bradford City AFC (Valley Pde.)
BD1
Depot
Bradford Bus. Pk.
Ind. Est.
Comm. Cen.
Nurs. Sch.
Retail Park
KING'S ROAD
BOLTON ROAD
QUEEN'S ROAD
LISTER LA.
VALLEY VIEW GRO.
NORTHCOTE RD.
OTLEY ROAD
VALLEY ROAD
KILLINGHALL
CANAL
A6176
A6177
A6037
A658
STATION RD.
HARROGATE
KING'S DRIVE

E
F
G
H
1
2
3
4
5
6
19
37
18
420
Thorpe Edge
Greengates
Superstore
Calverley Carr Farm
CARR RD.
A657
CARR HILL AV.
CARR HILL RD.
Carr Hills
Reservoir
CARR LA.
CROWTHER AVENUE
FRASER RD.
RAVENSCLIFFE
ROANS BRAE
COLLINDALE CL.
REIGHTON CROFT
ROUNDWOOD GLEN
RYTON DALE
ROKEBY GDNS.
ROWTON THORPE
RIMSWELL
REDCAR RD.
ROUNDWOOD
HOLBROOK AV.
JAMIE CT.
Swim. Pool
ROMANBY SHAW
ROWLESTONE RISE
ROOKWITH PDE.
RILLINGTON MEAD
Sch.
Mill
HARROGATE ROAD
A658
Bill Wood
Eccleshill Park
PARK ROAD
School
FLOWER GARTH
Bank Top
PARKSTONE DR.
BRIDGEGATE WY.
Playing Field
Round Hill
Round Wood
WOODHALL HILLS GOLF COURSE
Stanhope Rein
Low Rein
Beck
RANELAGH
ROUNDWOOD GLEN
OSTERLEY GR.
HALLWOOD GRN.
NORBURY AVENUE
Cavendish Prim. Sch.
Com. Cen.
The Oval
RAVENSCLIFFE
Ravenscliffe
36
STOTT TERRACE
CHAPEL ST.
TUNWELL ST.
WESTGATE
STONY LANE
Cem.
Rec. Grd.
Wks.
Works
PULLAN AVENUE
PULLAN DR.
Absolute Fitness Cen.
Res.
THACKERAY RD.
HAZELCROFT
BOWNESS AV.
DAMON AV.
WINSLOW RD.
LANGDALE AVENUE
FALKLAND RD.
Ravenscliffe Wood
Fagley Beck
Pudsey
LS28
Club House
PRIESTHORPE RD.
Woodhall Hills
Top Fm.
Woodhall Plantation
WOODHALL HILLS
Club Ho.
CALVERLEY GOLF COURSE
435
St. Luke's Prim. Sch.
Throstles Nest Farm
FAIRWOOD GROVE
Haigh Fold
Lower Fagley
Wks.
Stone Quarry
Cherry Tree Farm
Industrial Museum
Comm. Play. Cen. Fld.
Upper Fagley
FAGLEY ROAD
Fagley Prim. Sch.
St. Clare's RC Sch.
FLAXTON GREEN
FOLKTON HOLME
FOSTON LANE
Moor Side
Cricket Grd.
INTAKE ROAD
Fagley
Woodhall Farm
Playing Field
Woodhall Grange
THE GLADE
ROCKWOOD R.
Woodhall
Tennis Courts
Sports Ground
Playing Field
Thornbury Barracks
BRADFORD
LEEDS
WOODHALL ROAD
Bakery
SUNNYBANK LANE
Playing Field
Works
A647
BRADFORD RD.
KILLINGHALL ROAD
A6177
Killinghall Prim. Sch.
Boating Lake
Bowl. Grns.
Ten. Cts. Pav.
Bradford Moor Golf Course
BD2
BD10
Rec. Grd.
Superstore
THE WOODHALL RETAIL CEN.
LEEDS RD.
DICK LA.
Spts. Grd.
Club
Ckt. Grd.
Pudsey Bolton Royd Prim. Sch.
34
Odeon Cin.

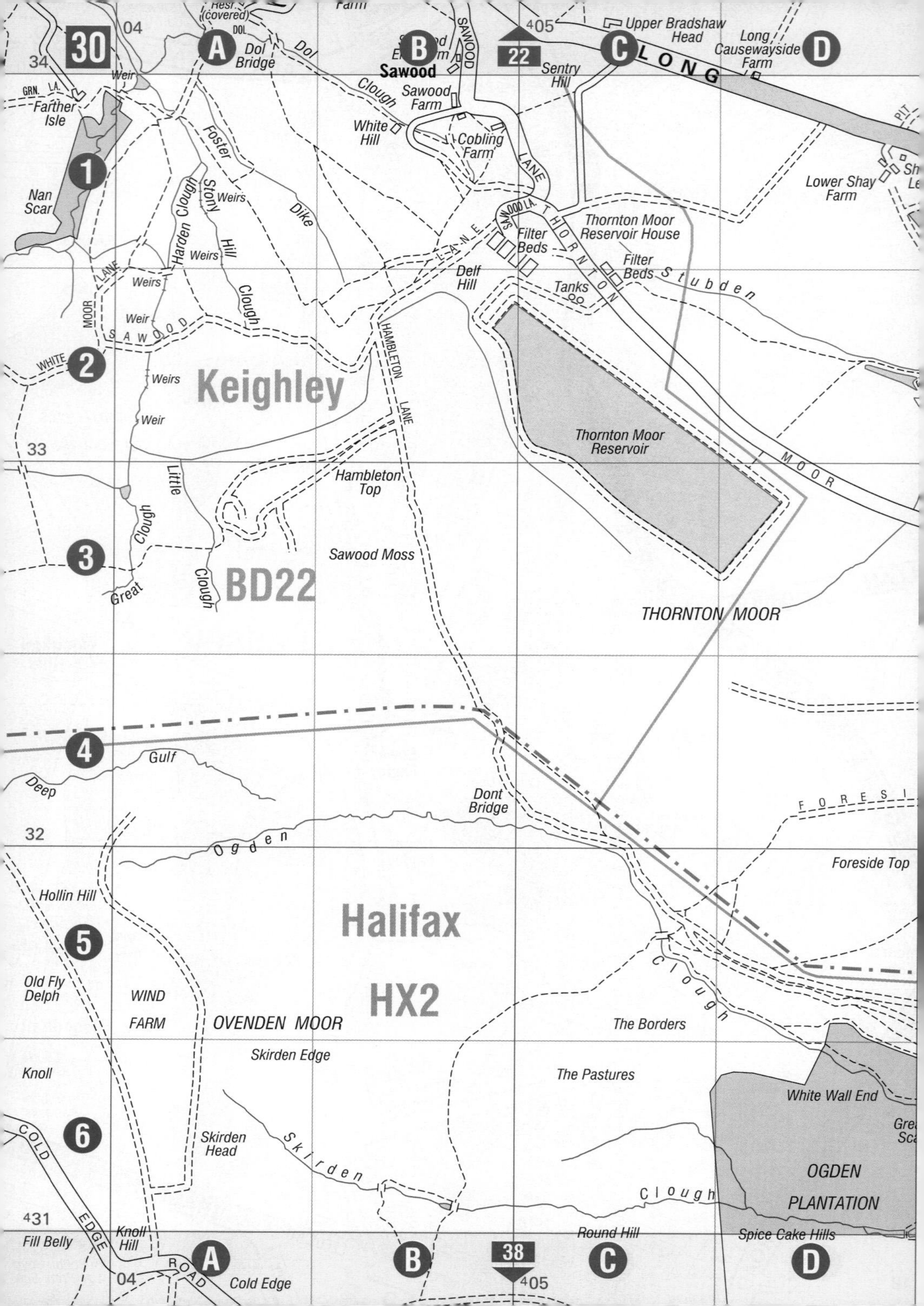

Keighley
BD22
Halifax
HX2
Sawood
Dol Bridge
Farther Isle
Nan Scar
White Hill
Sawood Farm
Cobling Farm
Sentry Hill
Upper Bradshaw Head
Long Causewayside Farm
Lower Shay Farm
Thornton Moor Reservoir House
Filter Beds
Delf Hill
Tanks
Thornton Moor Reservoir
THORNTON MOOR
Hambleton Top
Sawood Moss
Dont Bridge
Foreside Top
Hollin Hill
Old Fly Delph
WIND FARM
OVENDEN MOOR
Skirden Edge
Skirden Head
The Borders
The Pastures
White Wall End
OGDEN PLANTATION
Knoll
Knoll Hill
Fill Belly
Round Hill
Spice Cake Hills
Cold Edge
COLD EDGE ROAD
Gulf
Deep
Ogden Clough
Skirden Clough
Harden Clough
Stony Hill Clough
Little Clough
Great Clough
Foster Dike
Dol Clough
Stubden
SAWOOD LANE
HAMBLETON LANE
THORNTON MOOR
LONG
WHITE MOOR LANE
FORESIDE
22
38

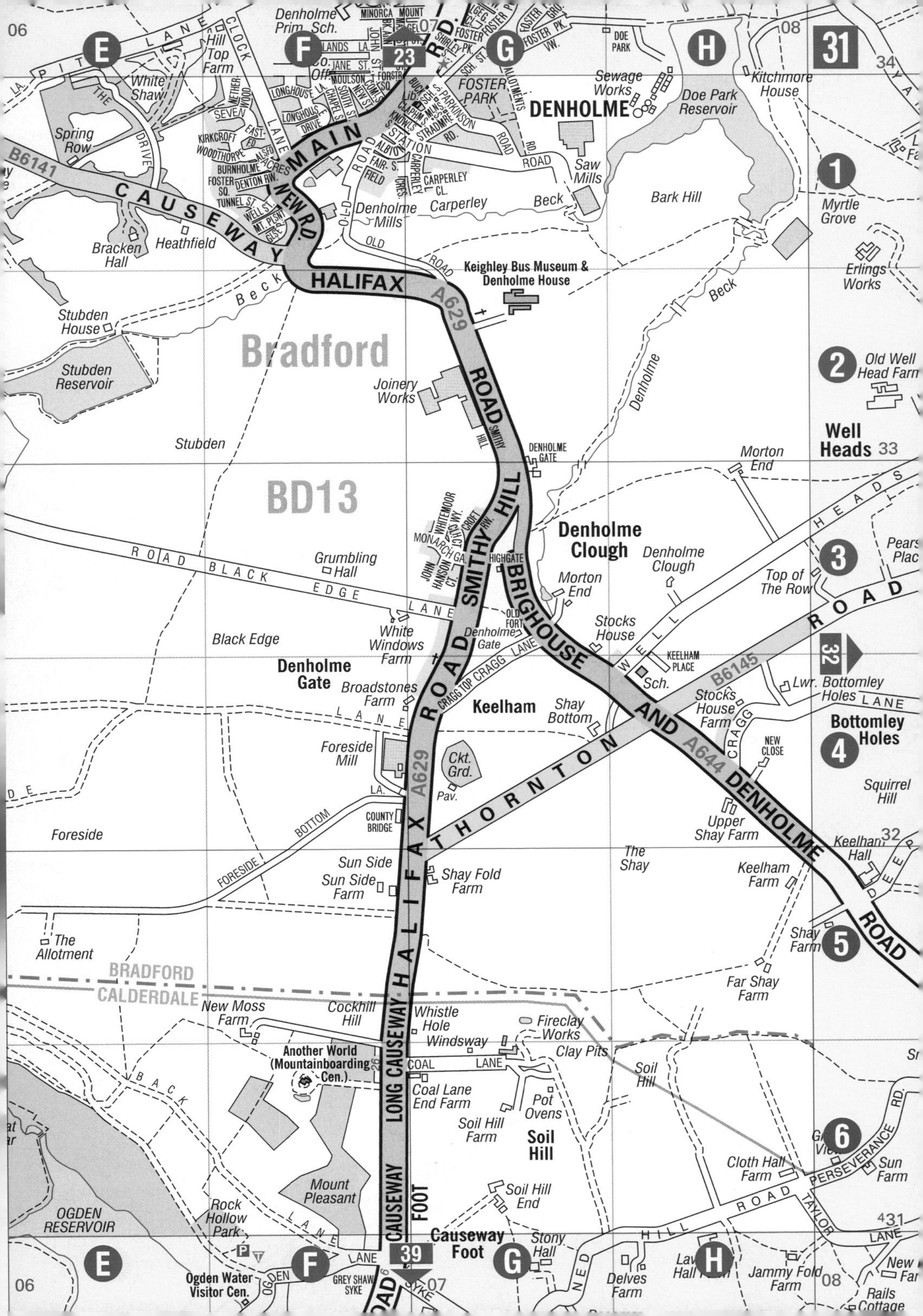

31
23
39
32
DENHOLME
Denholme Prim. Sch.
Foster Park
Doe Park Reservoir
Sewage Works
Kitchmore House
Spring Row
White Shaw
Hill Top Farm
Bracken Hall
Heathfield
Denholme Mills
Carperley
Bark Hill
Saw Mills
Myrtle Grove
Erlings Works
Keighley Bus Museum & Denholme House
Stubden House
Stubden Reservoir
Bradford
Joinery Works
Stubden
Old Well Head Farm
Well Heads
Morton End
BD13
Denholme Clough
Grumbling Hall
Top of The Row
Stocks House
Black Edge
White Windows Farm
Denholme Gate
Broadstones Farm
Keelham
Shay Bottom
Lwr. Bottomley Holes
Stocks House Farm
Bottomley Holes
Foreside Mill
Ckt. Grd.
Pav.
Squirrel Hill
Upper Shay Farm
Foreside
The Shay
Keelham Hall
Keelham Farm
Sun Side
Sun Side Farm
Shay Fold Farm
Shay Farm
The Allotment
Far Shay Farm
BRADFORD
CALDERDALE
New Moss Farm
Cockhill Hill
Whistle Hole
Fireclay Works
Windsway
Clay Pits
Another World (Mountainboarding Cen.)
Soil Hill
Coal Lane End Farm
Pot Ovens
Soil Hill Farm
Cloth Hall Farm
Sun Farm
Mount Pleasant
Soil Hill End
Rock Hollow Park
OGDEN RESERVOIR
Causeway Foot
Stony Hall
Delves Farm
Jammy Fold Farm
Ogden Water Visitor Cen.
Rails Cottage
HALIFAX ROAD
A629
SMITHY HILL
BRIGHOUSE AND DENHOLME ROAD
A644
THORNTON ROAD
B6145
CAUSEWAY
B6141
MAIN ST.
NEW RD.
OLD ROAD
BLACK EDGE LANE
LONG CAUSEWAY
CAUSEWAY FOOT
COAL LANE
FORESIDE BOTTOM LA.
CRAGG TOP
CRAGG LANE
WELL HEADS
PERSEVERANCE RD.
Beck
Denholme

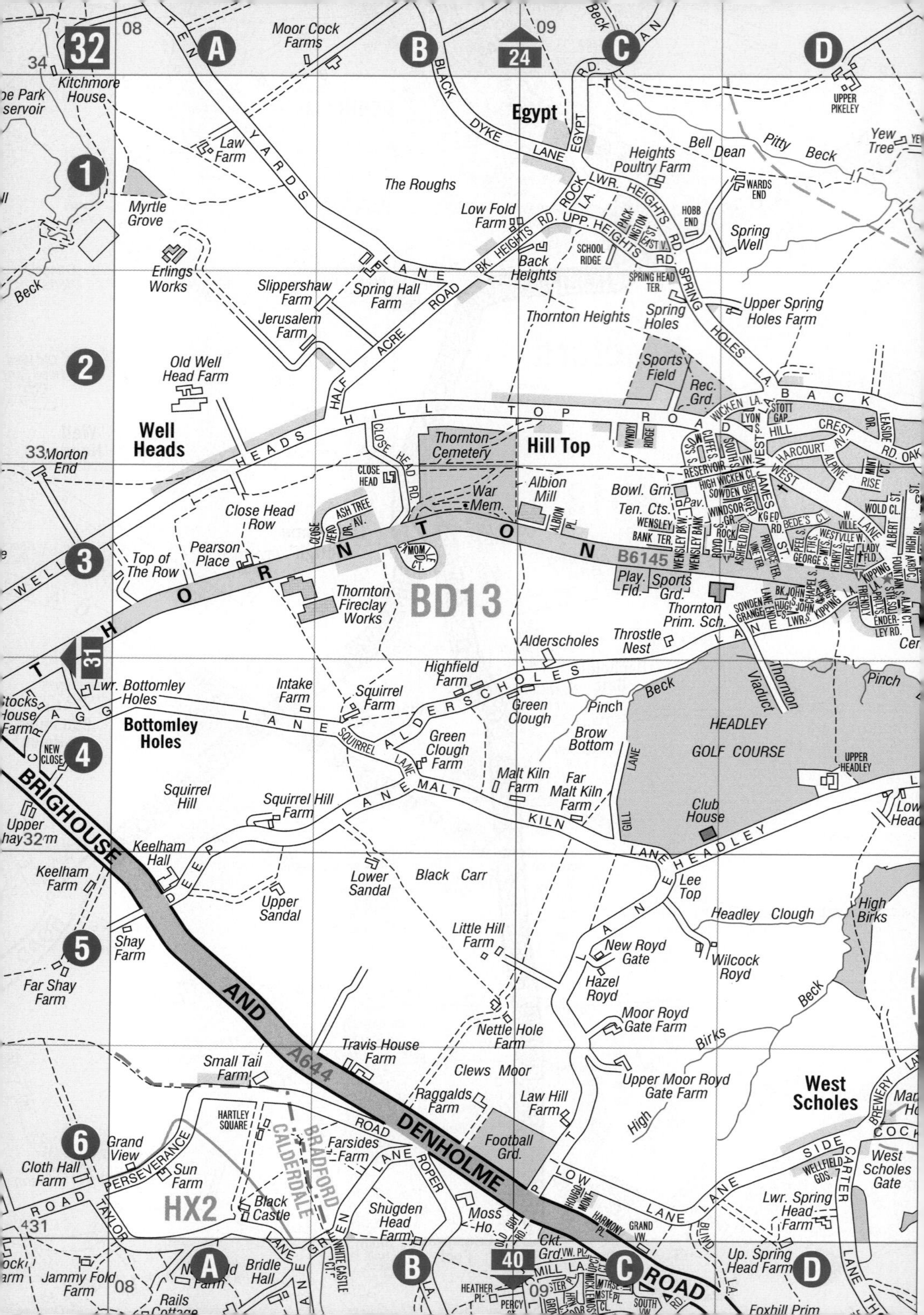
32
24
31
40
A
B
C
D
1
2
3
4
5
6
08
09
34
33
32
431
Kitchmore House
Moor Cock Farms
Upper Pikeley
Egypt
Black Dyke Lane
Ten Yards Lane
Law Farm
Myrtle Grove
Erlings Works
The Roughs
Low Fold Farm
Heights Poultry Farm
Bell Dean
Pitty Beck
Yew Tree
Wards End
Hobb End
Spring Well
Lwr. Heights Rd.
Upp. Heights Rd.
Bk. Heights Rd.
Rock La.
School Ridge
Back Heights
Spring Head Ter.
Spring Holes Lane
Upper Spring Holes Farm
Spring Holes
Thornton Heights
Slippershaw Farm
Spring Hall Farm
Jerusalem Farm
Half Acre Road
Old Well Head Farm
Sports Field
Rec. Grd.
Well Heads
Hill Top Road
Back Lane
Stott Gap
Lyon
Wicken La.
Hill Crest
Harcourt Av.
Alpine Rise
Leaside Dr.
Oak
Thornton Cemetery
Hill Top
Morton End
Heads Lane
Close Head Rd.
Close Head
Albion Mill
War Mem.
Bowl. Grn.
Ten. Cts.
Pav.
Reservoir
High Wicken Cl.
Sowden Gge.
Windsor Gr.
James St.
West La.
Wensley Bank Ter.
Bede's Cl.
Wold Cl.
Westville Lane
Albert St.
Close Head Row
Ash Tree Av.
Thornton Road
Top of The Row
Pearson Place
Well
B6145
Play. Fld.
Sports Grd.
Thornton Prim. Sch.
Thornton Fireclay Works
BD13
Kipping La.
Fountain St.
Alderscholes
Throstle Nest
Alderscholes Lane
Thornton Viaduct
Lwr. Bottomley Holes
Stocks House Farm
Cragg Lane
Highfield Farm
Intake Farm
Squirrel Farm
Green Clough
Pinch Beck
Bottomley Holes
Squirrel Lane
New Close
Green Clough Farm
Brow Bottom
Headley Golf Course
Upper Headley
Squirrel Hill
Squirrel Hill Farm
Malt Kiln Lane
Malt Kiln Farm
Far Malt Kiln Farm
Gill Lane
Club House
Low Headley
Upper Shay
Keelham Hall
Deep Lane
Headley Lane
Brighouse and Denholme Road
A644
Keelham Farm
Lower Sandal
Black Carr
Upper Sandal
Lee Top
Headley Clough
High Birks
Shay Farm
Little Hill Farm
New Royd Gate
Wilcock Royd
Far Shay Farm
Hazel Royd
Moor Royd Gate Farm
Beck
Birks
Nettle Hole Farm
Small Tail Farm
Travis House Farm
Clews Moor
Upper Moor Royd Gate Farm
West Scholes
Raggalds Farm
Law Hill Farm
High
Hartley Square
Bradford
Calderdale
Football Grd.
Brewery Lane
Cock Hill
Grand View
Cloth Hall Farm
Perseverance Road
Farsides Farm
Roper Lane
Low Lane
Side
West Scholes Gate
Sun Farm
Wellfield Gds.
HX2
Taylor Road
Black Castle
Shugden Head Farm
Moss Ho.
Harmony Pl.
Grand Vw.
Lwr. Spring Head Farm
Carter Lane
Green Lane
White Castle Ct.
Ckt. Grd.
Up. Spring Head Farm
Jammy Fold Farm
Bridle Hall
Mill La.
Heather Pl.
Percy
Rails Cottage
Foxhill Prim

33
E
F
G
H
25
41
34
1
2
3
4
5
6
410
11
12
431
BD15
BD14
Bradford
THORNTON
CLAYTON
Lower Grange
School Green
Town End
Lane End
Yews Green
Broad
THORNTON ROAD
B6145
Thornton Recreation Centre
Thornton Grammar Sch.
Sports Ground
Sandal
Bailey Fold
Old Cote Farm
Lower Pikeley
Aldersley
Allerton Upper Grn.
Upper Allerton La.
Long Lane
Dean House
Pitty Beck
Pitty Beck Bridge
Salt Pie
Cliffe Lane
Storrs
North Cliffe
Lower Hoyle Ing
Upper Hoyle Ing
Grandage Gate Farm
Broom Hill
Blue Weir
Allerton Lane
Ley Top Prim. Sch.
Allerton Grange
Cricket Grd.
Grave Yd.
Thornton Hall Farm
Nurs. Home
Mill Ponds
Weir
Mill Race
Pinch Beck
Mill Pond
Dye Royd Farm
Birks
High Birks
Chat Hill Farm
Chat Hill Road
Westfield Mews
Thorntree Farm
Valley Farm
Clayton Beck
Carr Ho. Farm
Cresswell House Farm
Cross Lea Farm
Hanging Fall Wood
Old Farm
Mavis Farm
Field House
Sun Wood Farm
Hole Bottom Beck
Hanging Falls
Mitchell Hall
Ashby Ho.
Green Head Farm
Yews Farm
Yews Grn. Farm
Hollingwell Hill
Hole Bottom Farm
The Towers
Fox Brow
Fall Top Farm
Ferncliffe Ho.
Brook Lane
Hole Bottom
Lanes Farm
Bridle Stile Farm
Willow Hall Farm
Old Ghyll Farm
Clayton Edge Farm
Low Fold
White Acres Farm
Brow Top Farm
Fiddler's Hill Farm
Sheep Hill
Baldwin Lane
Back Lane
Greenacres
Langberries
Upper Syke
Upper Penny Hill
Lwr. Penny Hill
Rec. Grd.
Play. Fld.
Ckt. Grd.
Victoria Pk.
Falls Farm
Holts Lane
Bradford Rd.
Leaventhorpe Lane
Southlands Av.
Hughendon Drive
Thorpe Av.
Old Road
Sapgate
Market St.
Highgate Mills Farm

34
A
B
C
D
26
13
1
2
3
4
5
6
Bradford Girls Grammar School
Allerton Rd.
Chellow Dean
Ladyhill Park
Bowling Green
Cricket Grd.
Chapel Grange Sch.
Tennis Cts.
Rhodesway Sch.
Rhodesway Pool
Allerton Grange
Lower Grange
Blue Weir
BD15
BD8
BD13
BD14
BD7
Recreation Ground
Four Lane Ends
Playing Field
Fairweather Green
Works
Crossley Hall
Green Side
Greenside Park
Thiefscore Bri.
Thornton Road
B6145
Middle Brook
Mill Race
Leaventhorpe Lane
Factory
Birks
Birks Fold
Scholemoor Crematorium
Scholemoor Cemetery
Scholemoor
Sports Ground
Leaventhorpe
Beck
Clayton
33
Bradford
Cemetery
Bull Greave Wood
Bull Greave Beck
Deep Lane
Middle Lane
Bradford Road
St. Anthony's RC Prim. Sch.
Clayton C of E Prim. School
Broad Folds
CLAYTON
Lidget Bridge
Clayton Lane
Sports Grd.
Ckt. Grd.
Football Grd.
Paradise Green
Brackenhill Park
Upper Green
Brackenhill Prim. Sch.
Thornaby Avenue
Pentland Avenue
Underhill Farm
Clayton Golf Course
Rec. Grd.
Club Ho.
Hollingwood Prim. Sch.
Horton Bank
Lwr. Penny Hill
Upper Penny Hill
Lane End
Horton Bank Country Park
Thornton View
Great Horton Road
A647
Highgate Mills Farm
Nab End
Pickles Hill
42
431
Spencer Road
Necropolis Road
Hollingwood Lane
Windermere Road

35
27
4
36
43
E
F
G
H
1
2
3
4
5
6
BRADFORD
Brown Royd
Warehouse
Lister Hills
Princeville
Warehouse
Shearbridge
University of Bradford
Sports Cen.
Bradford College
College
Little Horton Green
Nurses Home
Dirk Hill
Uni. of Bradford
Little Horton
Holme Top
Chapel Green
Great Horton
Horton Bank Bottom
Sellars Fold
Lidget Green
Superstore
St. William's RC Prim. Sch.
Warehouses
Depot
Factory
Beck
Bradford City Farm
Indoor Karting
Hockney Rd. Ind. Est.
Playing Fields
Schs.
Mills
Shires Bus. Park
Copthorne Prim. Sch.
Comm. Cen.
Works
Halls of Residence
ST. LUKE'S HOSPITAL
Academy of Ckt.
Cricket Grd.
Bowling Greens
HORTON PARK
Tennis Courts
Nutter House
Rec. Grd.
Horton Park Prim. Sch.
Grange Sports Cen.
Haycliffe School
Douglas Mills
Tech. Coll.
Newby Prim. Sch.
Ice Arena
Mus. & Cin.
Oastler Shop. Cen.
Drummond Trad. Est.
Listerhills Ind. Est.
Norcroft Ind. Est.
Listerhills Science Pk.
Phoenix Buildings
BD1
BD5
THORNTON ROAD
WHETLEY LANE
WHETLEY HILL
WHITE ABBEY RD.
WESTGATE
DREWTON
MANNINGHAM LANE
INGLEBY ROAD
A6177
HORTON GRANGE RD.
GT. HORTON RD.
MORLEY ST.
EASBY RD.
DIRKHILL RD.
A647
B6144
B6145
A650
A641
MANCHESTER RD.
HUDSON AV.
SOUTHFIELD LA.
SOUTHFIELD RD.
GREAT HORTON
PARK AVENUE
ALL SAINTS ROAD
LEGRAMS LANE
PRINCES WAY
GRATTAN RD.
CITY RD.

36
A
B
C
D
28
4
5
35
44
1
2
3
4
5
6
BRADFORD
Bradford Forster Sq.
Bradford Interchange
Transport Interchange
Barkerend
Eastbrook
Wapping
Broomfields
West Bowling
East Bowling
BOWLING
BD5
BD1
Forster Sq. Retail Pk.
Valley Rd. Retail Park
Kirkgate Cen.
Oastler Shop. Cen.
Inland Revenue
Cath.
Shop. Cen. (proposed)
City Hall
Crown Ct.
Hollywood Bowl
Cineworld
Mus. & Cin.
Ice Arena
Thtre.
Bradford College
St. James Business Park
St. James Abattoir
St. James's Market
Essex Pk. Ind. Est.
Bus Depot
Birksland Industrial Estate
Napoleon Bus. Park
Fowler St. Ind. Est.
Cityway Ind. Est.
Bradford Kart Racing
Mill La. Junc.
Bramall Bus. Pk.
Douglas Mills
Tech. Coll.
Newby Prim. Sch.
Bowling Park Prim. Sch.
Bowling Comm. Coll.
Bolling Hall (Mus.)
Bowling Swim. Pool
Bowling Park
Playing Fields
Fossil Tree
Bradford Cathedral Comm. Coll.
Bolling Spec. Sch.
Marie Curie Cen.
Leeds Rd. Hosp.
St. Luke's Hospital
Nurses Home
Barkerend Prim. Sch.
Byron Prim. Sch.
College
Pollard Park
Sikh Temple
Hindu Temple
Roughs
Hamm-Strasse
Shipley Airedale Road
Canal Rd.
Manningham La.
Drewton St.
Westgate
Godwin Street
Prince's Way
Hall Ings
Croft Street
Leeds Road
Wakefield Road
Bowling Old Lane
Manchester Road
Rooley Lane
Otley Rd.
New Otley Rd.
Barkerend Rd.
Morley St.
Little Horton Lane
Upper Castle Street
Parkside Road
Cross Street
A650
A6181
A6181
A658
A647
A641
A647
B6381

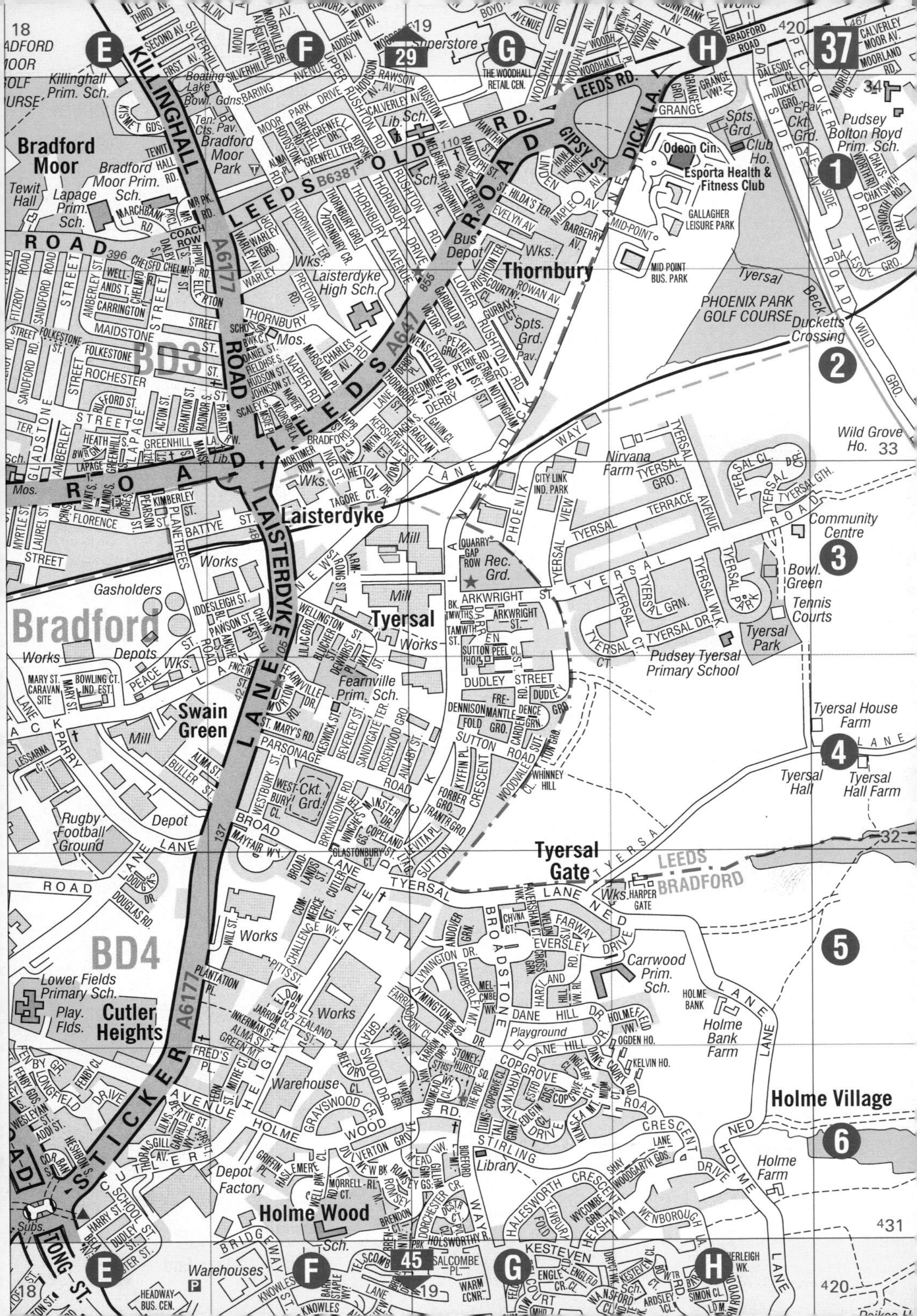
37
29
45
Bradford Moor
Bradford Moor Park
Bradford Moor Prim. Sch.
Killinghall Prim. Sch.
Lapage Prim. Sch.
Tewit Hall
KILLINGHALL RD.
LEEDS OLD RD.
LEEDS ROAD
A6177
A647
B6381
BD3
BD4
Thornbury
Laisterdyke
Laisterdyke High Sch.
LAISTERDYKE
Bradford
Tyersal
Tyersal Gate
Tyersal Park
Pudsey Tyersal Primary School
Fearnville Prim. Sch.
Swain Green
Odeon Cin.
Esporta Health & Fitness Club
GALLAGHER LEISURE PARK
MID POINT BUS. PARK
PHOENIX PARK GOLF COURSE
Ducketts Crossing
Pudsey Bolton Royd Prim. Sch.
Wild Grove Ho.
Nirvana Farm
CITY LINK IND. PARK
Community Centre
Tyersal House Farm
Tyersal Hall
Tyersal Hall Farm
LEEDS
BRADFORD
Carrwood Prim. Sch.
Holme Bank Farm
Holme Village
Holme Farm
Holme Wood
Rugby Football Ground
Lower Fields Primary Sch.
Cutler Heights
STICKER LANE
TONG ST.
Warehouses
HEADWAY BUS. CEN.
THE WOODHALL RETAIL CEN.
Superstore
Gasholders
MARY ST. CARAVAN SITE
BOWLING CT. IND. EST.

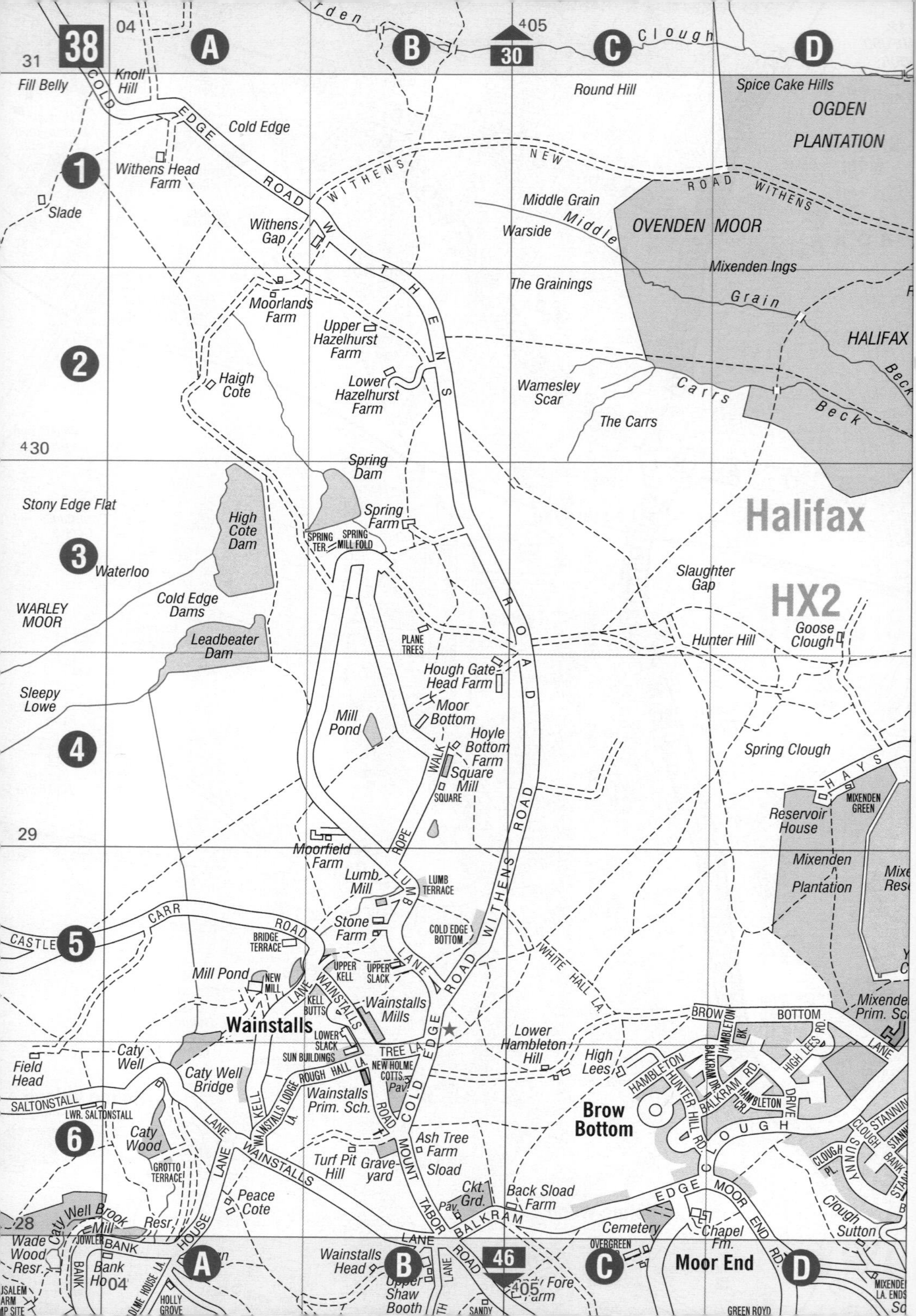

A
B
C
D
30
Clough
Fill Belly
Knoll Hill
COLD EDGE ROAD
Cold Edge
Round Hill
Spice Cake Hills
OGDEN PLANTATION
Withens Head Farm
Slade
NEW WITHENS ROAD
Withens Gap
Middle Grain
Warside
OVENDEN MOOR
Mixenden Ings
The Grainings
Moorlands Farm
Upper Hazelhurst Farm
Lower Hazelhurst Farm
Haigh Cote
Wamesley Scar
Carrs Beck
The Carrs
HALIFAX
Spring Dam
Spring Farm
Stony Edge Flat
High Cote Dam
SPRING TER.
SPRING MILL FOLD
Halifax
Waterloo
Slaughter Gap
HX2
WARLEY MOOR
Cold Edge Dams
Leadbeater Dam
PLANE TREES
Hunter Hill
Goose Clough
Hough Gate Head Farm
Sleepy Lowe
Mill Pond
Moor Bottom
Hoyle Bottom Farm
Spring Clough
WALK
Square Mill
SQUARE
HAYS
MIXENDEN GREEN
Reservoir House
ROPE
Moorfield Farm
Mixenden Plantation
Lumb Mill
LUMB TERRACE
LUMB LANE
WITHENS ROAD
CASTLE CARR ROAD
Stone Farm
BRIDGE TERRACE
COLD EDGE BOTTOM
WHITE HALL LA.
Mill Pond
NEW MILL
UPPER KELL
UPPER SLACK
KELL BUTTS
WAINSTALLS
Wainstalls Mills
Wainstalls
LOWER SLACK
COLD EDGE ROAD
BROW BOTTOM LANE
Lower Hambleton Hill
Mixenden Prim. Sch.
Field Head
Caty Well
TREE LA.
SUN BUILDINGS
Caty Well Bridge
ROUGH HALL LA.
NEW HOLME COTTS.
Pav.
High Lees
HAMBLETON
HUNTER HILL RD.
BALKRAM DR.
BALKRAM RD.
HIGH LEES RD.
SALTONSTALL
LWR. SALTONSTALL
KELL LANE
WAINSTALLS LODGE LA.
Wainstalls Prim. Sch.
ROAD
Brow Bottom
CLOUGH
DRIVE
Caty Wood
GROTTO TERRACE
Ash Tree Farm
Sload
Turf Pit Hill
Grave-yard
MOUNT TABOR
STANNINGLEY
CLOUGH PL.
Peace Cote
Ckt. Grd.
Back Sload Farm
EDGE MOOR END RD.
Clough Sutton
Caty Well Brook
Mill
Resr.
HOUSE LANE
WAINSTALLS LANE
BALKRAM ROAD
Cemetery
Chapel Fm.
OVERGREEN
Wade Wood Resr.
JOWLER
BANK
Bank
Wainstalls Head
46
Moor End
MIXENDEN LA. ENDS
Upper Shaw Booth
Fore Farm
HOLLY GROVE
SANDY
GREEN ROYD
04
405
31
430
29
28

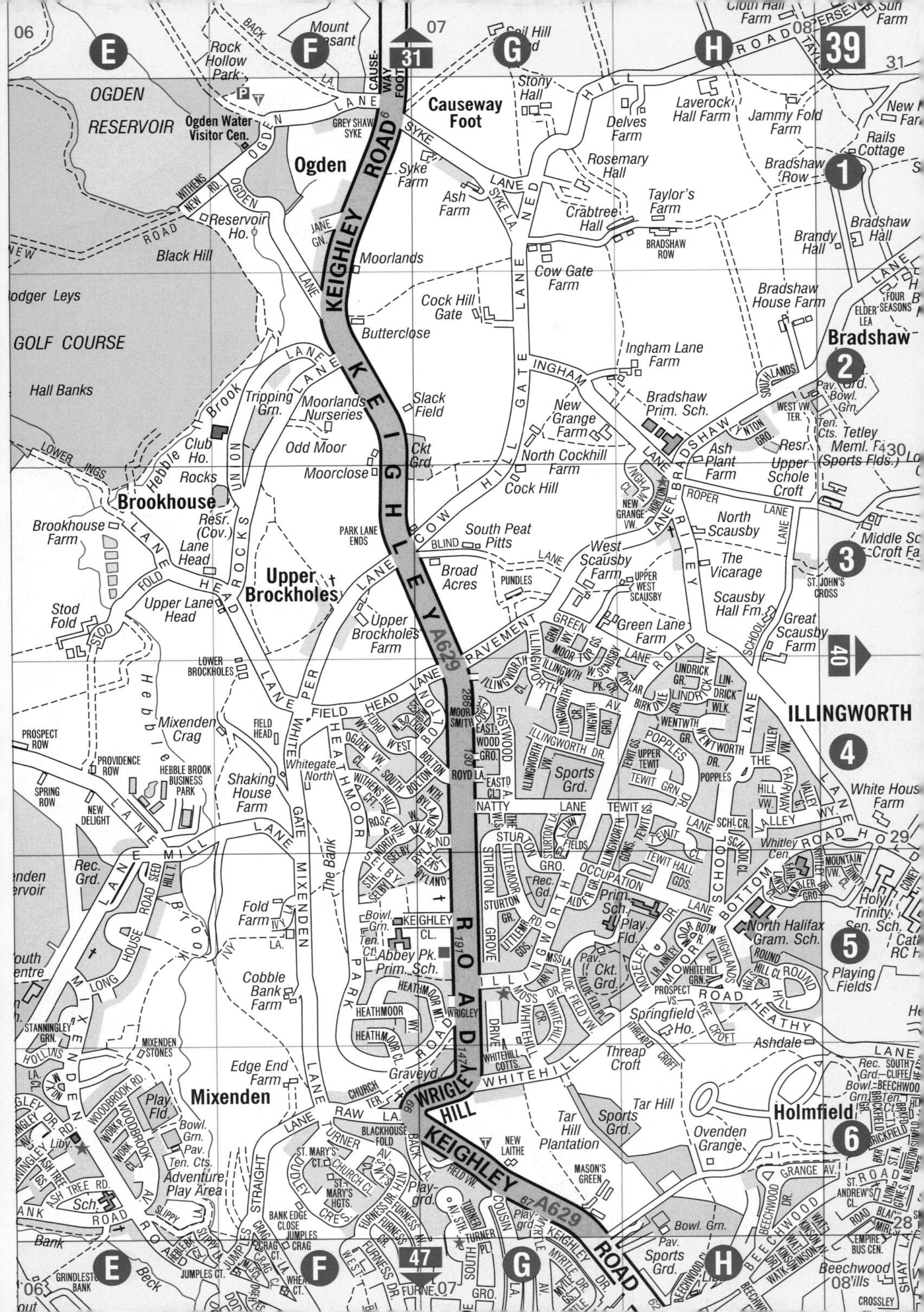

39
31
47
40
E
F
G
H
1
2
3
4
5
6
06
07
08
OGDEN
RESERVOIR
Ogden Water Visitor Cen.
Rock Hollow Park
Mount Pleasant
Soil Hill
Causeway Foot
Ogden
KEIGHLEY ROAD
Syke Farm
Ash Farm
Stony Hall
Delves Farm
Laverock Hall Farm
Jammy Fold Farm
Rails Cottage
Bradshaw Row
Rosemary Hall
Taylor's Farm
Crabtree Hall
Bradshaw Hall
Brandy Hall
Reservoir Ho.
Black Hill
Rodger Leys
GOLF COURSE
Hall Banks
Moorlands
Cow Gate Farm
Cock Hill Gate
Butterclose
Bradshaw House Farm
Ingham Lane Farm
Bradshaw
Tripping Grn.
Moorlands Nurseries
Slack Field
Odd Moor
Ckt Grd.
Moorclose
New Grange Farm
Bradshaw Prim. Sch.
North Cockhill Farm
Cock Hill
Club Ho.
Rocks
Brookhouse
Brookhouse Farm
Resr. (Cov.)
Lane Head
South Peat Pitts
Broad Acres
West Scausby Farm
North Scausby
The Vicarage
Scausby Hall Fm.
Great Scausby Farm
Upper Brockholes
Upper Lane Head
Stod Fold
Upper Brockholes Farm
Green Lane Farm
Ash Plant Farm
Upper Schole Croft
Tetley Meml. F. (Sports Flds.)
Middle Scholes Croft Fa
ILLINGWORTH
Mixenden Crag
Shaking House Farm
Whitegate North
Sports Grd.
White House Farm
Rec. Grd.
Fold Farm
The Bank
Cobble Bank Farm
Abbey Pk. Prim. Sch.
Whitley Cen.
Holy Trinity Sen. Sch.
North Halifax Gram. Sch.
Playing Fields
Prim. Sch.
Play. Fld.
Ckt. Grd.
Springfield Ho.
Ashdale
Threap Croft
Edge End Farm
Mixenden
Graveyd.
WRIGLEY HILL
Play. Fld.
Tar Hill
Tar Hill Plantation
Sports Grd.
Ovenden Grange
Holmfield
Adventure Play Area
Sch.
Bowl. Grn.
Pav. Sports Grd.
Beechwood Hills
A629
Bank
Beck

A
B
C
D
1
2
3
4
5
6
32
39
48
Black Castle
Sun Farm
Jammy Fold Farm
New Fold Farm
Bridle Hall
Rails Cottage
Saddle Hall Farm
Bradshaw Row
Bradshaw Hall
Brandy Hall
Bradshaw House Farm
Harper Bower Farm
Four Seasons
Elder Lea
Bradshaw
Crkt. Grd.
Pav.
Bowl. Grn.
Ten. Cts.
Tetley Meml. Pk. (Sports Flds.)
Resr.
Upper Schole Croft
Lower Schole Croft Farm
Middle Schole Croft Farm
North Scausby
The Vicarage
Scausby Hall Fm.
Great Scausby
St. John's Cross
HX2
ILLINGWORTH
Shugden Head Farm
Shugden Farm
Upper Fold
Small Clough Farm
Woodland Farm
May Royd Farm
Strines Beck
BRADFORD
CALDERDALE
Oats Royd
Royd Hill
The Gulf
Warmleigh Park
Warmleigh Hall
Warmleigh Farm
Warmleigh House
Roper Farm
Mickle Moss Farm
Mickle Moss
Ckt. Grd.
Mountain Res.
Upper Fleet Farm
Mountain
Foxhill Prim. Sch.
Clayton Edge
Queensbury Park
Hill Top Farm
Up. Spring Head Farm
Lwr. Spring Head Farm
Scholes Gate
Brighouse and Denholme Rd.
A644
Albert
West End
A647
Ford Hill
Upper Moor Cl.
Moor Close
Rec. Grd.
Cape of Good Hope
Shibden Head Prim. Sch.
West End
Shibden Brook
St. Elmo
Ambler Thorn
Folly Hall
Hazel Hurst Farm
Long Lane
Holmfield Industrial Estate
Works
Factory
Ambler Thorn Fireclay Works
Holdsworth
Victoria Wks.
Wks.
White House Farm
Whitley Cen.
Holy Trinity Sen. Sch.
St. Catherine's RC High Sch.
North Halifax Gra. Sch.
Playing Fields
School Cote Ter.
Windy Bank Lane
Priestley Hill
Shibden Head
Hanging Royd
Burnt Brow
Henacre Wood
Catherine Slack
Catherine Slack Farm
Twist Wood
Upper Shibden Hall
Holly Bank
Sewage Works
Shibden Brook
Netherton Mills
Heathy Ho.
Heathy Lane
Ashdale
Rec. Grd.
Bowl. Grn.
Ten. Ct.
Holmfield
Holmfield House
Empire Bus Cen.
Ovenden Brook
North Howcans
South Howcans
Beechwood Hills
Halifax Road
Queensbury Road
Slack End
Lower Shibden Hall
Halifax
Water Scout
Swales Moor
Swales Moor Mink Farm
Cross Point
Lower Lime House
Upper Lime House
Simm Carr La.
Bare Head
Crossley

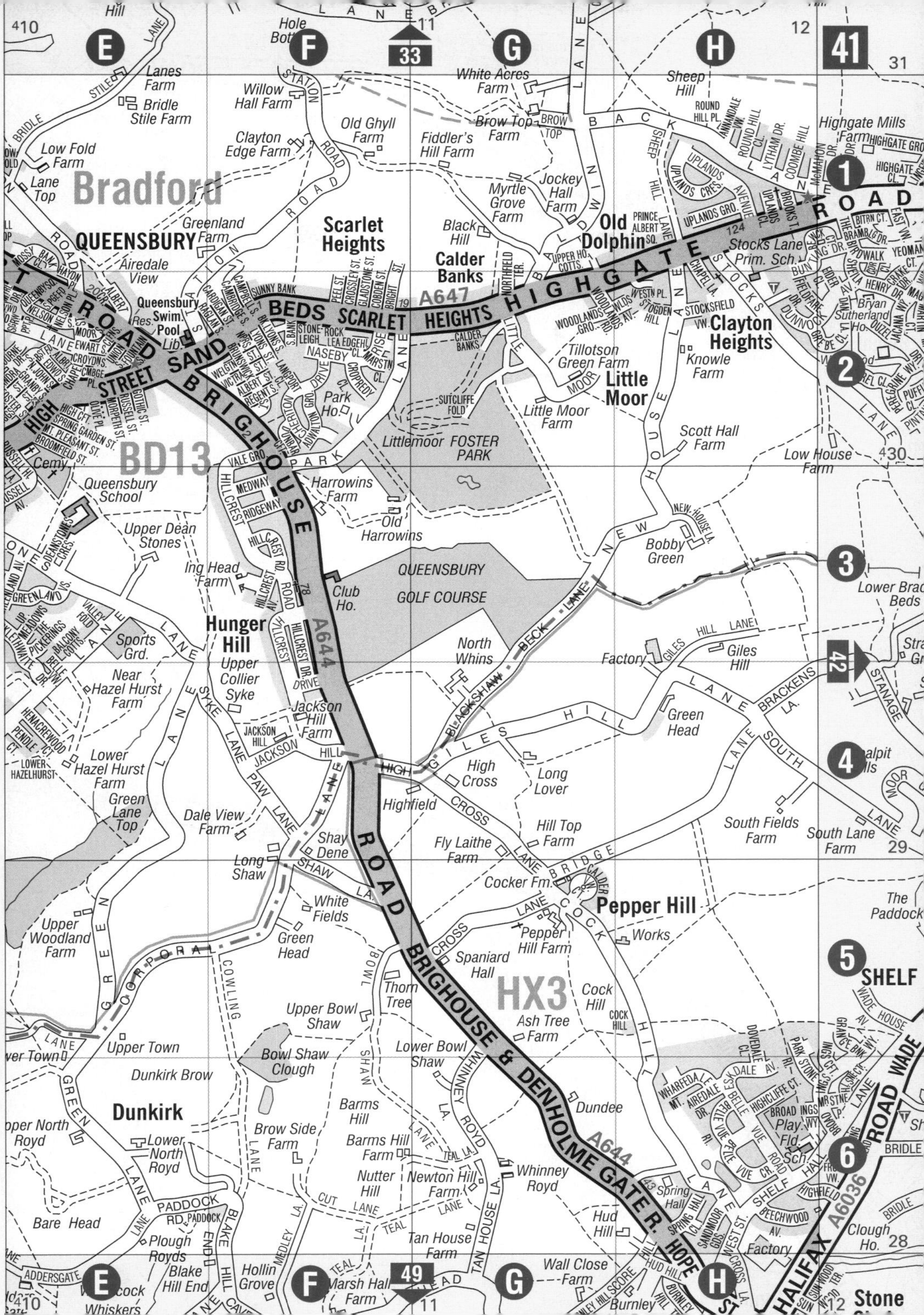
41
33
42
49
E
F
G
H
1
2
3
4
5
6
410
11
12
31
430
29
28
Bradford
QUEENSBURY
BD13
HX3
Scarlet Heights
Calder Banks
Old Dolphin
Clayton Heights
Little Moor
Hunger Hill
Pepper Hill
SHELF
Dunkirk
HIGHGATE ROAD
A647
BEDS SCARLET HEIGHTS
HIGH STREET
SAND
BRIGHOUSE ROAD
A644
BRIGHOUSE & DENHOLME GATE R.
HALIFAX ROAD
A6036
WADE HOUSE ROAD
Lanes Farm
Bridle Stile Farm
Low Fold Farm
Lane Top
Willow Hall Farm
Clayton Edge Farm
Old Ghyll Farm
White Acres Farm
Brow Top Farm
Fiddler's Hill Farm
Myrtle Grove Farm
Jockey Hall Farm
Sheep Hill
Highgate Mills Farm
Greenland Farm
Airedale View
Queensbury Swim Pool
Black Hill
Stocks Lane Prim. Sch.
Bryan Sutherland Ho.
Tillotson Green Farm
Knowle Farm
Little Moor Farm
Scott Hall Farm
Low House Farm
Park Ho.
Littlemoor FOSTER PARK
Harrowins Farm
Old Harrowins
Queensbury School
Upper Dean Stones
Ing Head Farm
QUEENSBURY GOLF COURSE
Club Ho.
Bobby Green
Lower Brad Beds
Sports Grd.
Near Hazel Hurst Farm
Upper Collier Syke
Jackson Hill Farm
North Whins
Factory
Giles Hill
Green Head
Lower Hazel Hurst Farm
Green Lane Top
Dale View Farm
High Cross
Long Lover
Highfield
Shay Dene
Long Shaw
Fly Laithe Farm
Hill Top Farm
South Fields Farm
South Lane Farm
Cocker Fm.
The Paddock
White Fields
Green Head
Pepper Hill Farm
Works
Upper Woodland Farm
Spaniard Hall
Thorn Tree
Upper Bowl Shaw
Cock Hill
Ash Tree Farm
Upper Town
Bowl Shaw Clough
Lower Bowl Shaw
Dunkirk Brow
Barms Hill
Dundee
Brow Side Farm
Barms Hill Farm
Lower North Royd
Nutter Hill
Newton Hill Farm
Whinney Royd
Spring Hall
Play. Fld.
Sch.
Bare Head
Plough Royds
Blake Hill End
Tan House Farm
Hud Hill
Factory
Clough Ho.
Hollin Grove
Marsh Hall Farm
Wall Close Farm
Burnley
Stone
Whiskers
CORPORAL LANE
NEW HOUSE LANE
GILES HILL LANE
BRACKENS LA.
SOUTH LANE
STANAGE
MOOR LANE
BLACKSHAW BECK LANE
CROSS LANE
BRIDGE
SHAW LA.
COWLING LANE
PADDOCK RD.
BLAKE HILL END
CUT LANE
TEAL LA.
TAN HOUSE LA.
WHINNEY ROYD LA.
PARK LANE
STATION ROAD
BACK LANE
BALDWIN LANE
STOCKS LANE
SHEEP HILL LANE
SHELF HALL LANE
HOPE

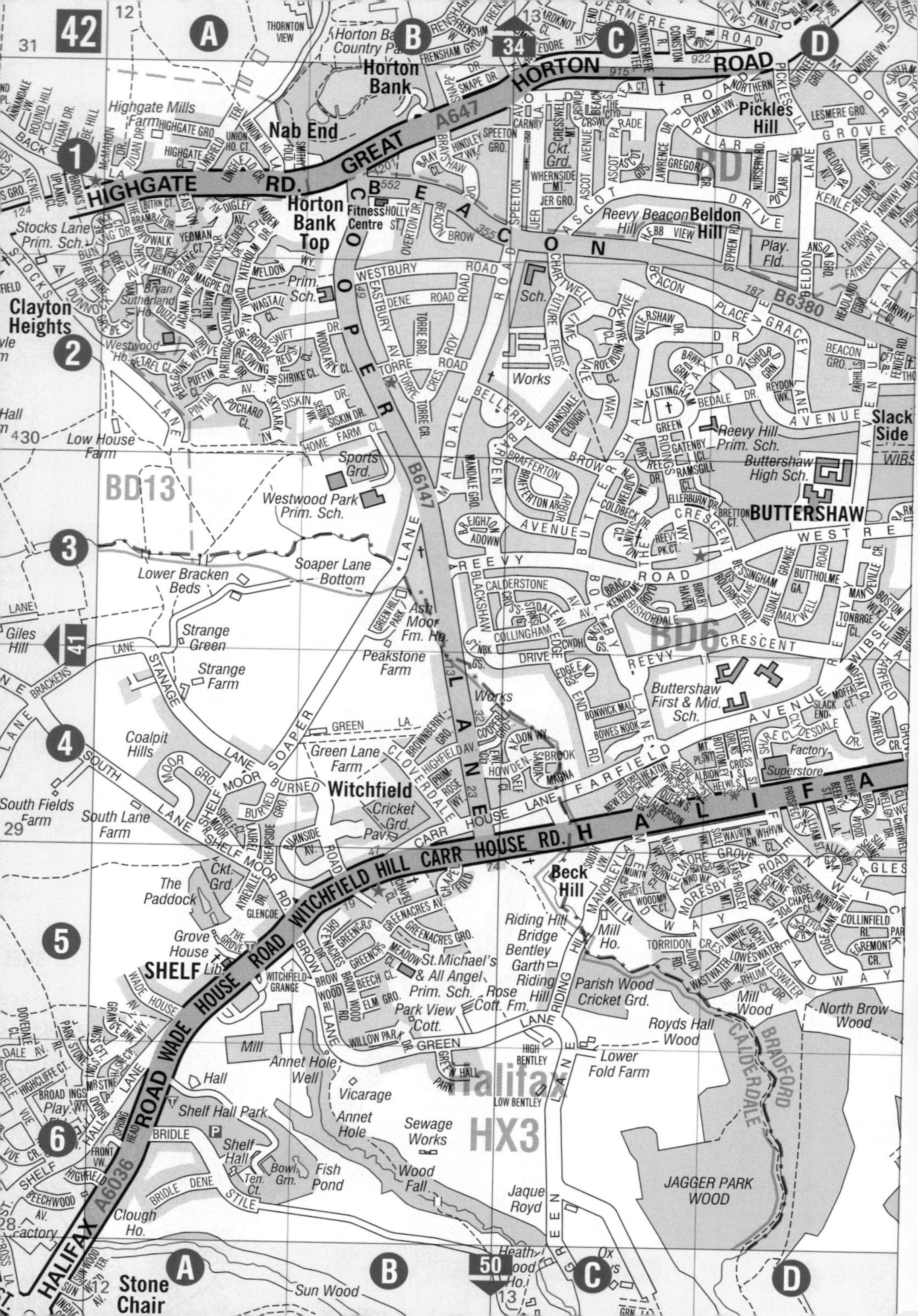

42
34
41
50
Horton Bank Country Park
Horton Bank
Nab End
Horton Bank Top
Highgate Mills Farm
GREAT HORTON ROAD
A647
HIGHGATE RD.
BEACON
B6380
Pickles Hill
Reevy Beacon Hill
Beldon Hill
BD7
Stocks Lane Prim. Sch.
Clayton Heights
Fitness Centre
Prim. Sch.
COOPER LANE
B6147
Low House Farm
BD13
Sports Grd.
Westwood Park Prim. Sch.
Reevy Hill Prim. Sch.
Buttershaw High Sch.
BUTTERSHAW
Slack Side
Soaper Lane Bottom
Lower Bracken Beds
Ash Moor Fm. Ho.
Strange Green
Strange Farm
Giles Hill
Peakstone Farm
BD6
Buttershaw First & Mid. Sch.
Works
Coalpit Hills
Green Lane Farm
Witchfield
Cricket Grd.
Superstore
Factory
South Fields Farm
South Lane Farm
CARR HOUSE RD.
HALIFAX
WITCHFIELD HILL
Beck Hill
The Paddock
Ckt. Grd.
Grove House
SHELF
St.Michael's & All Angel Prim. Sch.
Rose Cott. Fm.
Riding Hill Bridge
Bentley Garth
Riding Hill
Parish Wood Cricket Grd.
Mill Wood
North Brow Wood
WADE HOUSE ROAD
Park View Cott.
Royds Hall Wood
Lower Fold Farm
Annet Hole Well
Hall
Shelf Hall Park
Vicarage
Annet Hole
Sewage Works
Halifax
HX3
CALDERDALE
BRADFORD
Shelf Hall
Bowl. Grn.
Fish Pond
Wood Fall
JAGGER PARK WOOD
A6036
HALIFAX ROAD
Clough Ho.
Jaque Royd
Heath Wood Ho.
Sun Wood
Stone Chair

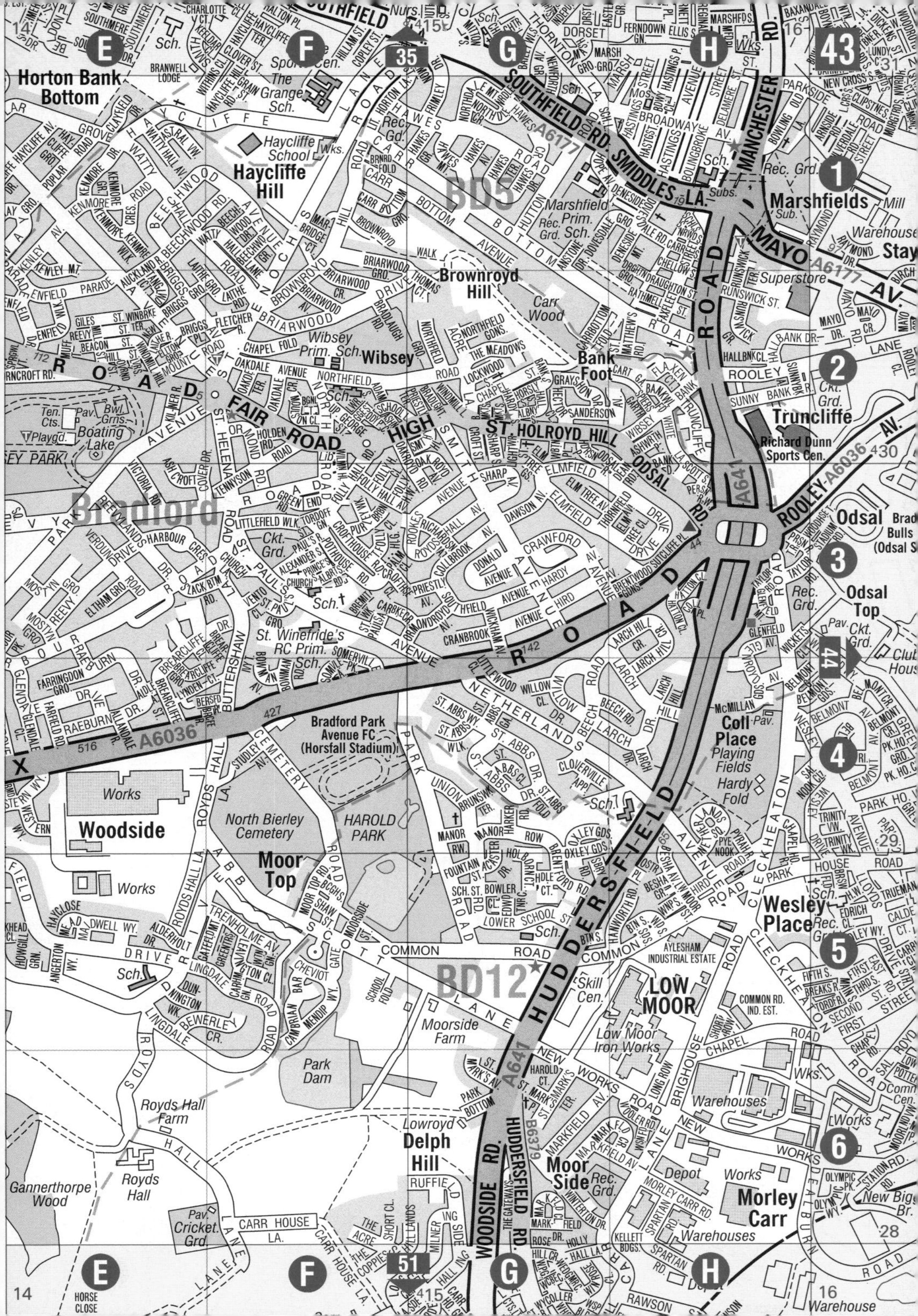
E
F
G
H
35
1
2
3
4
5
6
44
51
Horton Bank Bottom
Haycliffe Hill
Haycliffe School
The Grange Sch.
Marshfields
Marshfield Prim. Sch.
Brownroyd Hill
Carr Wood
Wibsey
Wibsey Prim. Sch.
Bank Foot
Truncliffe
Richard Dunn Sports Cen.
Odsal
Odsal Top
Bradford
BD5
BD12
Boating Lake
St. Winefride's RC Prim. Sch.
Bradford Park Avenue FC (Horsfall Stadium)
Woodside
North Bierley Cemetery
Harold Park
Moor Top
Coll Place
Playing Fields
Hardy Fold
Wesley Place
Aylesham Industrial Estate
Low Moor
Low Moor Iron Works
Common Rd. Ind. Est.
Moorside Farm
Park Dam
Royds Hall Farm
Royds Hall
Gannerthorpe Wood
Cricket Grd.
Delph Hill
Lowroyd
Moor Side
Morley Carr
Warehouses
Superstore
Skill Cen.
A6177
A6036
A641
B6379
HUDDERSFIELD RD.
MANCHESTER RD.
SMIDDLES LA.
SOUTHFIELD RD.
MAYO AV.
ROOLEY AV.
HIGH ST.
FAIR ROAD
HOLROYD HILL
ODSAL RD.
COMMON ROAD
CLECKHEATON ROAD
WOODSIDE RD.
CARR HOUSE LA.
NEW WORKS ROAD
HORSE CLOSE
14
16

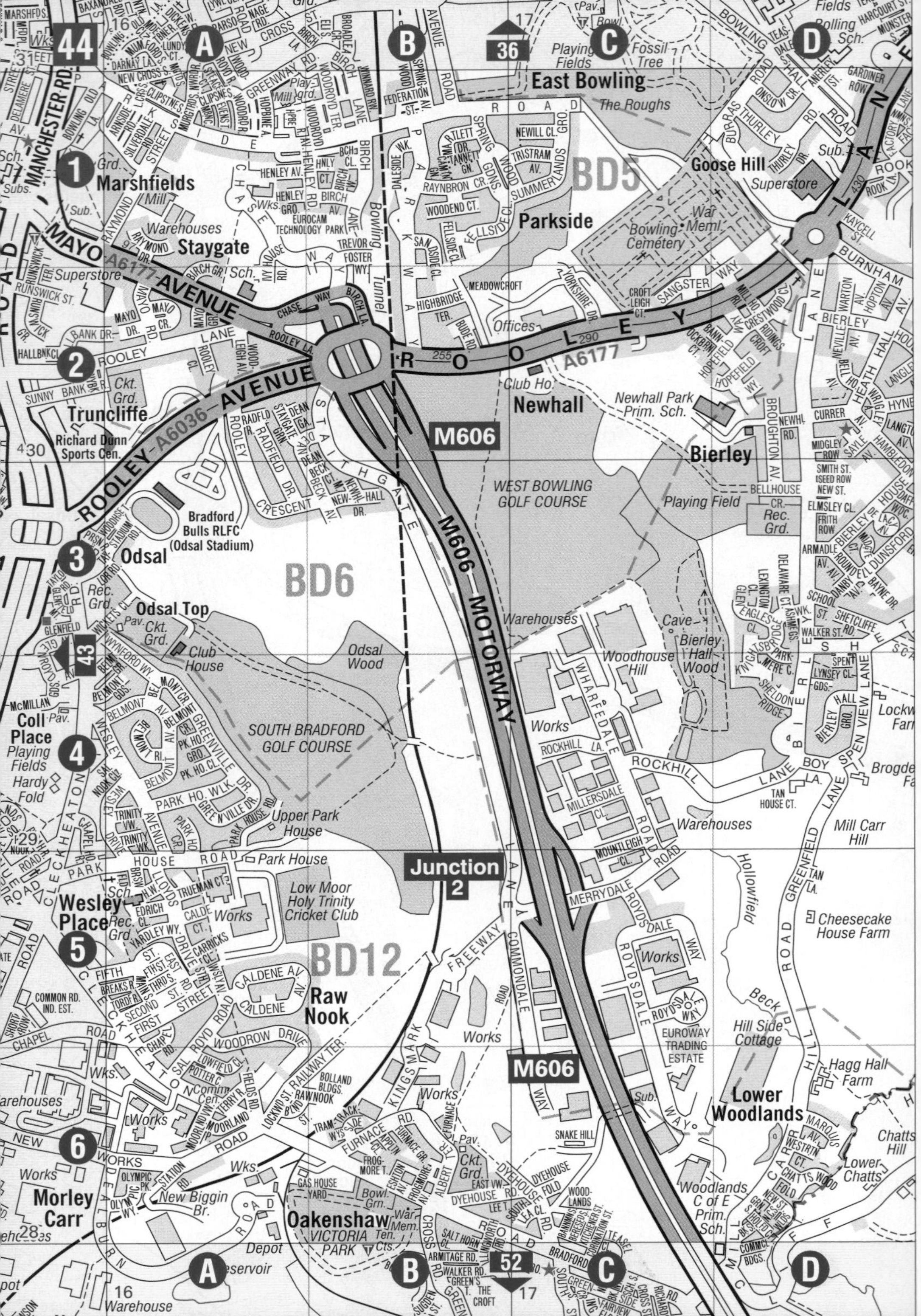
36
East Bowling
The Roughs
Fossil Tree
Playing Fields
Marshfields
Goose Hill
Superstore
BD5
Parkside
Bowling Cemetery
War Meml.
Staygate
Warehouses
Eurocam Technology Park
Bowling Tunnel
MAYO AVENUE
A6177
ROOLEY LANE
ROOLEY AVENUE
A6036
Truncliffe
Richard Dunn Sports Cen.
Newhall
Newhall Park Prim. Sch.
Bierley
M606
WEST BOWLING GOLF COURSE
Playing Field
Bradford Bulls RLFC (Odsal Stadium)
Odsal
BD6
Odsal Top
M606 MOTORWAY
Warehouses
Odsal Wood
Woodhouse Hill
Bierley Hall Wood
Cave
43
Coll Place
Playing Fields
Hardy Fold
SOUTH BRADFORD GOLF COURSE
Works
Upper Park House
Mill Carr Hill
Park House
Junction 2
Low Moor Holy Trinity Cricket Club
Wesley Place
Cheesecake House Farm
BD12
Raw Nook
EUROWAY TRADING ESTATE
Hill Side Cottage
Hagg Hall Farm
Lower Woodlands
Morley Carr
New Biggin Br.
Oakenshaw
VICTORIA PARK
Woodlands C of E Prim. Sch.
Lower Chatts
Chatts Hill
Reservoir
Warehouse
52
16
17
A
B
C
D
1
2
3
4
5
6

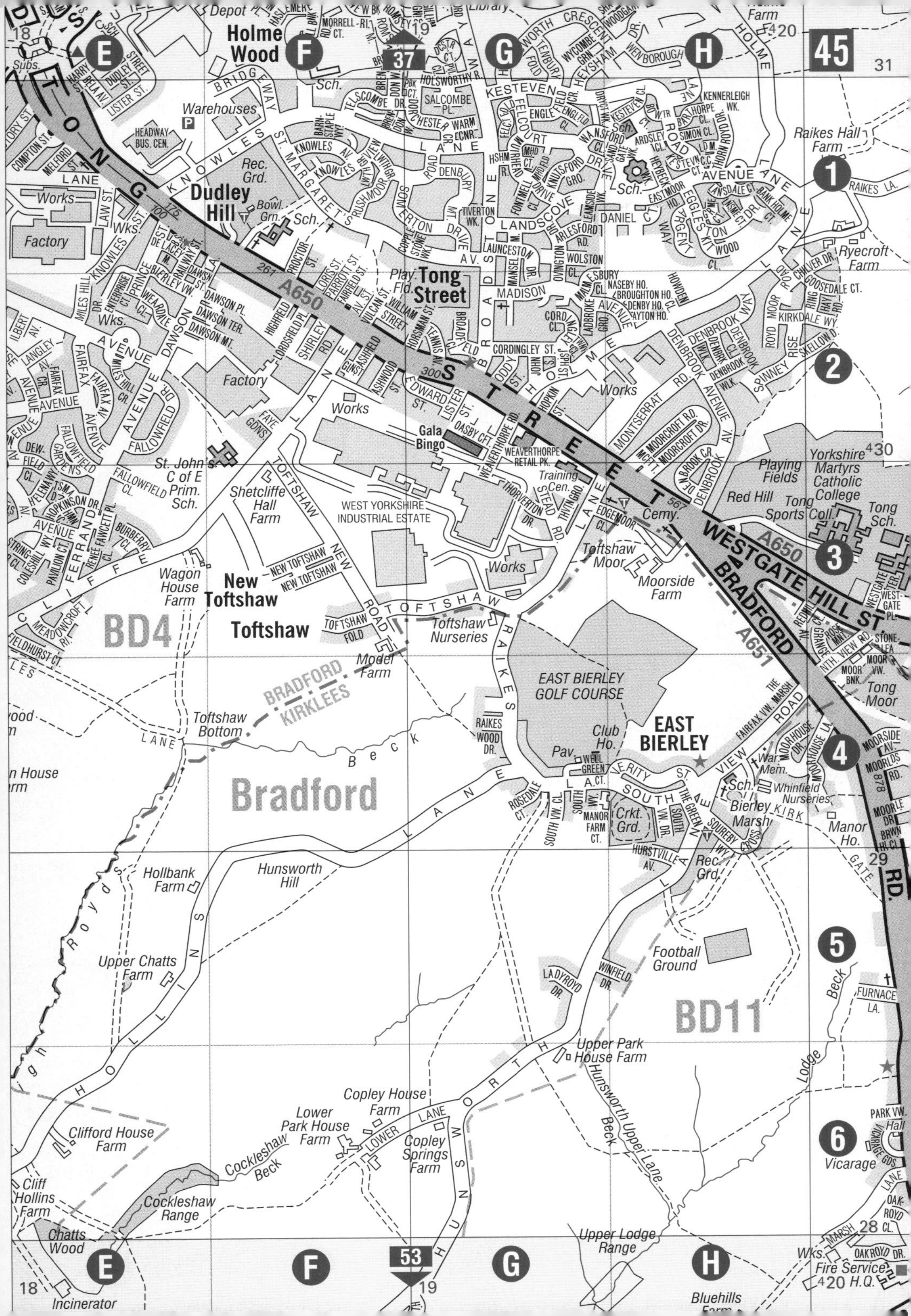

Holme Wood
Dudley Hill
Tong Street
New Toftshaw
Toftshaw
East Bierley
Bradford
BD4
BD11
West Yorkshire Industrial Estate
East Bierley Golf Course
Yorkshire Martyrs Catholic College
Tong Sports Coll.
Tong Sch.
Red Hill
Raikes Hall Farm
Ryecroft Farm
Tong Moor
Bierley Marsh
Toftshaw Moor
Moorside Farm
Shetcliffe Hall Farm
Wagon House Farm
Toftshaw Nurseries
Model Farm
Toftshaw Bottom
Hunsworth Hill
Hollbank Farm
Upper Chatts Farm
Football Ground
Upper Park House Farm
Copley House Farm
Lower Park House Farm
Copley Springs Farm
Clifford House Farm
Cliff Hollins Farm
Cockleshaw Beck
Cockleshaw Range
Chatts Wood
Upper Lodge Range
Incinerator
Fire Service H.Q.
Vicarage
Manor Ho.
Whinfield Nurseries
Gala Bingo
Weaverthorpe Retail Pk.
St. John's C of E Prim. Sch.
Factory
Works
Warehouses
A650
A651
Tong Street
Westgate Hill St.
Bradford Rd.
Knowles Lane
Cliffe Lane
Hunsworth Lane
Hollins Lane
Raikes Lane
Toftshaw Lane
Bradford Kirklees
37
53

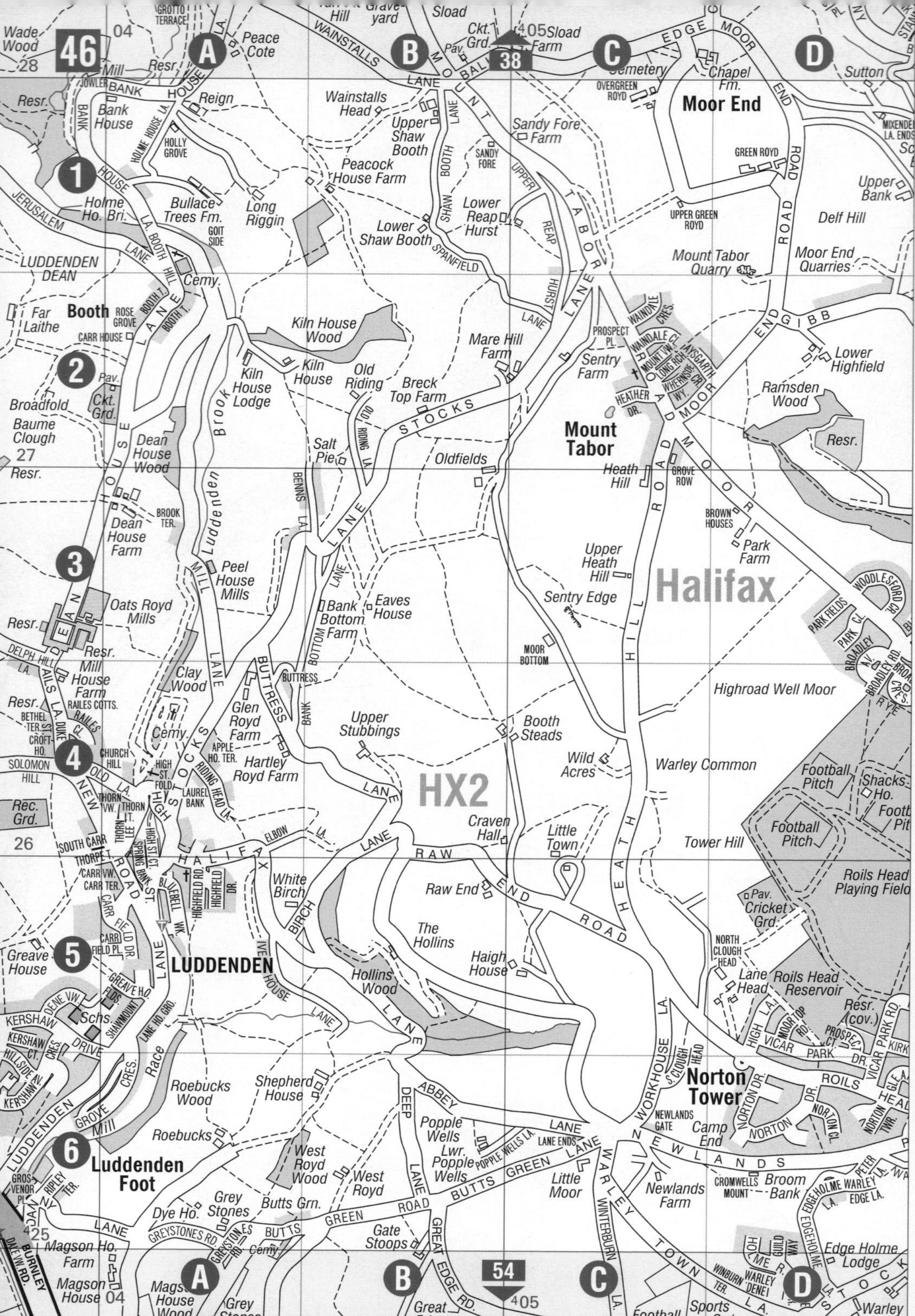

Grid references (top): **46** / 04 / **A** / **B** / 38 **C** / **D**

Grid references (left, top to bottom): 28 / **1** / 27 / **2** / **3** / 26 / **4** / 25 / **5** / **6**

Grid references (bottom): **A** / 54 405 **B** / **C** / **D**

Place names and features:

Wade Wood, Mill, GROTTO TERRACE, Peace Cote, Reign, WAINSTALLS, Grave yard, Sload, 405 Sload, Sload Farm, EDGE MOOR, Sutton, Mixenden, LA. ENDS, Sc...

HOWER BANK, Resr., HOLME HOUSE LA., Bank House, Wainstalls Head, Upper Shaw Booth, Peacock House Farm, Sandy Fore Farm, Pav., Ckt. Grd., Chapel Fm., Cemetery, Overgreen Royd, **Moor End**, Green Royd

JERUSALEM, HOUSE LA., Holme Ho. Bri., Bullace Trees Fm., Holly Grove, Long Riggin, GOIT SIDE, SHAW BOOTH, Lower Shaw Booth, SANDY FORE, Lower Reap Hurst, Upper, UPPER GREEN ROYD, Delf Hill, Upper Bank

LUDDENDEN DEAN, BOOTH HILL, Far Laithe, **Booth**, ROSE GROVE, CARR HOUSE, BOOTH T., Cemy., Kiln House Wood, STANFIELD, Mare Hill Farm, PROSPECT PL., Sentry Farm, WAINVALE, MANDALE CL., KINSGARTH, VINE TER., WHEATVALE, Lower Highfield, MOOR END QUARRIES, GIBB

BROOK, Pav., Ckt. Grd., Kiln House Lodge, Kiln House, Old Riding, Breck Top Farm, STOCKS, Mount Tabor Quarry, HEATHER DR., MOUNT TABOR ROAD, Ramsden Wood, Resr.

Broadfold, Baume Clough, LUDDENDEN BROOK, Dean House Wood, RIDING LA., Salt Pie, Oldfields, **Mount Tabor**, Heath Hill, GROVE ROW, BROWN HOUSES, Park Farm

Resr., MILL LANE, Dean House Farm, BROOK TER., Peel House Mills, Bank Bottom Farm, Eaves House, Upper Heath Hill, Sentry Edge, **Halifax**, PARK FIELDS, PARK CL., BRADLEY AV., BROADLEY RD.

DELPH HILL LA., Oats Royd Mills, Resr., Mill House Farm, RAILES COTTS., Clay Wood, BUTTRESS, Glen Royd Farm, BUTTRESS BANK, Upper Stubbings, MOOR BOTTOM, Highroad Well Moor, WOODLESFORD RD.

Resr., BETHEL TER., ST. DUKE LA., ST. RAILES, SOLOMON HILL, Cemy., APPLE HO. TER., Hartley Royd Farm, Booth Steads, Wild Acres, Warley Common, Tower Hill, Football Pitch, Shacks Ho., Football Pit...

Rec. Grd., CHURCH HILL, HIGH ST., LAUREL BANK, Craven Hall, Little Town, HEATH, Football Pitch, Roils Head Playing Field

SOUTH CARR, THORPE, CARR VW., CARR TER., NEW ROAD, OLD LA., THORN VW., THORN TT., JEFF..., RIDING HEAD LA., HALIFAX LANE, ELBOW LA., White Birch, RAW END, Raw End, The Hollins, HEATH ROAD, Pav. Cricket Grd., NORTH CLOUGH HEAD

Greave House, CARR, FIELD DR., FIELD PL., DENE VW., **LUDDENDEN**, HIGHFIELD RD., HIGHFIELD DR., BIRCH LA., Haigh House, Hollins Wood, Lane Head, Roils Head Reservoir, Resr. (cov.), VICAR PARK RD., PROSPECT DR.

KERSHAW, KERSHAW CRES., HILL SIDE, SCHS., SHINNROYD, GREAVE'S HO., LANE HO. GRO., Roebucks Wood, Shepherd House, ABBEY, DEEP LANE, Popple Wells, Lwr. Popple Wells, POPPLE WELLS LA., Little Moor, BUTTS GREEN LA., GREEN LANE, **Norton Tower**, NEWLANDS GATE, Camp End, Newlands Farm, CROMWELLS MOUNT, Broom Bank, EDGE HOLME LA., WARLEY, WINBURN, HOLME VW., MOOR ROYD, WORKHOUSE LA., S. CLOUGH HEAD, VICAR PARK, ROILS

GROSVENOR PL., RIPLEY TER., **Luddenden Foot**, GROVE, Mill, CRES., DRIVE, Race, Roebucks, West Royd Wood, West Royd, Butts Grn., GREEN ROAD, Gate Stoops, GREAT EDGE RD., WARLEY TOWN LANE, WINTERBURN LA., NEWLANDS, Newlands Mount, WARLEY DENE, WARLEY TER., Sports Grd.

BURNLEY, DALE VW. RD., Magson Ho. Farm, Magson House, Mags House Wood, Grey Stones, GREYSTONES RD., Dye Ho., Grey Stones, Cemy., BUTTS, Great..., Football, WINBURN, HOLME..., Edge Holme Lodge, PETER LA., EDGE LA., STOCK...

HX2

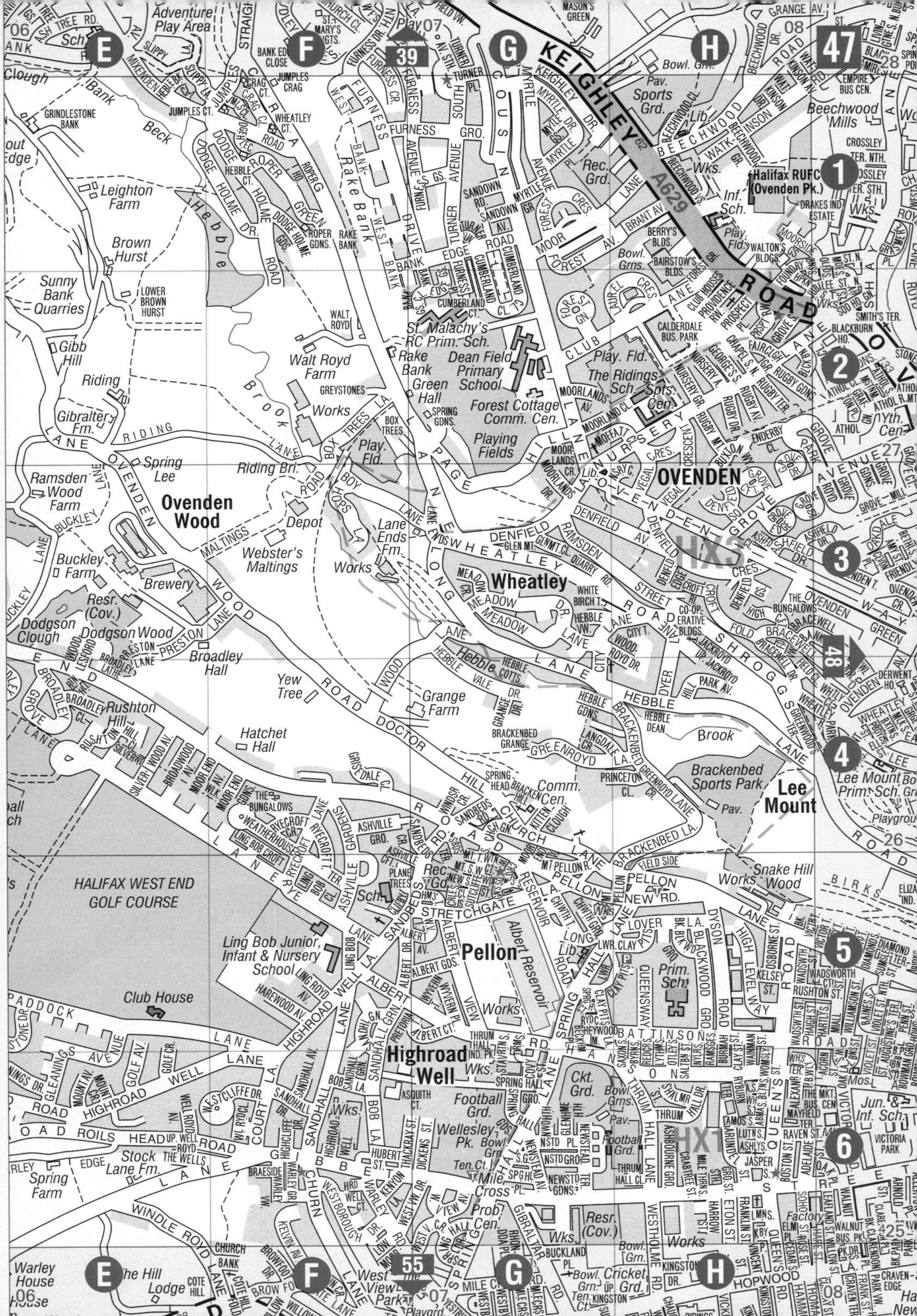

47
39
48
55
E
F
G
H
1
2
3
4
5
6
Adventure Play Area
Ovenden Wood
Wheatley
OVENDEN
HX3
Lee Mount
Pellon
Highroad Well
HX1
HALIFAX WEST END GOLF COURSE
KEIGHLEY ROAD
A629
Halifax RUFC (Ovenden Pk.)
Leighton Farm
Brown Hurst
Sunny Bank Quarries
Gibb Hill
Riding
Gibralter Fm.
Spring Lee
Ramsden Wood Farm
Buckley Farm
Brewery
Resr. (Cov.)
Dodgson Clough
Dodgson Wood
Broadley Hall
Rushton Hill
Yew Tree
Hatchet Hall
Grange Farm
Walt Royd Farm
Works
Depot
Webster's Maltings
Riding Bri.
Lane Ends Fm.
Rake Bank
Rake Bank Green Hall
St. Malachy's RC Prim. Sch.
Dean Field Primary School
Forest Cottage Comm. Cen.
Playing Fields
The Ridings Sch.
Calderdale Bus. Park
Beechwood Mills
Empire Bus Cen.
Drakes Ind. Estate
Hebble Brook
Brackenbed Sports Park
Comm. Cen.
Snake Hill Wood
Albert Reservoir
Ling Bob Junior, Infant & Nursery School
Club House
Football Grd.
Wellesley Pk.
Ckt. Grd.
Mile Cross
Prob. Cen.
Resr. (Cov.)
Cricket Grd.
Victoria Park
Lee Mount Prim. Sch.
Stock Lane Fm.
Spring Farm
Warley House
The Hill Lodge
West View Park
HIGHROAD WELL LANE
GIBBET ST.
SPRING HALL LANE
OVENDEN ROAD
SHROGGS ROAD
WHEATLEY LANE
HEBBLE LANE
DOCTOR HILL
OVENDEN WOOD ROAD
PELLON LANE
BATTINSON ROAD
QUEEN'S ROAD
HOPWOOD LANE

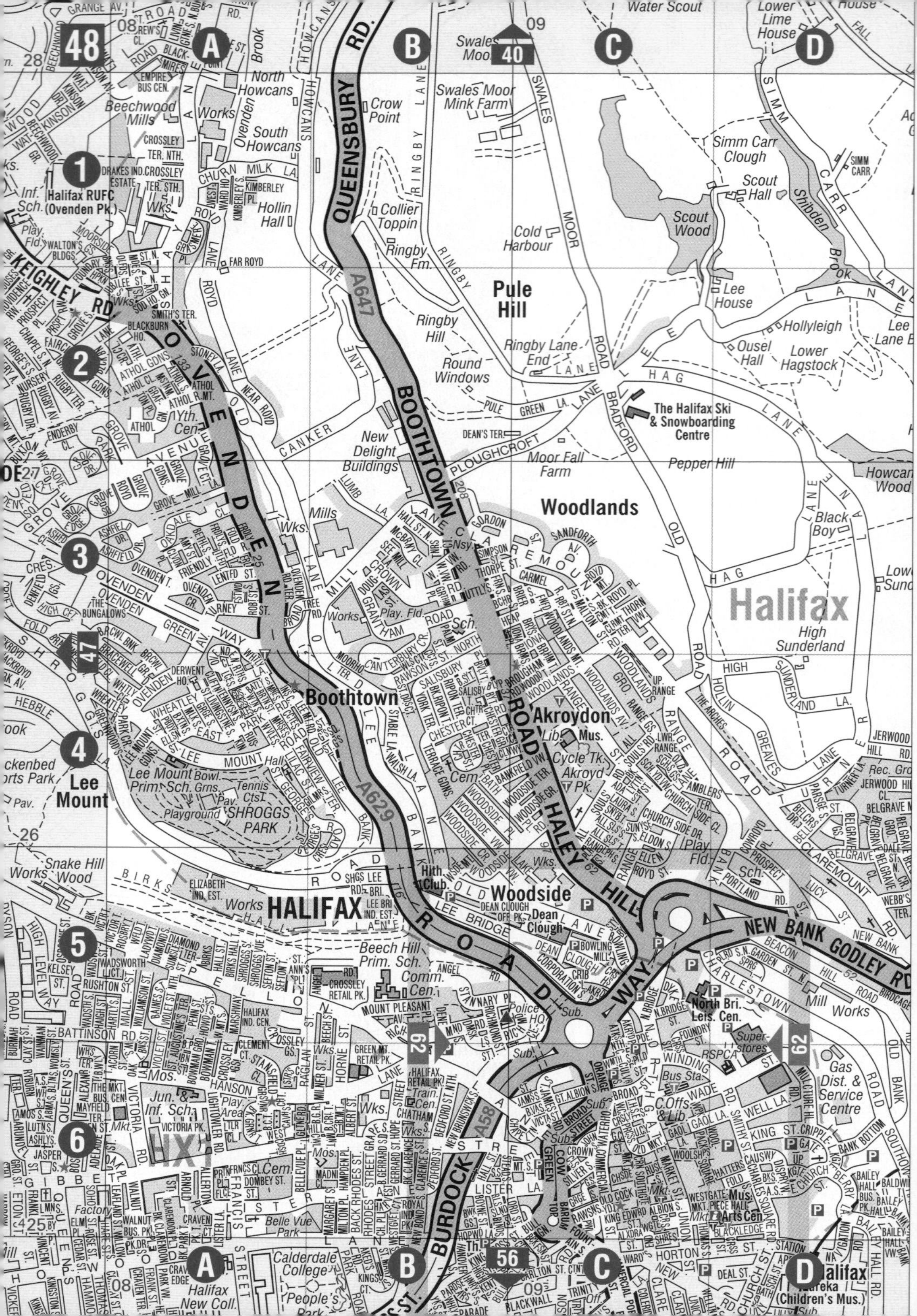

48
A
B
C
D
1
2
3
4
5
6
40
47
56
62
A647
A629
A58
QUEENSBURY RD.
BOOTHTOWN ROAD
OVENDEN ROAD
KEIGHLEY RD.
NEW BANK GODLEY RD.
HALEY HILL
BURDOCK WAY
Water Scout
Lower Lime House
Swales Moor
Swales Moor Mink Farm
North Howcans
South Howcans
Beechwood Mills
Works
Crow Point
Simm Carr Clough
Scout Hall
Scout Wood
Halifax RUFC (Ovenden Pk.)
Collier Toppin
Hollin Hall
Cold Harbour
Ringby Fm.
Pule Hill
Lee House
Hollyleigh
Ringby Hill
Ringby Lane End
Ousel Hall
Lower Hagstock
Round Windows
The Halifax Ski & Snowboarding Centre
New Delight Buildings
Moor Fall Farm
Pepper Hill
Woodlands
Mills
Black Boy
Halifax
High Sunderland
Boothtown
Akroydon
Lee Mount
Lee Mount Bowl.
Prim. Sch. Grns.
Tennis Cts.
SHROGGS PARK
Playground
Snake Hill Wood
HALIFAX
Woodside
Dean Clough
Beech Hill Prim. Sch.
Comm. Cen.
North Bri. Leis. Cen.
Mill Works
Gas Dist. & Service Centre
RSPCA
Bus Sta.
Halifax Retail Pk.
Train. Cen.
Jun. & Inf. Sch.
Belle Vue Park
Calderdale College
Halifax New Coll.
Piece Hall
Arts Cen.
Halifax Eureka (Children's Mus.)

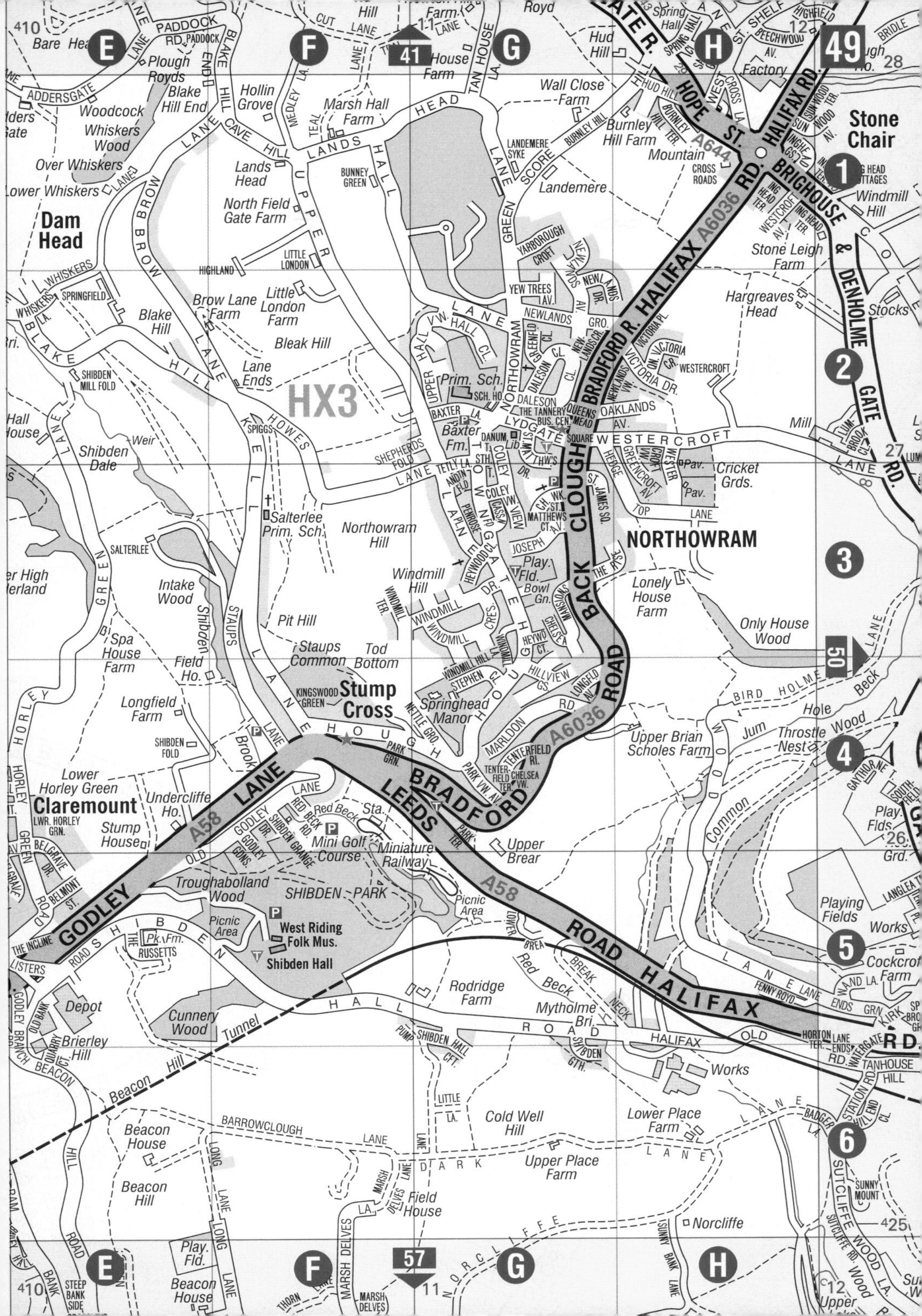
E
F
G
H
41
57
50
1
2
3
4
5
6
HX3
NORTHOWRAM
Stone Chair
Dam Head
Claremount
Stump Cross
Bare Head
Plough Royds
Blake Hill End
Hollin Grove
Marsh Hall Farm
House Farm
Hud Hill
Wall Close Farm
Burnley Hill Farm
Mountain
Cross Roads
Landemere
Woodcock
Whiskers Wood
Over Whiskers
Lower Whiskers
Lands Head
North Field Gate Farm
Little London
Little London Farm
Brow Lane Farm
Blake Hill
Bleak Hill
Lane Ends
Shibden Mill Fold
Hall House
Shibden Dale
Weir
Windmill Hill
Stone Leigh Farm
Hargreaves Head
Stocks
Westercroft
Mill
Cricket Grds.
Pav.
Prim. Sch.
Baxter Fm.
Lib.
Bus. Cen.
Square
Salterlee Prim. Sch.
Northowram Hill
Intake Wood
Play. Fld.
Bowl Gn.
Lonely House Farm
Only House Wood
Pit Hill
Stamps Common
Tod Bottom
Spa House Farm
Field Ho.
Longfield Farm
Springhead Manor
Upper Brian Scholes Farm
Jum Hole
Throstle Nest
Wood
Beck
Lower Horley Green
Undercliffe Ho.
Stump House
Red Beck Sta.
Mini Golf Course
Miniature Railway
Upper Brear
Troughabolland Wood
Shibden Park
Picnic Area
West Riding Folk Mus.
Shibden Hall
Pk. Fm.
Depot
Brierley Hill
Cunnery Wood
Tunnel
Rodridge Farm
Mythholme Bri.
Works
Playing Fields
Play. Flds.
Cockcroft Farm
Beacon Hill
Beacon House
Cold Well Hill
Lower Place Farm
Upper Place Farm
Field House
Norcliffe
Sunny Mount
Play. Fld.
A58
A6036
A644
GODLEY LANE
LEEDS ROAD
BRADFORD ROAD
HALIFAX ROAD
BACK CLOUGH
HOUGH
BRIGHOUSE & DENHOLME GATE RD.
HOPE ST.
WESTERCROFT LANE
LANDS HEAD LANE
UPPER LANDS
HALL LANE
GREEN LANE
SCORE HEAD
BROW LANE
BLAKE HILL
KELL LANE
STAUPS LANE
HOWES LANE
HORLEY GREEN
SHIBDEN HALL ROAD
BEACON HILL ROAD
BARROWCLOUGH LANE
DARK LANE
NORCLIFFE
MARSH DELVES LANE
LONG LANE
SUNNY BANK LANE
SUTCLIFFE WOOD LA.
OLD HALIFAX RD.
BIRD HOLME LANE
JUM HOLE COMMON
LANE ENDS
TANHOUSE HILL
STATION RD.
410
28
27
26
425
12
11

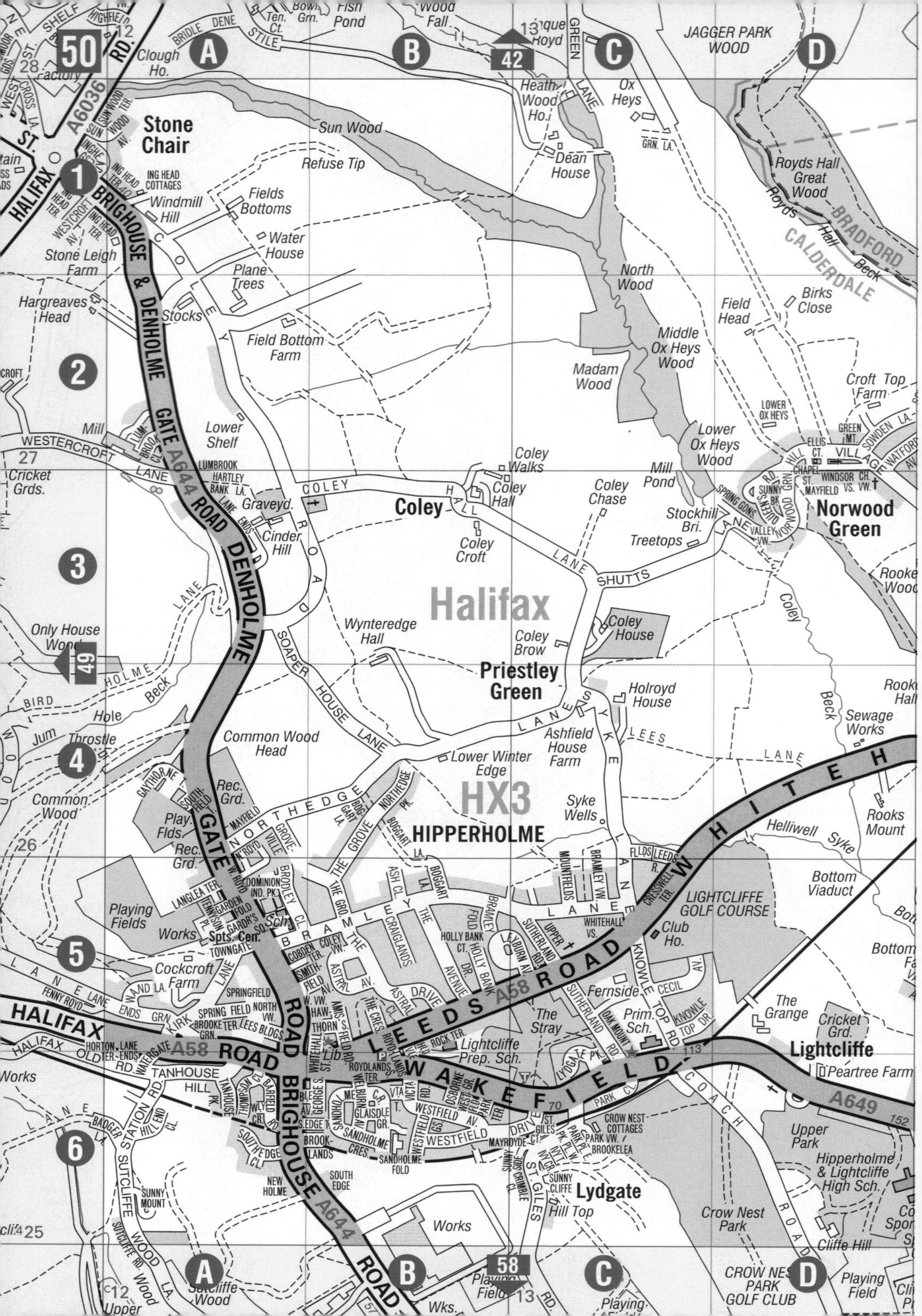

50
A
B
C
D
1
2
3
4
5
6
42
49
58
Stone Chair
Sun Wood
Refuse Tip
Clough Ho.
Bridle Dene
Stile
Fish Pond
Wood Fall
Heath Wood Ho.
Dean House
Ox Heys
Jagger Park Wood
Royds Hall Great Wood
Royds Hall Beck
BRADFORD
CALDERDALE
Ing Head Cottages
Windmill Hill
Fields Bottoms
Water House
Plane Trees
Stone Leigh Farm
Hargreaves Head
Stocks
Field Bottom Farm
North Wood
Middle Ox Heys Wood
Madam Wood
Field Head
Birks Close
Croft Top Farm
Lower Ox Heys Wood
Mill Pond
Lower Shelf
Mill
WESTERCROFT LANE
Cricket Grds.
Lumbrook
Graveyd.
Cinder Hill
COLEY ROAD
Coley
Coley Walks
Coley Hall
Coley Croft
Coley Chase
Stockhill Bri.
Treetops
Norwood Green
Village
Windsor Ch.
SHUTTS LANE
Halifax
Coley House
Coley Brow
Priestley Green
Wynteredge Hall
SOAPER HOUSE LANE
Only House Wood
HOLME
BIRD
Hole
Beck
Throstle
Common Wood Head
Holroyd House
Ashfield House Farm
Sewage Works
LEES LANE
SYKE LANE
Lower Winter Edge
HX3
Syke Wells
HIPPERHOLME
Rec. Grd.
Play. Flds.
Common Wood
NORTHEDGE
Rooks Mount
Helliwell Syke
Bottom Viaduct
LIGHTCLIFFE GOLF COURSE
Club Ho.
Playing Fields
Works
Spts. Cen.
Cockcroft Farm
Towngate
BRAMLEY LANE
LEEDS ROAD A58
WHITEHALL
Fernside
The Stray
Prim. Sch.
Lightcliffe Prep. Sch.
The Grange
Cricket Grd.
Lightcliffe
Peartree Farm
A649
HALIFAX ROAD A58
BRIGHOUSE ROAD
BRIGHOUSE & DENHOLME GATE ROAD A644
WAKEFIELD ROAD
TANHOUSE HILL
STATION RD.
BADGER LANE
SUTCLIFFE WOOD LA.
Sunny Mount
New Holme
South Edge
Westfield
Sandholme
Lydgate
Hill Top
St. Giles
Crow Nest Cottages
Crow Nest Park
COACH ROAD
Upper Park
Hipperholme & Lightcliffe High Sch.
Cliffe Hill
CROW NEST PARK GOLF CLUB
Playing Field
Sutcliffe Wood
Wks.

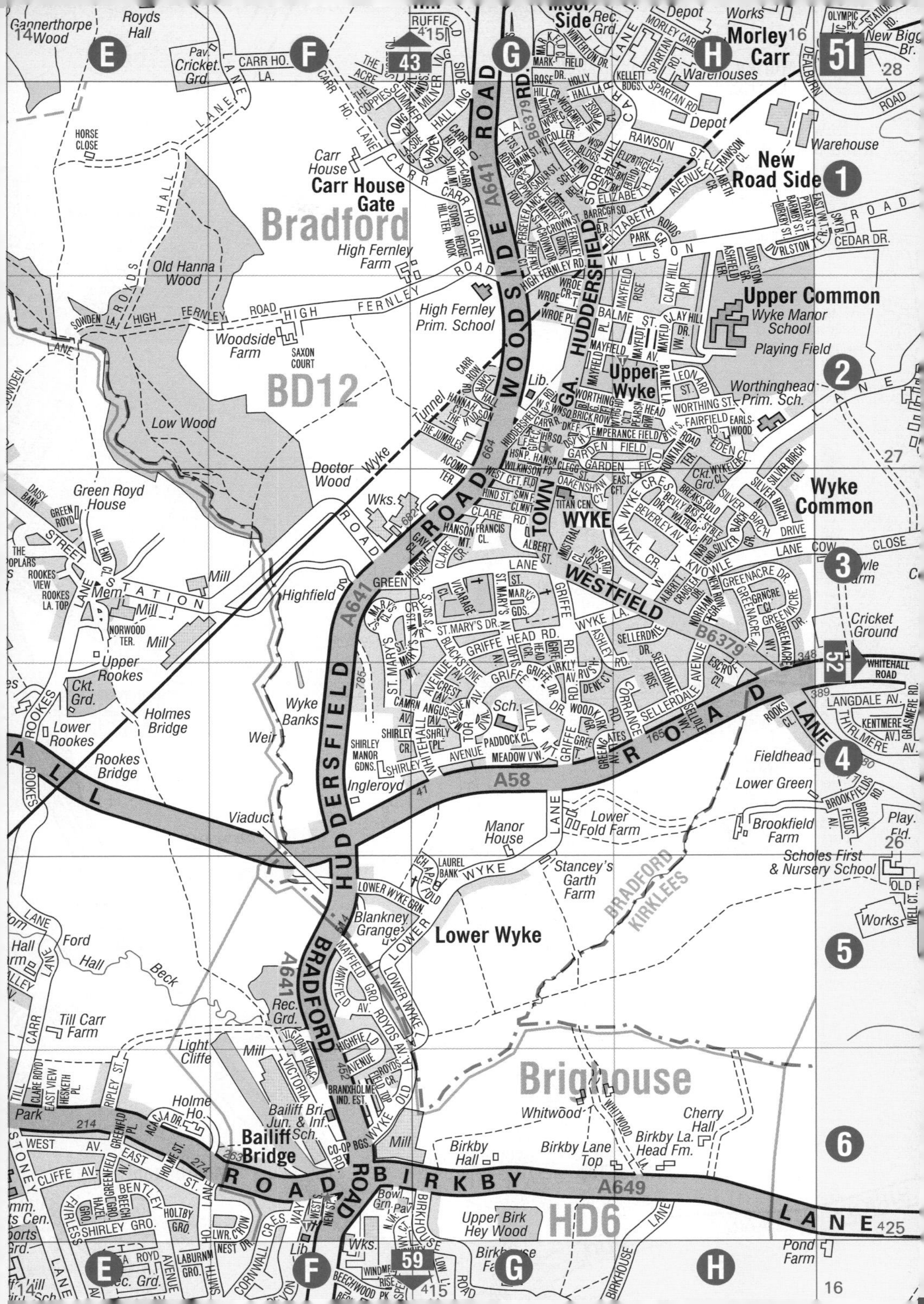

51
43
52
59
Bradford
BD12
HD6
Brighouse
Carr House Gate
New Road Side
Upper Common
Wyke Manor School
Upper Wyke
WYKE
Wyke Common
Lower Wyke
Bailiff Bridge
Morley Carr
Royds Hall
Old Hanna Wood
Low Wood
Doctor Wood
Woodside Farm
High Fernley Farm
High Fernley Prim. School
Worthinghead Prim. Sch.
Green Royd House
Upper Rookes
Lower Rookes
Holmes Bridge
Rookes Bridge
Wyke Banks
Highfield
Ingleroyd
Viaduct
Manor House
Lower Fold Farm
Stancey's Garth Farm
Brookfield Farm
Scholes First & Nursery School
Fieldhead
Lower Green
Cricket Ground
Blankney Grange
Ford Hall Beck
Till Carr Farm
Light Cliffe
Bailiff Bri. Jun. & Inf. Sch.
Whitwood
Birkby Hall
Birkby Lane Top
Birkby La. Head Fm.
Cherry Hall
Upper Birk Hey Wood
Pond Farm
WOODSIDE ROAD
HUDDERSFIELD ROAD
BRADFORD ROAD
BIRKBY LANE
WESTFIELD
WHITEHALL ROAD
HIGH FERNLEY ROAD
WILSON ROAD
A641
A58
A649
B6379
BRADFORD KIRKLEES

52
Morley Carr
New Biggin
Oakenshaw
Victoria Park
44
A
B
C
D
Woodlands C of E Prim. Sch.
Chatts Wood
Reservoir
Depot
Warehouses
New Road Side
1
2
3
4
5
6
Wilson Road
Cedar Dr.
Fearnley Farm
Mt. of Olives Fm.
Theaklands Farm
Threappleton Farm
Upper Common
Wyke Manor School
Playing Field
Worthing Head Prim. Sch.
Bradford
Bradford Kirklees
Chemical Works
Wyke Lane
BD12
Elm Cottage
Wyke Common
Cow Close Lane
Cow Close Cottages
Knowle Farm
Upper Cow Close
Cow Close Farm
The Nurseries
Cricket Ground
Oakenshaw Lane
M606
M606 Motorway
Bradford Road
Water Pollution Control Works
Woodlands Park
Club Ho.
Sugden Beck
Cleckheaton & District Golf Course
Stubs Beck
Road
51
Whitehall
A58
Junction 26 (M62)
Nursery
Westfield Lane
B6379
Lower Green
Brookfield Farm
Play. Fld.
Recn. Grd.
Scholes First & Nursery School
Branch Farm
Branch Road
Cemetery
Whitechapel
Chairbarrows Farm
The Royds
B6120
Road
Works
Scholes
Pav.
Playing Fields
Turnstead
Cricket & Athletic Ground
Longlands
New Popplewell
Brick Hill Farm
Whitcliffe Mount Sports Centre
Whitcliffe Mount School
M62
M62 Motorway
Calderdale Kirklees
West End
Hartshead Moor Top
Oldfieldnook
Wellands
Moorbottom
Lark Hill
Birkby Lane
A649
Halifax Road
Pond Farm
Manor Court
Whiteacre
16
17
425

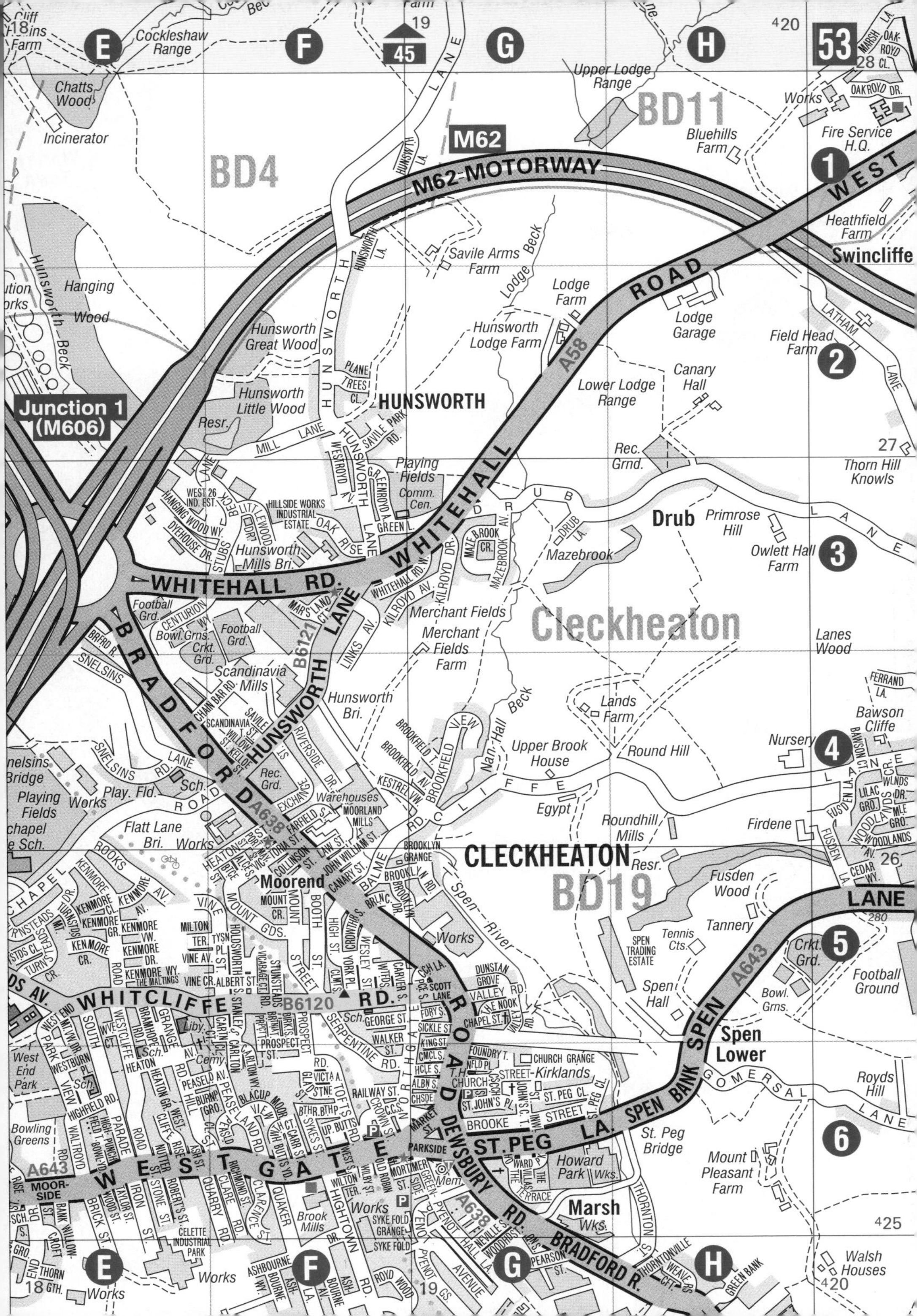
E
F
G
H
45
19
420
425
18
28
27
26
280
1
2
3
4
5
6
Cliff Hollins Farm
Cockleshaw Range
Chatts Wood
Incinerator
Upper Lodge Range
BD11
Works
Fire Service H.Q.
Bluehills Farm
M62
BD4
M62 MOTORWAY
WEST
ROAD
Heathfield Farm
Swincliffe
Hanging Wood
Hunsworth Beck
Savile Arms Farm
Lodge Beck
Lodge Farm
Lodge Garage
Field Head Farm
LATHAM LANE
Hunsworth Great Wood
Hunsworth Lodge Farm
A58
Canary Hall
Lower Lodge Range
Hunsworth Little Wood
HUNSWORTH
Junction 1 (M606)
Resr.
MILL LANE
HUNSWORTH LANE
PLANE TREES CL.
SAVILE PARK RD.
Rec. Grnd.
Thorn Hill Knowls
WESTROYD AV.
GREENROYD AV.
Playing Fields
Comm. Cen.
WHITEHALL
DRUB LANE
Drub
Primrose Hill
Owlett Hall Farm
WEST 26 IND. EST.
HILLSIDE WORKS INDUSTRIAL ESTATE
OAK RISE
GREEN L.
HANGING WOOD WY.
DYEHOUSE DR.
LITTLEWOOD DR.
STUBS BECK LANE
Hunsworth Mills Bri.
MAZEBROOK CR.
MAZEBROOK AV.
Mazebrook
WHITEHALL RD.
WHITEHALL RD. W.
KILROYD AV.
KILROYD DR.
Merchant Fields
Cleckheaton
Football Grd.
CENTURION WY.
Bowl. Grns.
Crkt. Grd.
MAR'S LAND CT.
LINKS AV.
Merchant Fields Farm
Lanes Wood
BRADFORD ROAD
B6121
HUNSWORTH LANE
Scandinavia Mills
SNELSINS
Hunsworth Bri.
FERRAND LA.
Lands Farm
Bawson Cliffe
CHAIN BAR RD.
SCANDINAVIA
SAVILE
WILLOW
ST. KELLOG
RIVERSIDE DR.
BROOKFIELD VIEW
BROOKFIELD AV.
Nan Hall Beck
Upper Brook House
Round Hill
Nursery
BAWSON CT.
Snelsins Bridge
SNELSINS RD.
LANE
Sch.
Rec. Grd.
Play. Fld.
KESTREL VW.
CLIFFE
Playing Fields
Works
ROAD
EXCHANGE
FAIRFIELD ST.
Warehouses
MOORLAND MILLS
Egypt
LANE
FUSDEN LA.
LILAC GRO.
WOODLANDS
Flatt Lane Bri.
A638
Roundhill Mills
Firdene
WOODLANDS AV.
ROOKS
HEATON ST.
VICTORIA ST.
COLLINSON ST.
LAW ST.
JOHN WILLIAM ST.
BROOKLYN GRANGE
CLECKHEATON
Resr.
CEDAR WY.
CHAPEL
KENMORE AV.
KENMORE
MOUNT GDS.
VINE
Moorend
CANARY ST.
BALME RD.
BROOKLYN RD.
Spen River
BD19
Fusden Wood
LANE
MILTON TER.
MOUNT CR.
MOUNT STREET
BOOTH ST.
HIGH ST.
Works
Tannery
TURNSTEADS
KENMORE CR.
KENMORE DR.
KENMORE WY.
THE MALTINGS
VINE AV.
VINE CR.
ALBERT ST.
HOLDSWORTH ST.
STUNSTEADS RD.
YORK PL.
WESLEY ST.
CARVER ST.
SPEN TRADING ESTATE
Tennis Cts.
Crkt. Grd.
DUNSTAN GROVE
VALLEY RD.
Spen Hall
A643
Football Ground
WHITCLIFFE RD.
B6120
SCOTT LANE
Bowl. Grns.
WEST END
WESTCLIFFE
BRAMHOPE
GRANGE
Liby.
STANLEY ST.
CARLTON ST.
PROSPECT ST.
Sch.
GEORGE ST.
THE NOOK
CHAPEL ST.
SPEN
Spen Lower
SICKLE ST.
KING ST.
SERPENTINE RD.
WALKER ST.
Cemy.
FOUNDRY T.
CHURCH GRANGE
West End Park
WESTBURN PL.
HEATON
Sch.
PEASELAND
CLIFFE
RAILWAY ST.
NORTHGATE
T.H.
CHURCH
STREET
Kirklands
ST. JOHN'S PL.
ST. PEG CL.
GOMERSAL LANE
Royds Hill
HIGHFIELD RD.
BLACUP MOOR VIEW
TOFTS RD.
CROWN ST.
BROOKE STREET
SPEN BANK
Bowling Greens
WALTROYD RD.
PARADE
ROAD
HIGH PUNCH
BOWL. YD.
NUTTER
RISE
ASH ST.
CARR ST.
SYKES ST.
UP. BUTTS
MARKET ST.
DEWSBURY
ST. PEG LA.
St. Peg Bridge
Mount Pleasant Farm
A643
MOORSIDE
WESTGATE
IRON ST.
STONE ST.
ROBERTS ST.
QUARRY RD.
RICHMOND ST.
CLARE RD.
CLARENCE ST.
QUAKER
OLD ROBIN
WILTON TER.
PARKSIDE
Mem.
WARD
THE VILLAS
THE TERRACE
Howard Park
Wks.
THORNTON
BANK WILLOW CROFT
BRICK ST.
WOOD ST.
TAYLOR ST.
CELETTE INDUSTRIAL PARK
Brook Mills
HIGHTOWN
Works
SYKE FOLD GRANGE
SYKE FOLD
PYENOT AVENUE
PYENOT HALL LA.
NEVILLE ST.
Marsh
Wks.
BRADFORD RD.
THORN GTH.
Works
ASHBOURNE WY.
ASHBOURNE AV.
ROYDS WOOD
PEARSON ST.
THORNTONVILLE
GREEN BANK
Walsh Houses
Works

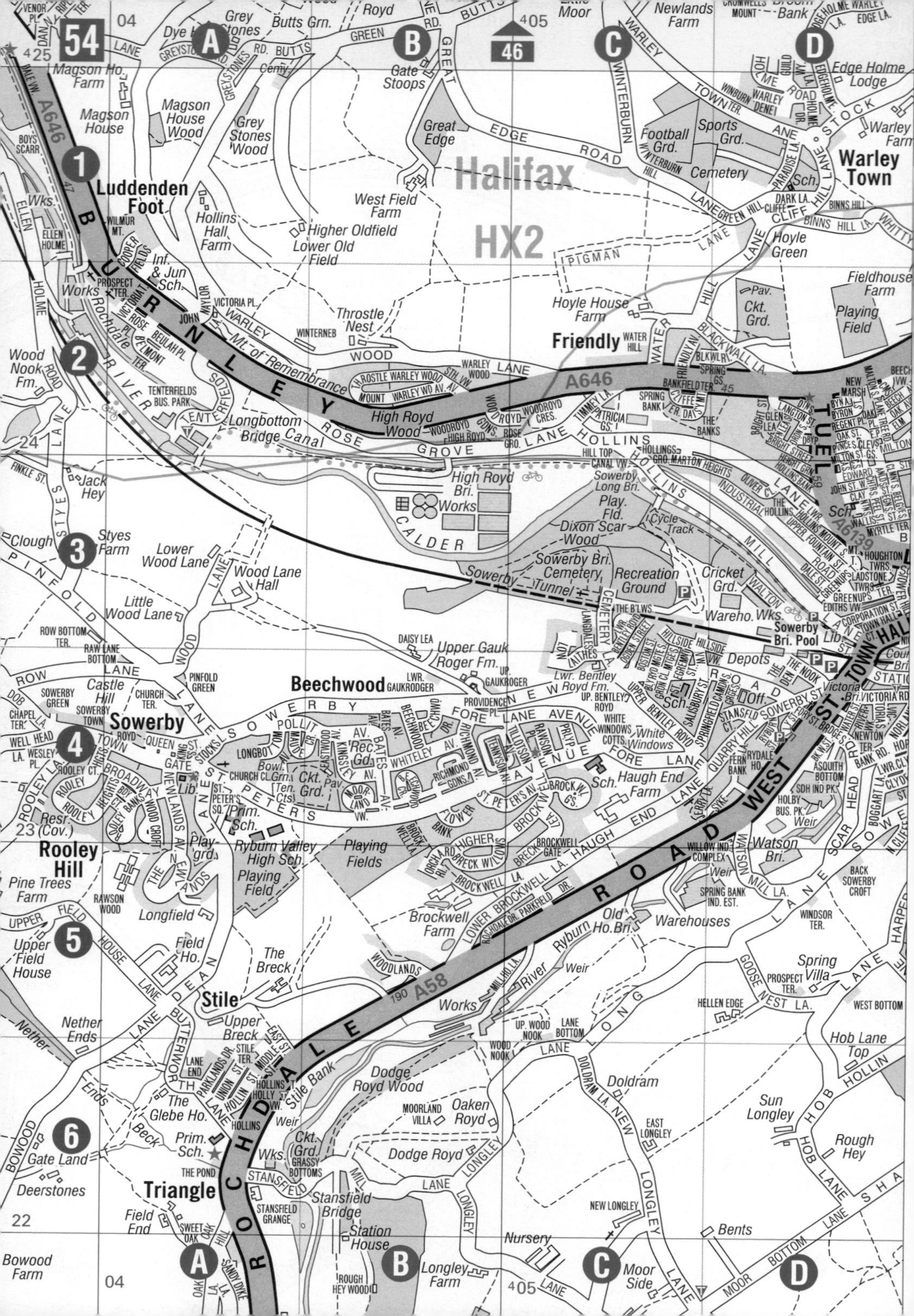

54
46
A
B
C
D
1
2
3
4
5
6
04
405
25
24
23
22
Halifax
HX2
Luddenden Foot
Warley Town
Friendly
Beechwood
Sowerby
Rooley Hill
Stile
Triangle
A646
A58
A6139
BURNLEY
ROCHDALE ROAD
ROCHDALE ROAD WEST
Magson Ho. Farm
Magson House
Magson House Wood
Grey Stones
Grey Stones Wood
Butts Grn.
Gate Stoops
Great Edge
EDGE ROAD
Newlands Farm
Edge Holme Lodge
Football Grd.
Sports Grd.
Cemetery
West Field Farm
Higher Oldfield
Lower Old Field
Hollins Hall Farm
Inf. & Jun Sch.
Works
Throstle Nest
Mt. of Remembrance
High Royd Wood
Hoyle House Farm
Hoyle Green
Fieldhouse Farm
Playing Field
Ckt. Grd.
Longbottom Bridge
Canal
River Calder
High Royd Bri. Works
Sowerby Long Bri.
Dixon Scar Wood
Cycle Track
Sowerby Bri. Cemetery
Recreation Ground
Cricket Grd.
Sowerby Tunnel
Wareho. Wks.
Sowerby Bri. Pool
Depots
Wood Nook Fm.
Jack Hey
Styes Farm
Lower Wood Lane
Wood Lane Hall
Little Wood Lane
Upper Gauk Roger Fm.
Lwr. Bentley Royd Fm.
White Windows
Haugh End Farm
Castle Hill
Ryburn Valley High Sch.
Playing Fields
Playing Field
Watson Bri.
Pine Trees Farm
Longfield
Upper Field House
Field Ho.
Brockwell Farm
The Breck
Old Ho. Bri.
Warehouses
River Ryburn
Weir
Spring Villa
Hob Lane Top
Nether Ends
Upper Breck
Dodge Royd Wood
Stile Bank
The Glebe Ho.
Oaken Royd
Doldram
Sun Longley
Rough Hey
Gate Land
Deerstones
Dodge Royd
Stansfield Bridge
Station House
Longley Farm
Nursery
Bents
Moor Side
Field End
Bowood Farm

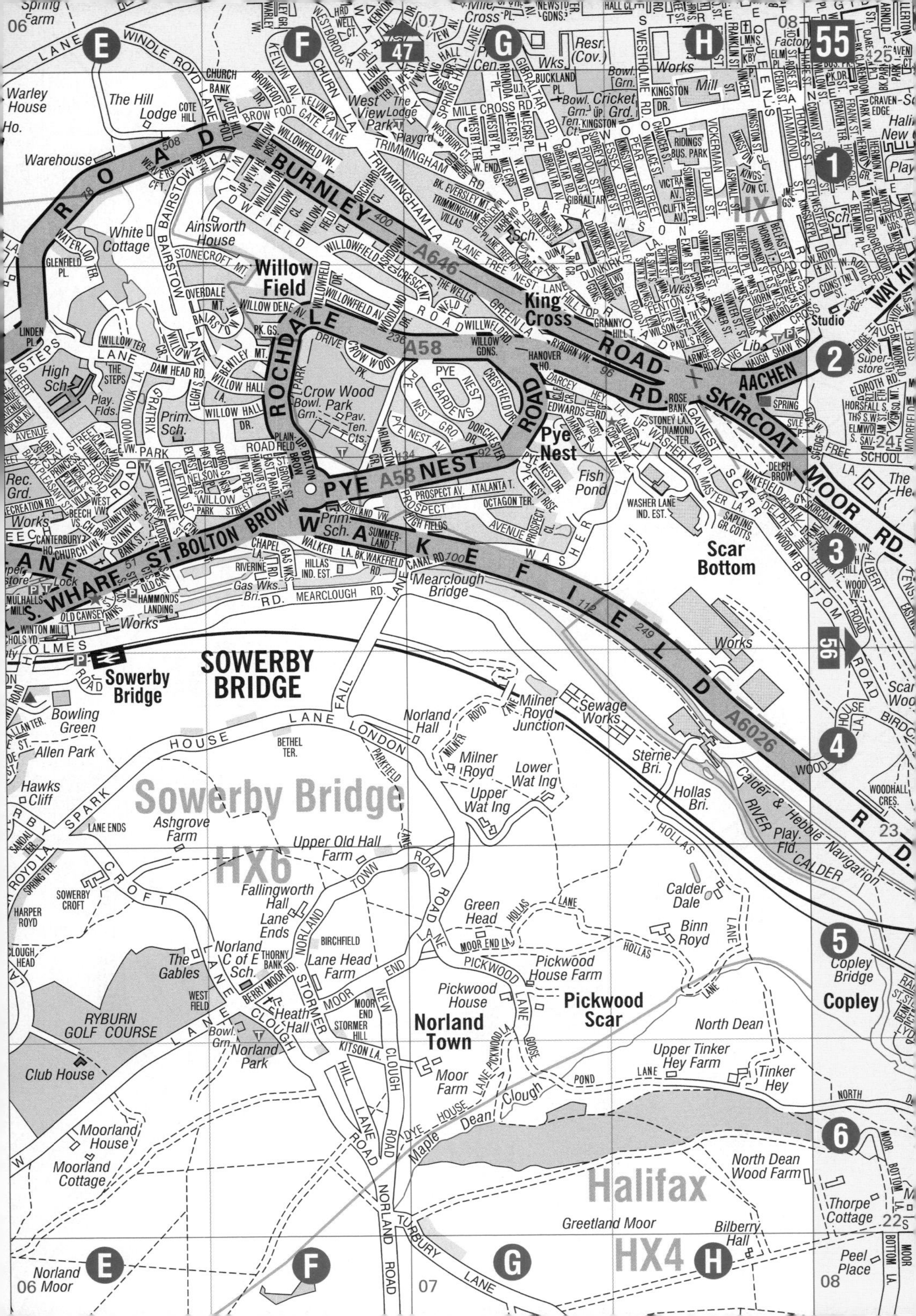

SOWERBY BRIDGE
Sowerby Bridge
HX6
Halifax
HX4
Willow Field
King Cross
Pye Nest
Scar Bottom
Copley
Norland Town
Pickwood Scar
BURNLEY ROAD
ROCHDALE ROAD
PYE NEST
WAKEFIELD RD
SKIRCOAT MOOR RD.
AACHEN
ST. BOLTON BROW
WHARF ST.
A646
A58
A6026
47
56
RYBURN GOLF COURSE
Club House
Norland Moor
Greetland Moor
North Dean
Sewage Works
Milner Royd Junction
Calder & Hebble Navigation
RIVER CALDER
Warley House
The Hill Lodge
White Cottage
Ainsworth House
Norland Hall
Milner Royd
Lower Wat Ing
Upper Wat Ing
Ashgrove Farm
Upper Old Hall Farm
Fallingworth Hall
Lane Ends
Lane Head Farm
Heath Hall
Norland Park
Moor Farm
Pickwood House
Pickwood House Farm
Green Head
Calder Dale
Binn Royd
Upper Tinker Hey Farm
Tinker Hey
North Dean Wood Farm
Thorpe Cottage
Bilberry Hall
Peel Place
Moorland House
Moorland Cottage
The Gables
Bowling Green
Allen Park
Hawks Cliff
Mearclough Bridge
Sterne Bri.
Hollas Bri.
Copley Bridge
Fish Pond
Crow Wood Park
High Sch.
Rec. Grd.
Works
Washer Lane Ind. Est.
Hillas Ind. Est.
Ridings Bus. Park

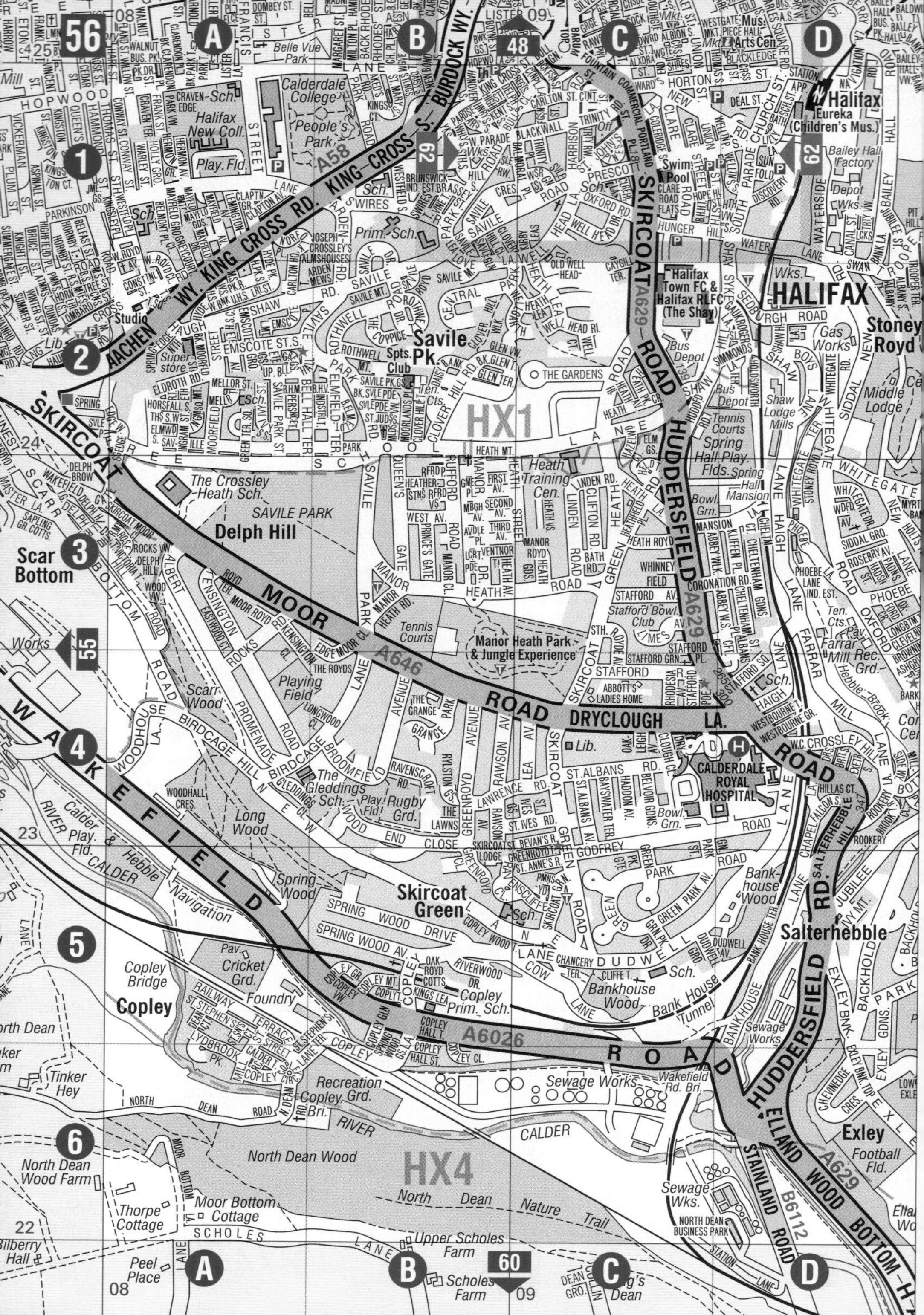

A
B
C
D
48
62
55
60
1
2
3
4
5
6
08
09
24
23
22
Calderdale College
People's Park
Halifax New Coll.
Play. Fld.
Belle Vue Park
Lister Lane
Burdock Wy.
A58
King Cross Rd.
Aachen Wy.
King Cross St.
Hopwood
Parkinson
Swires
Joseph Crossley's Almshouses
Prim. Sch.
Arts Cen.
Mus.
Piece Hall
Halifax
Eureka (Children's Mus.)
Bailey Hall Factory
Depot
Waterside
Swim. Pool
Skircoat Road
A629
Halifax Town FC & Halifax RLFC (The Shay)
Bus Depot
HALIFAX
Stoney Royd
Gas Works
Shaw Lodge Mills
Middle Lodge
Sedburgh Road
Savile Pk.
Spts. Club
The Gardens
HX1
Super store
Studio
Lib.
Spring
Skircoat
Free School Lane
Heath Training Cen.
Tennis Courts
Spring Hall Play. Flds.
Spring Hall Mansion
Bowl. Grn.
Huddersfield Road
The Crossley Heath Sch.
Savile Park
Delph Hill
Scar Bottom
Moor Road
A646
Manor Heath Park & Jungle Experience
Stafford Bowl. Club
Abbott's Ladies Home
Dryclough La.
Playing Field
Works
Scarr Wood
Promenade
Birdcage Hill
Woodhouse La.
The Gleddings Sch.
Rugby Grd.
Play. Fld.
Calderdale Royal Hospital
Long Wood
Wakefield Road
River Calder
Calder & Hebble Navigation
Calder Play. Fld.
Spring Wood
Skircoat Green
Spring Wood Drive
Spring Wood Av.
Dudwell Lane
Bankhouse Wood
Salterhebble
Salterhebble Hill
Copley Bridge
Copley
Cricket Grd.
Foundry
Copley Prim. Sch.
A6026
Bank House Tunnel
Sewage Works
Recreation Grd.
Copley Bri.
Wakefield Rd. Bri.
North Dean Road
North Dean Wood
HX4
North Dean Nature Trail
North Dean Wood Farm
Tinker Hey
Thorpe Cottage
Moor Bottom Cottage
Scholes Lane
Upper Scholes Farm
Scholes Farm
Peel Place
Bilberry Hall
Sewage Wks.
North Dean Business Park
Stainland Road
B6112
Elland Wood Bottom
Exley
Football Fld.
Farrar Mill Rec. Grd.
Hebble Brook
Jubilee

57
E
F
G
H
49
58
61
1
2
3
4
5
6
410
11
12
425
24
23
22
Beacon Hill
Upper Place Farm
Norcliffe
Play. Fld.
Beacon House
Caddy Field
Burial Grd.
Bank Top
Marsh Dene Farm
Upper Marsh Farm
Law Hill
Upper Marsh
Marsh Farm
Sunny Bank Quarries (Freestone)
Sunny Bank Farm
Sunny Bank Wood
Sunny Bank Clough
Upper Lake
Works
Sutcliffe Wood Bottom
Walter Clough Hall
Ivy House
Law
High Field Fm.
Withinfields Prim. Sch.
Pit Farm
Snydal Farm
Beaconsfield Centre
Cemetery
Pasture House Quarry (Stone)
Barker Royd
Res.
Pinnar Lane Quarries (Stone)
Halifax
Sion Hill
Wks.
SOUTHOWRAM
Lib.
Pasture House Farm
Hollins House
Backhold Royd
Siddal Top
Siddal Wells
Siddal
Jerusalem Square
Cote Hill Farm
Milking Hill
Works
Siddal Top Mine
Siddal Top
HX3
Cricket Grd.
Ashday Hall
Park Nook Farm
Boggart House
Binns Top
Wood Nook
Park Gate
Binns Wood
Ash Grove Cottage
Ash Grove Works
Cricket Grd.
South Halifax High Sch.
Playing Fields
ELLAND PARK WOOD
Park Wood Crematorium
A6025
ELLAND ROAD
PARK ROAD
Calder & Hebble Navigation
Exley Hall Farm
Upper Exley
Play. Fld.
Elland
HX5
Mills
Works
SOUTHOWRAM BANK
BEACON HILL ROAD
LONG LANE
MARSH LANE
MARSH DELVES LANE
STUB THORN LANE
NORCLIFFE LANE
SUNNY BANK LANE
WALTER CLOUGH LANE
WHITLEY LANE
LAW LANE
PINNAR LANE
TOP LANE
BROADWAY
SUN WAY
HIGGIN LANE
HIGH GROVE LANE
WHITEGATE TOP
SIDDAL TOP LA.
SIDDAL LANE
KESWICK CLOSE
COALPIT LANE
FAIRFAX CRESCENT
CROMWELL RD.
CAIN LANE
NEW STREET
CHURCH LANE
DARK LANE
WOOD LA.
TOWNGATE
ASHDAY LANE
BINNS TOP LANE
WEST LANE
LANE CHANGE
ROSEMARY LANE
BLAITHROYD LA.
CINDERHILLS LA.
GLADSTONE VW.
BACKHOLD DRIVE
RIVER BANK WAY
CALDER
LACY WAY
SAVILE WAY

A
B
C
D
1
2
3
4
5
6
50
57
Lydgate
Hill Top
Crow Nest Park
Cliffe Hill
CROW NEST PARK GOLF CLUB
Playing Field
BRIGHOUSE RD.
A644
HALIFAX RD.
Works
Wks.
Sutcliffe Wood
Upper Lake
SUTCLIFFE WOOD BOTTOM
Sunny Bank Farm
Sunny Bank Wood
Clough
Pearson Brow
BROW MILLS IND. EST.
Harley Head Fm.
Blakeboroughs Athletic FC
Giles House
Club House
Crowhurst
Rec. Grd.
Pinnell Bridge
WALTER CLOUGH LANE
Walter Clough Hall
Pond Quarries
UPPER GREEN LA.
WELL GREEN LANE
St. Joseph's RC Primary School
Hove Edge
Slead Syke Sports Centre
Brighouse High Sch.
Playing Fields
Lower Clay Royd Farm
Upper Clay Royd Farm
Red Beck
Sutcliffe Wood Farm
Sutcliffe Wood
Slead Syke Wood
The Nurseries
Pasture House Quarry (Stone)
Pasture Ho. Farm
Barker Royd
Res.
HOLLY ROYD
Hollins House
Halifax
HX3
Cross Platts Farm
CROSS PLATTS
THORN TREE COTTAGES
Birks Royd
Watson Quarries
Near Wood Bottom Farm
Slead Syke
CHURCH LANE
BROOKFOOT LANE
Cromwell Quarries (Sandstone)
Cote Hill Farm
Royd Quarry (Sandstone)
Brookfoot
Squire Hill Quarries (Sandstone)
Brookfoot Works
Brighouse Wood
Ashday
Ashday Hall
Cromwell Wood
Boggart House
ASHDAY LANE
CROMWELL WOOD LANE
Brookfoot Mills
Weir
Ganny Lock
Freeman's Wood
Brookfoot Lock
BROOKFOOT IND. EST.
ELLAND ROAD
A6025
Manor House Farm
The Lillands
Lillands Farm
Binns Wood
Ash Grove Cottage
Works
Cromwell Bottom
Freemans Cut
RIVER CALDER
Calder & Hebble Navigation
Cromwell Lock
Depot
Elland
Crowther Bridge
Freeman's Bridge
Pond
Great Dairy
Playing Fields
Rastrick Comm. Sports Cen.
Rastrick High School
Castlefields Inf. Sch.
Reins Wood
HX5
The William Henry Smith Sch.
Football Grd.
Boothroyd Farm
Harry Hill
Weir
LOWFIELDS WY.

E
F
G
H
51
BD19
HD6
Brighouse
BRIGHOUSE
Thornhills
Woolrow
Birkhouse
Birkhouse Farm
Upper Hey Wood
Pond Farm
Whitaker Pits Fm.
Whitaker Pits Wood
Clough
Rock Hole
Jay House Farm
JAY HOUSE LANE
Hole Bottom
Thorncliffe
Gospel Hall Farm
Lodge
Green Farm
Break Head Cottage
Cock Walk Farm
WILLOW VALLEY GOLF & COUNTRY CLUB
Football Grd.
Clifton
Clifton Wood
Motel
Alegar Bank Wood
Livingstone Works
CALDER TRADING ESTATE
Oak Gates
Hoyle House Beck
Cemetery
Ravensprings Park
Comm. Cen.
Oak Hill Bank
Viaduct
Ford
Clifton Beck
Wellholme Park
Pav. Cricket Grd.
COUNTY WORKSHOPS
Waring Green
Lane Head
Smith Art Gall.
Lib.
Bus Sta.
Mkt.
Pool
Super-store
Rastrick Bridge
Brighouse Bridge
Birds Royd
Brighouse
RASTRICK
Woodhouse
Woodhouse Bridge
Playing Field
Rec. Grd.
Warehouse
Depot
North Cut
Junc. 25
M62
BIRKBY LA.
BRADFORD ROAD
A641
HUDDERSFIELD ROAD
ELLAND ROAD
CLIFTON COMMON
HIGHMOOR LANE
A643
WAKEFIELD ROAD
A644
ARMYTAGE ROAD
BIRDS ROYD LANE
BRAMSTON ST.
COAL PIT LANE
TOWNGATE
DOLES LA.
BRIGGATE
CLIFFE RD.
WOODHOUSE GDNS.
DAISY ROAD
STRATTON PK.
HEALEY WOOD
SMITH HOUSE LANE
WHINNEY HILL PARK
LIGHTCLIFFE ROAD
RIVER CALDER
1
2
3
4
5
6
14
16
22
23
24
415
425

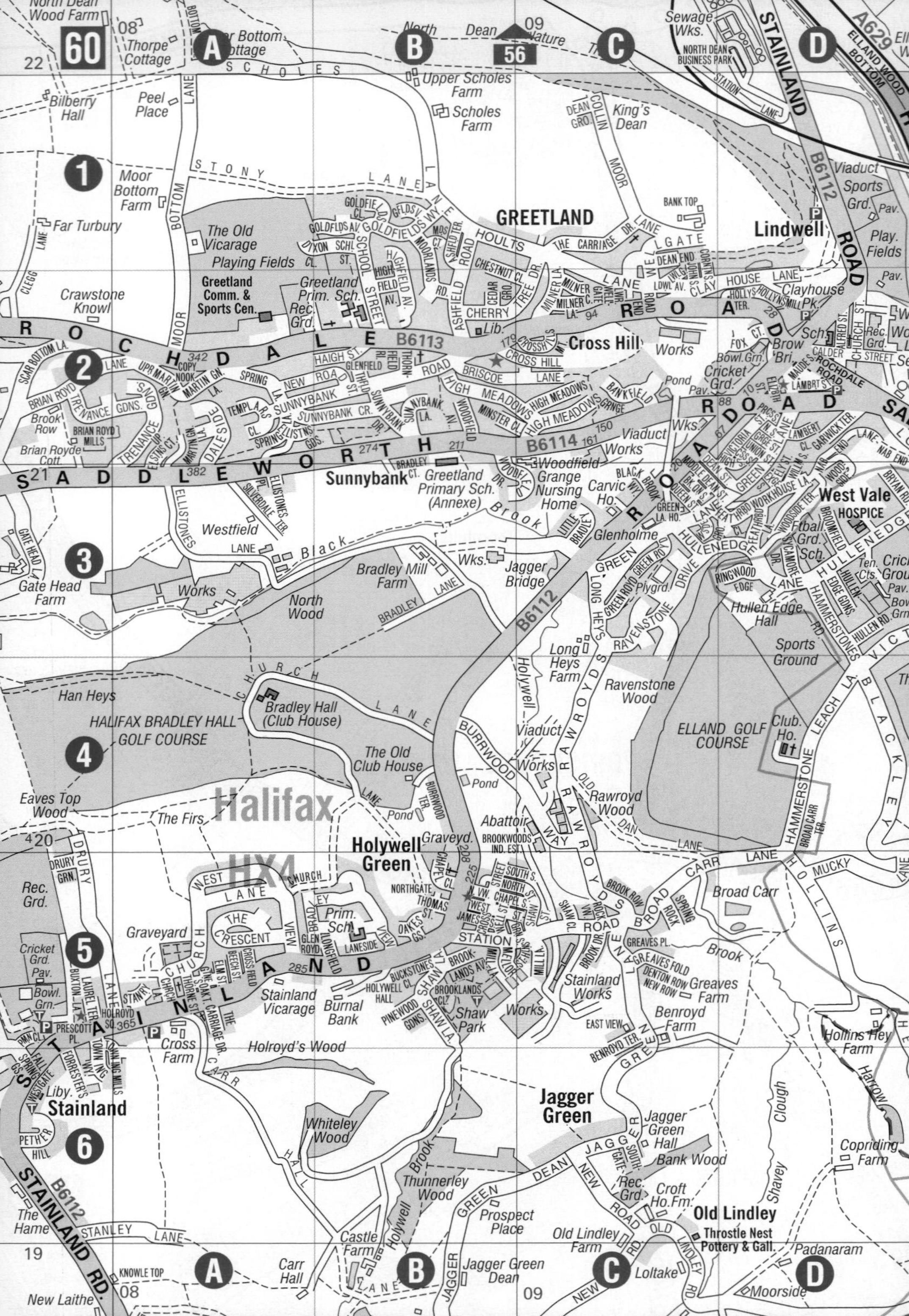
60
56
A
B
C
D
1
2
3
4
5
6
22
21
20
19
08
09
North Dean Wood Farm
Thorpe Cottage
Moor Bottom Cottage
North Dean Nature Trail
Sewage Wks.
NORTH DEAN BUSINESS PARK
STATION
STAINLAND
A629
ELLAND WOOD BOTTOM
SCHOLES
Upper Scholes Farm
Scholes Farm
Bilberry Hall
Peel Place
BOTTOM LANE
King's Dean
DEAN GRO.
COLIN
MOOR
STONY LANE
Moor Bottom Farm
Far Turbury
CLEGG LANE
MOOR BOTTOM
B6112
Viaduct Sports Grd.
Pav.
Play. Fields
BANK TOP
GREETLAND
Lindwell
ROAD
The Old Vicarage Playing Fields
Greetland Comm. & Sports Cen.
Greetland Prim. Sch.
Rec. Grd.
Crawstone Knowl
GOLDFIELDS CL.
GOLDFIELDS AV.
GOLDFIELDS WY.
SCHOOL STREET
HIGHFIELD AV.
MOORLANDS RD.
ASHFIELD ROAD
HOULTS
THE CARRIAGE DR.
WELLGATE
CLAY HOUSE LANE
Clayhouse Pk.
CHESTNUT CL.
CEDAR GRO.
CHERRY TREE DR.
Lib.
MILNER LA.
MILNER CL.
DEAN END
ROCHDALE ROAD
B6113
Cross Hill
CROSS HILL
Works
BRISCOE LANE
HIGH MEADOWS
MINSTER CL.
SCAR BOTTOM LA.
BRIAN ROYD LANE
COPY NOOK
UPR MARTIN GN.
MARTIN GN.
SPRING LA.
NEW ROAD
HAIGH ST.
GLENFIELD
SUNNYBANK
TRENANCE GDNS.
Brook Row
BRIAN ROYD MILLS
Brian Royde Cott.
DALESIDE
TEMPLARS CL.
SUNNYBANK CR.
SUNNYBANK AV.
WOODFIELD
Pond
BANKFIELD
Fox Ct.
Brow Bri.
Bowl. Grn.
Cricket Grd.
Pav.
Sch.
ALFRED ST.
CALDER STREET
CHURCH ST.
Rec. Grd.
SADDLEWORTH ROAD
B6114
Viaduct Works
Wks.
Sunnybank
BRADLEY CT.
Greetland Primary Sch. (Annexe)
Woodfield Grange Nursing Home
Carvic Ho.
BLACK BROOK WY.
GREEN LA. HO.
West Vale
HOSPICE
WORKHOUSE LA.
ELLISTONES
SILVERDALE
Westfield
Black Brook
LANE
GATE HEAD LA.
Gate Head Farm
Works
Bradley Mill Farm
BRADLEY LANE
Wks.
Jagger Bridge
LITTLE BRADLEY
Glenholme
GREEN ROYD
HULLENEDGE DRIVE
RINGWOOD EDGE
Ftball. Grd.
Sch.
HULLENEDGE LANE
Ten. Cts.
Pav.
North Wood
LONG HEYS
Plygrd.
RAVENSTONE
Hullen Edge Hall
HAMMERSTONES RD.
Sports Ground
Long Heys Farm
Ravenstone Wood
CHURCH LANE
Han Heys
Bradley Hall (Club House)
HALIFAX BRADLEY HALL GOLF COURSE
Holywell
Viaduct
RAWROYDS
ELLAND GOLF COURSE
Club. Ho.
LEACH LA.
BLACKLEY
Works
BURRWOOD
The Old Club House
Pond
Eaves Top Wood
Halifax
HX4
The Firs
Pond
BURRWOOD TER.
Rawroyd Wood
OLD RAWROYD WAY
Abattoir
BROOKWOODS IND. EST.
DAN LANE
HAMMERSTONE
BROAD CARR TER.
Holywell Green
Graveyd.
CARR LANE
HOLLINS
MUCKY
DRURY GRN.
DRURY
Rec. Grd.
WEST LANE
CHURCH
NORTHGATE
THOMAS ST.
CHAPEL
SOUTH S.
NORTH
BROOK ROW
BROAD
SPRING ROCK
Broad Carr
Graveyard
THE CRESCENT
VIEW
BRADLEY
Prim. Sch.
GLEN ROYD
LONGFIELD
LANESIDE
OAKES GS.
STATION ROAD
JAMES
WEST
GREAVES PL.
GREAVES FOLD
DENTON ROW
NEW ROW
Brook
Cricket Grd.
Pav.
Bowl. Grn.
STAINLAND
HOLROYD SQ.
PRESCOTT PL.
BUXTON LA.
LAUREL TER.
Stainland Vicarage
Burnal Bank
HOLYWELL CL.
HOLYWELL HALL
BUCKSTONES
BROOKLANDS
SHAW LA.
Shaw Park
PINEWOOD GDNS.
Works
MILL LA.
Stainland Works
Greaves Farm
Benroyd Farm
EAST VIEW
BENROYD TER.
Cross Farm
Holroyd's Wood
CARR
Hollins Hey Farm
Stainland
Liby.
PETHER HILL
WESTGATE
Jagger Green
Jagger Green Hall
Bank Wood
Whiteley Wood
Brook
Thunnerley Wood
HALL
DEAN
NEW ROAD
Rec. Grd.
Croft Ho. Fm.
Clough
Shavey
Copriding Farm
STAINLAND RD.
B6112
The Hame
STANLEY LANE
Prospect Place
Old Lindley Farm
OLD LINDLEY RD.
Old Lindley
Throstle Nest Pottery & Gall.
Padanaram
Castle Farm
Holywell
Carr Hall
KNOWLE TOP
New Laithe
JAGGER
Jagger Green Dean
Loltake
Moorside

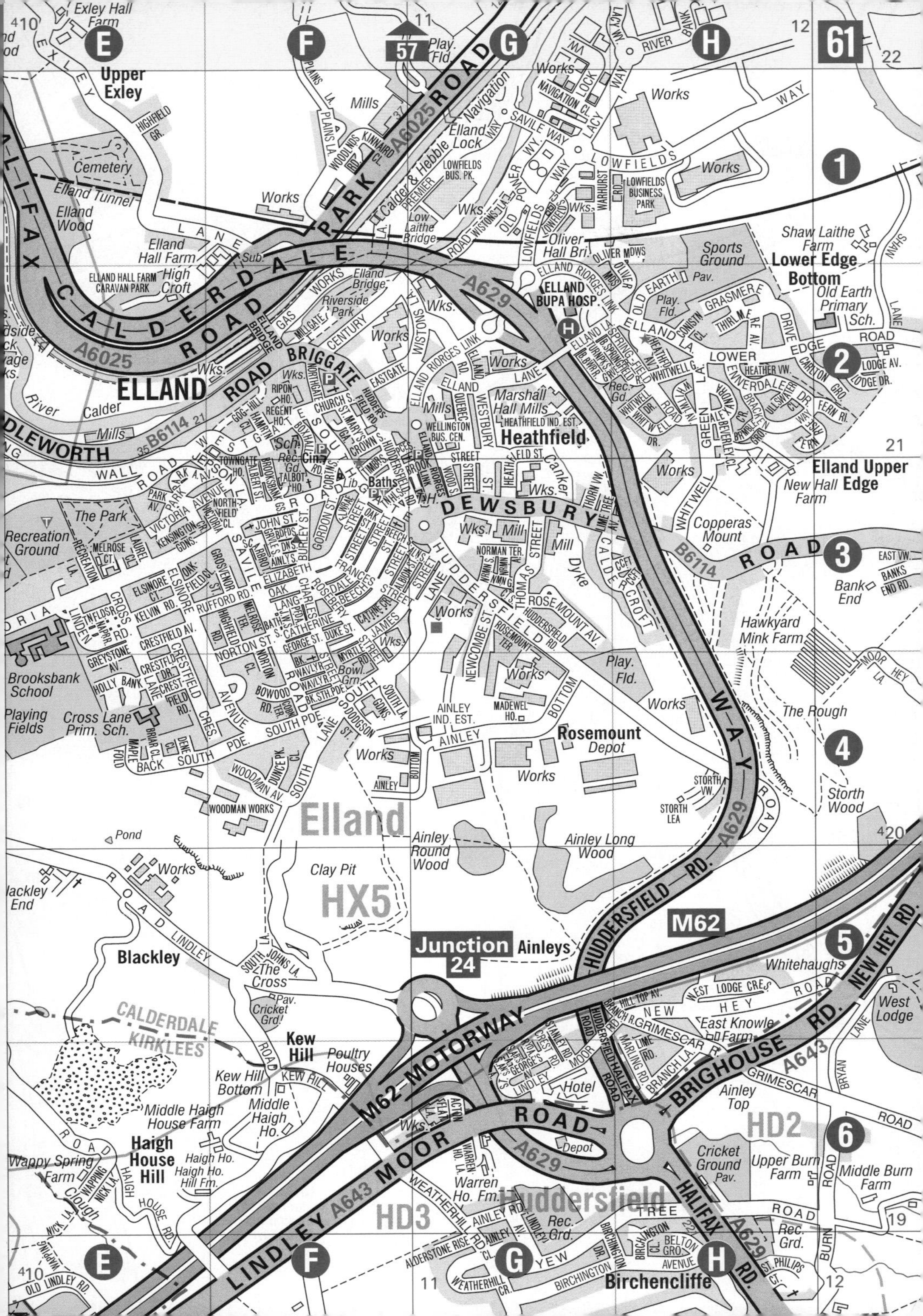

57
E
F
G
H
Upper Exley
Exley Hall Farm
Cemetery
Elland Tunnel
Elland Wood
Elland Hall Farm
Elland Hall Farm Caravan Park
High Croft
Works
Mills
Calder & Hebble Navigation
Elland Lock
Lowfields Bus. Pk.
Lowfields Business Park
Low Laithe Bridge
Oliver Hall Bri.
Elland Bridge
Riverside Park
CALDERDALE WAY
A6025
PARK ROAD
ELLAND ROAD
River Calder
ELLAND
BRIGGATE
Sports Ground
Shaw Laithe Farm
Lower Edge Bottom
Old Earth Primary Sch.
Elland BUPA Hosp.
Play. Fld.
Rec. Gd.
A629
Marshall Hall Mills
Heathfield
Heathfield Ind. Est.
Wellington Bus. Cen.
DEWSBURY ROAD
B6114
Elland Upper Edge
New Hall Farm
Copperas Mount
Bank End
Hawkyard Mink Farm
The Rough
Storth Wood
The Park
Recreation Ground
Brooksbank School
Playing Fields
Cross Lane Prim. Sch.
Baths
Lib.
Cin.
Sch.
Ainley Ind. Est.
Rosemount Depot
Woodman Works
Elland
Pond
Ainley Round Wood
Ainley Long Wood
Clay Pit
HX5
Blackley
Blackley End
HUDDERSFIELD RD.
M62
Junction 24
Ainleys
Whitehaughs
West Lodge
East Knowle Farm
CALDERDALE
KIRKLEES
Kew Hill
Kew Hill Bottom
Poultry Houses
Cricket Grd.
Pav.
The Cross
Middle Haigh House Farm
Middle Haigh Ho.
Haigh House Hill
Haigh Ho. Hill Fm.
Wappy Spring Farm
Clough
M62 MOTORWAY
LINDLEY MOOR ROAD
A643
BRIGHOUSE RD.
NEW HEY RD.
Hotel
Depot
Ainley Top
HD2
Cricket Ground
Upper Burn Farm
Middle Burn Farm
Warren Ho. Fm.
HD3
Huddersfield
Rec. Grd.
Birchencliffe
HALIFAX RD.
1
2
3
4
5
6
410
11
12
22
21
420
19

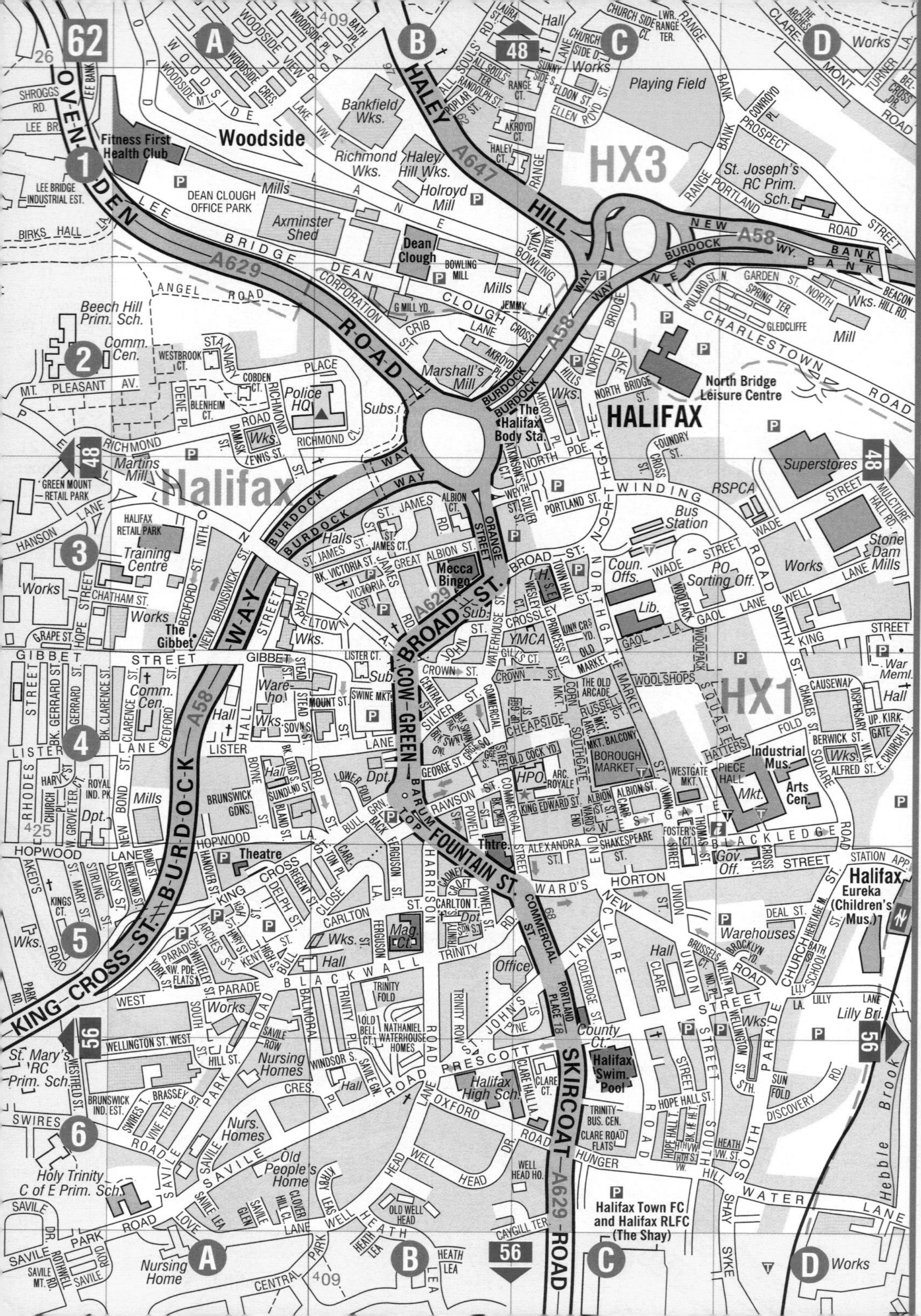

A
B
C
D
48
Woodside
Fitness First Health Club
Lee Bridge Industrial Est.
Dean Clough Office Park
Axminster Shed
Dean Clough
Bankfield Wks.
Richmond Wks.
Haley Hill Wks.
Holroyd Mill
Playing Field
HX3
St. Joseph's RC Prim. Sch.
Beech Hill Prim. Sch.
Comm. Cen.
Police HQ
Marshall's Mill
The Halifax Body Sta.
North Bridge Leisure Centre
HALIFAX
Halifax
Martins Mill
Green Mount Retail Park
Halifax Retail Park
Training Centre
Superstores
RSPCA
Bus Station
Coun. Offs.
PO Sorting Off.
Lib.
Works
Stone Dam Mills
Mecca Bingo
The Gibbet
YMCA
HX1
War Meml.
Borough Market
Piece Hall
Industrial Mus.
Arts Cen.
HPO
Theatre
Thtre.
Halifax Eureka (Children's Mus.)
Warehouses
Mag. Ct.
Office
County Ct.
Halifax Swim. Pool
Halifax High Sch.
Trinity Bus. Cen.
Clare Road Flats
Nursing Homes
Nurs. Homes
Old People's Home
Holy Trinity C of E Prim. Sch.
St. Mary's RC Prim. Sch.
Brunswick Ind. Est.
Halifax Town FC and Halifax RLFC (The Shay)
Nursing Home
Hebble Brook
Lilly Bri.
A629
A647
A58
OVENDEN ROAD
LEE BRIDGE
BURDOCK WAY
BROAD ST.
COW GREEN
FOUNTAIN ST.
KING CROSS ST.
SKIRCOAT ROAD
NORTHGATE
WINDING ROAD
WESTGATE
BLACKLEDGE
HORTON STREET
56

INDEX

Including Streets, Places & Areas, Hospitals & Hospices, Industrial Estates,
Selected Flats & Walkways, Stations and Selected Places of Interest.

HOW TO USE THIS INDEX

1. Each street name is followed by its Postcode District and then by its Locality abbreviation(s) and then by its map reference;
   e.g. **Aachen Way** HX1: Hal . . . .2H **55** is in the HX1 Postcode District and the Halifax Locality and is to be found in square 2H on page **55**.
   The page number is shown in bold type.

2. A strict alphabetical order is followed in which Av., Rd., St., etc. (though abbreviated) are read in full and as part of the street name;
   e.g. **Acrehowe Ri.** appears after **Acre Gro.** but before **Acre La.**

3. Streets and a selection of flats and walkways too small to be shown on the maps, appear in the index with the thoroughfare to which it is connected
   shown in brackets; e.g. **Abbots Wood** BD9: B'frd . . . .4E **27** (off Heaton Rd.)

4. Addresses that are in more than one part are referred to as not continuous.

5. Places and areas are shown in the index in BLUE TYPE and the map reference is to the actual map square in which the town centre or area is located
   and not to the place name shown on the map; e.g. ALLERTON 6H 25

6. An example of a selected place of interest is Bankfield Mus. & Gallery 4C 48

7. An example of a station is **Baildon Station (Rail)** 2A 18

8. An example of a hospital or hospice is **BINGLEY HOSPITAL** 2H 15

9. Map references shown in brackets; e.g **Acorn St.** BD3: B'frd . . . .3C **36** (5H **5**) refer to entries that also appear on the large scale pages **4-5** & **62**.

GENERAL ABBREVIATIONS

App. : Approach	**Ct.** : Court	**La.** : Lane	**Rd.** : Road
Arc. : Arcade	**Cres.** : Crescent	**Lit.** : Little	**Shop.** : Shopping
Av. : Avenue	**Cft.** : Croft	**Lwr.** : Lower	**Sth.** : South
Bk. : Back	**Dr.** : Drive	**Mnr.** : Manor	**Sq.** : Square
Bri. : Bridge	**E.** : East	**Mans.** : Mansions	**St.** : Street
B'way. : Broadway	**Est.** : Estate	**Mkt.** : Market	**Ter.** : Terrace
Bldgs. : Buildings	**Fld.** : Field	**Mdw.** : Meadow	**Twr.** : Tower
Bungs. : Bungalows	**Flds.** : Fields	**Mdws.** : Meadows	**Trad.** : Trading
Bus. : Business	**Gdn.** : Garden	**M.** : Mews	**Up.** : Upper
Cvn. : Caravan	**Gdns.** : Gardens	**Mt.** : Mount	**Va.** : Vale
C'way. : Causeway	**Gth.** : Garth	**Mus.** : Museum	**Vw.** : View
Cen. : Centre	**Ga.** : Gate	**Nth.** : North	**Vs.** : Villas
Chu. : Church	**Gt.** : Great	**No.** : Number	**Vis.** : Visitors
Circ. : Circle	**Grn.** : Green	**Pde.** : Parade	**Wlk.** : Walk
Cl. : Close	**Gro.** : Grove	**Pas.** : Passage	**W.** : West
Coll. : College	**Hgts.** : Heights	**Pl.** : Place	**Yd.** : Yard
Comn. : Common	**Ho.** : House	**Prom.** : Promenade	
Cnr. : Corner	**Ind.** : Industrial	**Ri.** : Rise	
Cotts. : Cottages	**Info.** : Information		

LOCALITY ABBREVIATIONS

Bail : **Baildon**	Ell : **Elland**	Oxen : **Oxenhope**	Wake : **Wakefield**
Bgly : **Bingley**	Hal : **Halifax**	Pud : **Pudsey**	Yead : **Yeadon**
B'frd : **Bradford**	Haw : **Haworth**	Ship : **Shipley**	
Brigh : **Brighouse**	Hud : **Huddersfield**	Stee : **Steeton**	
Cleck : **Cleckheaton**	Keigh : **Keighley**	Wads : **Wadsworth**	

1853 Art Gallery, The 4E **17**

A

Aachen Way HX1: Hal 2H **55**
Abaseen Cl. BD3: B'frd 2D **36**
Abbey Ct. BD8: B'frd 2A **4**
Abbey Court Leisure 2D **28**
Abbey La. HX2: Hal 6B **46**
Abbey Lea BD15: B'frd 1A **34**
Abbey Wlk. HX3: Hal 3C **56**
Abbey Wlk. Sth.
  HX3: Hal 3D **56**
Abbotside Cl. BD10: B'frd . . .1E **29**
Abbots Wood BD9: B'frd 4E **27**
  (off Heaton Rd.)
Abbott's Ladies Home
  HX3: Hal 4C **56**
Abbott's Ter. HX1: Hal 6A **48**
  (off Leafland St.)

Abb Scott La. BD6: B'frd 5F **43**
  BD12: B'frd 5F **43**
Abelia Mt. BD7: B'frd 3C **34**
Abel St. BD12: B'frd 1G **51**
Aberdeen BD22: Oxen 6F **21**
Aberdeen Pl. BD7: B'frd 4E **35**
Aberdeen Ter. BD7: B'frd 3E **35**
  BD14: B'frd 5B **34**
Aberford Rd. BD8: B'frd 6F **27**
Abingdon St. BD8: B'frd 6F **27**
Abram St. BD5: B'frd 5A **36**
Absolute Fitness Cen. 3F **29**
Acacia Dr. BD15: B'frd 3F **25**
  HX3: Hal 6E **51**
Acacia Pk. Cres.
  BD10: Yead 3H **19**
Acacia Pk. Dr. BD10: Yead . . .3H **19**
Acacia Pk. Ter. BD10: Yead . .3H **19**
Acaster Dr. BD12: B'frd 5G **43**
Acer Way BD19: Cleck 5B **52**
Ackroyd Ct. BD13: B'frd 3D **32**
Ackroyd Pl. BD13: B'frd 2D **40**
Ackroyd Sq. BD13: B'frd 2H **41**
  (off Highgate Rd.)

Ackworth St. BD5: B'frd 5A **36**
Acomb Ter. BD12: B'frd 2G **51**
Acorn Cl. BD6: B'frd 5C **42**
Acorn Pk. BD17: Bail 3A **18**
Acorn Pk. Ind. Est.
  BD17: Bail 3A **18**
Acorn St. BD3: B'frd . . .3C **36** (5H **5**)
  BD21: Keigh 6D **6**
  HX1: Hal 6A **48**
Acre, The BD12: B'frd 6F **43**
Acre Av. BD2: B'frd 2D **28**
Acre Cl. BD2: B'frd 2D **28**
Acre Cres. BD2: B'frd 2D **28**
Acre Dr. BD2: B'frd 2D **28**
Acre Gro. BD2: B'frd 2D **28**
Acrehowe Ri. BD17: Bail 1A **18**
Acre La. BD2: B'frd 3D **28**
  (not continuous)
  BD6: B'frd 2G **43**
  BD16: Bgly 3E **9**
  BD20: Keigh 3E **9**
  BD22: Haw 6G **11**
Acre Pl. BD6: B'frd 2G **43**
  (off Acre La.)

Acre Ri. BD17: Bail 1G **17**
Acres St. BD21: Keigh 5D **6**
Acton Flat La. HD3: Hud 6G **61**
Acton St. BD3: B'frd 2E **37**
Adam Cft. BD13: B'frd 1F **23**
Adam St. BD6: B'frd 2F **43**
Ada St. BD13: B'frd 2D **40**
  BD17: Bail 3A **18**
  BD18: Ship 5D **16**
  BD21: Keigh 4C **6**
  HX3: Hal 4C **48**
Addersgate La. HX3: Hal 1E **49**
Addison Av. BD3: B'frd 6F **29**
Addison Dr. BD22: Haw 1G **21**
Addi St. BD4: B'frd 6E **37**
Adelaide Ho. BD16: Bgly 3H **15**
Adelaide Ri. BD17: Bail 4G **17**
  (off John St.)
Adelaide St.
  BD5: B'frd 4A **36** (6D **4**)
  HX1: Hal 6H **47**
Adgil Cres. HX3: Hal 3G **57**
Adgil Gro. HX3: Hal 3H **57**
Adwalton Gro. BD13: B'frd . . .2F **41**

Agar St. BD8: B'frd 1D **34**
(not continuous)
Agar Ter. BD8: B'frd 1D **34**
Agnes St. BD20: Keigh 2E **7**
Ailsa Ho. *BD10: B'frd 6E* ***19***
(off Fairhaven Grn.)
Ails La. HX2: Hal 4A **46**
Ainley Bottom HX5: Ell 4F **61**
Ainley Cl. HD3: Hud 6G **61**
Ainley Ind. Est. HX5: Ell 4G **61**
Ainley Rd. HD3: Hud 6G **61**
AINLEYS 5G **61**
Ainley St. HX5: Ell 3F **61**
Ainsbury Av. BD10: B'frd 3D **18**
(not continuous)
Ainsdale Gro. BD13: B'frd 1G **23**
Airebank BD16: Bgly 2F **15**
Aire Cl. BD17: Bail 4F **17**
Airedale Av. BD16: Bgly 6G **15**
Airedale Coll. Mt.
BD3: B'frd 6C ***28***
(off Airedale College Rd.)
BD5: B'frd 6A ***36***
(off Darnay La.)
Airedale Coll. Rd.
BD3: B'frd 6C **28**
Airedale Coll. Ter.
BD3: B'frd 6C **28**
Airedale Cres. BD3: B'frd 6C **28**
Airedale Dr. HX3: Hal 6H **41**
Airedale Mt. BD20: Keigh 3C **8**
Airedale Pl. BD17: Bail 3A **18**
Airedale Rd. BD3: B'frd 6B **28**
BD21: Keigh 3H **7**
Airedale Shop. Cen.
BD21: Keigh 4E **7**
Airedale St. BD2: B'frd 4D **28**
BD16: Bgly 2F **15**
BD21: Keigh 3G **7**
Airedale Ter. BD17: Bail 3H **17**
Aire St. BD10: B'frd 4C **18**
BD16: Bgly 5E **9**
BD21: Keigh 3F **7**
BD22: Haw 6H **11**
HD6: Brigh 6F **59**
Aire Valley Bus. Cen.
BD21: Keigh 4E **7**
Aire Valley Ct.
BD16: Bgly 3F **15**
Aire Valley Rd.
BD21: Keigh 3G **7**
Aire Vw. BD20: Keigh 1H **7**
Aire Vw. Av. BD16: Bgly 5H **15**
Aireview Cres. BD17: Bail 4E **17**
Aire Vw. Dr. BD20: Keigh 4C **8**
Aire Vw. Nth. BD18: Ship 5E **17**
Aireview Ter. BD21: Keigh 5G **7**
Aireville Av. BD9: B'frd 2F **27**
BD18: B'frd 2F **27**
Aireville Cl. BD18: B'frd 2F **27**
BD20: Keigh 1C **6**
Aireville Cres. BD9: B'frd 3F **27**
Aireville Dr. BD18: B'frd 2F **27**
Aireville Grange
BD18: B'frd 2F **27**
Aireville Gro. BD18: B'frd 2F **27**
Aireville Mt. BD20: Keigh 3C **8**
Aireville Ri. BD9: B'frd 2F **27**
Aireville Rd. BD9: B'frd 2F **27**
Aireville St. BD20: Keigh 1C **6**
Aire Way BD17: Bail 4E **17**
AIREWORTH 3G **7**
Aireworth Cl. BD21: Keigh 2G **7**
Aireworth Gro. BD21: Keigh ...3G **7**
Aireworth Rd. BD21: Keigh 2G **7**
Aireworth St. BD21: Keigh 5D **6**
Airey St. BD21: Keigh 4C **6**
AJ's Workhouse *5F* ***17***
(off Charles St.)
Akam Rd.
BD1: B'frd 2H **35** (3A **4**)
Aked's Rd.
HX1: Hal 1B **56** (5A **62**)
Aked St. BD1: B'frd 2B **36** (4F **5**)
Akroyd Ct. HX3: Hal 1B **62**

AKROYDON 4C **48**
Akroyd Pl.
HX1: Hal 5C **48** (2B **62**)
Akroyd Ter. HX2: Hal 2H **55**
Alabama St. HX1: Hal 6H **47**
Alanby Dr. BD10: B'frd 6E **19**
Alban St. BD4: B'frd 5D **36**
Albany Ct. BD20: Keigh 3C **6**
Albany St. BD5: B'frd 5A **36**
BD6: B'frd 2G **43**
HX3: Hal 2D **56**
Albany Ter. HX3: Hal 2D **56**
Albert Av. BD10: B'frd 5E **19**
BD18: Ship 4C **16**
HX2: Hal 5G **47**
Albert Bldgs. BD10: B'frd 1D **28**
Albert Ct. HX2: Hal 5G **47**
Albert Cres. BD13: B'frd 2E **41**
Albert Dr. HX2: Hal 5F **47**
Albert Edward St.
BD13: B'frd 2E **41**
Albert Gdns. HX2: Hal 5G **47**
Albert Pl. BD3: B'frd 1G **37**
Albert Prom. HX3: Hal 3A **56**
Albert Rd. BD13: B'frd 1D **40**
BD18: Ship 5D **16**
HX2: Hal 5F **47**
HX6: Hal 2E **55**
Albert St. BD6: B'frd 3F **43**
BD10: B'frd 1D **28**
BD12: B'frd 3G **51**
BD13: B'frd 2F **41**
(Brighouse Rd.)
BD13: B'frd 3D **32**
(Kipping La.)
BD15: B'frd 3C **24**
BD17: Bail 4G **17**
BD19: Cleck 5F **53**
BD21: Keigh 4D **6**
BD22: Haw 5B ***12***
(off Bingley Rd.)
HD6: Brigh 5G **59**
HX1: Hal 6B **48**
HX5: Ell 3F **61**
Albert Ter. BD12: B'frd 3H **51**
(Craiglea Dr.)
BD12: B'frd 6B **44**
(Dyehouse Rd.)
BD18: Ship 4D **16**
Albert Vw. HX2: Hal 5G **47**
Albert Wlk. BD18: Ship 5C **16**
Albion Ct.
BD1: B'frd 2A **36** (4D **4**)
HX1: Hal 3B **62**
Albion Fold BD15: B'frd 2C **24**
Albion Pl. BD13: B'frd 3C **32**
HD6: Brigh 4E ***59***
(off Waterloo Rd.)
Albion Rd. BD10: B'frd 5D **18**
Albion St.
BD1: B'frd 2A **36** (4C **4**)
BD6: B'frd 4C **42**
BD13: B'frd 2D **40**
(Alma St.)
BD13: B'frd 1F **31**
(Station Rd.)
BD19: Cleck 6G **53**
BD22: Haw 5A **12**
HD6: Brigh 4E **59**
HX1: Hal 6C **48** (4C **62**)
(not continuous)
HX5: Ell 3G **61**
Albion Yd.
BD1: B'frd 2A **36** (4D **4**)
Alcester Gth.
BD3: B'frd 1D **36** (2H **5**)
Alder Av. BD21: Keigh 6G **7**
Alder Carr BD17: Bail 2F **17**
Alder Gro. HX2: Hal 5G **39**
Alderholt Dr. BD6: B'frd 5E **43**
Aldermanbury
BD1: B'frd 2A **36** (5C **4**)
Alderscholes Cl.
BD13: B'frd 3D ***32***
(off Alderscholes La.)

Alderscholes La.
BD13: B'frd 4B **32**
Alderson St. BD6: B'frd 4C **42**
Alderstone Ri. HD3: Hud 6G **61**
Alegar St. HD6: Brigh 5G **59**
Alexander Ct. BD20: Keigh 4D **8**
Alexander Sq. BD14: B'frd 5H **33**
Alexander St. BD6: B'frd 3F **43**
Alexander Ter. HX1: Hal 6H **47**
Alexandra Cl. HX6: Hal 3E **55**
Alexandra Cres. HX5: Ell 2H **61**
Alexandra Rd. BD2: B'frd 2E **29**
BD18: Ship 6E **17**
Alexandra Sq. BD18: Ship 5D **16**
Alexandra St. BD7: B'frd 4G **35**
BD13: B'frd 2D **40**
HX1: Hal 6C **48** (5C **62**)
Alexandra Ter. BD2: B'frd 5E **29**
Alford Ter. BD7: B'frd 2E **35**
Alfred St. HD6: Brigh 4F **59**
HX1: Hal 6H **47**
HX4: Hal 2D **60**
Alfred St. E.
HX1: Hal 6D **48** (4D **62**)
Alhambra Theatre & Studio
............3A **36** (5C **4**)
Alice St. BD8: B'frd ...1H **35** (1A **4**)
BD19: Cleck 5F **53**
BD21: Keigh 4E **7**
BD22: Haw 1G **21**
Alkincote St. BD21: Keigh 5E **7**
All Alone BD10: B'frd 6C **18**
All Alone Rd. BD10: B'frd 6B **18**
Allanbridge Cl. BD10: B'frd ...6E **19**
Allandale Av. BD6: B'frd 4E **43**
Allandale Rd. BD6: B'frd 4E **43**
Allan St. BD3: B'frd 3D **36**
Allan Ter. HX6: Hal 4E **55**
Allerby Grn. BD6: B'frd 4D **42**
ALLERTON 6H **25**
Allerton Cl. BD15: B'frd 6H **25**
Allerton Grange Dr.
BD15: B'frd 6H **25**
Allerton La. BD13: B'frd 2G **33**
BD15: B'frd 6G **25**
Allerton Pl. HX1: Hal 6A **48**
Allerton Rd. BD8: B'frd 6B **26**
BD15: B'frd 6D **24**
(Dean La.)
BD15: B'frd 6H **25**
(Meadowbank Av.)
Allerton Up. Grn.
BD15: B'frd 1E **33**
Allison La. BD2: B'frd 3H **27**
Alloe Fld. Pl. HX2: Hal 5G **39**
Alloe Fld. Vw. HX2: Hal 5G **39**
Allotments Rd. BD13: B'frd ...6G **23**
All Saints Ct. BD21: Keigh 4D **6**
All Saints Rd. BD7: B'frd 4F **35**
All Saints Ter. BD21: Keigh 4D **6**
All Souls' Rd.
HX3: Hal 4C **48** (1B **62**)
All Souls' St. HX3: Hal 4C **48**
All Souls' Ter.
HX3: Hal 4C **48** (1B **62**)
Alma Cotts. *BD13: B'frd 3C* ***40***
(off Moor Cl. La.)
Alma Gro. BD18: Ship 5H **17**
Alma Pl. BD3: B'frd 1F **37**
BD21: Keigh 6E **7**
Alma St. BD4: B'frd 4E **37**
(Buller St.)
BD4: B'frd 5F **37**
(Inkerman St.)
BD13: B'frd 2D **40**
BD18: Ship 5H **17**
BD21: Keigh 1E **13**
(not continuous)
BD22: Haw 5G **11**
HX5: Ell 3G ***61***
(off James St.)
Alma Ter. BD20: Keigh 2E **9**
BD21: Keigh 6E **7**
Almond St. BD3: B'frd 3E **37**
Almscliffe Pl. BD2: B'frd 3F **29**

Almsford BD13: B'frd 1F **31**
Alpha St. BD21: Keigh 4F **7**
Alpine Ri. BD13: B'frd 2D **32**
Alston Cl. BD9: B'frd 6B **26**
Alston Retail Pk.
BD21: Keigh 2F **7**
Alston Rd. BD21: Keigh 2F **7**
Altar Dr. BD9: B'frd 4E **27**
BD20: Keigh 2A **8**
Altar La. BD16: Bgly 1H **13**
Altar Vw. *BD16: Bgly 6E* ***9***
(off Sleningford Rd.)
BD20: Keigh 1H **7**
Altar Vs. BD20: Keigh 2H **7**
Althorpe Gro. BD10: B'frd 1C **28**
Alton Gro. BD9: B'frd 4D **26**
BD18: Ship 2F **27**
Alum Ct. BD9: B'frd 4E **27**
Alum Dr. BD9: B'frd 4E **27**
Alvanley Ct. BD8: B'frd 1B **34**
Alva Ter. BD18: Ship 1F **27**
Amberley Ct. *BD3: B'frd 3E* ***37***
(off Amberley St.)
Amberley St. BD3: B'frd 2E **37**
(not continuous)
Ambler Gro. HX2: Hal 5H **39**
Amblers Cft. BD10: B'frd 3D **18**
Amblers M. BD17: Bail 1G **17**
BD20: Keigh 3D **8**
Amblers Row BD17: Bail 1G **17**
Amblers Ter. HX3: Hal 4C **48**
Ambler St. BD8: B'frd 6G **27**
BD21: Keigh 4F **7**
AMBLER THORN 4C **40**
Ambler Way BD13: B'frd 4C **40**
Ambleside Av. BD9: B'frd 5D **26**
Amble Tonia BD13: B'frd 6G **23**
Ambleton Way BD13: B'frd ...3C **40**
Amelia St. BD18: Ship 4D **16**
America La. HD6: Brigh 5G **59**
AMF Bowling
Keighley 2F **7**
Amisfield Rd. HX3: Hal 5B **50**
Amos St. HX1: Hal 6H **47**
Amport Cl. HD6: Brigh 6F **59**
Amundsen Av. BD2: B'frd 2C **28**
Amyroyce Dr. BD18: Ship 6A **18**
Amy St. BD16: Bgly 2G **15**
HX3: Hal 3A **48**
Anchorage, The BD16: Bgly ...1F **15**
Anchor Ct. BD8: B'frd 2A **4**
Anderson Ho. *BD17: Bail 4F* ***17***
(off Fairview Ct.)
Anderson St. BD8: B'frd 6G **27**
Anderton Fold HX3: Hal 3G **49**
Andover Grn. BD4: B'frd 5G **37**
Andrew Cl. HX3: Hal 3G **57**
Anerley St. BD4: B'frd 1D **44**
Angel Pl. BD16: Bgly 6G **9**
Angel Rd. HX1: Hal 5B **48**
(Crossley Retail Pk.)
HX1: Hal 5B **48** (2A **62**)
(Stannary Pl.)
Angel St. BD17: Bail 1H **17**
Angel Way
BD7: B'frd 2H **35** (4A **4**)
Angerton Way BD6: B'frd 5E **43**
Anglesea Pl. BD22: Haw 2G **21**
Angram Rd. BD20: Keigh 1C **6**
Angus Av. BD12: B'frd 4G **51**
Anlaby St. BD4: B'frd 4F **37**
Annandale Vw.
BD13: B'frd 1H **41**
Anne Ga. BD1: B'frd ...2B **36** (3F **5**)
Anne's Ct. HX3: Hal 3G **57**
Anne St. BD7: B'frd 6D **34**
Annie St. BD18: Ship 1G **27**
BD21: Keigh 2E **7**
BD22: Haw 5B **12**
HX6: Hal 3D **54**
Annison St.
BD3: B'frd 2C **36** (4G **5**)
Ann Pl. BD5: B'frd 4A **36** (6C **4**)
Ann St. BD21: Keigh 5D **6**
BD22: Haw 6H **11**

Another World (Mountainboarding Cen.)—Bk. Broomfield Rd.

Another World (Mountainboarding Cen.) . . . 6F 31
Anson Gro. BD7: B'frd . . . 1D 42
Anstone Dr. BD5: B'frd . . . 1G 43
Anthony La. BD16: Bgly . . . 3B 14
Anvil Ct. BD8: B'frd . . . 6F 27 (off Carlisle St.)
BD13: B'frd . . . 2F 23
Anvil St. BD8: B'frd . . . 6F 27 (not continuous)
HD6: Brigh . . . 4E 59
APPERLEY BRIDGE . . . 5F 19
Apperley Gdns.
BD10: B'frd . . . 5G 19
Apperley La.
BD10: B'frd, Yead . . . 5G 19
LS19: Yead . . . 4H 19
Apperley Rd. BD10: B'frd . . . 5E 19 (not continuous)
Appleby Cl. BD13: B'frd . . . 2C 40
Applegarth BD14: B'frd . . . 6A 34
Applehaigh Cl. BD10: B'frd . . . 6E 19
Apple Ho. Ter. HX2: Hal . . . 4A 46
Apple St. BD21: Keigh . . . 2C 12
BD22: Oxen . . . 5G 21
Appleton Cl. BD12: B'frd . . . 6B 44
BD16: Bgly . . . 6H 9
Aprilia Ct. BD14: B'frd . . . 4B 34
Apsley Cres. BD8: B'frd . . . 6G 27
Apsley St. BD21: Keigh . . . 6D 6
BD22: Haw . . . 6H 11
BD22: Keigh . . . 2H 11
Apsley Ter. BD22: Keigh . . . 2H 11 (off Green La.)
Apsley Vs. BD8: B'frd . . . 6H 27
Arc. Royale HX1: Hal . . . 4C 62 (off Commercial St.)
Arcadia St. BD21: Keigh . . . 6D 6
Archbell Av. HD6: Brigh . . . 6F 59
Archer Rd. HD6: Brigh . . . 6H 59
Arches, The
HX3: Hal . . . 4C 48 (1D 62)
Arches St.
HX1: Hal . . . 1B 56 (5A 62)
Archibald St. BD7: B'frd . . . 2G 35
Arctic Pde. BD7: B'frd . . . 5E 35
Arctic St. BD20: Keigh . . . 1D 6
BD22: Haw . . . 5A 12
Arden Ho. HX1: Hal . . . 2B 56 (off Arden Rd.)
Arden M. HX1: Hal . . . 2B 56
Ardennes Cl. BD2: B'frd . . . 3B 28
Arden Rd. BD8: B'frd . . . 2A 34
HX1: Hal . . . 1B 56
Ardsley Cl. BD4: B'frd . . . 1H 45 (not continuous)
Argent Way BD4: B'frd . . . 1H 45
Argyle St. BD4: B'frd . . . 6D 36
BD21: Keigh . . . 4D 6
Argyll Cl. BD17: Bail . . . 3A 18
Arkendale M. BD7: B'frd . . . 6C 34
Arkwright St. BD4: B'frd . . . 3G 37
BD14: B'frd . . . 5H 33
Arlesford Rd. BD4: B'frd . . . 1G 45
Arlington Cres. HX2: Hal . . . 2F 55
Arlington St. BD3: B'frd . . . 3D 36
Armadale Av. BD4: B'frd . . . 3D 44
Armgill La. BD2: B'frd . . . 3H 27
Armidale Way BD2: B'frd . . . 4B 28
Armitage, The BD20: Keigh . . . 3B 8
Armitage Rd. BD12: B'frd . . . 1B 52
HX1: Hal . . . 2H 55
Armstrong St. BD4: B'frd . . . 3F 37
Armytage Rd. HD6: Brigh . . . 5G 59
Armytage Way HD6: Brigh . . . 6H 59
Arncliffe Av. BD22: Keigh . . . 5C 6
Arncliffe Gro. BD22: Keigh . . . 6C 6
Arncliffe Path BD22: Keigh . . . 5C 6 (off Arncliffe Av.)
Arncliffe Pl. BD22: Keigh . . . 5C 6 (off Arncliffe Av.)
Arncliffe Rd. BD22: Keigh . . . 6C 6
Arncliffe Ter. BD7: B'frd . . . 3F 35
Arndale Ho. BD1: B'frd . . . 4D 4
Arndale Shop. Cen.
BD18: Ship . . . 6F 17 (off Market St.)
Arnford Cl.
BD3: B'frd . . . 1B 36 (1F 5)
Arnold Pl. BD8: B'frd . . . 1G 35
Arnold St. BD8: B'frd . . . 6G 27
HX1: Hal . . . 6A 48
HX6: Hal . . . 3D 54
Arnside Av. BD20: Keigh . . . 2G 7
Arnside Rd. BD5: B'frd . . . 1A 44
Arthington St. BD8: B'frd . . . 1G 35
Arthur Av. BD8: B'frd . . . 2A 34
Arthur St. BD10: B'frd . . . 1D 28
BD16: Bgly . . . 1F 15
BD22: Keigh . . . 3G 11
HD6: Brigh . . . 5G 59
Arum St. BD5: B'frd . . . 6G 35
Arundel St. HX1: Hal . . . 6H 47
Ascot Av. BD7: B'frd . . . 1C 42
Ascot Dr. BD7: B'frd . . . 1C 42
Ascot Gdns. BD7: B'frd . . . 1C 42
Ascot Gro. HD6: Brigh . . . 6C 58
Ascot Pde. BD7: B'frd . . . 1C 42
Ashbourne Av. BD2: B'frd . . . 4B 28
BD19: Cleck . . . 6F 53
Ashbourne Bank
BD2: B'frd . . . 4B 28
Ashbourne Cl. BD2: B'frd . . . 3B 28
Ashbourne Cres.
BD2: B'frd . . . 4B 28
BD13: B'frd . . . 2D 40
Ashbourne Dr. BD2: B'frd . . . 4B 28
BD19: Cleck . . . 6F 53
Ashbourne Gdns.
BD2: B'frd . . . 4B 28
Ashbourne Gth. BD2: B'frd . . . 3C 28
Ashbourne Gro. BD2: B'frd . . . 4B 28
HX1: Hal . . . 6H 47
Ashbourne Haven
BD2: B'frd . . . 4B 28
Ashbourne Mt. BD2: B'frd . . . 4B 28
Ashbourne Oval
BD2: B'frd . . . 4B 28
Ashbourne Ri. BD2: B'frd . . . 4B 28
Ashbourne Rd. BD2: B'frd . . . 4B 28
BD21: Keigh . . . 1C 12
Ashbourne Way BD2: B'frd . . . 3B 28
BD19: Cleck . . . 6F 53
Ashburn Gro. BD17: Bail . . . 1G 17
Ashburnham Gro.
BD9: B'frd . . . 4F 27
Ashby St. BD4: B'frd . . . 5C 36
Ash Cl. HX3: Hal . . . 5B 50
Ash Ct. BD19: Cleck . . . 5B 52
Ash Cft. BD6: B'frd . . . 3E 43
Ashday La. HX3: Hal . . . 4G 57
Ashdene Ct. BD13: B'frd . . . 1F 23
Ashdown Cl. BD6: B'frd . . . 2F 43
HX2: Hal . . . 1F 55
Ashdown Ct. BD18: Ship . . . 6E 17
Ashdowne Pl. BD8: B'frd . . . 6G 27 (off E. Squire La.)
Ashfield BD4: B'frd . . . 2F 45
Ashfield Av. BD9: Ship . . . 2F 27
Ashfield Cl. HX3: Hal . . . 3H 47
Ashfield Ct. BD16: Bgly . . . 3G 15
Ashfield Cres. BD16: Bgly . . . 3G 15
Ashfield Dr. BD9: Ship . . . 2F 27
BD17: Bail . . . 1H 17
HX3: Hal . . . 3H 47
Ashfield Gro. BD9: B'frd . . . 2E 27
Ashfield Pl. BD2: B'frd . . . 5F 29
Ashfield Rd. BD10: B'frd . . . 4D 18
BD13: B'frd . . . 3D 32
BD18: Ship . . . 6C 16
HX4: Hal . . . 2B 60
Ashfield St. BD21: Keigh . . . 5D 6 (off Minnie St.)
Ashfield Ter. BD12: B'frd . . . 1H 51
BD16: Bgly . . . 3G 15
BD19: Cleck . . . 6G 53 (off Neville St.)
BD22: Haw . . . 1G 21
HX4: Hal . . . 1B 60
Ashford Grn. BD6: B'frd . . . 2D 42
Ash Ghyll Gdns.
BD16: Bgly . . . 1F 15
Ash Gro. BD2: B'frd . . . 4E 29
BD16: Bgly . . . 4G 15
BD19: Cleck . . . 6D 52
BD21: Keigh . . . 1C 12
HD6: Brigh . . . 4G 59
Ashgrove
BD7: B'frd . . . 3H 35 (6A 4)
BD10: B'frd . . . 6G 19
Ashgrove Av. HX3: Hal . . . 4D 56
Ashgrove Pl. HX3: Hal . . . 4E 57
Ashgrove Rd. BD20: Keigh . . . 1C 6
Ash Gro. Ter. HD6: Brigh . . . 6E 59 (off Thomas St.)
Ash Hill Wlk. BD4: B'frd . . . 5D 36
Ashington Cl. BD2: B'frd . . . 4F 29
Ashlar Cl. BD22: Haw . . . 6H 11
Ashlar Gro. BD13: B'frd . . . 4D 40
Ashlea Av. HD6: Brigh . . . 6F 59
Ashlea Cl. HD6: Brigh . . . 6F 59
Ashleigh St. BD21: Keigh . . . 3E 7
HX3: Hal . . . 2A 48
Ashley La. BD17: Ship . . . 5F 17
Ashley Rd. BD12: B'frd . . . 3G 51
BD16: Bgly . . . 3G 15
Ashley St. BD18: Ship . . . 5F 17
HX1: Hal . . . 6H 47
Ash M. BD10: B'frd . . . 6G 19
Ashmore Gdns. BD4: B'frd . . . 3D 44
Ash Mt. BD7: B'frd . . . 4F 35
BD21: Keigh . . . 6C 6
Ashmount BD7: B'frd . . . 5B 34
Ashmount Pl. BD22: Haw . . . 6G 11
Ash St. BD19: Cleck . . . 6E 53
BD22: Oxen . . . 4G 21
Ash Ter. BD16: Bgly . . . 3F 15
BD19: Cleck . . . 5F 53 (off Whitcliffe Rd.)
Ashton Av. BD7: B'frd . . . 4C 34
Ashton Ho. BD5: B'frd . . . 4A 36 (off Crosscombe Wlk.)
Ashton St.
BD1: B'frd . . . 2H 35 (3A 4)
Ashton Wlk. BD10: B'frd . . . 6C 18
Ash Tree Av. BD13: B'frd . . . 3B 32
Ash Tree Gdns. HX2: Hal . . . 6E 39
Ashtree Gro. BD7: B'frd . . . 1D 42
Ash Tree Rd. HX2: Hal . . . 6E 39
Ashville Cft. HX2: Hal . . . 5F 47
Ashville Gdns. HX2: Hal . . . 5F 47
Ashville Gro. HX2: Hal . . . 4F 47
Ashville St. HX3: Hal . . . 4A 48
Ashville Ter. BD22: Keigh . . . 3H 11
Ashwell La. BD9: B'frd . . . 3E 27
Ashwell Rd. BD8: B'frd . . . 6F 27
BD9: B'frd . . . 3E 27
Ashwood Dr. BD20: Keigh . . . 2A 8
Ashwood St. BD4: B'frd . . . 2F 45
Ashworth Pl. BD6: B'frd . . . 2H 43
Askrigg Dr. BD2: B'frd . . . 4D 28
Aspen Cl. BD21: Keigh . . . 6G 7
Aspen Ri. BD15: B'frd . . . 3F 25
Aspinall St. HX1: Hal . . . 1H 55
Asprey Dr. BD15: B'frd . . . 1H 33
Asquith Bottom HX6: Hal . . . 4D 54
Asquith Bldgs. BD12: B'frd . . . 6B 44 (off Cleckheaton Rd.)
Asquith Ct. HX2: Hal . . . 6F 47
Asquith Ter. HX6: Hal . . . 4D 54
Aston Rd. BD5: B'frd . . . 6A 36
Astral Av. HX3: Hal . . . 5B 50
Astral Cl. HX3: Hal . . . 5B 50
Astral Vw. BD6: B'frd . . . 1E 43
Atalanta Ter. HX2: Hal . . . 3G 55
Atamco Ho. BD19: Cleck . . . 6G 53 (off Albion St.)
Atherstone Rd.
BD15: B'frd . . . 1H 33
Athol Cl. HX3: Hal . . . 2A 48
Athol Cres. HX3: Hal . . . 2A 48
Athol Gdns. HX3: Hal . . . 2A 48
Athol Grn. HX3: Hal . . . 2A 48
Athol Mt. HX3: Hal . . . 2A 48
Athol Rd. BD9: B'frd . . . 5F 27
HX3: Hal . . . 2A 48
Athol St. BD21: Keigh . . . 2G 7
HX3: Hal . . . 2A 48
Atkinson's Ct.
HX1: Hal . . . 5C 48 (3B 62)
Atkinson St. BD18: Ship . . . 5F 17
Atlas Mill Rd. HD6: Brigh . . . 5E 59
Atlas St. BD8: B'frd . . . 6F 27
Auckland Rd. BD6: B'frd . . . 2E 43
Aurelia Ho. BD8: B'frd . . . 5G 27
Austell Ho. BD5: B'frd . . . 5H 35 (off Park La.)
Austin Av. HD6: Brigh . . . 3D 58
Austin St. BD21: Keigh . . . 3F 7
Autumn St. HX1: Hal . . . 2H 55
Avenel Rd. BD15: B'frd . . . 6H 25
Avenel Ter. BD15: B'frd . . . 1H 33
Avenham Way
BD3: B'frd . . . 1C 36 (2G 5)
Avenue, The BD10: B'frd . . . 2G 19 (not continuous)
BD14: B'frd . . . 6G 33
BD15: B'frd . . . 3D 24
BD16: Bgly . . . 5H 15
BD17: B'frd . . . 2G 19
HX3: Hal . . . 5B 50
Avenue No. 1 HD6: Brigh . . . 6E 59
Avenue No. 2 HD6: Brigh . . . 6E 59
Avenue Rd. BD5: B'frd . . . 6B 36
Avenue St. BD4: B'frd . . . 2F 45
Averingcliffe Rd.
BD10: B'frd . . . 1F 29
Avocet Cl. BD8: B'frd . . . 2A 34
Avondale BD20: Keigh . . . 3C 6
Avondale Cres. BD18: Ship . . . 6E 17
Avondale Gro. BD18: Ship . . . 6E 17
Avondale Mt. BD18: Ship . . . 6E 17
Avondale Pl. HX3: Hal . . . 3B 56
Avondale Rd. BD18: Ship . . . 6C 16
Aydon Way HX3: B'frd . . . 4C 42
Aygill Av. BD9: B'frd . . . 4B 26
Aylesbury St. BD21: Keigh . . . 1C 12
Aylesham Ind. Est.
BD12: B'frd . . . 5H 43
Aynsley Gro. BD15: B'frd . . . 5H 25
Ayresome Oval
BD15: B'frd . . . 2G 33
Ayreville Dr. HX3: Hal . . . 5A 42
Ayrton Cres. BD16: Bgly . . . 2G 15
Aysgarth Av. HX3: Hal . . . 1E 59
Aysgarth Cl. BD12: B'frd . . . 3G 51
Aysgarth Cres. HX2: Hal . . . 2C 46
Ayton Cl. BD3: B'frd . . . 1C 36 (2H 5)
Ayton Ho. BD4: B'frd . . . 2H 45
Azealea Ct.
BD3: B'frd . . . 1D 36 (2H 5) (not continuous)

B

Bk. Ada St. BD21: Keigh . . . 4C 6 (off Devonshire St.)
Bk. Aireview Ter.
BD21: Keigh . . . 5G 7
Bk. Aireville St.
BD20: Keigh . . . 1C 6
Bk. Ann St. BD13: B'frd . . . 6F 23
Bk. Ashgrove W.
BD7: B'frd . . . 3H 35 (6A 4)
Bk. Aylesbury St.
BD21: Keigh . . . 1C 12 (off Queen's Rd.)
Bk. Baker St. BD18: Ship . . . 5E 17
Bk. Balfour St. BD16: Bgly . . . 3F 15
BD21: Keigh . . . 5D 6
Bk. Beech St. BD16: Bgly . . . 3F 15
Bk. Blackwood Gro.
HX1: Hal . . . 5H 47
Bk. Blenheim Mt.
BD8: B'frd . . . 5G 27
Bk. Bower Rd. HX5: Ell . . . 2G 61
Bk. Broomfield Rd.
BD21: Keigh . . . 4D 6

Bk. Broomfield St.
BD21: Keigh 4D **6**
Bk. Buxton St. *BD21: Keigh* 4F **7**
(off Buxton St.)
Bk. Byrl St. *BD21: Keigh* 2E **7**
(off Byrl St.)
Bk. Caister St.
BD21: Keigh 1D **12**
(off Oakfield Rd.)
Bk. Caledonia Rd.
BD21: Keigh 3F **7**
(off Caledonia Rd.)
Bk. Cartmel Rd.
BD21: Keigh 4C **6**
(off Devonshire Rd.)
Bk. Castle Rd. BD21: Keigh . . .3D **6**
Bk. Cavendish Rd.
BD10: B'frd 6D **18**
Bk. Cavendish St.
BD21: Keigh 4E **7**
Bk. Cavendish Ter.
HX1: Hal 6A **48**
Bk. Chapel St.
BD1: B'frd 2B **36** (4F **5**)
Bk. Charles St. *HD6: Brigh* 4E **59**
(off Charles St.)
Bk. Claremount Ter.
HX3: Hal 3C **48**
Bk. Clarence St.
HX1: Hal 6B **48** (4A **62**)
Bk. Clarendon Pl.
HX1: Hal 6A **48**
Bk. Cliffe Ter. BD21: Keigh . . .1E **13**
Bk. Clock Vw. St.
BD20: Keigh 1D **6**
(off Eel Holme Vw. St.)
Bk. Clough HX3: Hal 3G **49**
Bk. Colenso Rd.
BD21: Keigh 2G **7**
(off Aireworth Rd.)
Bk. Commercial St.
HX1: Hal 4B **62**
Bk. Compton St.
BD21: Keigh 3F **7**
(off Compton St.)
Bk. Crag Rd. BD18: Ship 6G **17**
Bk. Croft Ho. La.
BD20: Keigh 1C **6**
Bk. Cromer Av.
BD21: Keigh 6D **6**
(off Cromer Rd.)
Bk. Cromer Gro.
BD21: Keigh 6D **6**
(off Cromer Rd.)
Bk. Cromwell Ter.
HX1: Hal 6B **48**
Bk. Cross La. *HX5: Ell* 3E **61**
(off Linden Rd.)
Bk. Dudley Hill Rd.
BD2: B'frd 5D **28**
Bk. Eaton St. *BD21: Keigh* . . .1C **12**
(off Queen's Rd.)
Bk. Edensor Rd.
BD21: Keigh 4C **6**
(off Devonshire Rd.)
Bk. Elizabeth St.
BD5: B'frd 4A **36**
Bk. Elmfield Ter. HX1: Hal . . .2B **56**
Bk. Emily St. *BD21: Keigh* 3E **7**
(off Cross Emily St.)
Bk. Eric St. BD21: Keigh 3E **7**
(off Eric St.)
Bk. Eversley Mt. HX2: Hal 1G **55**
Bk. Ferguson St.
HX1: Hal 1C **56** (4B **62**)
Back Fld. BD13: B'frd 3E **33**
(off Havelock Sq.)
Bk. Field Ct. BD13: B'frd 3D **32**
(off Bk. High St.)
Bk. Florist St. BD21: Keigh . . .2G **7**
(off Florist St.)
Back Fold BD14: B'frd 4H **33**
Bk. Foster Rd.
BD21: Keigh 1D **12**
(off Oakfield Rd.)

Bk. Gerard St.
HX1: Hal 6B **48** (4A **62**)
Bk. Giles St. Nth.
BD5: B'frd 4H **35**
Bk. Giles St. Sth.
BD5: B'frd 4H **35**
Bk. Girlington Rd.
BD8: B'frd 6D **26**
Bk. Gladstone Rd.
HX1: Hal 6B **48**
Bk. Gladstone St.
BD16: Bgly 3F **15**
Bk. Glen Ter. HX1: Hal 2B **56**
Bk. Gooder La. HD6: Brigh . . .6F **59**
Bk. Grant St. BD21: Keigh 4C **6**
Bk. Grassington Ter.
BD21: Keigh 3E **7**
(off Lawkholme La.)
Bk. Gt. Russell St.
BD7: B'frd 2G **35**
Bk. Greaves St. BD5: B'frd . . .6H **35**
(off Greaves St.)
Bk. Grosvenor Ter.
HX1: Hal 6A **48**
Bk. Grouse St. *BD21: Keigh* . . .3F **7**
(off Parson St.)
Bk. Hanson La. *HX1: Hal* 5G **47**
(off Hanson La., not continuous)
Bk. Heights Rd.
BD13: B'frd 1B **32**
Bk. High St. BD13: B'frd 3E **33**
Bk. Hird St. BD21: Keigh 5D **6**
Backhold HX3: Hal 4E **57**
Backhold Av. HX3: Hal 5E **57**
Backhold Dr. HX3: Hal 5D **56**
Backhold Hall HX3: Hal 4E **57**
Backhold La. HX3: Hal 5D **56**
Backhold Rd. HX3: Hal 5E **57**
Bk. Hope Hall Ter.
HX1: Hal 1C **56** (6C **62**)
Bk. Hyde Gro. *BD21: Keigh* 3F **7**
(off Kirby St.)
Bk. Irwell St. BD4: B'frd 4C **36**
Bk. John St. BD13: B'frd 3D **32**
Bk. Kensington St.
BD8: B'frd 6E **27**
(off Kensington St.)
Bk. Kirby St. *BD21: Keigh* 3F **7**
(off Kirby St.)
Bk. Kirkgate BD18: Ship 6E **17**
Bk. Laisteridge La.
BD7: B'frd 3G **35** (6A **4**)
Back La. BD9: B'frd 3E **27**
BD10: B'frd 5D **18**
BD13: B'frd 1H **41**
(Sheep Hill La.)
BD13: B'frd 2D **32**
(West La.)
BD14: B'frd 5A **34**
BD15: B'frd 5D **24**
BD20: Keigh 2D **8**
BD22: Haw 2A **20**
HX2: Hal 6E **31**
(Causeway Foot)
HX2: Hal 6F **39**
(Keighley Rd.)
Bk. Lime St. *BD21: Keigh* 2D **12**
(off Ivy St. Sth.)
Bk. Lindum Ter.
BD8: B'frd 5G **27**
(off Oak La.)
Bk. Lord St.
HX1: Hal 6B **48** (4A **62**)
Bk. Lyons St. BD13: B'frd 2F **41**
Bk. Lytton St. HX3: Hal 4C **48**
Bk. Malt St. *BD22: Keigh* 1C **12**
(off Bracken Rd.)
Bk. Mannville Rd.
BD21: Keigh 5C **6**
(off Malsis Rd.)
Bk. Manor St. BD2: B'frd 4D **28**
Bk. Market St. BD6: B'frd 2G **43**
Bk. Mill Hey *BD22: Haw* 6H **11**
(off Mill Hey)
Bk. Milton Ter. HX1: Hal 6B **48**

Bk. Mitchell Ter.
BD16: Bgly 3F **15**
Bk. Moorfield St. HX1: Hal . . .2A **56**
Bk. Morning St.
BD21: Keigh 1D **12**
(off Morning St.)
Bk. Mount Royd BD8: B'frd . .5G **27**
Bk. Muff St. BD4: B'frd 4D **36**
Bk. Myrtle Av. BD16: Bgly 3F **15**
Bk. Myrtle Ter. BD22: Haw . . .4B **12**
Bk. New St. *BD12: B'frd* 6D **44**
(off Mill Carr Hill St.)
Bk. Northfield Pl.
BD8: B'frd 6G **27**
(off Carlisle Rd.)
Bk. North St. BD12: B'frd 1C **52**
Bk. of the Mill BD16: Bgly 4A **14**
Bk. Otterburn St.
BD21: Keigh 3E **7**
(off Ashleigh St.)
Bk. Paget St. *BD21: Keigh* 4C **6**
(off Devonshire St.)
Bk. Park Ter. HX1: Hal 1A **56**
Bk. Pelham Rd.
BD2: B'frd 4D **28**
Bk. Pleasant St. HX6: Hal 3E **55**
Bk. Prospect Pl.
BD21: Keigh 5D **6**
Bk. Queen St. HX4: Hal 3C **60**
Bk. Rhodes St. HX1: Hal 6B **48**
Bk. Ribble St. *BD21: Keigh* 3H **7**
(off Ribble St.)
Bk. Richardson St.
BD12: B'frd 1C **52**
(off Richardson St.)
Bk. Ripley St. BD20: Keigh 2H **7**
(off Ripley St.)
Bk. Ripon St. HX1: Hal 1G **55**
Bk. Ripon Ter. HX3: Hal 4B **48**
Bk. River St. BD22: Haw 6H **11**
Back Rd. BD3: B'frd 6C **28**
BD12: B'frd 1G **51**
Bk. Rowsley St.
BD21: Keigh 4F **7**
(off Rowsley St.)
Bk. Roydwood Ter.
BD13: B'frd 1F **23**
Bk. Rupert St. *BD21: Keigh* 3E **7**
(off Rupert St.)
Bk. Russell St.
BD5: B'frd 4H **35** (6B **4**)
Bk. Rydal St. BD22: Keigh 5C **6**
Bk. Rylstone St.
BD21: Keigh 3G **7**
Bk. St Paul's Rd.
BD18: Ship 6E **17**
Bk. Salisbury Ter.
HX3: Hal 4B **48**
Bk. Saltaire Rd.
BD18: Ship 5E **17**
Bk. Saltaire Rd. Nth.
BD18: Ship 5E **17**
Bk. Savile Pde. HX1: Hal 2B **56**
Bk. Shaw La. BD21: Keigh 1F **13**
Bk. Simpson St.
BD21: Keigh 4C **6**
Bk. Sladen St. BD21: Keigh 4C **6**
Bk. Smith Row BD5: B'frd . . .6G **35**
Bk. Southfield Sq.
BD8: B'frd 6G **27**
(off Southfield St.)
Bk. South Pde. HX5: Ell 4E **61**
(not continuous)
Bk. Sowerby Cft. HX6: Hal . . .5D **54**
Bk. Springfield Pl.
BD1: B'frd 1B **4**
Bk. Springfield Rd.
HX5: Ell 2G **61**
Bk. Stone Hall Rd.
BD2: B'frd 3D **28**
Bk. Sycamore Av.
BD16: Bgly 3F **15**
Bk. Tamworth St.
BD4: B'frd 3G **37**
Bk. Trinity Ter. BD5: B'frd 4H **35**

Bk. Unity St. Nth.
BD16: Bgly 3F **15**
Bk. Unity St. Sth.
BD16: Bgly 3F **15**
Bk. Victoria St.
HX1: Hal 6C **48** (3B **62**)
Bk. Victor Ter. HX1: Hal 5H **47**
Bk. Violet Ter. *HX6: Hal* 3E **55**
(off Violet Ter.)
Bk. Wakefield Rd. HX6: Hal . . .3F **55**
Bk. Walnut St. *BD21: Keigh* . . .1D **12**
(off Walnut St.)
Bk. Waverley Rd. HX5: Ell 4F **61**
Bk. West St. HX6: Hal 4D **54**
Bk. Wheat St. *BD22: Keigh* . . .1C **12**
(off Bracken Rd.)
Bk. William St. *HD6: Brigh* . . .6E **59**
(off William St.)
Bk. Winterburn St.
BD21: Keigh 3E **7**
(off Ashleigh St.)
Bk. Wolseley Ter.
HX1: Hal 6H **47**
Bk. Wright Av.
BD22: Keigh 2H **11**
Bk. York Cres. *HX2: Hal* 2H **55**
(off Up. Washer La.)
Baddeley Gdns.
BD10: B'frd 4C **18**
Baden St. BD22: Haw 5G **11**
Baden Ter. *BD19: Cleck* 6F **53**
(off Tofts Rd.)
Badger Ga. BD15: B'frd 3C **24**
Badgergate Av.
BD15: B'frd 3C **24**
Badger La. HX3: Hal 6H **49**
Badgerstone Cl.
BD20: Keigh 2D **8**
Badgers Way BD2: B'frd 3A **28**
Badsworth Ct. BD14: B'frd . . .4B **34**
Bagnall Ter. BD6: B'frd 2F **43**
BAILDON 2G **17**
Baildon Bri. BD17: Ship 5F **17**
BAILDON GREEN 3F **17**
BAILDON HOLMES 4G **17**
Baildon Holmes
BD17: Bail 4G **17**
Baildon Mills *BD17: Bail* 1G **17**
(off Straits)
Baildon Recreation Cen. 4F **17**
Baildon Rd. BD17: Bail 2G **17**
Baildon Station (Rail) 2A **18**
BAILDON WOOD BOTTOM . . .4G **17**
Baildon Wood Ct.
BD17: Bail 4G **17**
Bailey Hall Bank HX3: Hal . . .6D **48**
Bailey Hall Rd. HX3: Hal 1D **56**
Bailey Hall Vw. HX3: Hal 6D **48**
Bailey Hills Rd. BD16: Bgly . . .1E **15**
Bailey St. BD4: B'frd 4B **36**
Bailey Wells Av.
BD5: B'frd 6G **35**
BAILIFF BRIDGE 6F **51**
Baines St. HX1: Hal 5A **48**
Baird St. BD5: B'frd 5A **36**
Bairstow Ct. HX6: Hal 1E **55**
Bairstow La. HX6: Hal 1E **55**
Bairstow Mt. HX6: Hal 2F **55**
Bairstow's Bldgs. HX2: Hal . . .1H **47**
Bairstow St. BD15: B'frd 4G **25**
Baker Fold *HX1: Hal* 6A **48**
(off Crossley Gdns.)
Baker St. BD2: B'frd 5D **28**
BD18: Ship 5E **17**
Baker St. Nth. HX2: Hal 6A **40**
Bakes St. BD7: B'frd 5E **35**
Balcony BD22: Haw 1F **21**
Balcony Cotts. BD13: B'frd . . .3E **41**
Balcony Ter. *BD22: Haw* 5B **12**
(off Halifax Rd.)
Baldwin La. BD13: B'frd 1G **41**
Baldwin Ter. HX3: Hal 6D **48**
Bale Dr. BD10: B'frd 5B **18**

Balfour St.—Beldon Pk. Cl.

Balfour St. BD4: B'frd 5C 36
BD16: Bgly 3F 15
BD21: Keigh 5D 6
Balk La. BD7: B'frd 5F 35
Balkram Dr. HX2: Hal 6D 38
Balkram Edge HX2: Hal 6B 38
Balkram Rd. HX2: Hal 6D 38
Ballantyne Rd. BD10: B'frd ...3C 18
Ball St. BD13: B'frd 3E 33
Balme La. BD12: B'frd 2H 51
Balme Rd. BD19: Cleck 5F 53
Balme St.
BD1: B'frd 2B 36 (3E 5)
BD12: B'frd 2G 51
Balmoral Pl. BD13: B'frd 4C 40
HX1: Hal 1C 56 (5A 62)
Bamford Ho. *BD4: B'frd 2G 45*
(off Tong St.)
Bamlett Brow BD22: Haw 5H 11
Bancroft St. *BD22: Haw 5B 12*
(off Halifax Rd.)
Bank BD10: B'frd 2E 29
BD22: Oxen 6A 22
Bank Bottom HX3: Hal 6D 48
Bank Bottom La. HX2: Hal 4B 46
Bank Cl. BD10: B'frd 2E 29
Bank Crest BD17: Bail 2G 17
Bankcrest Ri. BD18: Ship 6A 16
Bank Dr. BD6: B'frd 2H 43
Bank Edge Cl. HX2: Hal 6F 39
Bank Edge Gdns. HX2: Hal ...2G 47
Bank Edge Rd. HX2: Hal 1G 47
Bankfield Av. BD18: Ship 6B 16
Bankfield Dr. BD18: Ship 6B 16
BD22: Keigh 4A 6
Bankfield Gdns. HX3: Hal 1F 57
Bankfield Grange HX4: Hal ...2C 60
Bankfield Gro. BD18: Ship ...1B 26
Bankfield Mt. BD22: Keigh 3A 6
Bankfield Mus. & Gallery ...4C 48
Bankfield Rd. BD18: Ship 6B 16
BD22: Keigh 3A 6
Bankfield St. BD22: Keigh 3A 6
Bankfield Ter. BD17: Bail 3H 17
HX6: Hal 2C 54
Bankfield Vw. HX3: Hal 4B 48
Bankfield Wlk. BD22: Keigh ...3A 6
Bankfield Yd. *HX3: Hal 4B 48*
(off Boothtown Rd.)
BANK FOOT 2G 43
Bank Gdns. Cl. HX2: Hal 2G 47
Bank Holme Ct. BD4: B'frd ...1H 45
Bank Ho. BD3: B'frd 2G 5
Bank Ho. La. HX2: Hal 1A 46
Bankhouse La. HX3: Hal 5D 56
Bank Ho. Ter. HX3: Hal 5D 56
Bank La. BD22: Keigh 4A 6
(Braithwaite Rd.)
BD22: Keigh 3F 11
(Windsor Rd.)
BD22: Oxen 5C 20
Bank Rd. HX6: Hal 4D 54
(not continuous)
Banks, The HX6: Hal 2C 54
Banks End Rd. HX5: Ell 3H 61
Bank Side BD17: Bail 2G 17
Bankside Ter. BD17: Bail 3F 17
Banks La. BD20: Keigh 1G 7
Bank St. BD1: B'frd ...2A 36 (4D 4)
(not continuous)
BD6: B'frd 2G 43
BD18: Ship 6F 17
BD19: Cleck 6E 53
BD21: Keigh 4E 7
(off Airedale Shop. Cen.)
BD22: Haw 6G 11
(off Main St.)
HD6: Brigh 5E 59
Banks Vw. *BD22: Keigh 3F 11*
(off Low Banks La.)
Bank Ter. *HX2: Hal 5A 46*
(off High St.)
BANK TOP
Bradford 2E 29
Halifax 2F 57
Bank Top HX3: Hal 1E 57
HX4: Hal 1C 60
Bank Top Dr. BD20: Keigh 1H 7
Bank Top Way BD21: Keigh 5H 7
Bank Vw. BD17: Bail 3F 17
Bank Vw. Ho. *BD17: Bail 3G 17*
(off Bank Vw.)
Bank Wlk. BD17: Bail 2G 17
Bankwell Fold BD6: B'frd 2H 43
Bannerman St.
BD12: B'frd 6C 44
Banner St.
BD3: B'frd 3C 36 (5H 5)
Bannockburn Ct.
BD5: B'frd 2D 44
Bantree Ct. BD10: B'frd 3C 18
Baptist Fold BD13: B'frd 2E 41
Baptist Pl.
BD1: B'frd 2H 35 (3B 4)
Barberry Av. BD3: B'frd 1G 37
Barber St. HD6: Brigh 4F 59
Barclay Cl. BD13: B'frd 1G 23
BARCROFT 5B 12
Barcroft BD22: Haw 5B 12
Barden Av. BD6: B'frd 2B 42
Barden Dr. BD16: Bgly 1A 16
Barden St. BD8: B'frd 6F 27
Bardsey Cres.
BD3: B'frd 2C 36 (4H 5)
Bardsey Ho. *BD4: B'frd 4F 37*
(off Parsonage Rd.)
Bare Head La. HX3: Hal 6D 40
Barfield Rd. HX3: Hal 6A 50
Bargrange Av. BD18: Ship 1F 27
Barham Ter. BD10: B'frd 3F 29
Bar Ho. La. BD20: Keigh 1B 6
Baring Av. BD3: B'frd 1F 37
Barker Cl. HX3: Hal 4E 57
BARKEREND 2D 36
Barkerend Rd.
BD1: B'frd 2B 36 (3F 5)
BD3: B'frd 2C 36 (3F 5)
Barker Ho. HX3: Hal 4E 57
Barkston Wlk. BD15: B'frd ...2G 33
Bar La. BD20: Keigh 2H 7
Barley Cote BD20: Keigh 1A 8
Barley Cote Av.
BD20: Keigh 1H 7
Barley Cote Gro.
BD20: Keigh 1A 8
Barley Cote Rd.
BD20: Keigh 1A 8
Barley St. BD22: Keigh 1C 12
Barlow Rd. BD21: Keigh 3D 6
Barlow St. BD3: B'frd 2D 36
Barmby Pl. BD2: B'frd 6D 28
Barmby Rd. BD2: B'frd 6D 28
Barmby St. BD12: B'frd 1H 51
Barmouth Ter. BD3: B'frd 6B 28
Barnaby Rd. BD16: Bgly 1A 16
Barnard Rd. BD4: B'frd 4C 36
Barnard Ter. BD4: B'frd 4C 36
Barnby Av. BD8: B'frd 2A 34
Barnes Rd. BD8: B'frd 1D 34
Barnsley Beck Gro.
BD17: Bail 2H 17
Barnstaple Way BD4: B'frd ...1F 45
Barn St. BD22: Oxen 5G 21
Barraclough Bldgs.
BD10: B'frd 6G 19
Barraclough Sq.
BD12: B'frd 1G 51
Barraclough St. BD12: B'frd ...5F 43
Barran St. BD16: Bgly 2G 15
Barrington Cl. HX3: Hal 3G 57
Barrowclough La. HX3: Hal ...6F 49
Barr Ter. *BD8: B'frd 1D 34*
(off Washington St.)
Barry St. BD1: B'frd ...2A 36 (4C 4)
Barthorpe Cl. BD4: B'frd 1H 45
Bartle Cl. BD7: B'frd 6D 34
Bartle Fold BD7: B'frd 5E 35
Bartle Gill Dr. BD17: Bail 1A 18
Bartle Gill Ri. BD17: Bail 1A 18
Bartle Gill Vw. BD17: Bail 1A 18
Bartle Gro. BD7: B'frd 6D 34
Bartle La. BD7: B'frd 6D 34
Bartle Pl. BD7: B'frd 6D 34
Bartles Bldgs. BD15: B'frd ...1C 24
Bartle Sq. BD7: B'frd 5E 35
Barton St. BD5: B'frd 6F 35
HD6: Brigh 4E 59
(off Manley St.)
Barum Top
HX1: Hal 6C 48 (4B 62)
Barwick Grn. BD6: B'frd 2C 42
Barwick Sq. BD22: Haw 5B 12
Basil St. BD5: B'frd 6F 35
Baslow Gro. BD9: B'frd 5D 26
Bateman Fold *BD12: B'frd 6D 44*
(off Mill Carr Hill St.)
Bateman St. BD8: B'frd 6H 27
Bates Av. HX6: Hal 4B 54
Bateson St. BD10: B'frd 6G 19
Bath Pl. BD19: Cleck 6F 53
HD6: Brigh 6E 59
HX3: Hal 4B 48 (1B 62)
Bath Rd. BD19: Cleck 6F 53
HX3: Hal 3C 56
Bath St. BD3: B'frd 2C 36 (4G 5)
BD21: Keigh 4D 6
HX1: Hal 1D 56 (5D 62)
HX5: Ell 3F 61
Batley Ct. BD17: Bail 1H 17
Batley St. HX3: Hal 4A 48
Battinson Rd. HX1: Hal 5H 47
Battinson's St. HX3: Hal 2E 57
Battye St. BD4: B'frd 3E 37
Bavaria Pl. BD8: B'frd 6F 27
Bawson Ct. BD19: Cleck 4H 53
Baxandall St. BD5: B'frd 6H 35
Baxter La. HX3: Hal 2G 49
Bayne Dr. BD4: B'frd 3D 44
Bay of Biscay BD15: B'frd 3G 25
Bayswater Gro. BD2: B'frd 5F 29
Bayswater Ter. HX3: Hal 4C 56
Beacon Brow BD6: B'frd 1B 42
Beacon Bus. Cen.
HX3: Hal 1E 57
Beacon Cl. BD16: Bgly 2H 15
Beacon Gro. BD6: B'frd 2D 42
Beacon Hill Rd.
HX3: Hal 5D 48 (2D 62)
(not continuous)
Beacon Pl. BD6: B'frd 2C 42
Beacon Rd. BD6: B'frd 1B 42
Beaconsfield Rd.
BD14: B'frd 5A 34
Beaconsfield St. HX3: Hal 1E 57
Beacon St. BD6: B'frd 2E 43
BD7: B'frd 1C 42
Beamsley Gro. BD16: Bgly ...2H 15
Beamsley Ho. *BD18: Ship 2F 27*
(off Bradford Rd.)
Beamsley Rd. BD9: B'frd 5F 27
BD18: Ship 2F 27
Beamsley Wlk. BD9: B'frd 5E 27
Beanland Ct. *BD18: B'frd 2F 27*
(off Aireville Av.)
Beatrice St. BD19: Cleck 5F 53
BD20: Keigh 2D 6
BD22: Oxen 5G 21
Beaufort Gro. BD2: B'frd 4C 28
Beaumont Rd. BD8: B'frd 6F 27
Beauvais Dr. BD20: Keigh 3B 8
Beaver Cl. BD22: Haw 5A 12
Beck Bottom LS28: Pud 1G 29
Beckenham Pl. HX1: Hal 5G 47
Beckfield Cl. HD6: Brigh 1F 59
Beckfield Rd. BD16: Bgly 6F 15
Beckfoot La. BD16: Bgly 3E 15
BECK HILL 4D 42
Beck Hill BD6: B'frd 4C 42
Beck Ho's. *BD16: Bgly 1G 15*
(off Gawthorpe La.)
Beck La. BD16: Bgly 6F 9
Beck Rd. BD16: Bgly 3E 9
Beck Side BD21: Keigh 5E 7
Beckside La. BD7: B'frd 5E 35
Beckside Rd. BD7: B'frd 4E 35
Becks Rd. BD21: Keigh 5C 6
Beck St. BD21: Keigh 5D 6
Beckwith Dr. BD10: B'frd 2F 29
Bedale Dr. BD6: B'frd 2C 42
Bede's Cl. BD13: B'frd 3D 32
Bedford St.
BD4: B'frd 3B 36 (6E 5)
BD19: Cleck 6E 53
(off Westgate)
BD21: Keigh 4D 6
HX1: Hal 6B 48 (4A 62)
HX5: Ell 3F 61
Bedford St. Nth.
HX1: Hal 6B 48 (3A 62)
Bedivere Rd. BD8: B'frd 2B 34
Beech Av. BD13: B'frd 4E 23
HX6: Hal 2D 54
BEECHCLIFFE 2D 6
Beech Cl. BD10: B'frd 3D 18
HX3: Hal 5B 42
Beech Cres. BD3: B'frd 6D 28
BD17: Bail 4D 16
Beech Cft. *BD17: Bail 4F 17*
(off Valley Vw.)
Beech Dr. BD13: B'frd 4E 23
Beecher St. BD21: Keigh 3G 7
HX3: Hal 3B 48
Beeches, The BD17: Bail 1H 17
BD19: Cleck 5B 52
(off Field Hurst)
BD19: Cleck 6B 52
(off Scholes La.)
Beeches Rd. BD21: Keigh 3G 7
Beechfield Ter. *BD19: Cleck ...6G 53*
(off Neville St.)
Beech Gro. BD3: B'frd 6D 28
BD14: B'frd 5A 34
BD16: Bgly 6H 9
HX3: Hal 6E 51
Beechmount Cl. BD17: Bail ...1H 17
Beech Rd. BD6: B'frd 4G 43
HX6: Hal 3E 55
Beechroyd Ter. BD16: Bgly ...3F 15
Beech Sq. BD14: B'frd 5A 34
Beech St. BD16: Bgly 3F 15
BD21: Keigh 3G 7
HX1: Hal 5B 48
HX4: Hal 5A 60
HX5: Ell 3F 61
Beech Ter. BD3: B'frd 1D 36
Beechtree Ct. BD17: Bail 3E 17
Beech Vw. HX6: Hal 2D 54
Beech Vs. HX6: Hal 3E 55
BEECHWOOD 4B 54
Beechwood Av. BD6: B'frd 1E 43
BD18: Ship 6C 16
BD20: Keigh 2H 7
HX2: Hal 6A 40
HX3: Hal 6H 41
HX6: Hal 4B 54
Beechwood Cl. HX2: Hal 1H 47
Beechwood Cres. HX6: Hal ...4B 54
Beechwood Dr. BD6: B'frd 1F 43
HX2: Hal 6H 39
HX6: Hal 4B 54
Beechwood Gro. BD6: B'frd ...1F 43
BD18: Ship 6C 16
HX2: Hal 1H 47
Beechwood Pk. HD6: Brigh ...1F 59
Beechwood Rd. BD6: B'frd ...1E 43
HX2: Hal 1H 47
Beechwood Vs. HX2: Hal 1H 47
Beecroft St. BD21: Keigh 4F 7
Beecroft Wlk. BD15: B'frd 2G 33
Beehive St. BD6: B'frd 4D 42
Beehive Yd. BD6: B'frd 4D 42
Behrens Warehouse
BD1: B'frd 4F 5
Bela Av. BD4: B'frd 1E 45
Belcross Dr.
HX3: Hal 4D 48 (1D 62)
BELDON HILL 1C 42
Beldon La. BD7: B'frd 2D 42
Beldon Pk. Av. BD7: B'frd 1D 42
Beldon Pk. Cl. BD7: B'frd 1D 42

A-Z Bradford 67

Beldon Pl.—Bolton Outlanes

Beldon Pl. BD2: B'frd 5D 28
Beldon Rd. BD7: B'frd 6E 35
Belfast St. HX1: Hal 1H 55
Belford Cl. BD4: B'frd 6F 37
Belgrave Av. HX3: Hal 5D 48
Belgrave Cl. HX3: Hal 5D 48
Belgrave Cres. HX3: Hal 5D 48
Belgrave Dr. HX3: Hal 4E 49
Belgrave Gdns. HX3: Hal 4D 48
Belgrave Gro. HX3: Hal 4D 48
Belgrave Mt. HX3: Hal 4D 48
Belgrave Pk. HX3: Hal 4D 48
Belgrave Rd. BD16: Bgly 1G 15
BD21: Keigh 3D 6
Belgrave St. HX6: Hal 3D 54
Bell Bank Vw. BD16: Bgly 1E 15
Bell Dean Rd. BD8: B'frd 1H 33
BD15: B'frd 1H 33
Belle Isle BD22: Haw 1G 21
Belle Isle Rd. BD22: Haw 6G 11
Bellerby Brow BD6: B'frd 2B 42
Belle Vw. BD13: B'frd 4E 41
Belle Vue BD2: B'frd 2E 29
BD8: B'frd 6H 27
Belle Vue Cres. HX3: Hal 6H 41
Bellevue Pl. HX1: Hal 6A 48
Belle Vue Ri. HX3: Hal 6H 41
Belle Vue Rd. HX3: Hal 6H 41
Belle Vue Ter. BD21: Keigh 5F 7
(off Feather St.)
Bellevue Ter. HX3: Hal 2E 57
Bell Hall Mt. HX1: Hal 2A 56
Bell Hall Ter. HX1: Hal 2A 56
Bell Hall Vw. HX1: Hal 2B 56
Bell Ho. Av. BD4: B'frd 2D 44
Bellhouse Cres.
BD4: B'frd 3D 44
Belloe St. BD5: B'frd 5H 35
Bell Row HD6: Brigh 6E 59
Bellshaw St. BD8: B'frd 2C 34
Bell St. BD12: B'frd 1G 51
HX3: Hal 4D 48
Belmont Av. BD12: B'frd 4A 44
BD17: Bail 2F 17
Belmont Cl. BD17: Bail 2F 17
Belmont Cres.
BD12: B'frd 4A 44
BD18: Ship 5E 17
Belmont Gdns. BD12: B'frd . . .4A 44
Belmont Gro. BD6: B'frd 4H 43
Belmont Pl. HX1: Hal 1A 56
Belmont Ri. BD12: B'frd 4A 44
BD17: Bail 2F 17
Belmont St. BD2: B'frd 2E 29
HX3: Hal 5E 49
HX6: Hal 3E 55
Belmont Ter. BD18: Ship 5E 17
HX2: Hal 2A 54
Belton Cl. BD7: B'frd 6E 35
Belton Gro. HD3: Hud 6H 61
Belvedere St. BD8: B'frd 6F 27
Belvedere Ter. BD8: B'frd 1F 35
Belvoir Gdns. HX3: Hal 4C 56
Bempton Ct. BD7: B'frd 5F 35
Bempton Ho. BD10: B'frd 1E 29
(off Savile Av.)
Bempton Pl. BD7: B'frd 5F 35
Benbow Av. BD10: B'frd 2G 29
Benn Av. BD7: B'frd 5D 34
Benn Cres. BD7: B'frd 5D 34
Bennett St. HX3: Hal 1E 57
Benns La. HX2: Hal 3A 46
Benroyd Ter. HX4: Hal 6C 60
(not continuous)
Benson's Mobile Home Pk.
BD20: Keigh 1B 8
Bentcliff Wlk. BD15: B'frd 2H 33
Bentfield Cotts.
BD14: B'frd 4A 34
Bentley Av. HX3: Hal 6E 51
Bentley Cl. BD17: Bail 1F 17
Bentley Mt. HX6: Hal 2F 55
Bentley Royd Cl. HX6: Hal 4C 54
Bentley St. BD12: B'frd 2H 51
Bents BD22: Oxen 3G 21
Bents Foot BD16: B'frd 6B 14
Bents La. BD15: B'frd 3A 24
Beresford Rd. BD6: B'frd 4F 43
Beresford St. BD12: B'frd 6C 44
Berkeley Ho. BD4: B'frd 6G 37
(off Stirling Cres.)
Berrington Way
BD22: Keigh 2F 11
Berry La. BD21: Keigh 6D 6
HX1: Hal 6D 48
Berry Moor Rd. HX6: Hal 5F 55
Berry's Bldgs. HX2: Hal 1H 47
Berry St. BD21: Keigh 4F 7
Bertie St. BD4: B'frd 6E 37
Bertram Dr. BD17: Bail 4F 17
Bertram St. BD8: B'frd 5G 27
Berwick St.
HX1: Hal 6D 48 (4D 62)
Bescaby Gro. BD17: Bail 2A 18
Besha Av. BD12: B'frd 5H 43
Besha Gro. BD12: B'frd 5H 43
Bessingham Gdns.
BD6: B'frd 3D 42
Best La. BD22: Oxen 5G 21
Beswick Cl. BD3: B'frd 2F 37
Bethel Rd. BD18: Ship 5H 17
Bethel St. BD20: Keigh 3D 8
HD6: Brigh 5F 59
HX3: Hal 3A 48
Bethel Ter. HX2: Hal 4A 46
HX6: Hal 4F 55
Beulah Pl. HX2: Hal 2A 54
Bevan Ct. BD7: B'frd 6D 34
Beverley Av. BD12: B'frd 3H 51
Beverley Cl. HX5: Ell 2H 61
Beverley Dr. BD12: B'frd 3H 51
Beverley Pl. HX3: Hal 4B 48
Beverley St. BD4: B'frd 4F 37
Beverley Ter. HX3: Hal 4B 48
(not continuous)
Bewerley Cres. BD6: B'frd 5E 43
Bewick Ct. BD13: B'frd 1H 41
Bideford Mt. BD4: B'frd 6G 37
BIERLEY 2D 44
Bierley Hall Gro.
BD4: B'frd 4D 44
Bierley Ho. Av. BD4: B'frd 2D 44
Bierley La. BD4: B'frd 4D 44
Bierley Vw. BD4: B'frd 2E 45
Bilberry Cl. BD14: B'frd 6A 34
Bilberry Ri. BD22: Haw 1H 21
Billingsley Ter. BD4: B'frd 5D 36
Billing Vw. BD10: B'frd 6E 19
Bilsdale Grange BD6: B'frd 3D 42
Bilsdale Way BD17: Bail 3E 17
Bilton Pl. BD8: B'frd 1G 35
BINGLEY 2F 15
Bingley Arts Cen. & Little Theatre
. . . . .2F 15
BINGLEY HOSPITAL 2H 15
Bingley Pool 3F 15
Bingley Relief Rd.
BD16: Bgly 5D 8
Bingley Rd. BD9: B'frd 2B 26
BD13: B'frd 1F 23
BD18: Ship 5B 16
BD21: Haw 5B 12
BD22: Haw 5B 12
Bingley Station (Rail) 2F 15
Bingley St. BD8: B'frd 2E 35
Binks Fold BD12: B'frd 3H 51
Binnie St.
BD3: B'frd 2D 36 (3H 5)
Binns Fold BD15: B'frd 2C 24
(off Main Rd.)
Binns Hill HX2: Hal 1D 54
Binns Hill La. HX6: Hal 1D 54
Binns La. BD7: B'frd 4D 34
Binns St. BD16: Bgly 1G 15
Binns Top La. HX3: Hal 4G 57
HX5: Hal 4G 57
Binswell Fold BD17: Bail 1G 17
Bircham Cl. BD16: Bgly 6H 9
Birch Av. BD5: B'frd 1B 44
Birch Cliff BD17: Bail 3F 17
Birch Cl. BD5: B'frd 1B 44
HD6: Brigh 4G 59
Birchdale BD16: Bgly 5F 9
BIRCHENCLIFFE 6H 61
Birchfield HX6: Hal 5F 55
Birch Gro. BD5: B'frd 2A 44
BD21: Keigh 1D 12
Birchington Av. HD3: Hud 6G 61
Birchington Cl. HD3: Hud 6H 61
Birchington Dr. HD3: Hud 6G 61
Birchlands Av. BD15: B'frd 1B 24
Birchlands Gro.
BD15: B'frd 1B 24
Birch La. BD5: B'frd 6A 36
(not continuous)
HX2: Hal 5A 46
Birch St. BD8: B'frd 1D 34
(not continuous)
Birch Tree Gdns.
BD21: Keigh 5G 7
Birch Way BD5: B'frd 1B 44
Birchwood Av. BD20: Keigh 1D 6
Birchwood Dr. BD20: Keigh 1C 6
Birchwood Rd. BD20: Keigh 1C 6
Birdcage HX3: Hal 5D 48
Birdcage Hill HX3: Hal 4A 56
Birdcage La. HX3: Hal 4A 56
Bird Holme La. HX3: Hal 4H 49
BIRDS ROYD 6F 59
Birds Royd La. HD6: Brigh 6F 59
Birdswell Av. HD6: Brigh 4H 59
Birdwalk, The BD13: B'frd 1A 42
Birkby Haven BD6: B'frd 3C 42
Birkby La. BD19: Brigh 6F 51
HD6: Brigh 6F 51
Birkby St. BD12: B'frd 1H 51
Birkdale Cl. BD13: B'frd 1G 23
Birkdale Ct. BD20: Keigh 1C 6
Birkdale Gro. HX2: Hal 4H 39
Birkett St. BD19: Cleck 5F 53
Birkhey Cl. HD6: Brigh 1G 59
Birkhouse La. HD6: Brigh 1G 59
Birkhouse Rd. HD6: Brigh 6G 51
Birklands Rd. BD18: Ship 6F 17
Birklands Ter. BD18: Ship 6F 17
Birk Lea St. BD5: B'frd 5B 36
BIRKS 3D 34
Birks Av. BD7: B'frd 4D 34
Birks Fold BD7: B'frd 3D 34
Birks Hall La.
HX1: Hal 5A 48 (1A 62)
Birkshall La. BD4: B'frd 3D 36
Birks Hall St. HX1: Hal 5A 48
Birks Hall Ter. HX1: Hal 5A 48
BIRKSHEAD 3D 24
Birksland Ind. Est.
BD4: B'frd 4D 36
Birksland St. BD3: B'frd 4D 36
Birnam Gro. BD4: B'frd 5C 36
Birr Rd. BD9: B'frd 4F 27
Bishopdale Holme
BD6: B'frd 3C 42
Bishop St. BD9: B'frd 4F 27
Bittern Ct. BD13: B'frd 1A 42
Blackberry Way
BD14: B'frd 6H 33
Blackbird Gdns. BD8: B'frd 2H 33
Black Brook Way HX4: Hal 3C 60
Blackburn Bldgs.
HD6: Brigh 5G 59
Blackburn Cl. BD8: B'frd 2B 34
HX3: Hal 2H 47
Blackburn Ho. HX3: Hal 2A 48
Blackburn Rd. HD6: Brigh 3D 58
Black Dyke La. BD13: B'frd 5B 24
Black Edge La. BD13: B'frd 3F 31
BLACK HILL 3B 6
Black Hill La. BD20: Keigh 2A 6
Blackhouse Fold HX2: Hal 6F 39
Blackledge
HX1: Hal 6D 48 (4D 62)
BLACKLEY 5E 61
Blackley Rd. HX5: Ell 4D 60
Blackmires BD13: B'frd 3D 40
HX2: Hal 6A 40
Black Moor Rd.
BD22: Oxen 5A 22
Black Moor Top
BD22: Haw 1H 21
Blackshaw Beck La.
BD13: B'frd 4G 41
Blackshaw Dr. BD6: B'frd 3B 42
Blacksmith Fold BD7: B'frd . . .5E 35
Blackstone Av. BD12: B'frd . . .3G 51
Black Swan Ginnell
HX1: Hal 4B 62
Black Swan Pas.
HX1: Hal 6C 48 (4B 62)
Blackwall
HX1: Hal 1C 56 (5B 62)
Blackwall La. HX6: Hal 2C 54
Blackwall Ri. HX6: Hal 2C 54
Blackwood Gro. HX1: Hal 5H 47
Blacup Moor Vw.
BD19: Cleck 6F 53
Blaithroyd Ct. HX3: Hal 1E 57
Blaithroyd La. HX3: Hal 1E 57
Blake Hill HX3: Hal 2E 49
Blakehill Av. BD2: B'frd 5E 29
Blake Hill End HX3: Hal 6F 41
Blakehill Ter. BD2: B'frd 5E 29
Blakelaw Dr. HD6: Brigh 4H 59
Blamires Pl. BD7: B'frd 6D 34
Blamires St. BD7: B'frd 6D 34
Blanche St. BD4: B'frd 3F 37
Bland St. HX1: Hal . . .6B 48 (4A 62)
Blantyre Ct. BD13: B'frd 1F 23
Blenheim Ct. HX1: Hal 2A 62
Blenheim Mt. BD8: B'frd 5G 27
Blenheim Pl. BD10: B'frd 4D 18
Blenheim Rd. BD8: B'frd 6G 27
Blenheim St. BD21: Keigh 6D 6
(off Victoria Rd.)
Blind La. BD13: B'frd 6C 32
BD16: Bgly 3C 14
HX2: Hal 3G 39
Blucher St. BD4: B'frd 3F 37
Bluebell Cl. BD15: B'frd 1H 33
BD18: Ship 2H 27
Bluebell Wlk. HX2: Hal 5A 46
Bluebird Wlk. BD16: Bgly 1A 16
Blue Hill BD13: B'frd 5F 23
Blythe Av. BD8: B'frd 1E 35
Blythe St.
BD7: B'frd 2G 35 (4A 4)
Bob La. BD15: B'frd 4D 24
HX2: Hal 6F 47
BOCKING 5B 12
Bodkin BD22: Oxen 5C 20
Bodkin La. BD22: Oxen 5B 20
Bodmin Av. BD18: Ship 6B 18
Bogart La. HX3: Hal 4B 50
(not continuous)
Boggart Wood Vw.
BD8: B'frd 2H 33
BOGTHORN 1B 12
Boland Ct. BD22: Keigh 2A 12
Boldron Holt BD6: B'frd 3D 42
Boldshay St. BD3: B'frd 1D 36
Bold St. BD8: B'frd 6G 27
Bolehill Pk. HD6: Brigh 1C 58
Bolingbroke Ct. BD5: B'frd . . .4A 36
(off Elsdon Gro.)
Bolingbroke St. BD5: B'frd . . .1H 43
Bolland Bldgs. BD12: B'frd . . .6B 44
Bolland St. BD12: B'frd 6A 44
Bolling Hall (Mus.) 6C 36
Bolling Rd.
BD4: B'frd 3B 36 (6E 5)
Boltby La. BD6: B'frd 3C 42
BOLTON 4B 28
Bolton Brow HX6: Hal 3E 55
Bolton Ct. BD3: B'frd 5C 28
Bolton Cres. BD2: B'frd 3D 28
Bolton Dr. BD2: B'frd 2D 28
Bolton Gro. BD2: B'frd 3D 28
Bolton Hall Rd. BD2: B'frd 2H 27
(not continuous)
Bolton La. BD2: B'frd 5H 27
BOLTON OUTLANES 3C 28

Bolton Rd.—Bremit Wlk.

Bolton Rd.
BD1: B'frd 2B **36** (3E **5**)
(not continuous)
BD2: B'frd 4C **28**
BD3: B'frd 5B **28** (1E **5**)
Bolton St.
BD3: B'frd 2C **36** (3G **5**)
BD12: B'frd 5G **43**
(not continuous)
BOLTON WOODS 3A **28**
Bond St. HD6: Brigh 4E **59**
HX1: Hal 5A **62**
Bonegate Av. HD6: Brigh 4F **59**
Bonegate Rd. HD6: Brigh 4E **59**
Bonn Rd. BD9: B'frd 5E **27**
Bonwick Mall BD6: B'frd 4C **42**
BOOTH 2A **46**
Bootham Pk. BD9: B'frd 5B **26**
Booth Hill HX2: Hal 1A **46**
Boothman Wlk.
BD21: Keigh 6C **6**
Booth Royd BD10: B'frd 4D **18**
Booth Royd Dr.
BD10: B'frd 4D **18**
Booth's Bldgs. *HD6: Brigh 6F **51***
(off Wyke Old La.)
Booth St. BD10: B'frd 6D **18**
BD13: B'frd 2D **40**
BD18: Ship 6H **17**
BD19: Cleck 5F **53**
Booth Ter. HX2: Hal 2A **46**
BOOTHTOWN 4A **48**
Boothtown Rd. HX3: Hal 2B **48**
Borough Mkt. HX1: Hal 4C **62**
Borrin's Way BD17: Bail 2H **17**
Boston St. HX1: Hal 6H **47**
HX6: Hal 4C **54**
Boston Wlk. BD6: B'frd 3D **42**
Bosworth Cl. BD15: B'frd 5H **25**
BOTANY 2E **9**
Botany Av. BD2: B'frd 3B **28**
Botany Dr. BD20: Keigh 1E **9**
BOTTOMLEY HOLES 4A **32**
Bottomley St. BD5: B'frd 5H **35**
BD6: B'frd 4D **42**
HD6: Brigh 3F **59**
Bottoms HX3: Hal 4D **56**
Boulevard, The *HX1: Hal 6A **62***
(off Park Rd.)
Boundary, The BD8: B'frd 6C **26**
Boundary Cl. BD17: Bail 1H **17**
Boundary Pl. *BD2: B'frd 5D **28***
(off Baker St.)
Bourbon Cl. BD6: B'frd 3F **43**
Bourne St. BD10: B'frd 4D **18**
Bowater Ct. BD4: B'frd 1H **45**
Bow Beck
BD4: B'frd 4C **36** (6H **5**)
Bowbridge Rd. BD5: B'frd 5A **36**
Bower Grn. BD3: B'frd 2E **37**
Bower St. BD5: B'frd 6C **4**
Bowes Nook BD6: B'frd 4C **42**
Bow Grn. BD14: B'frd 5B **34**
Bowland Av. BD17: Bail 4C **16**
(not continuous)
Bowland St.
BD1: B'frd 1H **35** (1A **4**)
Bowler Cl. BD12: B'frd 5G **43**
BOWLING 5D **36**
Bowling Bk. La. BD4: B'frd . . .4C **36**
Bowling Ct. HD6: Brigh 4D **58**
Bowling Ct. Ind. Est.
BD4: B'frd 4E **37**
Bowling Dyke
HX3: Hal 5C **48** (1C **62**)
Bowling Grn. Fold
BD12: B'frd 2G **51**
Bowling Hall Rd.
BD4: B'frd 5C **36**
Bowling Mill
HX3: Hal 5C **48** (2B **62**)
Bowling Old La.
BD5: B'frd 1H **43**
(not continuous)
Bowling Pk. Cl. BD4: B'frd . . .5B **36**
Bowling Pk. Dr.
BD4: B'frd 6B **36**
Bowling Swimming Pool 6C **36**
Bowl Shaw La. HX3: Hal 5F **41**
Bowman Av. BD6: B'frd 4F **43**
Bowman Gro. HX1: Hal 6A **48**
Bowman Pl. HX1: Hal 6A **48**
Bowman Rd. BD6: B'frd 4F **43**
Bowman St. HX1: Hal 6A **48**
Bowman Ter. HX1: Hal 6A **48**
Bowmere Dr. BD15: B'frd 1H **33**
Bowness Av. BD10: B'frd 3F **29**
Bowood La. HX6: Hal 6A **54**
Bow St. BD21: Keigh 4E **7**
Bowwood Dr. BD20: Keigh 3B **8**
Boxhall Rd. HX5: Ell 2F **61**
Box Tree Cl. BD8: B'frd 6C **26**
Box Tree Gro. BD21: Keigh 5G **7**
Box Trees HX2: Hal 2F **47**
Box Trees La. HX2: Hal 2F **47**
Boxwood Rd. HX5: Ell 4F **61**
Boyd Av. BD3: B'frd 6G **29**
Boy La. BD4: B'frd 4D **44**
HX3: Hal 3F **47**
Boyne St. HX1: Hal . . .6B **48** (4A **62**)
Boynton St. BD5: B'frd 6H **35**
(not continuous)
Boynton Ter. BD5: B'frd 6A **36**
Boys La. HX3: Hal 2D **56**
Boys Scarr HX2: Hal 1A **54**
Bracewell Av. BD15: B'frd 1G **33**
Bracewell Bank HX3: Hal 3H **47**
Bracewell Dr. HX3: Hal 3H **47**
Bracewell Gro. HX3: Hal 4A **48**
Bracewell Mt. *HX3: Hal 3H **47***
(off Bracewell Hill)
Bracewell St. BD21: Keigh 4G **7**
Bracken Av. HD6: Brigh 2E **59**
BRACKEN BANK 2B **12**
Bracken Bank Av.
BD22: Keigh 3B **12**
Bracken Bank Cres.
BD22: Keigh 2B **12**
Bracken Bank Gro.
BD22: Keigh 2B **12**
Bracken Bank Wlk.
BD22: Keigh 3B **12**
Bracken Bank Way
BD22: Keigh 2B **12**
Brackenbeck Rd.
BD7: B'frd 5D **34**
Brackenbed Grange
HX2: Hal 4G **47**
Brackenbed La. HX2: Hal 4H **47**
Brackenbed Ter. *HX2: Hal 4H **47***
(off Brackenbed La.)
Bracken Cl. HD6: Brigh 2E **59**
Brackendale BD10: B'frd 3B **18**
Brackendale Av.
BD10: B'frd 3C **18**
Brackendale Dr.
BD10: B'frd 3B **18**
Brackendale Gro.
BD10: B'frd 3B **18**
Brackendale Pde.
BD10: B'frd 3B **18**
Bracken Edge BD10: B'frd 6E **19**
Bracken Hall (Countryside Cen.)
. . . . .2C **16**
Brackenhall Ct. BD7: B'frd . . .5D **34**
Bracken Hill HX2: Hal 4G **47**
Brackenhill Dr. BD7: B'frd 6D **34**
Brackenholme Royd
BD6: B'frd 3C **42**
Bracken Pk. BD16: Bgly 2A **16**
(Gilstead La.)
BD16: Bgly 6H **9**
(Southway)
Bracken Rd. BD22: Keigh 1C **12**
HD6: Brigh 2E **59**
Brackens La. HX3: Hal 4H **41**
Bracken St. BD21: Keigh 1D **12**
Bracken Way HX5: Ell 2H **61**
Bradbeck Rd. BD7: B'frd 2D **34**
BRADFORD 2A **36** (3C **4**)
Bradford Bulls RLFC
(Odsal Stadium) 3A **44**
Bradford Bus. Pk.
BD1: B'frd 6A **28**
Bradford Cathedral Church of
St Peter 2B **36** (3E **5**)
Bradford City AFC (Valley Parade)
. . . . .6H **27**
Bradford City Farm 1F **35**
Bradford College
McMillan Building 4H **35**
McMillan Halls of Residence
. . . . .4H **35** (6B **4**)
Bradford Design Exchange 4F **5**
Bradford Forster Square
Station (Rail) . . .2A **36** (3D **4**)
Bradford Ice Arena . . .3A **36** (6C **4**)
Bradford Industrial &
Horses at Work Mus. . . .4F **29**
Bradford Interchange Station (Rail)
. . . . .3B **36** (5E **5**)
Bradford Kart Racing 4B **36**
Bradford La. BD3: B'frd 2F **37**
BRADFORD MOOR 1E **37**
Bradford Old Rd.
BD16: Bgly 6H **15**
(not continuous)
HX3: Hal 2C **48**
Bradford Pk. Avenue FC
(Horsfall Stadium) 4F **43**
Bradford Rd. BD3: Pud 6H **29**
BD4: B'frd 3H **45**
BD10: B'frd 2C **28**
BD11: B'frd 3H **45**
BD12: B'frd 1C **52**
BD14: B'frd 4A **34**
BD16: Bgly 3G **15**
BD18: Ship 6E **17**
BD19: Cleck 6G **53**
(Pearson St.)
BD19: Cleck 3E **53**
(Whitehall Rd.)
BD20: Keigh 2A **8**
BD21: Keigh 4F **7**
HD6: Brigh 5F **59**
(King St.)
HD6: Brigh 5F **51**
(Mayfield Gro.)
HX3: Hal 2G **49**
(Oaklands Av.)
HX3: Hal 4G **49**
(Pk. View Av.)
LS28: Pud 6H **29**
BRADFORD ROYAL INFIRMARY
. . . . .6C **26**
Bradford St. BD21: Keigh 3E **7**
Bradlaugh Rd. BD6: B'frd 2F **43**
Bradlaugh Ter. BD6: B'frd 2G **43**
Bradleigh Cl. BD21: Keigh 6G **7**
Bradley Ct. HX4: Hal 3B **60**
Bradley La. HX4: Hal 3B **60**
Bradley St. BD9: B'frd 3G **27**
BD16: Bgly 2F **15**
Bradley Vw. HX4: Hal 5A **60**
BRADSHAW 2H **39**
Bradshaw La. HX2: Hal 3H **39**
Bradshaw Row HX2: Hal 1H **39**
Bradshaw Vw. BD13: B'frd . . .2C **40**
*HX2: Hal 4G **39***
(off Moor Top Gdns.)
Brae Av. BD2: B'frd 4B **28**
Braeside HX2: Hal 6F **47**
Brafferton Arbor BD6: B'frd . . .3C **42**
BRAITHWAITE 3A **6**
Braithwaite Av. BD22: Keigh . . .4A **6**
Braithwaite Cres.
BD22: Keigh 4B **6**
Braithwaite Dr. BD22: Keigh . . .4B **6**
Braithwaite Edge Rd.
BD22: Keigh 3A **6**
Braithwaite Gro.
BD22: Keigh 4B **6**
Braithwaite Rd. BD22: Keigh . . .3A **6**
Braithwaite Wlk.
BD22: Keigh 4B **6**
Braithwaite Way
BD22: Keigh 4B **6**
Bramall Bus. Pk.
BD5: B'frd 5A **36**
Bramble Cl. BD14: B'frd 6A **34**
BD22: Haw 1H **21**
Bramble Gro. HX5: Ell 2H **61**
Brambling Dr. BD13: B'frd 1A **42**
Bramham Dr. BD17: Bail 1H **17**
Bramham Rd. BD16: Bgly 1G **15**
Bramhope Rd. BD19: Cleck . . .5E **53**
Bramley Cl. BD22: Keigh 2F **11**
Bramley Fold HX3: Hal 5B **50**
Bramley La. HX3: Hal 5A **50**
Bramley St. BD5: B'frd 4A **36**
(not continuous)
Bramley Vw. HX3: Hal 5C **50**
Bramston Gdns.
HD6: Brigh 6E **59**
Bramston St. HD6: Brigh 6E **59**
Bramwell Ho. BD3: B'frd 2F **5**
Branch La. HD2: Hud 6H **61**
Branch Rd. BD19: Cleck 4B **52**
HD2: Hud 5G **61**
Brander Cl. BD10: B'frd 1D **28**
Brandfort St. BD7: B'frd 4E **35**
Branksome Ct. BD9: B'frd 5D **26**
Branksome Cres.
BD9: B'frd 5D **26**
Branksome Dr. BD18: Ship . . .5A **16**
Branksome Gro.
BD18: Ship 5A **16**
Bransdale Cl. BD17: Bail 3E **17**
Bransdale Clough
BD6: B'frd 2C **42**
Branshaw Dr. BD22: Keigh 6A **6**
Branshaw Gro. BD22: Keigh . . .6A **6**
Branshaw Mt. BD22: Keigh 6A **6**
Bran St. BD21: Keigh 1D **12**
Brant Av. HX2: Hal 1H **47**
Brantcliffe Dr. BD17: Bail 1F **17**
Brantcliffe Way BD17: Bail . . .1G **17**
Brantdale Cl. BD9: B'frd 3A **26**
Brantdale Rd. BD9: B'frd 3A **26**
Brantwood Av. BD9: B'frd 3A **26**
Brantwood Cl. BD9: B'frd 3A **26**
Brantwood Cres.
BD9: B'frd 3H **25**
Brantwood Dr. BD9: B'frd 3A **26**
Brantwood Gro. BD9: B'frd . . .3H **25**
Brantwood Oval BD9: B'frd . . .3A **26**
Brantwood Rd. BD9: B'frd 3H **25**
Brantwood Vs. BD9: B'frd 3A **26**
Branwell Ct. BD9: B'frd 5C **26**
Branwell Dr. BD22: Haw 5G **11**
Branwell Lodge BD7: B'frd . . .6E **35**
Branxholme Ind. Est.
HD6: Brigh 6F **51**
Brassey Rd. BD4: B'frd 5C **36**
Brassey St.
HX1: Hal 1B **56** (6A **62**)
Brassey Ter. BD4: B'frd 5C **36**
Braybrook Ct. BD8: B'frd 4G **27**
Bray Cl. BD7: B'frd 1B **42**
Brayshaw Dr. BD7: B'frd 1B **42**
Brayshaw Fold BD12: B'frd . . .5A **44**
Break Neck HX3: Hal 5G **49**
Breaks Fold BD12: B'frd 3H **51**
Breaks Rd. BD12: B'frd 5A **44**
Brearcliffe Cl. BD6: B'frd 3F **43**
Brearcliffe Dr. BD6: B'frd 4E **43**
Brearcliffe Gro. BD6: B'frd . . .4E **43**
Brearcliffe Rd. BD6: B'frd 4F **43**
Brearcliffe St. BD6: B'frd 4E **43**
Brearton St.
BD1: B'frd 1A **36** (1C **4**)
Breck Lea HX6: Hal 5C **54**
Brecks BD14: B'frd 4B **34**
Brecks Rd. BD14: B'frd 4B **34**
Breck Willows HX6: Hal 5B **54**
Brecon Cl. BD10: B'frd 6D **18**
Bredon Av. BD18: Ship 6B **18**
Breighton Adown
BD6: B'frd 3B **42**
Bremit Wlk. BD6: B'frd 3F **43**

A-Z Bradford 69

Brendon Ct.—Brownroyd Wlk.

Brendon Ct. BD4: B'frd 6F **37**
Brendon Ho. *BD4: B'frd 1G **45***
(off Landscove Av.)
Brendon Wlk. BD4: B'frd 1F **45**
(not continuous)
Brentford Rd. BD12: B'frd 4G **43**
Brentwood Gdns.
BD6: B'frd 3H **43**
Bretton Ct. BD6: B'frd 3D **42**
Brewery La. BD13: B'frd 4C **40**
(Ambler Way)
BD13: B'frd 6D **32**
(Carter La.)
Brewery Rd. BD21: Keigh 2C **12**
Brewery St. BD21: Keigh 4F **7**
HX3: Hal 3C **48**
Brian Royd La. HX4: Hal 2A **60**
Brian Royd Mills HX4: Hal 2A **60**
Briar Cl. HX5: Ell 4E **61**
Briardale Rd. BD9: B'frd 3H **25**
Briarfield Av. BD10: B'frd 6C **18**
Briarfield Cl. BD10: B'frd 6C **18**
Briarfield Gdns.
BD18: Ship 1F **27**
Briarfield Gro. BD10: B'frd . . .6C **18**
Briarfield Rd. BD18: Ship 2G **27**
Briar Rhydding BD17: Bail 3A **18**
Briar Wood BD18: Ship 6A **18**
Briarwood Av. BD6: B'frd 2F **43**
BD20: Keigh 2H **7**
Briarwood Cres.
BD6: B'frd 2F **43**
Briarwood Dr. BD6: B'frd 2F **43**
Briarwood Gro. BD6: B'frd 1F **43**
Brick & Tile Ter.
HD6: Brigh 6E **59**
Brickfield Gro. HX2: Hal 6A **40**
Brickfield La. HX2: Hal 6A **40**
Brickfield Ter. HX2: Hal 6A **40**
Brick Row BD12: B'frd 2G **51**
Brick St. BD19: Cleck 6E **53**
BD21: Keigh 5E **7**
Brick Ter. HD6: Brigh 6F **59**
Bridge End HD6: Brigh 6E **59**
Bridgegate Way
BD10: B'frd 1F **29**
Bridgehouse La.
BD22: Haw 1G **21**
Bridge La. HX3: Hal 5G **41**
Bridge Rd. HD6: Brigh 5E **59**
Bridge St.
BD1: B'frd 3A **36** (5D **4**)
BD13: B'frd 3E **33**
BD21: Keigh 5D **6**
BD22: Keigh 3F **11**
HX6: Hal 4D **54**
Bridge Ter. HX2: Hal 5A **38**
Bridgewater Apartments
*BD5: B'frd 4A **36***
(off Park Rd.)
Bridgeway BD4: B'frd 1F **45**
Bridgwater Rd. BD9: B'frd 5E **27**
Bridle Dene HX3: Hal 6A **42**
Bridle Stile HX3: Hal 6A **42**
Bridle Stile La.
BD13: B'frd 1E **41**
Brier La. HD6: Brigh 5B **58**
Brierley Cl. BD18: Ship 1G **27**
Brier St. BD21: Keigh 1D **12**
HX3: Hal 3C **48**
Briery Fld. BD18: Ship 2F **27**
Briggate BD17: Ship 5F **17**
BD18: Ship 6F **17**
HD6: Brigh 5E **59**
(not continuous)
HX5: Ell 2F **61**
Brigg Gdns. BD22: Keigh 4B **6**
Briggland Ct. BD15: B'frd 2C **24**
Briggs Av. BD6: B'frd 2E **43**
Briggs Gro. BD6: B'frd 2E **43**
Briggs Pl. BD6: B'frd 2E **43**
Briggs St. BD13: B'frd 2D **40**
Briggs Vs. *BD13: B'frd 2E **41***
(off Briggs St.)
BRIGHOUSE **4E 59**
Brighouse & Denholme Ga. Rd.
HX3: Hal 5G **41**
(Pepper Hill)
HX3: Hal 1H **49**
(Stone Chair)
Brighouse & Denholme Rd.
BD13: B'frd 3G **31**
Brighouse Pool **5F 59**
Brighouse Rd. BD12: B'frd 6H **43**
BD13: B'frd 2F **41**
HD2: Hud 6H **61**
HX3: Hal 6A **50**
(Barfield Rd.)
HX3: Hal 2F **41**
(Brighouse & Denholme Ga. Rd.)
Brighouse Station (Rail) **6F 59**
Brighouse Wood La.
HD6: Brigh 4D **58**
Brighouse Wood Row
*HD6: Brigh 4D **58***
(off Brighouse Wood La.)
Brighton Gro. *HX1: Hal 5A **48***
(off Pellon La.)
Brighton St. BD10: B'frd 4C **18**
BD17: Ship 5F **17**
HX3: Hal 4A **48**
Brighton Ter. BD19: Cleck 5B **52**
Bright St. BD4: B'frd 1E **45**
BD13: B'frd 2F **41**
BD14: B'frd 5H **33**
BD15: B'frd 6H **25**
BD22: Haw 6H **11**
HX6: Hal 2D **54**
Brindley Gro. BD8: B'frd 2A **34**
Brisbane Av. BD2: B'frd 4A **28**
Briscoe La. HX4: Hal 2B **60**
Bristol Av. *BD20: Keigh 3B **8***
(off Ford Rd.)
Bristol St. HX3: Hal 4D **56**
Britannia Ho. *BD1: B'frd 5D **4***
(off Bridge St.)
Britannia St.
BD5: B'frd 3B **36** (6E **5**)
BD16: Bgly 2G **15**
Britannia Ter. BD19: Cleck 5F **53**
Broadacre Way BD17: Bail 1B **18**
Broad Carr La. HX4: Hal 5C **60**
Broad Carr Ter. HX4: Ell 4D **60**
Broad Dale Cl. BD20: Keigh . . .2B **8**
Broadfield Cl. BD4: B'frd 2G **45**
BROAD FOLDS **4A 34**
Broadfolds BD14: B'frd 5A **34**
Broad Head La.
BD22: Keigh 2A **10**
Broad Ings Way HX3: Hal 6A **42**
Broadlands BD20: Keigh 3B **6**
Broadlands St. BD4: B'frd 5F **37**
Broad La. BD4: B'frd 4F **37**
Broadlea Cres. BD5: B'frd 6B **36**
Broadley Av. HX2: Hal 4D **46**
Broadley Cl. HX2: Hal 4E **47**
Broadley Cres. HX2: Hal 4D **46**
Broadley Gro. HX2: Hal 4E **47**
Broadley Laithe HX2: Hal 4E **47**
Broadley Rd. HX2: Hal 4D **46**
Broad Oak HX3: Hal 1B **58**
Broad Oak La. HX3: Hal 1B **58**
Broad Oak Pl. HX3: Hal 1B **58**
Broad Oak St. HX3: Hal 1B **58**
Broad Oak Ter. HX3: Hal 1B **58**
Broadstones Pk.
BD16: Bgly 3B **16**
Broadstone Way
BD4: B'frd 2G **45**
Broad St.
BD1: B'frd 2A **36** (3D **4**)
HX1: Hal 6C **48** (4B **62**)
Broad Tree Rd. HX3: Hal 3A **48**
Broadwater Dr. BD2: B'frd 2A **28**
BD18: Ship 2A **28**
Broadway
BD1: B'frd 3A **36** (5D **4**)
BD16: Bgly 2G **15**
HX3: Hal 2E **57**
HX6: Hal 4A **54**
Broadway Av. BD5: B'frd 1H **43**
Broadway Cl. BD5: B'frd 1H **43**
Broadway Ct. HX6: Hal 4A **54**
Broadwood Av. HX2: Hal 4E **47**
Brocklesby Dr. BD15: B'frd . . .1H **33**
Brocklyn Yd. HX1: Hal 5D **62**
Brockwell Gdns. HX6: Hal 4C **54**
Brockwell Ga. HX6: Hal 4C **54**
Brockwell La. HX6: Hal 4B **54**
(not continuous)
Brodley Cl. HX3: Hal 5A **50**
Broken Way *BD5: B'frd 1H **43***
(off Manchester Rd.)
Bromet Pl. BD2: B'frd 3D **28**
Bromford Rd. BD4: B'frd 5D **36**
Bromley Gro. BD22: Keigh 6A **6**
Bromley Rd. BD16: Bgly 1F **15**
BD18: Ship 5C **16**
Brompton Av. BD4: B'frd 6C **36**
Brompton Rd. BD4: B'frd 5C **36**
Brompton Ter. BD4: B'frd 5C **36**
Bronshill Gro. BD15: B'frd 6A **26**
Bronte Cl. BD9: B'frd 5C **26**
Bronte Dr. BD22: Keigh 2A **12**
Bronte Ho. *BD4: B'frd 5G **37***
(off Eversley Dr.)
Bronte Old Rd. BD13: B'frd . . .3E **33**
Bronte Parsonage Mus. **6F 11**
Bronte Pl. BD13: B'frd 3E **33**
Bronte St. BD21: Keigh 3F **7**
BD22: Haw 6F **11**
Bronte Vs. BD22: Haw 5B **12**
Brook Dr. HX4: Hal 5C **60**
Brooke Grn. HX3: Hal 5A **50**
Brooke St. BD19: Cleck 6G **53**
HD6: Brigh 6E **59**
Brookeville *HX3: Hal 6B **50***
(off Brighouse Rd.)
Brookeville Av. HX3: Hal 6A **50**
Brookfield Av. BD18: Ship 5H **17**
BD19: Cleck 4F **53**
Brookfield Rd.
BD3: B'frd 1C **36** (2H **5**)
BD18: Ship 5H **17**
Brookfields Av.
BD12: Cleck 4A **52**
Brookfields Rd.
BD12: Cleck 4A **52**
Brookfield Ter.
BD19: Cleck 4G **53**
Brookfield Vw.
BD19: Cleck 4G **53**
BROOKFOOT **4D 58**
Brookfoot Bus. Pk.
HD6: Brigh 4D **58**
Brookfoot Ind. Est.
HD6: Brigh 5D **58**
Brookfoot La. HD6: Brigh 4D **58**
HX3: Brigh 4B **58**
Brookfoot Old La.
HD6: Brigh 4D **58**
Brook Grain Hill
HD6: Brigh 6E **59**
BROOK HILL **2H 17**
Brook Hill BD17: Bail 2H **17**
BROOKHOUSE **3E 39**
Brookhouse Gdns.
BD10: B'frd 5H **19**
Brooklands HX3: Hal 6B **50**
Brooklands Av. BD13: B'frd . . .3F **33**
HX4: Hal 5B **60**
Brooklands Cl. *HX4: Hal 5B **60***
(off Shaw La.)
Brook La. BD14: B'frd 6G **33**
Brooklea HX3: Hal 6C **50**
Brooklyn Ct. BD19: Cleck 5F **53**
Brooklyn Dr. BD19: Cleck 5F **53**
Brooklyn Grange
BD19: Cleck 4G **53**
Brooklyn Rd. BD19: Cleck 5F **53**
Brooklyn St. BD20: Keigh 1C **6**
Brooklyn Ter. HD6: Brigh 2C **58**
Brook Row BD22: Keigh 4H **11**
HX4: Hal 5C **60**
Brookroyd Av. HD6: Brigh 1F **59**
Brooksbank Av. BD7: B'frd 4C **34**
Brooksbank Gdns. HX5: Ell . . .3F **61**
Brookside BD13: B'frd 1F **23**
Brookside Fold
BD22: Oxen 5G **21**
Brooks Ter. BD13: B'frd 1H **41**
Brook St. BD12: B'frd 6D **44**
BD21: Keigh 6D **6**
*HX2: Hal 4A **46***
(off High St.)
HX5: Ell 3G **61**
Brook Ter. HX2: Hal 3A **46**
Brookwater Cl. HX3: Hal 4D **56**
Brookwoods Ind. Est.
HX4: Hal 4C **60**
Broom Cft. BD14: B'frd 5H **33**
Broome Av. BD2: B'frd 4A **28**
Broomfield BD14: B'frd 6G **33**
*BD19: Cleck 6E **53***
(off W. End Dr.)
HX5: Ell 3D **60**
Broomfield Av. HX3: Hal 4B **56**
Broomfield Pl. BD14: B'frd . . .6G **33**
BD21: Keigh 4D **6**
Broomfield Rd. BD21: Keigh . . .4D **6**
BROOMFIELDS **4A 36**
Broomfield St. BD13: B'frd . . .2E **41**
BD21: Keigh 4D **6**
Broomfield Ter.
BD19: Cleck 6D **52**
Broomhill BD21: Keigh 4H **7**
Broomhill Av. BD21: Keigh 6C **6**
Broomhill Dr. BD21: Keigh 6C **6**
Broomhill Gro. BD21: Keigh . . .6C **6**
Broomhill Mt. BD21: Keigh 6C **6**
Broomhill St. BD21: Keigh . . .1C **12**
Broomhill Wlk. BD21: Keigh . . .6C **6**
Broomhill Way BD21: Keigh . . .6C **6**
Broom St.
BD4: B'frd 3B **36** (6E **5**)
BD19: Cleck 6D **52**
Broom Ter. BD22: Keigh 2H **11**
Broster Av. BD22: Keigh 4B **6**
Brougham Rd. HX3: Hal 4C **48**
Brougham St. HX3: Hal 4C **48**
Brougham Ter. HX3: Hal 3C **48**
Broughton Av. BD4: B'frd 2D **44**
Broughton Ho. BD4: B'frd 2H **45**
Brow, The *BD17: Bail 2G **17***
(off Bank Wlk.)
BROW BOTTOM **6C 38**
Brow Bottom La. HX2: Hal 5C **38**
Brow Cotts. HD6: Hal 2B **58**
Browfield Vw. BD22: Keigh 6A **6**
Browfoot BD18: Ship 5H **17**
Browfoot Dr. HX2: Hal 1F **55**
Brow Foot Ga. *HX2: Hal 1F **55***
(off Brow Foot Ga. La.)
Brow Foot Ga. La.
HX2: Hal 1F **55**
Browgate BD17: Bail 2G **17**
Brow La. BD14: B'frd 6E **33**
HX3: Hal 5A **40**
(Holmfield Ind. Est. Rd.)
HX3: Hal 1E **49**
(Whiskers La.)
HX3: Hal 5B **42**
(Witchfield Hill)
Brow Mills Ind. Est.
HX3: Hal 1B **58**
Brownberry Gro. HX3: Hal 4B **42**
Brown Hill Cl. BD11: B'frd . . .4H **45**
Brown Ho's. HX2: Hal 3D **46**
Browning Av. HX3: Hal 4D **56**
Browning St.
BD3: B'frd 2D **36** (4H **5**)
Brown Lee La. BD15: B'frd . . .3A **24**
BROWN ROYD **2F 35**
Brownroyd Fold BD5: B'frd . . .1F **43**
BROWNROYD HILL **1G 43**
Brownroyd Hill Rd.
BD6: B'frd 2F **43**
Brownroyd St. BD7: B'frd 3F **35**
BD8: B'frd 1F **35**
Brownroyd Wlk. BD6: B'frd . . .1F **43**

Chatsworth St. BD21: Keigh 4F 7
Chatts Wood Fold
BD12: B'frd 6D 44
Chaucer St. HX1: Hal 1H 55
Cheapside
BD1: B'frd 2A 36 (3D 4)
BD19: Cleck 6G 53
HX1: Hal 6C 48 (4C 62)
HX3: Hal 5A 42
Cheddington Gro.
BD15: B'frd 1H 33
Chellowfield Ct. BD9: B'frd . . .4A 26
Chellow Gdns. BD15: B'frd . . .5G 25
(off Deanwood Cres.)
Chellow Grange Rd.
BD9: B'frd 4A 26
Chellow La. BD9: B'frd 5A 26
Chellow St. BD5: B'frd 1H 43
Chellow Ter. BD9: B'frd 6B 26
Chelmsford Rd. BD3: B'frd . . .1E 37
(not continuous)
Chelmsford Ter. BD3: B'frd . . .2E 37
Chelsea Mans. HX3: Hal 3G 49
Chelsea Rd. BD7: B'frd 5D 34
Chelsea St. BD21: Keigh 5D 6
Chelsea Vw. HX3: Hal 4G 49
(off Bradford Rd.)
Cheltenham Ct. HX3: Hal 3D 56
Cheltenham Gdns.
HX3: Hal 3D 56
Cheltenham Pl. HX3: Hal 3D 56
Cheltenham Rd. BD2: B'frd . . .2B 28
Chelwood Dr. BD15: B'frd 2G 33
Cheriton Dr. BD13: B'frd 2F 41
Cherry Ct. HX1: Hal 5A 48
(off Crossley Gdns.)
Cherry Flds. BD2: B'frd 3A 28
Cherry St. BD21: Keigh 3G 7
BD22: Haw 5A 12
Cherry Tree Av. BD10: B'frd . . .6F 19
Cherry Tree Dr. HX4: Hal 2B 60
Cherry Tree Gdns.
BD10: B'frd 4B 18
Cherry Tree Ri. BD21: Keigh . . .6F 7
Cherry Tree Row
BD16: B'frd 6B 14
Chervana Ct. BD4: B'frd 5G 37
Cherwell Dr. BD6: B'frd 4D 42
Chesham St. BD21: Keigh 4F 7
Chester Cl. HX3: Hal 4B 48
Chester Ct. HX3: Hal 4B 48
Chester Gro. HX3: Hal 4B 48
Chester Pl. HX3: Hal 4B 48
Chester Rd. HX3: Hal 4B 48
Chester St.
BD5: B'frd 3A 36 (5B 4)
BD7: B'frd 3H 35 (6C 4)
HX3: Hal 4B 48
HX6: Hal 3D 54
Chester Ter. HX3: Hal 4B 48
Chestnut Cl. BD22: Keigh 5B 6
HX4: Hal 2B 60
Chestnut Ct. BD18: Ship 6D 16
Chestnut Gro. BD2: B'frd 3A 28
Chestnut St. HX1: Hal 1H 55
Chevet Mt. BD15: B'frd 2G 33
Chevinedge Cres. HX3: Hal . . .6D 56
Cheviot Ga. BD12: B'frd 5F 43
Cheyne Wlk. BD22: Keigh 5C 6
Childs La. BD18: Ship 1A 28
Chilver Dr. BD4: B'frd 1H 45
Chippendale Ri. BD8: B'frd . . .1B 34
Chislehurst Pl. BD5: B'frd 6G 35
Chrisharben Pk.
BD14: B'frd 5A 34
Chrismoor BD10: B'frd 6C 18
Christopher St. BD5: B'frd 6G 35
Christopher Ter. BD5: B'frd . . .6G 35
Church Bank
BD1: B'frd 2B 36 (4E 5)
HX2: Hal 1F 55
HX6: Hal 3E 55
Church Cl. BD22: Keigh 3F 11
(off Commercial St.)
HX2: Hal 6F 39
Church Cl. HX6: Hal 4A 54
Church Ct. BD7: B'frd 4D 34
BD20: Keigh 1H 7
Church Flds. BD2: B'frd 5F 29
Churchfields Rd.
HD6: Brigh 4E 59
Church Grange
BD19: Cleck 6G 53
Church Grn. BD8: B'frd 6G 27
(off Conduit St.)
HX2: Hal 4G 47
Church Hill BD17: Bail 1H 17
HX2: Hal 4A 46
Church Ho. HX5: Ell 2F 61
(off Church St.)
HX5: Ell 2F 61
(off Southgate)
Churchill Rd. BD13: B'frd 3F 33
Church La. BD6: B'frd 3F 43
HD6: Brigh 4E 59
(Churchfields Rd.)
HD6: Brigh 5E 59
(Gooder St.)
HX2: Hal 4G 47
HX3: Hal 3H 57
HX4: Hal 5A 60
(not continuous)
Church M. BD6: B'frd 4C 42
(off Church St.)
Church Paddocks
HD6: Brigh 5H 59
Church Pl.
HX1: Hal 6B 48 (4A 62)
Church Rd. BD6: B'frd 3F 43
Church Side Cl.
HX3: Hal 4C 48 (1C 62)
Church Side Dr.
HX3: Hal 4C 48 (1C 62)
CHURCH STREET 3G 11
Church St. BD6: B'frd 4C 42
BD8: B'frd 6F 27
BD13: B'frd 1F 23
BD16: Bgly 3G 15
BD18: Ship 5H 17
BD19: Cleck 6G 53
BD21: Keigh 4F 7
(Bradford Rd.)
BD21: Keigh 5D 6
(Water La.)
BD22: Haw 6F 11
HX1: Hal 6D 48 (4D 62)
(Berry La.)
HX1: Hal 1D 56 (5D 62)
(Lily La.)
HX4: Hal 2D 60
HX5: Ell 2F 61
Church Ter. HX2: Hal 6F 39
HX6: Hal 4A 54
Church Vw. BD19: Cleck 5D 52
HX3: Hal 3D 50
HX6: Hal 3E 55
Church Wlk. HX3: Hal 3G 49
Church Way BD21: Keigh 5E 7
Churn La. HX2: Hal 6F 47
Churn Milk La. HX3: Hal 1A 48
Cinderhills La. HX3: Hal 4E 57
Cineworld 3B 36 (5F 5)
City La. HX3: Hal 4G 47
City Link Ind. Pk.
BD4: Pud 3G 37
City Rd. BD1: B'frd 1G 35
BD8: B'frd 1G 35 (2A 4)
City Sports 2D 36
(in Greystone Mill)
City Ter. HX3: Hal 3H 47
Cityway Ind. Est.
BD4: B'frd 4D 36
Clapham St. BD13: B'frd 1G 31
Clapton Av. HX1: Hal 1A 56
Clapton Gro. HX1: Hal 1A 56
Clapton Mt. HX1: Hal 1A 56
(off King Cross St.)
Clara Dr. LS28: Pud 6H 19
Clara Rd. BD2: B'frd 2B 28
Clara St. HD6: Brigh 6E 59
Clare Ct. HX1: Hal 6C 62
Clare Cres. BD12: B'frd 3G 51
Clare Hall La.
HX1: Hal 1C 56 (6C 62)
Claremont
BD7: B'frd 3H 35 (6A 4)
BD12: B'frd 3G 51
Claremont Av. BD18: Ship 1A 28
Claremont Cres.
BD18: Ship 1A 28
Claremont Gdns.
BD16: Bgly 1G 15
Claremont Gro. BD18: Ship . . .1B 28
Claremont Rd. BD18: Ship . . .1A 28
Claremont St. BD19: Cleck . . .5F 53
HX5: Ell 3G 61
HX6: Hal 2E 55
Claremont Ter.
BD7: B'frd 3H 35 (6B 4)
Claremont Vs. HX6: Hal 3E 55
(off Victoria Av.)
CLAREMOUNT 5D 48
Claremount Ho. HX3: Hal 5D 48
(off Claremount Rd.)
Claremount Rd.
HX3: Hal 3B 48 (1D 62)
Claremount Ter. HX3: Hal 3C 48
Clarence Rd. BD18: Ship 5D 16
Clarence St. BD19: Cleck 6F 53
HX1: Hal 6B 48 (4A 62)
Clarendon Pl. BD13: B'frd 3C 40
HX1: Hal 6A 48
Clarendon Rd. BD16: Bgly . . .1H 15
Clarendon St. BD21: Keigh 6D 6
BD22: Haw 1G 21
Clare Rd. BD12: B'frd 3G 51
BD19: Cleck 6F 53
HX1: Hal 1C 56 (5C 62)
Clare Rd. Flats
HX1: Hal 1C 56 (6C 62)
Clare Royd HX3: Hal 6E 51
Clare St. HX1: Hal . . .1C 56 (5C 62)
Clarges St. BD5: B'frd 6G 35
Classic Gym, The 3C 4
Clay Brow BD22: Haw 5G 11
(off Nth. View Ter.)
Clayfield Dr. BD7: B'frd 1E 43
Clay Hill Dr. BD12: B'frd 2H 51
(not continuous)
Clay Ho. La. HX4: Hal 2C 60
Clay Pits La. HX1: Hal 5G 47
Clay Royd La. HX3: Hal 2A 58
Clay St. HX1: Hal 6H 47
HX6: Hal 3E 55
(Bk. Pleasant St.)
HX6: Hal 3D 54
(John St. W.)
CLAYTON 5H 33
CLAYTON EDGE 1D 40
CLAYTON HEIGHTS 2H 41
Clayton La. BD5: B'frd 5A 36
BD14: B'frd 6H 33
Clayton Ri. BD20: Keigh 3C 6
Clayton Rd. BD7: B'frd 5C 34
Clayton Ter. BD13: B'frd 2F 23
CLECKHEATON 6F 53
Cleckheaton Rd.
BD6: B'frd 5H 43
BD12: B'frd 5H 43
Clegg La. HX4: Hal 2A 60
Clegg St. BD12: B'frd 3G 51
Clement Ct. HX1: Hal 6A 48
Clement St. BD8: B'frd 1D 34
HX6: Hal 3D 54
Clervaux Ct. BD14: B'frd 4B 34
Cleveden Pl. HX3: Hal 3A 48
Clevedon Ho. BD8: B'frd 6G 27
(off Trenton Dr.)
Cleveland Av. HX3: Hal 3D 56
Cleveland Rd. BD9: B'frd 4F 27
Cleveland Ter. BD16: Bgly . . .2G 15
(off Elizabeth St.)
Cleveleys Av. HX6: Hal 2D 54
(off Edward St.)
Cleveleys Gdns. HX6: Hal 2D 54
Clifby HX2: Hal 5F 47
Cliff Cres. HX2: Hal 2G 55
Cliffe HX2: Hal 1D 54
Cliffe Av. BD16: Bgly 4A 14
BD17: Bail 3G 17
HX3: Hal 6E 51
Cliffe Castle (Mus.) 2D 6
Cliffe Cres. BD20: Keigh 3B 8
Cliffe Dr. LS19: Yead 2H 19
(not continuous)
Cliffe Gdns. BD18: Ship 1F 27
Cliffe La. BD13: B'frd 2E 33
BD17: Bail 4G 17
BD19: Cleck 4G 53
Cliffe La. Sth. BD17: Bail 4G 17
Cliffe La. W. BD17: Bail 3G 17
Cliffe Mill Fold BD20: Keigh . . .3E 9
Cliffe Rd. BD3: B'frd 5B 28
BD21: Keigh 1D 12
HD6: Brigh 5E 59
Cliffestone Dr. BD20: Keigh . . .3D 8
Cliffe St. BD13: B'frd 2C 32
BD21: Keigh 3D 6
Cliffe Ter. BD8: B'frd 6H 27
BD13: B'frd 1G 31
(off Station Rd.)
BD17: Bail 4G 17
BD21: Keigh 1E 13
HX3: Hal 5C 56
HX6: Hal 2C 54
Cliffe Vw. BD15: B'frd 5G 25
Cliffe Vs. BD16: Bgly 2A 26
Cliffe Wood Av. BD18: Ship . . .1F 27
Cliffe Wood Cl. BD9: B'frd 4C 26
Cliff Gdns. HX2: Hal 2G 55
Cliff Hill La. HX2: Hal 1D 54
Cliff Hollins La. BD4: B'frd . . .1D 52
BD12: B'frd 1D 52
Clifford Cl. BD2: B'frd 2H 27
Clifford Rd. BD17: Bail 3G 17
Clifford St.
BD5: B'frd 4A 36 (6D 4)
Cliff St. BD22: Haw 6H 11
Cliff Va. Rd. BD18: Ship 2F 27
CLIFTON 5H 59
Clifton Av. HX1: Hal 1H 55
Clifton Comn. HD6: Brigh 5G 59
Clifton Pl. BD18: Ship 1F 27
Clifton Rd. HD6: Brigh 5F 59
(not continuous)
HX3: Hal 3C 56
Clifton St. BD8: B'frd 6H 27
BD13: B'frd 2E 41
BD22: Keigh 5C 6
HX3: Hal 4A 48
HX6: Hal 3E 55
CLIFTON VILLAS 6G 27
Clifton Vs. BD8: B'frd 6H 27
Clipstone St. BD5: B'frd 1A 44
Cliveden Av. BD13: B'frd 2E 33
Clive Pl. BD7: B'frd 4F 35
Clive Ter. BD7: B'frd 4F 35
Clock La. BD13: B'frd 6F 23
Clock Vw. St. BD20: Keigh 1D 6
Clog Sole Rd. HD6: Brigh 3D 58
Cloisters, The HX1: Hal 2A 56
(off Constitutional St.)
Close, The BD2: B'frd 1B 28
Close Head BD13: B'frd 3B 32
Close Head Dr. BD13: B'frd . . .3B 32
Close Head Rd.
BD13: B'frd 2B 32
Close Lea HD6: Brigh 6D 58
Close Lea Av. HD6: Brigh 6D 58
Close Lea Dr. HD6: Brigh 6D 58
Close Lea Way HD6: Brigh . . .6D 58
Closes Pl. HD6: Brigh 6E 59
(off Closes Rd.)
Closes Rd. HD6: Brigh 6D 58
Cloudsdale Av. BD5: B'frd 5A 36
Clough Bank HX2: Hal 6D 38
Clough Ct. BD13: B'frd 3G 31
Clough Ga. BD22: Keigh 3H 11
(off Clough La.)
Clough Head HX6: Hal 5E 55

Daleside Cl.—Drake St.

Daleside Cl. LS28: Pud 6H 29
Daleside Gro. BD12: B'frd 1B 52
LS28: Pud 1H 37
Dale Side Ho. BD8: B'frd 5H 27
Daleside Rd. BD18: Ship 4H 17
BD20: Keigh 2A 8
LS28: Pud 6H 29
Daleside Wlk. BD5: B'frd 1B 44
Daleson Cl. HX3: Hal 2G 49
Dale St. BD1: B'frd 2A 36 (3D 4)
BD18: Ship 6F 17
BD21: Keigh 2G 7
HX6: Hal 3D 54
Dalesway BD16: Bgly 6H 9
Dale Ter. HX6: Hal 3D 54 (off Greenups Ter.)
Dale Vw. HX2: Hal 6A 46
Dale Vw. Cl. BD21: Keigh 5G 7
Daleview Ct. BD17: Bail 3E 17
Dale Vw. Gro. BD21: Keigh 5G 7
Dale Vw. Rd. BD21: Keigh 6G 7
Dale Vw. Way BD21: Keigh 5G 7
Dallam Av. BD18: Ship 5C 16
Dallam Gro. BD18: Ship 4C 16
Dallam Rd. BD18: Ship 5C 16
Dallam Wlk. BD18: Ship 5D 16
Dalton La. BD21: Keigh 4F 7
Dalton Mills Bus. Complex BD21: Keigh 4G 7
Dalton Rd. BD21: Keigh 4G 7
Dalton St. HX6: Hal 2D 54
Dalton Ter. BD8: B'frd 1F 35
BD21: Keigh 3G 7 (off Surrey St.)
Damask St. HX1: Hal 5B 48 (2A 62)
Damems BD22: Keigh 3B 12
Damems La. BD22: Keigh 3B 12
Damems Rd. BD21: Keigh 3C 12
Damems Station Vintage Carriages Trust Mus. of Rail Travel 3C 12
DAM HEAD 2E 49
Dam Head Rd. HX6: Hal 2E 55
Damon Av. BD10: B'frd 3G 29
Damside BD21: Keigh 5D 6
Damson Ct. BD14: B'frd 6A 34
Danby Av. BD4: B'frd 3D 44
Dancroft BD22: Haw 1G 21
Danebury Rd. HD6: Brigh 6F 59
Dane Ct. Rd. BD4: B'frd 6G 37
Dane Hill Dr. BD4: B'frd 5G 37
Daniel Cl. BD21: Keigh 2C 12
Daniel Ct. BD4: B'frd 1H 45
Daniel St. BD3: B'frd 2F 37
Dan La. BD13: B'frd 2A 42
Danny La. HX2: Hal 6A 46
Danum Dr. BD17: Bail 3G 17
Danum Ter. HX3: Hal 2G 49
Darcey Hey La. HX2: Hal 2G 55
Darfield Ho. BD10: B'frd 1E 29 (off Summerfield Rd.)
Darfield St. BD1: B'frd 1H 35 (2B 4)
Dark La. BD22: Keigh 5D 10 (not continuous)
BD22: Oxen 4G 21
HX2: Hal 1D 54
HX3: Hal 6G 49 (Barrowclough La.)
HX3: Hal 3H 57 (Church La.)
Darley Mall BD1: B'frd 4D 4
Darley St. BD1: B'frd 2A 36 (3C 4) (not continuous)
BD20: Keigh 2D 6
Darnay La. BD5: B'frd 6A 36
Darnes Av. HX2: Hal 2G 55
Darren St. BD4: B'frd 3G 37
Dartmouth Ter. BD8: B'frd 5G 27
Darwin St. BD5: B'frd 6G 35
Davenport Ho. BD3: B'frd 2G 5
Dawnay Rd. BD5: B'frd 6F 35
Dawson Av. BD6: B'frd 3G 43
Dawson La. BD4: B'frd 2E 45
Dawson Mt. BD4: B'frd 2E 45
Dawson Pl. BD4: B'frd 2F 45
BD21: Keigh 6E 7
Dawson Rd. BD21: Keigh 6E 7
Dawson St. BD4: B'frd 1E 45
BD10: B'frd 4D 18
Dawson Ter. BD4: B'frd 2E 45
Dawson Way BD21: Keigh 6E 7
Dealburn Rd. BD12: B'frd 6H 43
Deal St. BD21: Keigh 3G 7
HX1: Hal 1D 56 (5D 62)
Dean Beck Av. BD6: B'frd 2A 44
Dean Beck Ct. BD6: B'frd 3B 44
Dean Cl. BD8: B'frd 6B 26
Dean Clough 5C 48 (1B 62)
Dean Clough HX3: Hal 5C 48 (2B 62)
Dean Clough Galleries 1B 62 (in Dean Clough)
Dean Clough Office Pk. HX3: Hal 5C 48 (1A 62)
Dean Ct. HX3: Hal 5A 56
Dean End HX4: Hal 1C 60
Deanery Gdns. BD10: B'frd 2E 29
Dean Ho. La. HX2: Hal 3A 46
Dean La. BD13: B'frd 6C 24
HX6: Hal 5A 54
Dean Rd. BD6: B'frd 3H 43
Dean's Ter. HX3: Hal 2B 48
Deanstones Cres. BD13: B'frd 3E 41
Deanstones La. BD13: B'frd 3D 40
Dean St. BD22: Haw 6H 11
HX4: Hal 3C 60
HX5: Ell 3F 61
Deanwood Av. BD15: B'frd 5G 25
Deanwood Cres. BD15: B'frd 4G 25
Deanwood Wlk. BD15: B'frd 5G 25
Dearden St. HX6: Hal 2D 54
Dee Ct. BD22: Keigh 3G 11
Deepdale Cl. BD17: Bail 3E 17
Deep La. BD13: B'frd 5A 32
BD14: B'frd 4A 34
HX2: Hal 6B 46
Defarge Ct. BD5: B'frd 6A 36 (off Newton St.)
De Lacy Av. BD4: B'frd 3D 44
Delamere St. BD5: B'frd 1H 43
Delaware Ct. BD4: B'frd 3D 44
Delf Cl. HX3: B'frd 4C 42
Delius Av. BD10: B'frd 2G 29
Dell, The BD13: B'frd 1F 23
Dellside Fold BD13: B'frd 1F 23
Delph Cres. BD14: B'frd 5H 33
Delph Cft. Vw. BD21: Keigh 5F 7
Delph Dr. BD14: B'frd 5H 33
Delph Gro. BD14: B'frd 5H 33
DELPH HILL
Bradford 6G 43
Halifax 3A 56
Delph Hill BD17: Bail 1G 17
HX2: Hal 3A 56
Delph Hill Fold HX2: Hal 3H 55
Delph Hill La. HX2: Hal 3A 46
Delph Hill Rd. HX2: Hal 3H 55
Delph Hill Ter. HX2: Hal 3H 55 (off Delph Hill Rd.)
Delph Ho. BD21: Keigh 6E 7
Delph St. HX1: Hal 1B 56 (5A 62)
Delph Ter. BD14: B'frd 5H 33
Delphwood Cl. BD16: Bgly 2A 16
Delverne Gro. BD2: B'frd 4E 29
Demontfort Ho. BD4: B'frd 5G 37 (off Ned La.)
Denbrook Av. BD4: B'frd 2H 45
Denbrook Cl. BD4: B'frd 2H 45
Denbrook Cres. BD4: B'frd 3H 45
Denbrook Wlk. BD4: B'frd 2H 45
Denbrook Way BD4: B'frd 2H 45
Denbury Mt. BD4: B'frd 1G 45
Denby Ct. BD22: Keigh 3F 11
Denby Dr. BD17: Bail 4F 17
DENBY HILL 3E 11
Denby Hill Rd. BD22: Keigh 3F 11
Denby Ho. BD4: B'frd 2H 45
BD17: Bail 4G 17 (off Denby Dr.)
Denby La. BD15: B'frd 6H 25
Denby Mt. BD22: Oxen 5G 21
Denby Pl. HX6: Hal 2D 54
Denby Rd. BD21: Keigh 6E 7
Denby St. BD8: B'frd 1G 35
Dence Grn. BD4: B'frd 4G 37
Dendrum Cl. BD22: Keigh 2G 11
Dene Bank BD16: Bgly 5G 9
Dene Cl. HX5: Ell 4E 61
Dene Cres. BD7: B'frd 5C 34
Dene Hill BD17: Bail 2D 16
Denehill BD9: B'frd 6B 26
Dene Mt. BD15: B'frd 6A 26
Dene Pl. HX1: Hal 5B 48 (2A 62)
Dene Rd. BD6: B'frd 2B 42
Deneside Mt. BD5: B'frd 1H 43
Deneside Ter. BD5: B'frd 1H 43
Dene Vw. HX2: Hal 5A 46
Denfield Av. HX3: Hal 3G 47
Denfield Cres. HX3: Hal 3H 47
Denfield Edge HX3: Hal 3H 47
Denfield Gdns. HX3: Hal 3H 47
Denfield La. HX3: Hal 3G 47
Denfield Sq. HX3: Hal 3H 47
Denham St. HD6: Brigh 6E 59
DENHOLME 6G 23
DENHOLME CLOUGH 3G 31
DENHOLME GATE 4F 31
Denholme Ga. BD13: B'frd 2G 31
Denholme Ga. Rd. HX3: Hal 3A 50
Denholme House 2G 31
Denholme Rd. BD22: Oxen 5H 21
Dennison Fold BD4: B'frd 4G 37
Denton Dr. BD16: Bgly 1A 16
Denton Row BD13: B'frd 1F 31
HX4: Hal 5C 60
Derby Pl. BD3: B'frd 2F 37
Derby Rd. BD3: B'frd 2G 37
Derby St. BD7: B'frd 5F 35
BD13: B'frd 2D 40
BD14: B'frd 5H 33
HX6: Hal 3F 55
Derby Ter. BD10: B'frd 5G 19
Derwent Av. BD15: B'frd 3C 24
BD17: Bail 4C 16 (not continuous)
Derwent Ho. HX3: Hal 4A 48
Derwent Pl. BD13: B'frd 1C 40
Derwent Rd. BD2: B'frd 4C 28
Derwent St. BD21: Keigh 3H 7
Devonshire St. BD21: Keigh 4C 6
Devonshire St. W. BD21: Keigh 4C 6
Devonshire Ter. BD9: B'frd 5G 27
Devon St. HX1: Hal 1H 55
Devon Way HD6: Brigh 1F 59
Dewfield Cl. BD4: B'frd 2E 45
Dewhirst Cl. BD17: Bail 3H 17
Dewhirst Pl. BD4: B'frd 4F 37
Dewhirst Rd. BD17: Bail 3H 17
HD6: Brigh 3E 59
Dewhirst St. BD15: B'frd 2C 24
Dewsbury Rd. BD19: Cleck 6G 53
HX5: Ell 3G 61
Diamond St. BD22: Keigh 1C 12
HX1: Hal 5A 48
Diamond Ter. HX1: Hal 5A 48
HX2: Hal 2H 55
Dickens St. BD5: B'frd 6A 36
HX2: Hal 6G 47
Dick La. BD3: B'frd 2G 37
BD4: B'frd 5F 37
Digley Av. BD6: B'frd 1A 42
Dimples La. BD20: Keigh 3D 8
BD22: Haw 6F 11
DIRK HILL 4G 35
Dirkhill Rd. BD7: B'frd 4G 35
Dirkhill St. BD7: B'frd 4F 35
Discovery Rd. HX1: Hal 1D 56 (6D 62)
Dispensary Wlk. HX1: Hal 6D 48 (4D 62)
Dixon Av. BD7: B'frd 4D 34
Dixon Cl. HX4: Hal 1A 60
Dobb Kiln La. BD16: Bgly 4H 15
Dob La. HX6: Hal 4A 54
Dobrudden Cvn. Pk. BD17: Bail 1D 16
Dockfield Ind. Pk. BD17: Ship 4H 17
Dockfield Pl. BD17: Ship 5G 17
Dockfield Rd. BD17: Ship 5G 17
Dockfield Ter. BD17: Ship 5G 17
Dock La. BD17: Ship 4G 17
BD18: Ship 5G 17
Dockroyd BD22: Keigh 4H 11
Dockroyd La. BD22: Keigh 3G 11
Doctor Hill BD10: B'frd 6D 18 (Evesham Gro.)
BD10: B'frd 1C 28 (Highfield Rd.)
HX2: Hal 4F 47
Doctor La. BD10: B'frd 4D 18
Dodge Holme Cl. HX2: Hal 1F 47
Dodge Holme Ct. HX2: Hal 1F 47 (off Dodge Holme Rd.)
Dodge Holme Dr. HX2: Hal 1E 47
Dodge Holme Gdns. HX2: Hal 1F 47
Dodge Holme Rd. HX2: Hal 1F 47
Dodgson St. HX5: Ell 4F 61
Doe Pk. BD13: B'frd 6H 23
Dog Kennel La. HX3: Hal 2E 57
Dol BD22: Oxen 6A 22
Doldram La. HX6: Hal 6C 54
Doles La. HD6: Brigh 3H 59
Dole St. BD13: B'frd 3E 33
Doll La. BD13: B'frd 3G 23
Dolphin La. BD16: B'frd 5G 13
Dolphin Ter. BD13: B'frd 3C 40
Dombey St. HX1: Hal 6A 48
Dominion Ind. Pk. HX3: Hal 5A 50
Donald Av. BD6: B'frd 3G 43
Doncaster St. HX3: Hal 4D 56
Donisthorpe St. BD5: B'frd 6H 35
Don St. BD21: Keigh 3D 6
Dorchester Ct. BD4: B'frd 6G 37
Dorchester Cres. BD4: B'frd 6G 37
BD17: Bail 1B 18
Dorchester Dr. HX2: Hal 2G 55
Dorian Cl. BD10: B'frd 1F 29
Dorothy St. BD21: Keigh 2C 12
Dorset Cl. BD5: B'frd 6G 35
Dorset St. BD5: B'frd 6G 35
Douglas Cres. BD18: Ship 1H 27
Douglas Dr. BD4: B'frd 5E 37
Douglas Rd. BD4: B'frd 5E 37
Douglas St. BD22: Haw 5A 12
HX3: Hal 3B 48
Douglas Towers BD5: B'frd 6C 4
Dovedale Cl. HX3: Hal 6H 41
Dover St. BD3: B'frd 6B 28
Dovesdale Gro. BD5: B'frd 1G 43
Dovesdale Rd. BD5: B'frd 1H 43
Dove St. BD18: Ship 5D 16
BD22: Haw 6H 11
Dowker St. HX1: Hal 2H 55
DOWLEY GAP 3A 16
Dowley Gap La. BD16: Bgly 4H 15
Downham St. BD3: B'frd 3C 36 (5H 5)
Downing Cl. BD3: B'frd 2D 36 (3H 5)
Downside Cres. BD15: B'frd 6G 25
Dracup Av. BD7: B'frd 4C 34
Dracup Rd. BD7: B'frd 6D 34
Drake Fold BD12: B'frd 2G 51
Drakes Ind. Est. HX3: Hal 1A 48
Drake St. BD1: B'frd 3B 36 (5E 5)
BD21: Keigh 3E 7

76 A-Z Bradford

Draughton Gro.—Ellinthorpe St.

Draughton Gro. BD5: B'frd . . .2H **43**
Draughton St. BD5: B'frd 2H **43**
Draycott Wlk. BD4: B'frd 1G **45**
Drewry Rd. BD21: Keigh 4D **6**
Drewton St.
BD1: B'frd 2H **35** (3B **4**)
Drill Pde. BD8: B'frd 6H **27**
Drill St. BD21: Keigh 4E **7**
BD22: Haw 1G **21**
Drive, The BD10: B'frd 1F **29**
BD13: B'frd 1E **31**
BD16: Bgly 5E **9**
HX3: Hal 5B **50**
Drove Rd. Ho. *BD5: B'frd 6A 36*
(off Bowling Old La.)
Drovers Way BD2: B'frd 3A **28**
DRUB 3G **53**
Drub La. BD19: Cleck 3G **53**
Druids St. BD14: B'frd 5H **33**
Druids Vw. Av. BD16: Bgly 4D **8**
Drummond Rd. BD8: B'frd . . .6G **27**
Drummond Trad. Est.
BD8: B'frd 1H **35** (1A **4**)
Drury La. HX4: Hal 5A **60**
Dryclough Cl. HX3: Hal 4C **56**
Dryclough La. HX3: Hal 4C **56**
Dryden St.
BD1: B'frd 3B **36** (6F **5**)
BD16: Bgly 2F **15**
Dubb La. BD16: Bgly 2F **15**
Duchy Av. BD9: B'frd 4C **26**
Duchy Cres. BD9: B'frd 4C **26**
Duchy Dr. BD9: B'frd 5C **26**
(not continuous)
Duchy Gro. BD9: B'frd 4C **26**
Duchy Vs. BD9: B'frd 4C **26**
Duchywood BD9: B'frd 4C **26**
Ducie St. BD10: B'frd 4D **18**
Duckett Gro. LS28: Pud 1H **37**
Duckett La.
BD1: B'frd 2A **36** (3C **4**)
Ducking Well Cl.
BD22: Haw 1G **21**
Duckworth Gro. BD9: B'frd . . .5D **26**
Duckworth La. BD9: B'frd 6C **26**
Duckworth Ter. BD9: B'frd 5D **26**
Dudley Cres. HX2: Hal 6F **39**
Dudley Gro. BD4: B'frd 4G **37**
DUDLEY HILL 1E **45**
Dudley Hill Rd. BD2: B'frd . . .4D **28**
Dudley St. BD4: B'frd 4G **37**
(Dennison Fold)
BD4: B'frd 6E **37**
(School St.)
BD4: B'frd 6E **37**
(Wakefield Rd.)
Dudwell Av. HX3: Hal 5D **56**
Dudwell Gro. HX3: Hal 5C **56**
Dudwell La. HX3: Hal 5C **56**
Duich Rd. BD6: B'frd 5C **42**
Duinen St. BD5: B'frd 4B **36**
Duke St. BD1: B'frd . . .2A **36** (3D **4**)
BD20: Keigh 2D **6**
BD22: Haw 6H **11**
HX2: Hal 4A **46**
HX5: Ell 3F **61**
Dulverton Gro. BD4: B'frd 6F **37**
Dunbar Cft. BD13: B'frd 2F **41**
Duncan St. BD5: B'frd 4A **36**
Dunce Pk. Cl. HX5: Ell 4F **61**
Duncombe Rd. BD8: B'frd 2D **34**
Duncombe St. BD8: B'frd 2E **35**
Duncombe Way BD8: B'frd . . .2E **35**
Dundas St. BD21: Keigh 5F **7**
HX1: Hal 2H **55**
Dunkhill Cft. BD10: B'frd 6D **18**
DUNKIRK 6E **41**
Dunkirk Cres. HX1: Hal 1G **55**
Dunkirk Gdns. HX1: Hal 2G **55**
Dunkirk La. HX1: Hal 2G **55**
Dunkirk Ri. BD20: Keigh 1G **7**
Dunkirk St. HX1: Hal 1G **55**
Dunkirk Ter. HX1: Hal 1H **55**
Dunlin Way BD8: B'frd 2A **34**
Dunmore Av. BD13: B'frd 2C **40**
Dunnington Wlk.
BD6: B'frd 5E **43**
Dunnock Av. BD13: B'frd 2H **41**
Dunsford Av. BD4: B'frd 3D **44**
Dunstan Gro. BD19: Cleck 5G **53**
Durham Rd. BD8: B'frd 6E **27**
Durham St. HX2: Hal 5G **47**
Durham Ter. BD8: B'frd 6E **27**
Durkheim Ct. *BD3: B'frd 2E 37*
(off Amberley St.)
Durley Av. BD9: B'frd 4E **27**
Durling Dr. BD18: Ship 6A **18**
Durlston Gro. BD12: B'frd 1H **51**
Durlston Ter. BD12: B'frd 1H **51**
Durrance St. BD22: Keigh 5B **6**
Dye Ho. BD15: B'frd 2B **24**
Dyehouse Dr. BD19: Cleck 3E **53**
Dyehouse Fold BD12: B'frd . . .6C **44**
Dye Ho. La. HX6: Hal 6G **55**
Dyehouse La. BD15: B'frd 2A **24**
HD6: Brigh 6F **59**
Dyehouse Rd. BD12: B'frd 6B **44**
Dyer La. HX3: Hal 4H **47**
Dyke BD22: Haw 6D **10**
Dyke Nook BD22: Oxen 6E **21**
Dyson Pl. *HX3: Hal 4E 57*
(off Ashgrove Av.)
Dyson Rd. HX1: Hal 5H **47**
Dyson St.
BD1: B'frd 2H **35** (3A **4**)
BD9: B'frd 3E **27**
HD6: Brigh 4E **59**

E

Eaglesfield Dr. BD6: B'frd 5D **42**
Eagle St. BD21: Keigh 4D **6**
BD22: Haw 6H **11**
Earl St. BD21: Keigh 3D **6**
BD22: Haw 1G **21**
Earlswood BD12: B'frd 2H **51**
Earl Ter. HX3: Hal 3A **48**
Easby Rd.
BD7: B'frd 4H **35** (6A **4**)
East Av. BD21: Keigh 3E **7**
(not continuous)
EAST BIERLEY 4H **45**
East Bolton HX2: Hal 4G **39**
Eastbourne Rd. BD9: B'frd 2F **27**
EAST BOWLING 1C **44**
EASTBROOK 3B **36** (5F **5**)
Eastbury Av. BD6: B'frd 2B **42**
East Byland HX2: Hal 5G **39**
East Cft. BD12: B'frd 3H **51**
East Croft M. *BD12: B'frd 3H 51*
(off Garden Fld.)
Eastfield BD13: B'frd 1F **31**
Eastfield Gdns. BD4: B'frd . . .6G **37**
E. Fountains *HX2: Hal 4F 39*
(off Field Head La.)
Eastgate HX5: Ell 2F **61**
Easthorpe Ct. BD2: B'frd 3F **29**
Eastleigh Gro. BD5: B'frd 6G **35**
E. Longley HX6: Hal 6C **54**
E. Manywells BD13: B'frd 3G **23**
Eastmoor Ho. BD4: B'frd 1H **45**
EAST MORTON 3D **8**
East Mt. HD6: Brigh 4E **59**
E. Mount Pl. HD6: Brigh 4E **59**
East Pde. BD1: B'frd . . .2B **36** (4F **5**)
(not continuous)
BD17: Bail 1H **17**
BD21: Keigh 4E **7**
HX6: Hal 3F **55**
E. Park Rd. HX3: Hal 4A **48**
East Riddlesden Hall 2H **7**
East Rd. BD12: B'frd 5A **44**
East Royd BD22: Keigh 3H **11**
HX3: Hal 4A 50
(off Groveville)
E. Squire La. BD8: B'frd 6G **27**
East St. HD6: Brigh 6E **59**
HX3: Hal 6E **51**
East St. HX6: Hal 5A **54**
East Ter. BD22: Haw 5A **12**
East Vw. BD12: B'frd 6B **44**
BD13: B'frd 1A **42**
(Lingfield Ter.)
BD13: B'frd 1C **32**
(Up. Heights Rd.)
HX3: Hal 6E **51**
HX4: Hal 5C **60**
HX5: Ell 3H **61**
HX6: Hal 2E **55**
East Vw. Ter. BD12: B'frd 1A **52**
Eastwood Av. HX2: Hal 4G **39**
HX6: Hal 4B **54**
Eastwood Cl. HX2: Hal 4G **39**
Eastwood Ct. HX3: Hal 3A **56**
Eastwood Cres. BD16: Bgly . . .5H **15**
Eastwood Gro. HX2: Hal 4G **39**
Eastwood's Farm *HX2: Hal . . .4G 39*
(off Causeway Foot)
Eastwood St. BD4: B'frd 4B **36**
HD6: Brigh 4F **59**
HX3: Hal 3A **48**
Eaton St. BD21: Keigh 1C **12**
Ebenezer Pl. BD7: B'frd 5E **35**
Ebenezer St.
BD1: B'frd 3B **36** (5E **5**)
Ebor Ct. *BD21: Keigh 5D 6*
(off Aireworth St.)
Ebor La. BD22: Haw 5G **11**
Ebridge Ct. *BD16: Bgly 2G 15*
(off Edward St.)
Eccles Ct. BD2: B'frd 3D **28**
ECCLESHILL 2D **28**
Eccleshill Swimming Pool . . .1F **29**
Edale Gro. BD13: B'frd 3C **40**
Edderthorpe St.
BD3: B'frd 3C **36** (5H **5**)
Eden Cl. BD12: B'frd 2H **51**
Edensor Rd. BD21: Keigh 4C **6**
Edgar St. BD14: B'frd 5B **34**
Edgebank Av. BD6: B'frd 5D **42**
Edge Bottom BD13: B'frd 6F **23**
Edge End BD13: B'frd 6G **23**
Edge End Gdns.
BD6: B'frd 4C **42**
Edge End Rd. BD6: B'frd 3C **42**
Edgehill Cl. BD13: B'frd 2F **41**
Edgeholme La. HX2: Hal 6D **46**
Edgemoor Cl. BD4: B'frd 3G **45**
HX3: Hal 3B **56**
Edge Nook *BD6: B'frd 2E 43*
(off Windmill Hill)
Ediths Vw. HX6: Hal 3D **54**
Edlington Cl. BD4: B'frd 6G **37**
Edmund St.
BD5: B'frd 3H **35** (6B **4**)
Edrich Cl. BD12: B'frd 5A **44**
Edward Cl. HX3: Hal 3G **57**
Edwards Rd. HX2: Hal 2G **55**
Edward St.
BD4: B'frd 3B **36** (6E **5**)
(Bedford St.)
BD4: B'frd 2G **45**
(Lister St.)
BD16: Bgly 2G **15**
BD18: Ship 4D **16**
HD6: Brigh 5G **59**
(Albert St.)
HD6: Brigh 4E **59**
(Lightcliffe Rd.)
HX6: Hal 3D **54**
Edward Turner Cl.
BD12: B'frd 5G **43**
Eel Holme Vw. St.
BD20: Keigh 1D **6**
Effingham Rd. BD16: Bgly 4A **14**
Egerton Gro. BD15: B'frd 6G **25**
Egerton St. HX6: Hal 3D **54**
Eggleston Dr. BD4: B'frd 1H **45**
Egham Grn. *BD10: B'frd 6D 18*
(off Ley Fleaks Rd.)
Egremont Cres. BD6: B'frd . . .5D **42**
Egremont St. HX6: Hal 4C **54**
Egremont Ter. *HX6: Hal 4C 54*
(off Egremont St.)
EGYPT 1C **32**
Egypt Rd. BD13: B'frd 1C **32**
Eider Cl. BD13: B'frd 2A **42**
Elam Grange BD20: Keigh 1E **7**
Elam Wood BD20: Keigh 1F **7**
Elam Wood Rd.
BD20: Keigh 1F **7**
Eland Ho. *HX5: Ell 2F 61*
(off Southgate)
Elbow La. BD2: B'frd 5D **28**
HX2: Hal 4A **46**
Elder Bank *BD13: B'frd 1F 23*
(off Keighley Rd.)
Elderberry Cl. BD20: Keigh 2B **8**
Elder Lea HX2: Hal 2A **40**
Elder St. BD10: B'frd 6G **19**
BD20: Keigh 1C **6**
Elderwood Gdns.
BD10: B'frd 2G **29**
Eldon Pl. BD1: B'frd . . .1H **35** (2B **4**)
BD4: B'frd 5F **37**
BD19: Cleck 6G 53
(off Dewsbury Rd.)
Eldon St. HX3: Hal . . .5C **48** (1C **62**)
Eldon Ter.
BD1: B'frd 1H **35** (2B **4**)
Eldroth Mt. HX1: Hal 2A **56**
Eldroth Rd. HX1: Hal 2A **56**
ELDWICK 1H **15**
Eleanor Dr. LS28: Pud 6H **19**
Eleanor St. HD6: Brigh 6E **59**
Elia St. BD21: Keigh 3F **7**
Eli St. BD5: B'frd 6B **36**
Elizabeth Av. BD12: B'frd 1H **51**
Elizabeth Cl. BD12: B'frd 1H **51**
Elizabeth Cres. BD12: B'frd . . .1H **51**
Elizabeth Dr. BD12: B'frd 1H **51**
Elizabeth Ho. *HX2: Hal 1G 47*
(off Furness Pl.)
Elizabeth Ind. Est.
HX3: Hal 5A **48**
Elizabeth St. BD5: B'frd 4A **36**
BD12: B'frd 1H **51**
BD16: Bgly 2G **15**
BD21: Keigh 4G **7**
BD22: Keigh 3H **11**
HX4: Hal 2D **60**
HX5: Ell 3F **61**
ELLAND 3F **61**
Elland Baths 3F **61**
Elland Bri. HX5: Ell 2F **61**
ELLAND BUPA HOSPITAL 2G **61**
Elland Fitness Cen. 3F 61
(off Southgate)
Elland Hall Farm Cvn. Pk.
HX4: Ell 2E **61**
Elland La. HD6: Brigh 5E **59**
HX5: Ell 2G **61**
(not continuous)
Elland Riorges Link
HX5: Ell 2G **61**
Elland Rd. HD6: Brigh 4D **58**
HX5: Ell 2G **61**
(Elland Riorges Link)
HX5: Ell 6G **57**
(Park Rd.)
ELLAND UPPER EDGE 3H **61**
Elland Wood Bottom
HX3: Hal 6D **56**
HX4: Hal 6D **56**
Ellar Carr Rd. BD10: B'frd 3E **19**
BD13: B'frd 6E **13**
Ella St. BD21: Keigh 3F **7**
Ellen Holme HX2: Hal 1A **54**
Ellen Holme Rd. HX2: Hal 1A **54**
Ellen Royd St.
HX3: Hal 5C **48** (1C **62**)
Ellen St. BD16: Bgly 2G **15**
Ellenthorpe Rd. BD17: Bail . . .3C **16**
Ellerburn Dr. BD6: B'frd 3C **42**
Ellercroft Av. BD7: B'frd 3E **35**
Ellercroft Rd. BD7: B'frd 3E **35**
Ellercroft Ter. BD7: B'frd 3E **35**
Ellerton St. BD3: B'frd 2E **37**
Ellinthorpe St. BD4: B'frd 4D **36**

Elliot Ct. BD13: B'frd 2D 40
Elliott St. BD18: Ship 5E 17
Ellis Ct. HX3: Hal 2D 50
Ellison Fold BD17: Bail 1G 17
Ellison St. HX3: Hal 4A 48
Ellis St. BD5: B'frd 6H 35
Ellistones Gdns. HX4: Hal 2A 60
Ellistones La. HX4: Hal 3A 60
Ellistones Pl. HX4: Hal 3A 60
Ellton Gro. BD6: B'frd 2E 43
Elm Av. HX6: Hal 2D 54
Elm Ct. BD15: B'frd 3C 24
Elm Cres. BD20: Keigh 3D 8
Elmfield BD17: Bail 1H 17
Elmfield Dr. BD6: B'frd 3G 43
Elmfield Ter. HX1: Hal 2B 56
Elm Gdns. HX3: Hal 2C 56
Elm Gro. BD18: Ship 6A 18
BD20: Keigh 3D 8
BD21: Keigh 1C 12
HX3: Hal 5B 42
Elm Pl. HX1: Hal 6H 47
HX6: Hal 2D 54
Elm Rd. BD18: Ship 6H 17
Elm St. BD22: Oxen 5G 21
HX4: Hal 5A 60
Elm Ter. HD6: Brigh 2F 59
Elm Tree Av. BD6: B'frd 3G 43
Elm Tree Cl. BD6: B'frd 3H 43
BD21: Keigh 5F 7
Elm Tree Gdns. BD6: B'frd . . .2G 43
Elm Vw. *HX3: Hal 3C 56*
(off Skircoat Grn. Rd.)
Elmwood Dr. BD22: Keigh 1B 12
HD6: Brigh 4D 58
Elmwood Pl. *BD2: B'frd 6E 29*
(off Fagley Rd.)
Elmwood Rd. BD22: Keigh . . .2B 12
Elm Wood St. HD6: Brigh 3F 59
Elmwood St. HX1: Hal 2A 56
Elmwood Ter. BD22: Keigh . . .1B 12
Elsdon Gro. BD5: B'frd 4A 36
Elsie St. BD20: Keigh 1D 6
BD22: Haw 5B 12
Elsinore Av. HX5: Ell 3E 61
Elsinore Ct. HX5: Ell 3E 61
Elston Dr. *BD20: Keigh 3B 8*
(off Ford Rd.)
Elsworth Av. BD3: B'frd 6F 29
Elsworth St. BD4: B'frd 4C 36
Eltham Gro. BD6: B'frd 3E 43
Elvey Cl. BD2: B'frd 3F 29
Elwell Cl. HX3: B'frd 4B 42
Elwyn Gro. BD5: B'frd 6A 36
Elwyn Rd. BD5: B'frd 6B 36
Ely St. HX4: Hal 3D 60
Emblem Ct. BD13: B'frd 3D 40
Emerald St. BD22: Keigh 1C 12
Emerson Av. BD9: B'frd 4B 26
Emily Ct. *BD7: B'frd 6F 35*
(off Oakwell Cl.)
Emily Hall Gdns.
BD15: B'frd 2C 24
Emily St. BD21: Keigh 3E 7
BD22: Haw 6H 11
(off Victoria Rd.)
Emmeline Cl. BD10: B'frd 5D 18
Emmfield Dr. BD9: B'frd 3E 27
Emm La. BD9: B'frd 4E 27
Emmott Farm Fold
BD22: Haw 1G 21
Empire Bus. Cen. HX2: Hal . . .1A 48
Empsall Row *HD6: Brigh 4F 59*
(off Camm St.)
Emscote Av. HX1: Hal 2A 56
Emscote Gdns. HX1: Hal 2A 56
Emscote Gro. HX1: Hal 2A 56
Emscote Pl. HX1: Hal 2A 56
Emscote St. Sth. HX1: Hal 2A 56
Emsley Cl. BD4: B'frd 3D 44
Enderby Cl. HX3: Hal 2H 47
Enderley Rd. BD13: B'frd 3D 32
Endsleigh Pl. BD14: B'frd 5H 33
Enfield Dr. BD6: B'frd 2E 43
Enfield Pde. BD6: B'frd 2E 43
Enfield Rd. BD17: Bail 3G 17
Enfield Side Rd.
BD22: Haw 2B 20
Enfield St. BD21: Keigh 4D 6
Enfield Wlk. BD6: B'frd 2E 43
Englefield Cl. BD4: B'frd 1G 45
Englefield Cres. BD4: B'frd . . .1G 45
Ennerdale Dr. BD2: B'frd 4D 28
HX5: Ell 2H 61
Ennerdale Rd. BD2: B'frd 4C 28
Enterprise 5 La. Ends
BD10: B'frd 1D 28
Enterprise Ct. BD4: B'frd 2E 45
Enterprise Way
BD10: B'frd 1D 28
Epworth Pl. BD22: Keigh 2F 11
Equity Chambers BD1: B'frd . . .3D 4
Eric St. BD21: Keigh 3E 7
Escroft Cl. BD12: B'frd 4H 51
Esholt Hall Est.
BD17: B'frd 1G 19
Esholt La. BD17: Bail, B'frd . . .1B 18
Eshton Av. BD12: B'frd 6B 44
Eskdale Av. HX3: Hal 6H 41
Eskdale Ho. *HX6: Hal 4D 54*
(off Quarry Hill)
Eskdale Ri. BD15: B'frd 1H 33
Eskine Pde. BD6: B'frd 5D 42
Esmond St. BD7: B'frd 6D 34
Esporta Health & Fitness Club
Bradford 1H 37
Essex Pk. Ind. Est.
BD4: B'frd 3C 36 (6G 5)
Essex St. BD4: B'frd . . .3C 36 (6G 5)
HX1: Hal 1H 55
Estcourt Gro. BD7: B'frd 4E 35
Estcourt Rd. BD7: B'frd 4E 35
Ethel St. BD20: Keigh 2D 6
Etna St. BD7: B'frd 6D 34
Eton St. HX1: Hal 6H 47
Eureka Children's Mus.
. . . . .1D 56 (5D 62)
Eurocam Technology Pk.
BD5: B'frd 1A 44
Euroway Trad. Est.
BD4: B'frd 5C 44
Evans Towers BD5: B'frd 6D 4
Evelyn Av. BD3: B'frd 1G 37
Evelyn Ter. BD13: B'frd 1C 40
Evens Ter. BD5: B'frd 1A 44
Everest Av. BD18: Ship 6A 18
Evergreen Wlk. *BD16: Bgly 6E 9*
(off Canal Rd.)
Eversley Dr. BD4: B'frd 5G 37
Eversley Mt. *HX2: Hal 1G 55*
(off Bk. Eversley Mt.)
Eversley Pl. HX2: Hal 1G 55
Evesham Gro. BD10: B'frd . . .6D 18
Ewart Pl. BD7: B'frd 6E 35
Ewart St. BD7: B'frd 6E 35
BD13: B'frd 2E 41
Exchange St. BD19: Cleck 4F 53
HX4: Hal 3D 60
Exe St. BD5: B'frd 6G 35
Exeter St. HX3: Hal 4D 56
HX6: Hal 3E 55
Exhibition Rd. BD18: Ship 5D 16
EXLEY 6D 56
Exley Av. BD21: Keigh 1C 12
Exley Bank HX3: Hal 5D 56
Exley Bank Top HX3: Hal 6D 56
Exley Cres. BD21: Keigh 6C 6
(not continuous)
Exley Dr. BD21: Keigh 6C 6
Exley Gdns. HX3: Hal 6D 56
Exley Gro. BD21: Keigh 6C 6
EXLEY HEAD 6B 6
Exley Head Vw.
BD22: Keigh 3A 6
Exley La. HX3: Hal 6D 56
HX5: Hal 6D 56
Exley Mt. BD7: B'frd 3D 34
BD21: Keigh 6C 6
Exley Rd. BD21: Keigh 6C 6
Exley St. BD22: Keigh 5C 6
Exley Way BD21: Keigh 1C 12
(not continuous)
Exmoor St. HX1: Hal 1H 55
Exmouth Pl. BD3: B'frd 6B 28

F

Factory La. BD4: B'frd 1D 44
Factory St. BD4: B'frd 1E 45
FAGLEY 6E 29
Fagley Cres. BD2: B'frd 5E 29
Fagley Cft. BD2: B'frd 5F 29
Fagley Dr. BD2: B'frd 5E 29
Fagley La. BD2: B'frd 3F 29
Fagley Pl. BD2: B'frd 6E 29
Fagley Rd. BD2: B'frd 6E 29
Fagley Ter. BD2: B'frd 6E 29
Fair Bank BD18: Ship 1G 27
Fairbank Pl. *BD18: Ship 1G 27*
(off Fair Bank)
Fairbank Rd. BD8: B'frd 6E 27
Fairbank Ter. BD8: B'frd 6E 27
Fairburn Ct. HX3: Hal 3G 57
Fairburn Gdns. BD2: B'frd 3E 29
Fairclough Gro. HX3: Hal 2H 47
Fairfax Av. BD4: B'frd 2E 45
Fairfax Cres. BD4: B'frd 2E 45
HX3: Hal 2G 57
Fairfax Ho. BD1: B'frd 3F 5
Fairfax Rd. BD13: B'frd 6F 13
BD16: Bgly 6F 9
Fairfax St. BD4: B'frd 4B 36
BD22: Haw 6H 11
Fairfax Vw. BD4: B'frd 4H 45
Fairfield BD13: B'frd 1F 31
Fairfield Ct. BD17: Bail 1A 18
Fairfield Dr. BD17: Bail 1A 18
Fairfield Ri. HD6: Brigh 1F 59
Fairfield Rd. BD8: B'frd 6F 27
BD12: B'frd 2H 51
Fairfield St. BD4: B'frd 2F 45
Fairfield Ter. *BD19: Cleck 6G 53*
(off Neville St.)
Fairford Ct. BD2: B'frd 4D 28
Fairhaven Grn. BD10: B'frd . . .6E 19
Fair Isle Ct. *BD21: Keigh 4E 7*
(off Alice St.)
Fairlands Cl. HX2: Hal 5H 39
Fairless Av. HX3: Hal 6E 51
Fairmount BD9: B'frd 5G 27
Fairmount Pk. BD18: Ship 6C 16
(not continuous)
Fairmount Ter. BD21: Keigh . . .5H 7
Fair Rd. BD6: B'frd 2F 43
Fairview BD12: B'frd 1C 52
Fairview Ct. BD17: Bail 4F 17
Fairview Ter. HX3: Hal 4A 48
Fairway BD7: B'frd 2D 42
BD10: Yead 4H 19
BD18: Ship 6D 16
Fairway, The HX2: Hal 4H 39
Fairway Av. BD7: B'frd 2D 42
Fairway Cl. BD7: B'frd 2D 42
Fairway Cres. BD22: Haw 1H 21
Fairway Dr. BD7: B'frd 1D 42
Fairway Gro. BD7: B'frd 1D 42
Fairways, The BD9: B'frd 2C 26
BD20: Keigh 1C 6
Fairway Wlk. BD7: B'frd 1D 42
FAIRWEATHER GREEN 2B 34
Fairweather M. BD8: B'frd . . .2C 34
Fairwood Gro. BD10: B'frd . . .4G 29
Fairy Dell BD16: Bgly 6G 15
Falcon M. BD8: B'frd 1A 34
Falcon Rd. BD16: Bgly 6F 9
Falcon St. BD7: B'frd 4F 35
HX3: Hal 4D 56
Falkland Ct. BD16: Bgly 2G 15
Falkland Rd. BD10: B'frd 3G 29
Fall Brow Cl. BD14: B'frd 6G 33
Fall La. HX3: Hal 6D 40
HX6: Hal 4F 55
Fallowfield Cl. BD4: B'frd 3E 45
Fallowfield Dr. BD4: B'frd 2E 45
Fallowfield Gdns.
BD4: B'frd 2E 45
Fall Spring Gdns. HX4: Hal . . .6A 60
Fallwood St. BD22: Haw 1H 21
Falmouth Av. BD3: B'frd 6B 28
Falsgrave Av. BD2: B'frd 5F 29
Faltis Sq. BD10: B'frd 1E 29
Fanny St. BD18: Ship 4D 16
BD21: Keigh 5D 6
Farcliffe Pl. BD8: B'frd 6F 27
Farcliffe Rd. BD8: B'frd 6F 27
Farcliffe Ter. BD8: B'frd 6F 27
Far Crook BD10: B'frd 4B 18
Fardew Ct. BD16: Bgly 1F 15
Farfield Av. BD6: B'frd 4C 42
Farfield Cres. BD6: B'frd 4D 42
Farfield Gro. BD6: B'frd 4D 42
Farfield Rd. BD6: B'frd 4E 43
BD17: Bail 3H 17
BD18: Ship 6D 16
Farfield St. BD9: B'frd 5E 27
BD19: Cleck 4F 53
Farfield Ter. BD9: B'frd 5E 27
Far High Fld. BD22: Keigh . . .2G 11
Farhills BD6: B'frd 2D 42
Farlea Dr. BD2: B'frd 4E 29
Farleton Dr. BD2: B'frd 5F 29
Farley Cres. BD22: Keigh 2F 11
Far Low Bank *BD22: Keigh . . .2F 11*
(off Kelburn Gro.)
Farm Hill Ct. BD10: B'frd 2D 28
Farm Hill Rd. BD10: B'frd 1D 28
Farmstead Rd. BD10: B'frd . . .1E 29
Farndale Rd. BD15: B'frd 3C 24
BD17: Bail 3E 17
Farnham Cl. BD17: Bail 1H 17
Farnham Rd. BD7: B'frd 4F 35
Farrar Bldgs. *BD12: B'frd 2G 51*
(off Brick Row)
Farrar Mill La. HX3: Hal 3D 56
Farra St. BD22: Oxen 5G 21
Farriers Cft. BD2: B'frd 3B 28
Farringdon Cl. BD4: B'frd 5F 37
Farringdon Dr. BD4: B'frd 6G 37
Farringdon Gro. BD6: B'frd . . .4E 43
Farringdon Sq. BD4: B'frd 5G 37
Far Royd HX3: Hal 1A 48
Farside Grn. BD5: B'frd 6G 35
Far Vw. HX2: Hal 5G 39
Farway BD4: B'frd 5G 37
Fascination Pl. *BD13: B'frd . . .1C 40*
(off Mill La.)
Faulkland Ho. BD8: B'frd 1A 4
Faversham Wlk. BD4: B'frd . . .5G 37
Fawcett Pl. BD4: B'frd 3E 45
Faxfleet St. BD5: B'frd 2H 43
Faye Gdns. BD4: B'frd 2F 45
Fearnsides St. BD8: B'frd 1F 35
Fearnsides Ter. BD8: B'frd 1F 35
Fearnville Dr. BD4: B'frd 4F 37
Featherbed Cl. HX4: Hal 3D 60
Featherbed La. HX4: Hal 3D 60
Feather Rd. BD3: B'frd 2D 36
Feather St. BD21: Keigh 5F 7
Federation St. BD5: B'frd 1B 44
Felbrigg Av. BD22: Keigh 5B 6
Felcourt Dr. BD4: B'frd 1G 45
Felcourt Fold BD4: B'frd 1G 45
Fell Cres. BD22: Keigh 6B 6
Fell Gro. BD22: Keigh 5B 6
Fell La. BD22: Keigh 6A 6
Fellside Cl. BD5: B'frd 1B 44
Fellwood Av. BD22: Haw 5A 12
Fellwood Cl. BD22: Haw 5A 12
Fenby Av. BD4: B'frd 5D 36
(not continuous)
Fenby Cl. BD4: B'frd 6E 37
(not continuous)
Fenby Gdns. BD4: B'frd 6E 37
Fenby Gro. BD4: B'frd 6E 37
Fencote Cres. BD2: B'frd 4F 29
Fencote Ho. *BD10: B'frd 1E 29*
(off Rowantree Dr.)
Fender Rd. BD6: B'frd 2D 42
Fenned Rd. BD17: Bail 1A 18

Fenny Royd—Frodingham Vs.

Fenny Royd HX3: Hal 5H **49**
Fenton Ct. BD13: B'frd 1F **23**
Fenton Fold BD12: B'frd 1B **52**
Fenton Rd. HX1: Hal 2H **55**
Fenwick Dr. BD6: B'frd 4D **42**
Fenwick Ho. *BD5: B'frd 2B 44*
(off Parkway)
Ferguson St.
HX1: Hal 1C **56** (5B **62**)
Fern Bank HX6: Hal 4D **54**
Fernbank Av. BD16: Bgly 2H **15**
BD22: Keigh 1B **12**
Fernbank Dr. BD16: Bgly 2G **15**
BD17: Bail 4E **17**
Fernbank Rd. BD3: B'frd 6D **28**
Fernbank St. BD16: Bgly 2G **15**
Fernbank Ter. BD16: Bgly 2G **15**
FERNCLIFFE **2H 15**
Ferncliffe Ct. BD18: Ship 5D **16**
Ferncliffe Dr. BD17: Bail 2F **17**
BD20: Keigh 1B **6**
Ferncliffe Rd. BD16: Bgly 2F **15**
BD18: Ship 5D **16**
Fern Ct. BD20: Keigh 1C **6**
Ferndale BD14: B'frd 6G **33**
Ferndale Av. BD14: B'frd 6G **33**
Ferndale Gro. BD9: B'frd 3G **27**
Ferndene BD16: Bgly 2H **15**
Ferndown Grn. BD5: B'frd 6H **35**
Fernfield Ter. HX3: Hal 3C **48**
Fernhill BD16: Bgly 6G **9**
Fern Hill Av. BD18: Ship 6D **16**
Fern Hill Gro. BD18: Ship 6D **16**
Fern Hill Mt. BD18: Ship 6D **16**
Fern Hill Rd. BD18: Ship 6D **16**
Ferniehurst BD17: Bail 4G **17**
Fern Lea *BD13: B'frd 2F 41*
(off Scarlet Hgts.)
Fern Lea St. HX6: Hal 2D **54**
Fernley Gdns. BD12: B'frd . . . 1G **51**
Fern Pl. *BD18: Ship 5D 16*
(off George St.)
Fern Ri. HX5: Ell 2H **61**
Fern St. BD4: B'frd 6F **37**
BD21: Keigh 3E **7**
HX3: Hal 3B **48**
Fern Ter. BD8: B'frd 5G **27**
BD20: Keigh 2H 7
(off Carr La.)
Ferrand Av. BD4: B'frd 3E **45**
Ferrand La. BD16: Bgly 2F **15**
BD19: Cleck 4H **53**
Ferrand Rd. BD18: Ship 5D **16**
Ferrands Cl. BD16: Bgly 4B **14**
Ferrands Pk. Way
BD16: Bgly 4B **14**
Ferriby Cl. BD2: B'frd 4F **29**
Festival Av. BD18: Ship 2H **27**
Feversham St.
BD3: B'frd 3C **36** (5G **5**)
Field Cl. HX3: Hal 4H **47**
Field Ct. BD13: B'frd 3E **33**
Fieldedge La. BD20: Keigh 1A **8**
Fieldfare Dr. BD13: B'frd 2H **41**
Fieldgate Rd. BD10: B'frd 6F **19**
Field Head BD22: Oxen 2F **21**
HX2: Hal 4F **39**
Fieldhead Bus. Cen.
BD7: B'frd 2G 35
(off Gt. Russell Ct.)
Fld. Head La. BD22: Oxen 2E **21**
HX2: Hal 4F **39**
Fieldhead St. BD7: B'frd 3G **35**
Fld. Head Way HX2: Hal 4F **39**
Field Ho. Cotts. *HX1: Hal 2A 56*
(off Carlton Ho. Ter.)
Fieldhouse Ct. BD14: B'frd . . . 6A **34**
Fieldhouse St. BD3: B'frd 2F **37**
Field Hurst BD19: Cleck 6B **52**
Fieldhurst Ct. BD4: B'frd 3E **45**
Field Side HX1: Hal 5H **47**
Fieldside BD13: B'frd 1F **23**
Fields Rd. BD12: B'frd 6A **44**
Field St. BD1: B'frd 2B **36** (4E **5**)
Field Top HD6: Brigh 6F **51**
Fld. Top Rd. HD6: Brigh 6D **58**
Field Vw. HX2: Hal 6G **39**
HX3: Hal 3H **47**
Fieldway BD14: B'frd 4H **33**
Fife St. BD22: Haw 6H **11**
Fifth Av. BD3: B'frd 6E **29**
Fifth St. BD12: B'frd 5H **43**
Filey St. BD1: B'frd 3B **36** (5F **5**)
Finch Cl. BD16: Bgly 1A **16**
Finchley St. BD5: B'frd 6H **35**
Finch St. BD5: B'frd 5H **35**
Findon Ter. BD10: B'frd 3G **29**
Finkil St. HD6: Brigh 2C **58**
Finkle St. HX6: Hal 3A **54**
Finsbury Dr. BD2: B'frd 2B **28**
Firbank Grn. BD2: B'frd 4F **29**
Firbeck BD16: Bgly 5B **14**
Firethorn Cl. BD8: B'frd 1E **35**
First Av. BD3: B'frd 6E **29**
BD21: Keigh 5D **6**
HX3: Hal 3B **56**
Fir St. BD21: Keigh 1D **12**
BD22: Haw 1G **21**
First St. BD12: B'frd 5A **44**
Firth Av. HD6: Brigh 4E **59**
Firth Carr BD18: B'frd 2F **27**
Firth La. BD15: B'frd 2C **24**
Firth Rd. BD9: B'frd 4E **27**
Firths Ter. *HX3: Hal 3H 47*
(off Ramsden St.)
Firth St. BD13: B'frd 3D **32**
HD6: Brigh 6E **59**
Fir Tree Gdns. BD10: B'frd 1F **29**
Fitness Fast *. 3F 61*
(off Burley St.)
Fitness Finesse Health & Exercise Cen. **1B 42**
Fitness First Health Club Halifax . . . . **5B 48 (1A 62)**
Fitness Studio, The *. 5F 59*
(off Park Row)
Fitzgerald St. BD5: B'frd 4H **35**
Fitzroy Rd. BD3: B'frd 2D **36**
(not continuous)
Fitzwilliam St. BD4: B'frd 4B **36**
FIVE LANE ENDS **1D 28**
Five Oaks BD17: Bail 3E **17**
Five Ri. BD16: Bgly 6F **9**
Fixby Av. HX2: Hal 2G **55**
FLAPPIT SPRINGS **1C 22**
Flasby Av. *BD20: Keigh 3B 8*
(off Ford Rd.)
Flasby St. BD21: Keigh 3E **7**
Flat Nook BD16: Bgly 2H **15**
Flawith Dr. BD2: B'frd 5F **29**
Flaxen Ct. BD6: B'frd 2H **43**
Flaxman Rd. BD2: B'frd 3E **29**
Flaxton Grn. BD2: B'frd 5F **29**
Flaxton Pl. BD7: B'frd 3F **35**
Fleece St. BD6: B'frd 4D **42**
BD21: Keigh 4E **7**
Fleet La. BD13: B'frd 1D **40**
Fletcher La. BD2: B'frd 3H **27**
Fletcher Rd. BD6: B'frd 2F **43**
Fletton Ter. BD2: B'frd 5D **28**
Flinton Gro. BD2: B'frd 4F **29**
Flockton Av. BD4: B'frd 5C **36**
Flockton Cl. BD4: B'frd 5C **36**
Flockton Cres. BD4: B'frd 5C **36**
Flockton Dr. BD4: B'frd 5C **36**
Flockton Gro. BD4: B'frd 5C **36**
Flockton Rd. BD4: B'frd 5C **36**
Flockton Ter. BD4: B'frd 5C **36**
Florence Av. BD15: B'frd 1B **24**
Florence St. BD3: B'frd 3E **37**
HX1: Hal 6A **48**
Florida Rd. BD15: B'frd 3G **25**
Florist St. BD21: Keigh 2G **7**
Flower Acre HX5: Ell 3F **61**
Flower Bank BD2: B'frd 3B **28**
HX6: Hal 4B **54**
Flower Ct. BD2: B'frd 5E **29**
Flower Cft. BD21: Keigh 6B **6**
Flowerfields HX3: Hal 4C **50**
Flower Gth. BD10: B'frd 1F **29**
Flower Haven BD9: B'frd 3B **26**
Flower Hill BD9: B'frd 3D **26**
Flower Mt. BD17: Bail 1H **17**
Flowerpot La. BD13: B'frd 3C **40**
Floyd St. BD5: B'frd 6F **35**
Fold, The BD22: Haw 6F **11**
Foldings Av. BD19: Cleck 5B **52**
Foldings Cl. BD19: Cleck 5A **52**
Foldings Ct. BD19: Cleck 5A **52**
Foldings Gro. BD19: Cleck 5A **52**
Foldings Pde.
BD19: Cleck 5A **52**
Foldings Rd. BD19: Cleck 5A **52**
Folkestone St. BD3: B'frd 2D **36**
(not continuous)
Folkton Holme BD2: B'frd 5F **29**
Folly Hall Av. BD6: B'frd 3F **43**
Folly Hall Cl. BD6: B'frd 3F **43**
Folly Hall Gdns., The
BD6: B'frd 3F **43**
Folly Hall Rd. BD6: B'frd 3F **43**
Folly Hall Wlk. BD6: B'frd 3F **43**
Folly Vw. Rd. BD22: Haw 1H **21**
Fontmell Cl. BD4: B'frd 1G **45**
Forber Gro. BD4: B'frd 4G **37**
Forbes Ho. *BD4: B'frd 6G 37*
(off Stirling Cres.)
Ford BD13: B'frd 3C **40**
Ford Hill BD13: B'frd 3C **40**
Ford St. BD21: Keigh 2G **7**
Fore La. HX6: Hal 4C **54**
Fore La. Av. HX6: Hal 4B **54**
Foreside Bottom La.
BD13: B'frd 5F **31**
Foreside La. BD13: B'frd 4D **30**
Forest Av. HX2: Hal 1G **47**
Forest Cres. HX2: Hal 1G **47**
Forester Ct. *BD13: B'frd 1F 31*
(off Main Rd.)
Forester Sq. BD13: B'frd 1F **31**
Forest Grn. HX2: Hal 2G **47**
Forest Gro. HX2: Hal 2H **47**
Forge Gym **4B 4**
Forrester's Ter. HX4: Hal 6A **60**
Forster Ct.
BD1: B'frd 2A **36** (3E **5**)
Forster Sq.
BD1: B'frd 2B **36** (4E **5**)
Forster Sq. Retail Pk.
BD1: B'frd 1A **36** (2D **4**)
Foster Av. BD13: B'frd 3F **33**
Foster Gdns. BD22: Keigh 4B **6**
Foster Pk. BD13: B'frd 6G **23**
Foster Pk. Gro.
BD13: B'frd 6G **23**
Foster Pk. Rd. BD13: B'frd . . . 6G **23**
Foster Pk. Vw. BD13: B'frd . . . 6G **23**
(not continuous)
Foster Rd. BD21: Keigh 1D **12**
Foster's Ct. HX1: Hal 4C **62**
Foster Sq. BD13: B'frd 1F **31**
Foster St. BD13: B'frd 2E **41**
Foston Cl. BD2: B'frd 5G **29**
Foston La. BD2: B'frd 5F **29**
Foulds Ter. BD16: Bgly 1G **15**
Foundry Hill BD16: Bgly 2F **15**
Foundry La. BD4: B'frd 4D **36**
Foundry St. BD19: Cleck 5G **53**
HD6: Brigh 6G **59**
HX1: Hal 5C **48** (2C **62**)
HX6: Hal 4D **54**
Foundry St. Nth. HX3: Hal 2H **47**
Foundry Ter. BD19: Cleck 6G **53**
Fountain St.
BD1: B'frd 2A **36** (3C **4**)
BD12: B'frd 5G **43**
BD13: B'frd 3D **32**
(Kipping La.)
BD13: B'frd 2E **41**
(Union St.)
HX1: Hal 6C **48** (5B **62**)
Fountain Ter. BD12: B'frd 2H **51**
Fountain Way BD18: Ship 6G **17**
FOURLANDS **5E 19**
Fourlands Ct. BD10: B'frd 5E **19**
Fourlands Cres.
BD10: B'frd 5E **19**
Fourlands Dr. BD10: B'frd 5E **19**
Fourlands Gdns.
BD10: B'frd 5E **19**
Fourlands Gro. BD10: B'frd . . . 5E **19**
Fourlands Rd. BD10: B'frd 5E **19**
FOUR LANE ENDS **1D 34**
Four Lanes Bus. Pk.
BD8: B'frd 1D **34**
Four Seasons HX2: Hal 2A **40**
Fourth Av. BD3: B'frd 6E **29**
BD21: Keigh 5C **6**
Fourth St. BD12: B'frd 5A **44**
Fowlers Gth. BD22: Haw 5H **11**
Fowler St. BD4: B'frd 4D **36**
Fowler St. Ind. Est.
BD4: B'frd 4D **36**
Fox Ct. HX4: Hal 2D **60**
Fox Cft. Cl. BD13: B'frd 4C **40**
Foxcroft Dr. HD6: Brigh 6D **58**
Fox Croft La. BD16: Bgly 6E **15**
Foxhill BD17: Bail 2F **17**
Foxhill Av. BD13: B'frd 2D **40**
Foxhill Cl. BD13: B'frd 2D **40**
Foxhill Dr. BD13: B'frd 2D **40**
Foxhill Gro. BD13: B'frd 2D **40**
Foxstone Ri. BD17: Bail 2A **18**
Fox St. BD16: Bgly 2F **15**
BD19: Cleck 6D **52**
Foxwood Ho. *BD4: B'frd 4F 37*
(off Westbury St.)
Fraisthorpe Mead
BD2: B'frd 5F **29**
Frances St. BD21: Keigh 3C **6**
HD6: Brigh 4E **59**
HX5: Ell 3F **61**
Francis Cl. BD12: B'frd 3G **51**
HX1: Hal 6A **48**
Francis Ho. *BD2: B'frd 5D 28*
(off Hatfield Rd.)
Francis Sq. *BD13: B'frd 1F 23*
(off Station Rd.)
Francis St.
BD4: B'frd 4C **36** (6G **5**)
HX1: Hal 6A **48**
Franklin Ho. BD3: B'frd 2F **5**
Franklin St. HX1: Hal 6H **47**
Frank Pl. BD7: B'frd 5F **35**
Frank St. BD7: B'frd 5F **35**
HX1: Hal 1A **56**
Fraser Rd. LS28: Pud 1H **29**
Fraser St. BD8: B'frd 1G **35**
Fred Atkinson Way
BD17: Bail 4H **17**
Frederick Cl. BD10: B'frd 4B **18**
Frederick St. BD21: Keigh 4F **7**
Fred's Pl. BD4: B'frd 6E **37**
Fred St. BD21: Keigh 5D **6**
Freeman Rd. HX3: Hal 2G **57**
Free School La. HX1: Hal 2A **56**
Fremantle Gro. BD4: B'frd . . . 4G **37**
Frensham Dr. BD7: B'frd 6B **34**
Frensham Gro. BD7: B'frd 6B **34**
Frensham Way BD7: B'frd 6B **34**
Freshfield Gdns.
BD15: B'frd 6H **25**
Friar Ct. BD10: B'frd 1E **29**
Friars Ind. Est. BD10: B'frd . . . 6D **18**
FRIENDLY **2D 54**
Friendly Av. HX6: Hal 2C **54**
Friendly Fold HX3: Hal 3A **48**
Friendly Fold Ho. *HX3: Hal . . . 3A 48*
(off Lentilfield St.)
Friendly Fold Rd. HX3: Hal . . . 3A **48**
Friendly St. BD13: B'frd 3D **32**
HX3: Hal 3A **48**
Frimley Dr. BD5: B'frd 1G **43**
Frith Row BD4: B'frd 3D **44**
Frith St. BD22: Haw 5A **12**
FRIZINGHALL **2G 27**
Frizinghall Rd. BD9: B'frd 4G **27**
Frizinghall Station (Rail) **3G 27**
Frizley Gdns. BD9: B'frd 3G **27**
Frodingham Vs. BD2: B'frd . . . 5F **29**

Frogmore Av.—Goose Hill

Frogmore Av. BD12: B'frd 6B **44**
Frogmore Ter. BD12: B'frd 6B **44**
Front Vw. HX3: Hal 6A **42**
Fruit St. BD21: Keigh 3G **7**
Fulford Wlk. BD2: B'frd 5F **29**
Fullerton St.
BD3: B'frd 3C **36** (5G **5**)
Fulmar M. BD8: B'frd 2A **34**
Fulton St.
BD1: B'frd 2H **35** (4C **4**)
Furnace Gro. BD12: B'frd 6B **44**
Furnace Inn St. BD4: B'frd 4F **37**
Furnace La. BD11: B'frd 5H **45**
Furnace Rd. BD12: B'frd 6B **44**
(not continuous)
Furness Av. HX2: Hal 6F **39**
Furness Cres. HX2: Hal 6F **39**
Furness Dr. HX2: Hal 6F **39**
Furness Gdns. HX2: Hal 1G **47**
Furness Gro. HX2: Hal 1F **47**
Furness Pl. HX2: Hal 2G **47**
Fusden La. BD19: Cleck 4H **53**
Future Flds. BD6: B'frd 2C **42**
Futures Way BD4: B'frd 4B **36**
Fyfe Cres. BD17: Bail 3H **17**
Fyfe Gro. BD17: Bail 3A **18**
Fyfe La. BD17: Bail 3A **18**

G

Gables, The *BD17: Bail 3A* ***18***
(off Dewhirst Rd.)
BD17: Bail 2A **18**
(Kirklands Rd.)
BD21: Keigh 4C ***6***
(off W. Leeds St.)
Gainest HX2: Hal 2H **55**
Gain La. BD3: B'frd 6F **29**
Gainsborough Cl.
BD3: B'frd 5C **28**
GAISBY 2H **27**
Gaisby La. BD2: Ship 3G **27**
Gaisby Mt. BD18: Ship 2H **27**
Gaisby Pl. BD18: Ship 1H **27**
Gaisby Ri. BD18: Ship 1H **27**
Gala Bingo
Tong Street 2G **45**
Galefield Grn. BD6: B'frd 5D **42**
Gale St. BD21: Keigh 3E **7**
BD22: Haw 5B **12**
Gallagher Leisure Pk.
BD3: Pud 1H **37**
Galloway Rd. BD10: B'frd 6F **19**
Galsworthy Av. BD9: B'frd 4A **26**
Gannerthorpe Cl.
BD12: B'frd 2G **51**
Ganny Rd. HD6: Brigh 5F **59**
Gant Pl. BD2: B'frd 4B **28**
Gaol La. HX1: Hal 6C **48** (3C **62**)
(not continuous)
Garden Cl. BD12: B'frd 1G **51**
Gardener's Sq. HX3: Hal 5A **50**
Garden Fld. BD12: B'frd 2G **51**
Garden Fold HX3: Hal 5A **50**
Garden La. BD9: B'frd 4D **26**
Garden Rd. HD6: Brigh 3D **58**
Gardens, The BD16: Bgly 2B **16**
HX1: Hal 2C **56**
Garden St. BD9: B'frd 3D **26**
BD22: Haw 5B **12**
Garden St. Nth.
HX3: Hal 5D **48** (2D **62**)
Garden Ter. BD9: B'frd 4E **27**
Garden Vw. BD15: B'frd 1C **24**
BD16: Bgly 2A **16**
Gardiner Row BD4: B'frd 1D **44**
Garfield Av. BD8: B'frd 5F **27**
Garfield Ho. *BD5: B'frd 5H* ***35***
(off Hutson St.)
Garfield Pl. *BD15: B'frd 6G* ***25***
(off North Vw.)
Garfield St. BD15: B'frd 6G **25**
HX3: Hal 4A **48**
Garforth Rd. BD21: Keigh 3G **7**
Garforth St. BD15: B'frd 6H **25**
Gargrave Ho. BD3: B'frd 2G **5**
Garibaldi St. BD3: B'frd 2G **37**
(not continuous)
Garnett St.
BD3: B'frd 2C **36** (4G **5**)
Garrowby Ho. *BD10: B'frd 5D* ***18***
(off Thorp Gth.)
Garsdale Av. BD10: B'frd 6E **19**
Garsdale Cres. BD17: Bail 1A **18**
Gth. Barn Cl. BD9: B'frd 4E **27**
Garth Fold BD10: B'frd 5D **18**
Garthland Way BD4: B'frd 6E **37**
Garth St. BD21: Keigh 4D **6**
Garthwaite Mt. BD15: B'frd . . .5H **25**
Garton Dr. BD10: B'frd 2F **29**
Garvey Vw. BD5: B'frd 5A **36**
Garwick Ter. HX4: Hal 2D **60**
Gas Ho. Yd. BD12: B'frd 6A **44**
Gas Works La. HX5: Ell 2F **61**
Gas Works Rd. BD21: Keigh . . .3H **7**
(not continuous)
HX6: Hal 3F **55**
Gatefield Mt. BD6: B'frd 5E **43**
Ga. Head La. HX4: Hal 3A **60**
Gatenby Cl. BD6: B'frd 2C **42**
Gatesway BD16: Bgly 4A **14**
Gateways, The BD12: B'frd . . .6G **43**
Gathorne St. BD7: B'frd 5F **35**
HD6: Brigh 4F **59**
Gaukroger La. HX1: Hal 2D **56**
Gavin Cl. BD3: B'frd 2G **37**
Gawcliffe Rd. BD18: Ship 1G **27**
Gawthorpe BD16: Bgly 6F **9**
Gawthorpe Av. BD16: Bgly 6G **9**
Gawthorpe Dr. BD16: Bgly 6G **9**
Gawthorpe La. BD16: Bgly . . .1G **15**
Gayle Cl. BD12: B'frd 3G **51**
Gaynor St.
BD1: B'frd 2H **35** (2A **4**)
Gaythorne Rd. BD2: B'frd 4E **29**
BD5: B'frd 6A **36**
Gaythorne Ter. BD14: B'frd . . .5A **34**
HX3: Hal 4A **50**
Geelong Cl. BD2: B'frd 4B **28**
George Sq.
HX1: Hal 6C **48** (4B **62**)
George's Sq. BD13: B'frd 1F **23**
BD21: Keigh 5D **6**
George's St. HX3: Hal 2H **47**
George St.
BD1: B'frd 3B **36** (5F **5**)
BD13: B'frd 6G **23**
(Foster Pk.)
BD13: B'frd 3D **32**
(James St.)
BD17: Bail 4G **17**
BD18: Ship 5D **16**
BD19: Cleck 5F **53**
HD6: Brigh 5G **59**
(Armytage Rd.)
HD6: Brigh 6E **59**
(Bryant St.)
HX1: Hal 6C **48** (4B **62**)
HX3: Hal 6B **50**
HX4: Hal 2D **60**
HX5: Ell 3F **61**
HX6: Hal 4D **54**
Geraldton Av. BD2: B'frd 4A **28**
Gerard Ho. *BD10: B'frd 6E* ***19***
(off Fairhaven Grn.)
Gerard St.
HX1: Hal 6B **48** (4A **62**)
Ghyll, The BD16: Bgly 5G **15**
Ghyll Dr. BD22: Haw 1G **21**
Ghyll Lodge BD16: Bgly 5G **15**
Ghyll Wood Dr. BD16: Bgly 5G **15**
Gibbet, The *3A* ***62***
Gibbet St.
HX1: Hal 6A **48** (4A **62**)
HX2: Hal 6F **47**
Gibb La. HX2: Hal 2D **46**
Gibraltar HX1: Hal 1G **55**
Gibraltar Av. HX1: Hal 1G **55**
Gibraltar Rd. HX1: Hal 6G **47**
Gibson St. BD3: B'frd 3D **36**
Giles Hill La. HX3: Hal 4G **41**
(not continuous)
Giles St. BD5: B'frd 4H **35**
BD6: B'frd 2E **43**
Giles' Wlk. BD16: Bgly 3A **16**
Gill Beck Cl. BD17: Bail 1A **18**
Gillingham Grn. BD4: B'frd . . .6G **37**
Gill La. BD13: B'frd 4C **32**
BD22: Keigh 1E **11**
LS19: Yead 1G **19**
Gillrene Av. BD15: B'frd 3D **24**
Gillroyd Ri. BD7: B'frd 2F **35**
Gill's Ct. HX1: Hal 6C **48** (4C **62**)
Gillstone Dr. BD22: Haw 6H **11**
Gilmour St. HX3: Hal 4A **48**
Gilpin St. BD3: B'frd 1D **36**
GILSTEAD 1A **16**
Gilstead Ct. BD16: Bgly 2A **16**
Gilstead Dr. BD16: Bgly 2A **16**
Gilstead La. BD16: Bgly 2H **15**
Gilynda Cl. BD8: B'frd 2C **34**
Gipsy St. BD3: B'frd 1G **37**
GIRLINGTON 6E **27**
Girlington Rd. BD8: B'frd 6D **26**
Gisburn St. BD21: Keigh 3D **6**
Glade, The BD17: Bail 3D **16**
LS28: Pud 5H **29**
Gladstone Pl. BD13: B'frd 1F **31**
BD22: Keigh 3H ***11***
(off Keighley Rd.)
Gladstone Rd. HX1: Hal 6A **48**
Gladstone St. BD3: B'frd 3E **37**
BD13: B'frd 2F **41**
BD15: B'frd 6H **25**
BD16: Bgly 3F **15**
BD19: Cleck 6F **53**
BD21: Keigh 5D **6**
HX4: Hal 5A **60**
Gladstone Vw. HX3: Hal 4E **57**
Glaisdale Ct. BD15: B'frd 4G **25**
Glaisdale Gro. HX3: Hal 6B **50**
Glastonbury Ct. BD4: B'frd . . .4F **37**
Glazier Rd. BD13: B'frd 1C **40**
Gleanings Av. HX2: Hal 6E **47**
Gleanings Dr. HX2: Hal 6D **46**
Glebe Fold BD20: Keigh 1H **7**
Glebe Gdns. HX1: Hal 2A **56**
Gledcliffe HX3: Hal 2D **62**
Gleddings Cl. HX3: Hal 4A **56**
Gledhill Rd. BD3: B'frd 3D **36**
Gledhills Yd. *HX1: Hal 2H* ***55***
(off King Cross Rd.)
Gledhow Dr. BD22: Oxen 3G **21**
Glenaire BD18: Ship 4A **18**
Glenaire Dr. BD17: Bail 4E **17**
Glenbrook Dr. BD7: B'frd 2C **34**
Glencoe HX3: Hal 5A **42**
Glendale BD16: Bgly 6F **15**
(Beckfield Rd.)
BD16: Bgly 2A **16**
(Gilstead La.)
Glendale Cl. BD6: B'frd 4E **43**
Glendale Dr. BD6: B'frd 4E **43**
Glendale Studio 2A **56**
Glendare Av. BD7: B'frd 3D **34**
Glendare Rd. BD7: B'frd 3D **34**
Glendare Ter. BD7: B'frd 3D **34**
Glendene BD16: Bgly 6F **15**
Glen Eagles Cl. BD4: B'frd . . .3D **44**
Glenfield BD18: Ship 4A **18**
HX4: Hal 2B **60**
Glenfield Av. BD6: B'frd 3H **43**
Glenfield Mt. BD6: B'frd 3H **43**
Glenfield Pl. HX6: Hal 1E **55**
Glen Gth. BD21: Keigh 6F **7**
Glenholm BD18: Ship 4A **18**
Glenholme Heath HX1: Hal . . .6G **47**
Glenholme Pk. BD14: B'frd . . .6A **34**
Glenholme Rd. BD8: B'frd 6F **27**
Glenholm Rd. BD17: Bail 3G **17**
Glenhurst BD4: B'frd 2F **45**
Glenhurst Av. BD21: Keigh 6E **7**
Glenhurst Dr. BD21: Keigh 6F **7**
Glenhurst Gro. BD21: Keigh 6F **7**
Glenhurst Rd. BD18: Ship 5C **16**
Glen Lea HX6: Hal 2D **54**
Glen Lee La. BD21: Keigh 1F **13**
Glenlee Rd. BD7: B'frd 2D **34**
Glenlyon Av. BD20: Keigh 2C **6**
Glenlyon Dr. BD20: Keigh 2C **6**
Glenmore Cl. BD2: B'frd 6E **29**
Glen Mt. HX3: Hal 3G **47**
Glenmount BD16: Bgly 6F **15**
Glen Mt. Cl. HX3: Hal 3G **47**
Glen Ri. BD17: Bail 3D **16**
Glen Rd. BD16: Bgly 1A **16**
BD17: Bail 1B **16**
Glenrose Dr. BD7: B'frd 3C **34**
Glen Royd HX4: Hal 5A **60**
Glenroyd BD18: Ship 4A **18**
Glenroyd Av. BD6: B'frd 3H **43**
Glenside Av. BD18: Ship 4A **18**
Glenside Rd. BD18: Ship 4A **18**
Glenstone Gro. BD7: B'frd . . .2D **34**
Glen Ter. HX1: Hal 2B **56**
HX3: Hal 6A ***50***
(off Waverley Cres.)
Glenton Sq. BD9: B'frd 5F **27**
Glen Vw. BD16: Bgly 4B **14**
HX1: Hal 2B **56**
Glenview Av. BD9: B'frd 4C **26**
Glenview Cl. BD18: Ship 6A **16**
Glenview Dr. BD18: Ship 1A **26**
Glenview Gro. BD18: Ship 6B **16**
Glen Vw. Rd. BD16: Bgly 6H **9**
Glenview Rd. BD18: Ship 1A **26**
Glenview Ter. BD18: Ship 5D **16**
Glen Way BD16: Bgly 1B **16**
Glenwood Av. BD17: Bail 4C **16**
Globe Fold BD8: B'frd 1G **35**
Gloucester Av. BD3: B'frd 6F **29**
Gloucester Rd. BD16: Bgly . . .3H **15**
Glover Ct. BD5: B'frd 5A **36**
Glydegate
BD5: B'frd 3A **36** (5C **4**)
Glyndon Ct. HD6: Brigh 6F **59**
Glynn Ter. BD8: B'frd 1F **35**
G Mill Yd. *HX1: Hal 2B* ***62***
(off Corporation St.)
Gobind Marg
BD3: B'frd 2C **36** (4G **5**)
Godfrey Rd. HX3: Hal 5C **56**
Godfrey St. BD8: B'frd 2B **34**
Godley Branch Rd.
HX3: Hal 5E **49**
Godley Gdns. HX3: Hal 4F **49**
Godley La. HX3: Hal 5E **49**
Godley Rd. HX3: Hal 5D **48**
Godwin St.
BD1: B'frd 2A **36** (4C **4**)
Goff Well La. BD16: Keigh 2E **13**
BD21: Keigh 2E **13**
Gog Hill HX5: Ell 2F **61**
Goit Side BD1: B'frd . . .2H **35** (4B **4**)
(not continuous)
HX2: Hal 1A **46**
Goit Stock La. BD16: Bgly 5B **14**
Goit Stock Ter. BD16: Bgly . . .5B **14**
Goldcrest Av. BD8: B'frd 2H **33**
Golden Vw. Dr. BD21: Keigh . . .5H **7**
Goldfields Av. HX4: Hal 1B **60**
Goldfields Cl. HX4: Hal 1B **60**
Goldfields Vw. HX4: Hal 1B **60**
Goldfields Way HX4: Hal 1B **60**
Golf Av. HX2: Hal 6E **47**
Golf Cres. HX2: Hal 6E **47**
Gomersal La. BD19: Cleck . . .6H **53**
Gondal Ct. BD5: B'frd 6G **35**
Gooder La. HD6: Brigh 6E **59**
Gooder St. HD6: Brigh 5E **59**
GOODLEY 2G **11**
Goodwin Ho. *BD13: B'frd 2E* ***41***
(off Minstrel Dr.)
Goose Cote La.
BD22: Keigh 2A **12**
Goose Cote Way
BD22: Keigh 2A **12**
Goosedale Ct. BD4: B'frd 2H **45**
GOOSE HILL 1D **44**

Goose Nest La.—Gresham Av.

Goose Nest La. HX6: Hal 5D **54**
Goose Pond La. HX6: Hal 6G **55**
Gordon St. BD5: B'frd 4B **36**
BD14: B'frd 5H **33**
BD21: Keigh 4D **6**
BD22: Haw 5A **12**
HX3: Hal 3B **48**
HX5: Ell 3F **61**
HX6: Hal 4C **54**
Gordon Ter. BD10: B'frd 4D **18**
Gorse Av. BD17: Bail 4C **16**
Gothic St. BD13: B'frd 2E **41**
Gotts Ter. BD20: Keigh 1C **6**
Gott St. BD22: Haw 5B **12**
Goulbourne St. BD21: Keigh . . .5D **6**
Gower St. BD5: B'frd 5A **36**
Gracechurch St.
BD8: B'frd 1H **35** (2A **4**)
Grace St. BD21: Keigh 4F **7**
Gracey La. BD6: B'frd 2D **42**
Grady Cl. BD10: B'frd 1D **28**
Grafton Cl. BD17: Bail 1H **17**
Grafton Pl. HX3: Hal 2A **48**
Grafton Rd. BD21: Keigh 6C **6**
Grafton St. BD5: B'frd 4A **36**
BD21: Keigh 6D **6**
Graham St. BD9: B'frd 5E **27**
Grain St. BD5: B'frd 1F **43**
Grammar School St.
BD1: B'frd 1A **36** (2C **4**)
Granary Ct. BD2: B'frd 2E **29**
Granby Dr. BD20: Keigh 2H **7**
Granby La. BD20: Keigh 2H **7**
Granby St.
BD4: B'frd 4B **36** (6E **5**)
(not continuous)
BD13: B'frd 2E **41**
Grandage Ter. BD8: B'frd 1F **35**
Grandsmere Pl. HX3: Hal 3B **56**
Grand Vw. BD13: B'frd 6C **32**
HX3: Hal 4A 48
(off Ovenden Av.)
HX6: Hal 4D 54
(off Clyde St.)
Grange, The HX3: Hal 4B **56**
Grange Av. BD3: Pud 1H **37**
BD4: B'frd 3H **45**
BD15: B'frd 1A **34**
BD18: Ship 5C **16**
HX2: Hal 6H **39**
Grange Bank HX3: Hal 5A **42**
Grange Cotts. BD13: B'frd 1G **23**
BD19: Cleck 5E 53
(off Whitcliffe Rd.)
Grange Ct. BD16: Bgly 6G **15**
HX3: Hal 4G **57**
Grange Cres. BD20: Keigh 2G **7**
Grange Dr. BD15: B'frd 1A **34**
Grange Fold BD15: B'frd 1H **33**
Grange Gro. BD3: Pud 1H **37**
BD20: Keigh 2G **7**
Grange Hgts. HX3: Hal 4G **57**
Grange La. BD22: Keigh 2C **10**
HD6: Brigh 5H **59**
Grange Pk. BD17: Bail 2A **18**
HX3: Hal 4B **56**
Grange Pk. Dr. BD16: Bgly . . .5G **15**
Grange Pk. Rd. BD16: Bgly . . .5G **15**
Grange Rd. BD15: B'frd 1A **34**
BD16: Bgly 1H **15**
BD19: Cleck 5E **53**
BD20: Keigh 2G **7**
Grange Sports Cen. 1F **43**
Grange St. BD21: Keigh 3E **7**
HX3: Hal 4A **48**
Grange Ter. BD15: B'frd 1A **34**
BD18: Ship 1F **27**
Grange Vw. BD3: Pud 1H **37**
Grange Way BD15: B'frd 1A **34**
Grange Yd. *HX6: Hal 3E 55*
(off Wharf St.)
Granny Hall Gro.
HD6: Brigh 3D **58**
Granny Hall La.
HD6: Brigh 3D **58**
Granny Hall Pk.
HD6: Brigh 3D **58**
Granny Hill HX2: Hal 2G **55**
Grantham Pl. BD7: B'frd 4G **35**
HX3: Hal 3B **48**
Grantham Rd.
BD7: B'frd 4G **35** (6A **4**)
HX3: Hal 3B **48**
Grantham Ter. BD7: B'frd 4G **35**
Granton St. BD3: B'frd 2E **37**
Grant St. BD3: B'frd . . .2C **36** (3H **5**)
BD21: Keigh 4C **6**
BD22: Oxen 5G **21**
Granville Pl. BD15: B'frd 6H **25**
Granville Rd. BD9: B'frd 2F **27**
BD18: B'frd 2F **27**
Granville St. BD14: B'frd 4A **34**
BD21: Keigh 4D 6
(off Drewery Rd.)
HX5: Ell 3F **61**
Granville Ter. BD16: Bgly 2G **15**
BD18: Ship 2F **27**
Grape St. BD15: B'frd 6A **26**
BD21: Keigh 3G **7**
HX1: Hal 6B **48** (3A **62**)
Grasleigh Av. BD15: B'frd 5G **25**
Grasleigh Way BD15: B'frd . . .5F **25**
Grasmere Dr. HX5: Ell 2H **61**
Grasmere Pl. HX3: Hal 1A **48**
Grasmere Rd. BD2: B'frd 4C **28**
BD12: Cleck 4A **52**
Grass Rd. BD20: Keigh 1D **8**
Grassy Bottoms HX6: Hal 6B **54**
Gratrix La. HX6: Hal 2E **55**
Grattan Rd.
BD1: B'frd 2H **35** (4A **4**)
Gray Av. BD18: Ship 2H **27**
Grayshon Dr. BD6: B'frd 2G **43**
Grayswood Cres.
BD4: B'frd 6F **37**
Grayswood Dr. BD4: B'frd 5F **37**
Gt. Albion St.
HX1: Hal 6C **48** (3B **62**)
Gt. Cross St.
BD1: B'frd 3B **36** (5E **5**)
Gt. Edge Rd. HX2: Hal 6B **46**
Greater Elland Historical Society
. . . .*2F 61*
(off Northgate)
GREAT HORTON 5E **35**
Gt. Horton Rd.
BD7: B'frd 1B **42** (6A **4**)
Gt. Northern Rd.
BD21: Keigh 5E **7**
Gt. Russell Ct. BD7: B'frd 2G **35**
Gt. Russell St. BD7: B'frd 2F **35**
Greave Ho. Flds. HX2: Hal . . .5A **46**
Greaves Fold HX4: Hal 5C **60**
Greaves Pl. HX4: Hal 5C **60**
Greaves St. BD5: B'frd 6H **35**
Grebe Cl. BD13: B'frd 2A **42**
Green, The BD4: B'frd 4H **45**
BD10: B'frd 5D **18**
BD16: Bgly 5G **9**
(College Rd.)
BD16: Bgly 2B **16**
(Gardens, The)
BD16: Bgly 4E **9**
(Victoria St.)
Greenacre Av. BD12: B'frd . . .3H **51**
Green Acre Cl. BD17: Bail 2H **17**
Greenacre Cl. BD12: B'frd 3H **51**
Greenacre Dr. BD12: B'frd . . .3H **51**
Greenacres HX3: Hal 5B **42**
Greenacres Av. HX3: Hal 5B **42**
Greenacres Dr. BD20: Keigh . . .2C **6**
HX3: Hal 5B **42**
Greenacres Gro. HX3: Hal 5B **42**
Greenacre Way
BD12: B'frd 3H **51**
Greenaire Pl.
BD1: B'frd 2H **35** (4B **4**)
Green Bank BD19: Cleck 6H **53**
Greenbank BD17: Bail 4F **17**
Greenbank Rd. BD15: B'frd . . .1A **34**
Greencliffe Av. BD17: Bail 2F **17**
Green Cl. BD8: B'frd 1C **34**
Green Ct. BD7: B'frd 4D **34**
BD19: Cleck 5B **52**
Greencroft Av. HX3: Hal 2H **49**
Greencroft Cl. BD10: B'frd 6C **18**
GREEN END 2E **9**
Green End BD14: B'frd 5H **33**
HD6: Brigh 6E **59**
Grn. End Rd. BD6: B'frd 3F **43**
BD20: Keigh 2E **9**
Greenfell Cl. BD22: Keigh 5B **6**
Greenfield BD22: Haw 6G **11**
Greenfield Av. BD18: Ship . . .1G **27**
HX3: Hal 6E **51**
Greenfield Cl. HX3: Hal 2G **49**
Greenfield Ct. BD21: Keigh 4C **6**
Greenfield Cres.
BD13: B'frd 1G **23**
Greenfield Dr. BD19: Cleck . . .5B **52**
Greenfield La. BD4: B'frd 5D **44**
BD7: B'frd 5D **34**
BD10: B'frd 4D **18**
Greenfield Pl. BD8: B'frd 6G **27**
HX3: Hal 6E **51**
Greenfield Ter. BD22: Haw . . .6G **11**
Greenfinch Way
BD15: B'frd 2H **33**
Green Fold BD17: Bail 3F **17**
Greengate Rd. BD21: Keigh 5E **7**
GREENGATES 6G **19**
Greengates Av. BD12: B'frd . . .4G **51**
Green Hall Pk. HX3: Hal 6B **42**
Greenhead Athletics Track . . .2D **6**
Green Head Av. BD20: Keigh . . .1C **6**
Green Head Dr. BD20: Keigh . . .1C **6**
Green Head La. BD20: Keigh . . .1C **6**
Green Head Rd.
BD20: Keigh 1C **6**
Green Hill HX2: Hal 1D **54**
Greenhill Dr. BD16: Bgly 4E **9**
Greenhill La. BD3: B'frd 2E **37**
BD16: Bgly 5F **9**
Grn. Hill Pk. HX3: Hal 3B **42**
Greenhill St. BD3: B'frd 2E **37**
Greenholme Ct. BD4: B'frd . . .1H **45**
Greenland Av. BD13: B'frd 3E **41**
Greenland Vs. BD13: B'frd . . .3E **41**
Green La. BD2: B'frd 4F **29**
BD7: B'frd 4E **35**
BD8: B'frd 6G **27** (1A **4**)
BD10: B'frd 5E **19**
(Apperley Rd.)
BD10: B'frd 6C **18**
(Sandhill Fold)
BD12: B'frd 3F **51**
(Huddersfield Rd.)
BD12: B'frd 1B **52**
(Walker Rd.)
BD13: B'frd 3E **33**
(Bronte Old Rd.)
BD13: B'frd 5E **41**
(Corporal La.)
BD13: B'frd 1B **40**
(White Castle Ct.)
BD17: Bail 4E **17**
(Green Rd., not continuous)
BD17: Bail 1E **17**
(Somerset Av.)
BD19: Cleck 3F **53**
BD22: Keigh 3H **11**
(Keighley Rd.)
BD22: Keigh 1D **10**
(Whitehill Rd.)
BD22: Oxen 5C **20**
(Bodkin La.)
BD22: Oxen 6H **21**
(Isle La.)
HD6: Brigh 2C **58**
HX2: Hal 3G **39**
(Pavement La.)
HX2: Hal 2G **55**
(Ryburn Vw.)
HX3: Hal 1E **57**
(Bank Top)
Green La. HX3: Hal 6E **41**
(Paddock Rd.)
HX3: Hal 4B **42**
(Soaper La.)
HX3: Hal 5B **42**
(Willow Pk. Dr.)
HX4: Hal 3C **60**
Green La. Ho. HX4: Hal 3C **60**
Greenley Hill BD15: B'frd 3B **24**
Green Mdw. BD15: B'frd 3D **24**
Green Mt. BD4: B'frd 6F **37**
BD17: Bail 3E **17**
HX3: Hal 2D **50**
Green Mt. Retail Pk.
HX1: Hal 6B **48** (3A **62**)
Green Mt. Rd. BD13: B'frd . . .3E **33**
Green Pk. Av. HX3: Hal 5C **56**
Green Pk. Dr. HX3: Hal 5C **56**
Green Pk. Ga. HX3: Hal 5C **56**
Green Pk. Rd. HX3: Hal 5C **56**
Green Pk. St. HX3: Hal 4C **56**
Green Pl. BD2: B'frd 5D **28**
Green Rd. BD17: Bail 3E **17**
Green Row BD10: B'frd 1D **28**
Green Royd HX2: Hal 1D **46**
HX3: Hal 3E **51**
HX4: Hal 3C **60**
(not continuous)
Greenroyd Av. BD19: Cleck . . .3F **53**
HX3: Hal 4B **56**
Greenroyd Cl. HX3: Hal 5B **56**
Greenroyd Cres. HX2: Hal 4H **47**
Greenroyd La. HX2: Hal 4G **47**
Greenroyd Ter. HX3: Hal 5C **56**
Greens Health & Fitness 4H **17**
GREEN SIDE 2D **34**
Greenside BD12: B'frd 1C **52**
BD14: B'frd 5H **33**
BD19: Cleck 6G **53**
Greenside La. BD8: B'frd 2D **34**
BD13: B'frd 1F **23**
Greenside Pk. BD8: B'frd 2D **34**
Green's Sq. HX2: Hal 5G **47**
Green's Ter. BD12: B'frd 1B **52**
Green St. BD1: B'frd . . .2B **36** (4F **5**)
BD12: B'frd 6D **44**
BD22: Haw 1G **21**
BD22: Oxen 5G **21**
HX4: Hal 5C **60**
Green Ter. *BD2: B'frd 5D 28*
(off Idle Rd.)
Green Ter. Sq. HX1: Hal 2A **56**
Greenthwaite Cl.
BD20: Keigh 2C **6**
Greenton Av. BD19: Cleck 4A **52**
Greenton Cres. BD13: B'frd . . .3D **40**
Green Top St. BD8: B'frd 2C **34**
Greentrees BD6: B'frd 5F **43**
Greenups Mill *HX6: Hal 3E 55*
(off Old Cawsey)
Greenups Ter. HX6: Hal 3D **54**
Greenville Dr. BD12: B'frd 4A **44**
Green Way HX2: Hal 3G **39**
Greenway
BD3: B'frd 1C **36** (1G **5**)
Greenway Dr. BD15: B'frd 2H **33**
Greenway Rd. BD5: B'frd 1A **44**
Greenwell Row
BD14: B'frd 5H **33**
Greenwood Av. BD2: B'frd 2C **28**
Greenwood Ct.
BD1: B'frd 3A **36** (5E **5**)
Greenwood Dr. BD2: B'frd . . .3C **28**
Greenwood Mt. BD2: B'frd . . .3C **28**
Greenwood Rd. BD17: Bail . . .4F **17**
Greenwood's Ter. HX3: Hal . . .4H **47**
GREETLAND 2B **60**
Greetland Community &
Sports Cen. 2A **60**
Gregory Ct. BD14: B'frd 5A **34**
Gregory Cres. BD7: B'frd 1C **42**
Grenfell Dr. BD3: B'frd 1F **37**
Grenfell Rd. BD3: B'frd 1F **37**
Grenfell Ter. BD3: B'frd 1F **37**
Gresham Av. BD2: B'frd 3B **28**

Hions Cl.—Iddesleigh St.

Hions Cl. HD6: Brigh ... 6E **59**
HIPPERHOLME ... 5B **50**
Hipswell St. BD3: B'frd ... 1E **37**
Hird Av. BD6: B'frd ... 3G **43**
Hird Rd. BD12: B'frd ... 5H **43**
Hird St. BD17: Ship ... 5F **17**
BD21: Keigh ... 6C **6**
(not continuous)
Hirst Fold *BD12: B'frd ... 2G **51***
(off Town Ga.)
Hirst La. BD18: Ship ... 4C **16**
Hirst Lodge Ct. BD2: B'frd ... 2B **28**
Hirst Mill Cres. BD18: Ship ... 4C **16**
Hirst Wood Cres.
BD18: Ship ... 5C **16**
Hirst Wood Rd. BD18: Ship ... 5B **16**
Hive St. BD22: Keigh ... 5C **6**
Hobb End BD13: B'frd ... 1C **32**
Hob Cote La. BD22: Keigh ... 4D **10**
Hob Hill BD22: Haw ... 1A **20**
Hob La. BD22: Haw ... 6A **10**
HX6: Hal ... 6D **54**
Hobson Fold BD12: B'frd ... 3H **51**
Hockney Rd. BD8: B'frd ... 1F **35**
Hockney Rd. Ind. Est.
BD8: B'frd ... 1F **35**
Hodgson Av. BD3: B'frd ... 1F **37**
Hodgson Fold BD2: B'frd ... 3B **28**
Hodgson Yd. BD2: B'frd ... 2E **29**
Holborn Ct. BD12: B'frd ... 5G **43**
Holby Bus. Pk. HX6: Hal ... 4D **54**
Holden La. BD17: Bail ... 1H **17**
(not continuous)
BD22: Oxen ... 6D **20**
Holden Rd. BD6: B'frd ... 2F **43**
HOLDSWORTH ... 5A **40**
Holdsworth Bldgs.
*BD2: B'frd ... 3F **29***
(off Elvey Cl.)
*BD12: B'frd ... 1G **51***
(off Huddersfield Rd.)
Holdsworth Ct. BD19: Cleck ... 6F **53**
Holdsworth Rd. HX2: Hal ... 4A **40**
Holdsworth Sq. BD2: B'frd ... 3F **29**
Holdsworth St.
BD1: B'frd ... 1B **36** (2E **5**)
BD18: Ship ... 1G **27**
BD19: Cleck ... 5F **53**
Holdsworth Ter. HX1: Hal ... 2D **56**
Holdsworth Yd. *BD1: B'frd ... 4B **4***
(off Thornton Rd.)
Hole BD22: Haw ... 1F **21**
Holker St. BD8: B'frd ... 1F **35**
BD21: Keigh ... 3E **7**
Hollas La. HX6: Hal ... 5G **55**
(not continuous)
Hollin Cl. La. BD2: B'frd ... 4A **28**
(not continuous)
Hollin Ct. BD18: Ship ... 1G **27**
Holling Gro. HX6: Hal ... 2C **54**
Hollin Greaves La.
HX3: Hal ... 4D **48**
Hollings Rd. BD8: B'frd ... 6F **27**
Hollings Sq. BD8: B'frd ... 1F **35**
Hollings St. BD8: B'frd ... 1F **35**
BD16: Bgly ... 6H **15**
Hollings Ter. BD8: B'frd ... 1F **35**
Hollingwood Av. BD7: B'frd ... 5D **34**
Hollingwood Ct. BD7: B'frd ... 6C **34**
Hollingwood Dr. BD7: B'frd ... 5C **34**
Hollingwood La. BD7: B'frd ... 6B **34**
Hollingwood Mt.
BD7: B'frd ... 5C **34**
Hollin Hall Rd. BD18: Ship ... 1C **26**
Hollin Head BD17: Bail ... 1B **18**
Hollin La. BD18: Ship ... 1H **27**
HX6: Hal ... 6D **54**
Hollin Ri. BD18: Ship ... 1G **27**
Hollin Rd. BD18: Ship ... 1G **27**
Hollins HX6: Hal ... 6A **54**
Hollins, The HX6: Hal ... 3D **54**
Hollins Bank HX6: Hal ... 3D **54**
Hollins Cl. BD20: Keigh ... 1B **6**
Hollins Hey Rd. HX5: Hal ... 5D **60**
Hollins Hill BD17: Bail ... 1C **18**
Hollins La. BD20: Keigh ... 1B **6**
HX2: Hal ... 6E **39**
HX6: Hal ... 2C **54**
Hollins Mill La. HX6: Hal ... 3C **54**
Hollins Ter. HX6: Hal ... 6A **54**
Hollin St. HX6: Hal ... 6A **54**
Hollin Ter. BD18: Ship ... 1G **27**
Hollin Wood Cl.
BD18: Ship ... 6C **16**
Hollinwood Vw. BD16: Bgly ... 4D **8**
Hollowfield Cft.
BD12: B'frd ... 6D **44**
Holly Bank HX5: Ell ... 4E **61**
Holly Bank Ct. HX3: Hal ... 5B **50**
Holly Bank Dr. HX3: Hal ... 5B **50**
Hollybank Gdns. BD7: B'frd ... 6C **34**
Hollybank Gro. BD7: B'frd ... 6C **34**
Hollybank Rd. BD7: B'frd ... 6C **34**
Hollycroft St. BD21: Keigh ... 5D **6**
Holly Gro. HX1: Hal ... 1A **56**
HX2: Hal ... 1A **46**
Holly Hall La. BD12: B'frd ... 1G **51**
Holly Mt. *HX3: Hal ... 2E **57***
(off High Gro. La.)
Hollynsmill HX4: Hal ... 2D **60**
Hollyns Ter. HX4: Hal ... 2D **60**
Holly Pk. Dr. BD7: B'frd ... 5C **34**
Holly Pk. Gro. BD7: B'frd ... 5C **34**
Holly Royd HX3: Hal ... 3A **58**
Holly St. BD6: B'frd ... 1B **42**
Holly Vw. HX6: Hal ... 6A **54**
Hollywood Bowl
Bradford ... 3B **36** (5E **5**)
Holme Bank BD4: B'frd ... 5H **37**
Holmecarr Ct. BD16: Bgly ... 1G **15**
Holme Dr. HX2: Hal ... 1D **54**
Holmefield Vw. BD4: B'frd ... 5H **37**
Holme Ho. La.
BD22: Keigh ... 1F **11** & 6A **6**
(not continuous)
HX2: Hal ... 1A **46**
Holme La. BD4: B'frd ... 6H **37**
Holme Mill La. BD22: Keigh ... 5B **6**
Holme Rd. HX2: Hal ... 1D **54**
Holmes Rd. HX6: Hal ... 3E **55**
Holmes St.
BD1: B'frd ... 1H **35** (2A **4**)
Holme's Ter. HX2: Hal ... 5G **47**
Holme St. BD5: B'frd ... 5H **35**
BD22: Oxen ... 5G **21**
HX3: Hal ... 6E **51**
HOLME TOP ... 5H **35**
Holme Top La. BD5: B'frd ... 5H **35**
Holme Top St. BD5: B'frd ... 5H **35**
HOLME VILLAGE ... 6H **37**
HOLME WOOD ... 6F **37**
Holme Wood BD22: Keigh ... 5C **6**
Holme Wood Rd.
BD4: B'frd ... 6F **37**
BD22: Keigh ... 5B **6**
HOLMFIELD ... 6A **40**
Holmfield BD22: Oxen ... 6G **21**
Holmfield Ct. BD1: B'frd ... 4B **4**
Holmfield Gdns. HX2: Hal ... 6A **40**
Holmfield Ho. HX3: Hal ... 6A **40**
Holmfield Ind. Est.
HX2: Hal ... 4A **40**
Holmfield Ind. Est. Rd.
HX2: Hal ... 5A **40**
Holmfield St.
BD1: B'frd ... 2H **35** (4B **4**)
Holroyd Hill BD6: B'frd ... 2G **43**
Holroyd Mill La. BD16: Bgly ... 3E **9**
Holroyd Sq. HX4: Hal ... 5A **60**
Holsworthy Rd. BD4: B'frd ... 1G **45**
Holt, The BD18: Ship ... 5G **17**
Holtby Gro. HX3: Hal ... 6E **51**
Holt Gdns. BD10: B'frd ... 5C **18**
Holts La. BD14: B'frd ... 4H **33**
Holts Ter. HX3: Hal ... 3D **56**
Holybrook Av. BD10: B'frd ... 1F **29**
HOLY CROFT ... 5D **6**
Holyoake Av. BD16: Bgly ... 4F **15**
Holywell Ash La.
BD8: B'frd ... 6H **27**
HOLYWELL GREEN ... 5B **60**
Holywell Hall HX4: Hal ... 5B **60**
Home Farm Cl. BD6: B'frd ... 2B **42**
Home Vw. Ter. BD8: B'frd ... 6F **27**
Honey Pot BD15: B'frd ... 4C **24**
Honey Pot La. BD17: Bail ... 2E **17**
Hoopoe M. BD15: B'frd ... 2H **33**
Hopbine Av. BD5: B'frd ... 1A **44**
Hopbine Rd. BD5: B'frd ... 1A **44**
Hope Av. BD5: B'frd ... 1G **43**
BD18: Ship ... 5H **17**
Hopefield Way BD5: B'frd ... 2D **44**
Hope Hall St.
HX1: Hal ... 1C **56** (6C **62**)
Hope Hall Ter. HX1: Hal ... 6C **62**
Hope Hill Vw. BD16: Bgly ... 6G **15**
Hope La. BD17: Bail ... 1F **17**
Hope Pl. BD21: Keigh ... 6E **7**
Hope St. HX1: Hal ... 6B **48** (3A **62**)
HX3: Hal ... 1H **49**
HX6: Hal ... 4D **54**
Hope Vw. BD18: Ship ... 6H **17**
Hopkinson Bldgs. *HX3: Hal ... 2H **47***
(off Foundry St. Nth.)
Hopkinson Dr. BD4: B'frd ... 3E **45**
Hopkinson St. HX3: Hal ... 2H **47**
Hopkin St. BD4: B'frd ... 2G **45**
Hops La. HX3: Hal ... 3F **47**
Hopton Av. BD4: B'frd ... 2D **44**
Hopwood La.
HX1: Hal ... 1G **55** (5A **62**)
(not continuous)
Horley Grn. La. HX3: Hal ... 4E **49**
Horley Grn. Rd. HX3: Hal ... 4E **49**
Hornbeam Cl. BD15: B'frd ... 3F **25**
Hornby St. HX1: Hal ... 1H **55**
Hornby Ter. HX1: Hal ... 1H **55**
Horncastle St. BD19: Cleck ... 6G **53**
Horner's Bldgs. *HX2: Hal ... 6A **40***
(off Shay La.)
Horners Fold BD20: Keigh ... 2D **8**
Horne St. HX1: Hal ... 6B **48**
Hornsea Dr. BD15: B'frd ... 3C **24**
Horse Cl. BD12: B'frd ... 1E **51**
Horseshoe Ct. BD15: B'frd ... 3B **24**
Horsfall Stadium ... 4F **43**
Horsfall St. HX1: Hal ... 2A **56**
Horsham Ct. BD22: Keigh ... 6A **6**
Horsham Rd. BD4: B'frd ... 1G **45**
Horsley Fold HD6: Brigh ... 5H **59**
Horsley St. BD6: B'frd ... 2G **43**
Horsman St. BD4: B'frd ... 2G **45**
HORTON BANK ... 6B **34**
HORTON BANK BOTTOM ... 1E **43**
Horton Bank Country Pk. ... 6B **34**
Horton Grange Rd.
BD7: B'frd ... 3F **35**
Horton Hall Cl. BD5: B'frd ... 4H **35**
Horton Ind. Est. BD7: B'frd ... 6E **35**
Horton Pk. Av. BD7: B'frd ... 4F **35**
Horton Pl. HX2: Hal ... 3H **39**
Horton St.
HX1: Hal ... 1C **56** (5C **62**)
Horton Ter. HX3: Hal ... 5H **49**
Hospital Rd. BD20: Keigh ... 2H **7**
Hough HX3: Hal ... 4F **49**
Houghton Pl.
BD1: B'frd ... 1H **35** (2B **4**)
Houghton St. HD6: Brigh ... 4F **59**
Houghton Towers HX6: Hal ... 3D **54**
Hougomont BD13: B'frd ... 6C **32**
Hoults La. HX4: Hal ... 1B **60**
HOVE EDGE ... 2D **58**
Howard Pk. BD19: Cleck ... 6G **53**
Howards Dean BD22: Haw ... 5H **11**
Howard St.
BD5: B'frd ... 3H **35** (6B **4**)
HX1: Hal ... 5A **48**
Howarth Av. BD2: B'frd ... 2C **28**
Howarth Cres. BD2: B'frd ... 2C **28**
Howbeck Av. BD20: Keigh ... 2A **8**
Howbeck Dr. BD20: Keigh ... 3A **8**
Howcans La. HX3: Hal ... 6A **40**
Howden Av. BD20: Keigh ... 1C **6**
Howdenbrook HX3: B'frd ... 4C **42**
Howden Cl. BD4: B'frd ... 2H **45**
Howes La. HX3: Hal ... 2F **49**
Howgate BD10: B'frd ... 5E **19**
Howgate Hill HX3: Hal ... 2F **57**
Howgill Grn. BD6: B'frd ... 5E **43**
Hoxton St. BD8: B'frd ... 1E **35**
Hoyle Ct. Av. BD17: Bail ... 2A **18**
Hoyle Ct. Dr. BD17: Bail ... 2A **18**
Hoyle Ct. Rd. BD17: Bail ... 2A **18**
Hoyle Fold BD22: Keigh ... 6B **6**
Hoyle Ing Rd. BD13: B'frd ... 3F **33**
Hoyle Syke BD22: Oxen ... 3F **21**
Hubert St. BD3: B'frd ... 3D **36**
HX2: Hal ... 6F **47**
Huddersfield Rd.
BD6: B'frd ... 5G **43**
BD12: B'frd, Brigh ... 5F **51**
(not continuous)
HD3: Hud ... 6G **61**
HD6: Brigh ... 6F **59**
HX3: Hal ... 2C **56**
(not continuous)
HX5: Ell ... 5G **61**
Hud Hill HX3: Hal ... 1H **49**
Hudson, The BD12: B'frd ... 2G **51**
Hudson Av. BD7: B'frd ... 5F **35**
Hudson Cl. BD7: B'frd ... 6F **35**
Hudson Cres. BD7: B'frd ... 6F **35**
Hudson Gdns. BD7: B'frd ... 6F **35**
Hudson St. BD3: B'frd ... 2F **37**
Hughendon Dr. BD13: B'frd ... 3G **33**
Hughendon Wlk.
BD13: B'frd ... 3G **33**
Hugill St. BD13: B'frd ... 3D **32**
Hulbert St. BD16: Bgly ... 3G **15**
Hullenedge Gdns. HX5: Ell ... 3D **60**
Hullenedge La. HX4: Hal ... 3C **60**
Hullenedge Rd. HX5: Ell ... 3D **60**
Hullen Rd. HX5: Ell ... 3D **60**
Hulme St. *HX6: Hal ... 4D **54***
(off Syke La.)
Humboldt St.
BD1: B'frd ... 2C **36** (3G **5**)
HUNGER HILL ... 3F **41**
Hunger Hill
HX1: Hal ... 1C **56** (6C **62**)
HUNSWORTH ... 3F **53**
Hunsworth La. BD4: B'frd ... 6G **45**
BD19: Cleck ... 4F **53**
Hunter Hill Rd. HX2: Hal ... 6C **38**
Hunters Ct. BD9: B'frd ... 3A **26**
Hunters Grn. BD13: B'frd ... 6F **13**
Hunters Pk. Av. BD14: B'frd ... 4B **34**
Huntingdon Rd. HD6: Brigh ... 6G **59**
Huntock Pl. HD6: Brigh ... 2D **58**
Huntsmans Cl. BD16: Bgly ... 1A **16**
BD20: Keigh ... 3C **6**
Hunt Yd. BD7: B'frd ... 5E **35**
Hurstville Av. BD4: B'frd ... 5H **45**
Hustlergate
BD1: B'frd ... 2A **36** (4D **4**)
Hustler St.
BD3: B'frd ... 6C **28** (1H **5**)
Hutchinson La. HD6: Brigh ... 5F **59**
Hutson St. BD5: B'frd ... 5H **35**
Hutton Rd. BD5: B'frd ... 1G **43**
Hutton Ter. BD2: B'frd ... 2F **29**
Huxley Mt. BD2: B'frd ... 2E **29**
Hydale Cl. BD21: Keigh ... 6G **7**
Hydale Ct. BD12: B'frd ... 5G **43**
Hyde Gro. *BD21: Keigh ... 3F **7***
(off Kirby St.)
Hyde Pk. HX1: Hal ... 1A **56**
Hyde Pk. Gdns. *HX1: Hal ... 2A **56***
(off Haugh Shaw Rd.)
Hyde Pk. Rd. HX1: Hal ... 2A **56**
Hyde Pk. St. HX1: Hal ... 2A **56**
Hyde St. BD10: B'frd ... 4D **18**
Hyne Av. BD4: B'frd ... 2D **44**

I

Ida St. BD5: B'frd ... 6G **35**
Iddesleigh St. BD4: B'frd ... 3F **37**

Idle—Kellymoor Wlk.

IDLE .5D 18
Idlecroft Rd. BD10: B'frd .5D 18
IDLE MOOR .6B 18
Idle Rd. BD2: B'frd .2C 28
Idlethorp Way BD10: B'frd .6E 19
Ilbert Av. BD4: B'frd .2E 45
Ilkley Rd. BD20: Keigh .1H 7
ILLINGWORTH .5G 39
Illingworth Av. HX2: Hal .3G 39
Illingworth Bldgs.
BD12: B'frd .1B 52
(off Illingworth Rd.)
Illingworth Cl. HX2: Hal .4G 39
Illingworth Cres. HX2: Hal .4G 39
Illingworth Dr. HX2: Hal .4G 39
Illingworth Gdns. HX2: Hal .5G 39
Illingworth Gro. HX2: Hal .4G 39
Illingworth La. HX2: Hal .5G 39
Illingworth Rd. BD12: B'frd .1B 52
Illingworth Way HX2: Hal .4G 39
Imax Bus. Cen.
BD19: Cleck .5F 53
(off Balme Rd.)
Imax Cinema .6C 4
Incline, The HX3: Hal .5E 49
Independent St. BD5: B'frd .6G 35
Industrial Mus. .6D 48 (4D 62)
Industrial Pl. HX1: Hal .5C 62
Industrial Rd. HX6: Hal .3D 54
Industrial St. BD16: Bgly .2F 15
BD19: Cleck .5B 52
BD22: Keigh .5C 6
HD6: Brigh .4F 59
Industrial Ter. HX1: Hal .2B 56
Infirmary St.
BD1: B'frd .1H 35 (3B 4)
(not continuous)
Ingester St. BD22: Haw .6F 11
(off West La.)
Ing Fld. BD12: B'frd .1C 52
Ingham Cl. HX2: Hal .3H 39
Ingham La. HX2: Hal .2G 39
Inghams Ct. HX3: Hal .4A 48
Ing Head Cotts. HX3: Hal .1A 50
Inghead Gdns. HX3: Hal .1H 49
Ing Head Ter. HX3: Hal .1H 49
(not continuous)
Ingleborough Cl.
BD4: B'frd .6G 37
Ingleby Pl. BD7: B'frd .3E 35
Ingleby Rd. BD7: B'frd .1E 35
BD8: B'frd .1E 35
Ingleby St. BD8: B'frd .2E 35
Ingleton Ho. BD4: B'frd .1G 45
(off Arlesford Rd.)
Ingram Sq. HX1: Hal .2A 56
Ingram St. BD21: Keigh .2D 12
HX1: Hal .2A 56
INGROW .1C 12
Ingrow Bri. BD21: Keigh .1D 12
Ingrow La. BD21: Keigh .1C 12
BD22: Keigh .1B 12
Ingrow West Station
Vintage Carriages Trust
Mus. of Rail Travel .1D 12
Ings, The HX3: Hal .1E 59
Ings Cft. HX3: Hal .6A 42
Ing St. BD3: B'frd .2F 37
Ings Way BD8: B'frd .1C 34
Ingwell Ter. BD19: Cleck .6G 53
Inkerman St. BD2: B'frd .3F 29
BD4: B'frd .5F 37
Innings, The BD10: B'frd .5C 18
Institute Rd. BD2: B'frd .2E 29
Intake BD22: Keigh .5A 6
Intake Gro. BD2: B'frd .5E 29
Intake Laithe BD22: Keigh .5A 10
Intake La. BD22: Oxen .6E 21
Intake Rd. BD2: B'frd .5E 29
Intake Ter. BD2: B'frd .6E 29
Iona Pl. HX3: Hal .3C 48
(off Iona St.)
Iona St. HX3: Hal .3C 48
Iqbal Ct. BD3: B'frd .3F 37
Ireland St. BD16: Bgly .2E 15
Ireland Ter. BD16: Bgly .2E 15
Ireton St. BD7: B'frd .3F 35
Irish La. BD22: Keigh .3E 11
Iron St. BD19: Cleck .6E 53
Irvine St. HX1: Hal .2H 55
Irving Ter. BD14: B'frd .6A 34
Irwell St. BD4: B'frd .4C 36
Isaac St. BD8: B'frd .1F 35
Isle La. BD22: Oxen .6H 21
Isles St. BD8: B'frd .1D 34
Ivanhoe Rd. BD7: B'frd .4F 35
Ivegate BD1: B'frd .2A 36 (4C 4)
Ive Ho. La. HX2: Hal .5A 46
Ives St. BD17: Ship .5F 17
(not continuous)
Ivey Way BD18: Ship .6E 17
Ivy Bank BD12: B'frd .1G 51
Ivy Bank Ct. BD17: Bail .3H 17
(off Dewhirst Cl.)
Ivy Bank La. BD22: Haw .1G 21
Ivy Cotts. HX1: Hal .2A 56
(off Ivy St.)
Ivy Cres. HX3: Hal .6C 50
Ivy Gro. BD18: Ship .6C 16
Ivy Ho. Rd. BD5: B'frd .1A 44
Ivy La. BD15: B'frd .6G 25
HX2: Hal .5F 39
Ivy Mt. HX3: Hal .5D 56
Ivy Pl. BD2: B'frd .3D 28
Ivy Rd. BD18: Ship .6C 16
BD21: Keigh .5G 7
Ivy St. BD21: Keigh .3D 6
HD6: Brigh .4D 58
HX1: Hal .2A 56
Ivy St. Sth. BD21: Keigh .1D 12
HX1: Hal .2A 56
Ivy Ter. BD6: B'frd .4F 43
BD21: Keigh .5H 7
HD6: Brigh .4D 58
(off Ivy St.)
HX1: Hal .2A 56
(off Ivy St.)
HX3: Hal .6C 50

J

Jacana Way BD6: B'frd .2A 42
Jackdaw Cl. BD15: B'frd .2H 33
Jackie Smart Rd.
BD5: B'frd .5A 36
Jackroyd HX3: Hal .3H 47
Jackson Hill BD13: B'frd .4F 41
(not continuous)
Jackson St.
BD3: B'frd .3C 36 (6H 5)
Jacky La. BD22: Haw .1G 21
Jacobs Cft. BD14: B'frd .5H 33
Jacobs La. BD22: Haw .5H 11
Jacob St. BD5: B'frd .5H 35
Jacobs Well
BD1: B'frd .3A 36 (5D 4)
JAGGER GREEN .6C 60
Jagger Grn. Dean HX4: Hal .6B 60
Jagger Grn. La. HX4: Hal .6C 60
James Ga.
BD1: B'frd .2A 36 (4C 4)
James St.
BD1: B'frd .2A 36 (3C 4)
BD13: B'frd .3D 32
BD15: B'frd .6A 26
BD22: Keigh .3F 11
HD6: Brigh .3E 59
HX4: Hal .5B 60
HX5: Ell .3F 61
James St. E. BD21: Keigh .5E 7
James St. Mkt. BD1: B'frd .3C 4
Jamie Ct. BD10: B'frd .1F 29
Jane Grn. HX2: Hal .1F 39
Jane Hills BD17: Ship .5E 17
(off Riverside Est.)
Jane St. BD13: B'frd .6F 23
BD18: Ship .5D 16
BD22: Haw .6H 11
(off Park St.)
Janet St. BD22: Haw .5A 12
Japonica Way BD3: B'frd .6E 29
Jardine Rd. BD16: Bgly .2G 15
Jardine St. BD16: Bgly .2G 15
Jarratt St. BD8: B'frd .6F 27
Jarratt St. E. BD8: B'frd .6F 27
Jarrom Cl. BD4: B'frd .5F 37
Jasmine Gdns. HX1: Hal .1H 55
Jasmin Ter. BD8: B'frd .1G 35
Jasper St. BD10: B'frd .5D 18
HX1: Hal .6H 47
Javelin Cl. BD10: B'frd .1D 28
Jay Ho. La. HD6: Brigh .2G 59
Jay St. BD22: Haw .6H 11
(not continuous)
Jemmy La. HX3: Hal .2C 62
Jennings Pl. BD7: B'frd .5E 35
Jennings St. BD7: B'frd .5E 35
Jenny La. BD17: Bail .1H 17
Jepson La. HX5: Ell .3F 61
Jer Gro. BD7: B'frd .1C 42
Jer La. BD7: B'frd .1C 42
Jermyn St.
BD1: B'frd .2B 36 (3F 5)
Jerry La. HX6: Hal .4C 54
Jerusalem La. HX2: Hal .1A 46
Jervaulx Cres.
BD8: B'frd .1G 35 (1A 4)
Jerwood Hill Cl. HX3: Hal .4D 48
Jerwood Hill Rd. HX3: Hal .4D 48
Jesmond Av. BD9: B'frd .5D 26
Jesmond Gro. BD9: B'frd .5D 26
Jesse St. BD5: B'frd .4A 36
BD8: B'frd .2B 34
Jester Pl. BD13: B'frd .1C 40
Jew La. BD22: Oxen .5G 21
Jim Laker Pl. BD18: Ship .6D 16
Jimmy Gees .5D 16
Jinnah Ct.
BD8: B'frd .1H 35 (1A 4)
Joba Av. BD3: B'frd .2D 36
John Escritt Rd.
BD16: Bgly .3G 15
John Hanson Ct.
BD13: B'frd .3G 31
John Naylor La. HX2: Hal .2A 54
Johns La. HX5: Ell .5F 61
Johnson St. BD3: B'frd .2F 37
BD16: Bgly .1F 15
John St. BD1: B'frd .2A 36 (3C 4)
BD4: B'frd .2G 45
BD13: B'frd .6F 23
(Longlands La.)
BD13: B'frd .3D 32
(Lwr. Kipping La.)
BD13: B'frd .1F 23
(Old La.)
BD14: B'frd .5A 34
BD17: Bail .4G 17
BD18: Ship .5E 17
BD22: Keigh .3H 11
HD6: Brigh .4E 59
HX1: Hal .6C 48 (4B 62)
HX4: Hal .2C 60
HX5: Ell .3F 61
John St. W. HX6: Hal .3D 54
John William St.
BD19: Cleck .5F 53
HX5: Ell .3F 61
Jonscroft BD13: B'frd .4D 40
Jordan Way BD2: B'frd .6E 29
Joseph Av. HX3: Hal .3G 49
Joseph Crossley's Almshouses
HX1: Hal .1B 56
Joseph St.
BD1: B'frd .2C 36 (4G 5)
(not continuous)
BD4: B'frd .2G 45
Joseph Wright Ct.
BD10: B'frd .4C 18
(off Greenfield La.)
Jowett Pk. Cres.
BD10: B'frd .3C 18
Jowett St.
BD1: B'frd .2G 35 (3A 4)
Jowler HX2: Hal .1A 46
Jubilee Ct. BD18: Ship .5G 17
Jubilee Dr. BD21: Keigh .6C 6
Jubilee Mt. HD6: Brigh .5D 58
Jubilee Rd. HX3: Hal .5D 56
Jubilee St.
BD8: B'frd .6H 27 (1B 4)
HX3: Hal .1D 56
Jubilee St. Nth. HX3: Hal .2A 48
Jubilee Ter. HX3: Hal .1D 56
(off Jubilee St.)
Jubilee Way BD18: Ship .5H 17
Julian Dr. BD13: B'frd .1A 42
Jumbles, The BD12: B'frd .2G 51
Jumples HX2: Hal .1F 47
Jumples Cl. HX2: Hal .1F 47
Jumples Ct. HX2: Hal .1E 47
Jumples Crag HX2: Hal .1F 47
Junction Rd. BD17: Ship .5G 17
Junction Row BD2: B'frd .3D 28
(off Bolton Rd.)
Junction Ter. BD2: B'frd .3D 28
(off Bolton Rd.)
June St. BD21: Keigh .3E 7
Juniper Cl. BD8: B'frd .1F 35

K

Katherine St. BD18: Ship .5D 16
Kaycell St. BD4: B'frd .1D 44
Kay St. BD18: Ship .2G 27
Keasden Cl. BD10: B'frd .3C 18
Keeble Ho. BD2: B'frd .5F 29
(off St Clare's Av.)
Keeldar Cl. BD7: B'frd .6F 35
KEELHAM .4G 31
Keelham La. BD20: Keigh .1C 6
Keelham Pl. BD13: B'frd .4H 31
KEIGHLEY .4E 7
Keighley & Worth Valley Railway
Exhibition Cen. .4G 21
Keighley Bus Mus. .1G 31
Keighley Cl. HX2: Hal .5F 39
Keighley Cougars RLFC
(Cougar Pk.) .2F 7
Keighley Crematorium
BD22: Keigh .2E 11
Keighley Dr. HX2: Hal .6G 39
Keighley Ind. Pk.
BD21: Keigh .2E 7
Keighley Leisure Cen. .3F 7
Keighley Playhouse .4D 6
Keighley Retail Pk.
BD21: Keigh .2E 7
Keighley Rd. BD8: B'frd .3F 27
BD9: B'frd .3F 27
BD13: B'frd .6E 13
(Ellar Carr Rd.)
BD13: B'frd .4E 23
(Manywells Brow)
BD16: Bgly .1H 13
(Altar La.)
BD16: Bgly .5D 8
(Croft Rd.)
BD16: B'frd .6E 13
(Ellar Carr Rd.)
BD22: Keigh .3H 11
BD22: Oxen .4G 21
HX2: Hal .2F 39
(not continuous)
HX3: Hal .6G 39
Keighley Station (Rail) .4F 7
Keilder Cres. BD6: B'frd .1A 42
Kelbrook Ho. BD4: B'frd .1G 45
(off Muirhead Dr.)
Kelburn Gro. BD22: Keigh .2F 11
Kell Butts HX2: Hal .5B 38
Kellett Bldgs. BD12: B'frd .6H 43
Kell La. HX2: Hal .6A 38
HX3: Hal .2F 49
Kelloe St. BD19: Cleck .4F 53
Kell St. BD16: Bgly .2G 15
Kellymoor Wlk.
BD10: B'frd .6B 18

Kelmore Gro.—Langela Ter.

Kelmore Gro. BD6: B'frd 5C **42**
Kelsall Ho. BD3: B'frd 2F **5**
Kelseys Ct. *HX2: Hal 5G 47*
(off Stretchgate La.)
Kelsey St. HX1: Hal 5H **47**
Kelton Ho. *BD5: B'frd 1C 44*
(off Spring Wood Gdns.)
Kelvin Av. HX2: Hal 6F **47**
Kelvin Cres. HX2: Hal 1F **55**
Kelvin Ho. BD4: B'frd 6H **37**
Kelvin Pl. BD4: B'frd 4C **36**
Kelvin Rd. HX5: Ell 3E **61**
Kelvin Way BD2: B'frd 5E **29**
Kendall Av. BD18: Ship 6C **16**
Kendal Mellor Ct.
BD21: Keigh 4D **6**
Kendal St. BD21: Keigh 5F **7**
Kenilworth Dr. HX3: Hal 1E **59**
Kenilworth St. BD4: B'frd 5D **36**
Kenley Av. BD6: B'frd 1E **43**
Kenley Mt. BD6: B'frd 1E **43**
Kenley Pde. BD7: B'frd 1D **42**
Kenmore Av. BD19: Cleck 5E **53**
Kenmore Cl. BD19: Cleck 5E **53**
Kenmore Cres. BD6: B'frd 1E **43**
BD19: Cleck 5E **53**
Kenmore Dr. BD6: B'frd 1E **43**
BD19: Cleck 5E **53**
Kenmore Gro. BD6: B'frd 1E **43**
BD19: Cleck 5E **53**
Kenmore Rd. BD6: B'frd 1E **43**
BD19: Cleck 5E **53**
Kenmore Vw. BD19: Cleck 5E **53**
Kenmore Wlk. BD6: B'frd 1E **43**
Kenmore Way BD19: Cleck . . .5E **53**
Kennedy Ho. *BD21: Keigh 1D 12*
(off Hainworth La.)
Kennel La. BD22: Oxen 5C **20**
(not continuous)
Kennerleigh Wlk.
BD4: B'frd 1H **45**
Kennion St. BD5: B'frd 4H **35**
Kensington Cl. HX3: Hal 3A **56**
Kensington Gdns. HX5: Ell 3E **61**
Kensington Rd. HX3: Hal 3A **56**
Kensington St. BD8: B'frd 6E **27**
BD21: Keigh 5D **6**
Kenstone Cres. BD10: B'frd . . .6C **18**
Kentmere BD2: B'frd 1B **28**
Kentmere Av. BD12: Cleck 4A **52**
Kent M. BD16: Bgly 3H **15**
Kenton Way BD4: B'frd 5F **37**
Kent Rd. BD16: Bgly 3H **15**
Kent St. BD1: B'frd 3A **36** (6D **4**)
HX1: Hal 1B **56** (5A **62**)
Kenya Mt. BD21: Keigh 3B **6**
Kenyon La. HX2: Hal 6F **47**
Kepler Ho. *BD4: B'frd 1E 45*
(off Railway St.)
Kershaw Ct. HX2: Hal 5A **46**
Kershaw Cres. HX2: Hal 6A **46**
Kershaw Dr. HX2: Hal 5A **46**
Kershaw St. BD3: B'frd 2F **37**
Kesteven Cl. BD4: B'frd 1H **45**
Kesteven Ct. BD4: B'frd 1H **45**
Kesteven Rd. BD4: B'frd 1G **45**
Kestrel Dr. BD2: B'frd 3C **28**
Kestrel Mt. BD2: B'frd 3C **28**
Kestrel Vw. BD19: Cleck 4F **53**
Keswick Cl. HX3: Hal 3E **57**
Keswick St. BD4: B'frd 4F **37**
Kettlewell Dr. BD5: B'frd 6F **35**
Keverne Ho. *BD5: B'frd 5H 35*
(off Hutson St.)
KEW HILL 5F **61**
Kew Hill HD3: Ell 6F **61**
Khalaq Ct. BD3: B'frd 1D **36**
Khus Wlk. BD21: Keigh 1E **13**
Kilburn Ho. BD10: B'frd 1E **29**
Kildare Cres. BD15: B'frd 6G **25**
Killinghall Av. BD2: B'frd 6D **28**
Killinghall Dr. BD2: B'frd 6D **28**
Killinghall Gro. BD2: B'frd . . .6D **28**
Killinghall Rd. BD2: B'frd 5D **28**
BD3: B'frd 5D **28**
Kiln Bank BD20: Keigh 1G **7**
Kilner Ho. *BD2: B'frd 5F 29*
(off St Clares Av.)
Kilner Rd. BD6: B'frd 2E **43**
(not continuous)
Kiln Fold HD6: Brigh 4H **59**
Kilnsea Mt. BD4: B'frd 6G **37**
Kilnsey M. BD17: Bail 2F **17**
Kilnsey Rd. BD3: B'frd 3D **36**
Kilroyd Av. BD19: Cleck 3F **53**
Kilroyd Dr. BD19: Cleck 3G **53**
Kimberley Pl. HX3: Hal 1A **48**
Kimberley St. BD3: B'frd 3E **37**
HD6: Brigh 4F **59**
HX3: Hal 1A **48**
Kinara Cl. BD21: Keigh 3G **7**
Kingcliff BD15: B'frd 1B **24**
KING CROSS 2G **55**
King Cross Rd. HX1: Hal 2H **55**
King Cross St.
HX1: Hal 1B **56** (5A **62**)
King Edward Rd.
BD13: B'frd 3D **32**
King Edward St.
HX1: Hal 6C **48** (4C **62**)
King Edward Ter.
BD13: B'frd 3D **32**
Kingfisher Ct. *BD21: Keigh 4E 7*
(off East Pde.)
Kingfisher Gro. BD8: B'frd 2A **34**
Kingsbury Pl. HX1: Hal 6H **47**
Kings Ct. BD16: Bgly 2F **15**
HX1: Hal 1B **56** (5A **62**)
Kingsdale Av. BD2: B'frd 4C **28**
Kingsdale Cres. BD2: B'frd . . .4C **28**
Kingsdale Dr. BD2: B'frd 4C **28**
Kingsdale Gro. BD2: B'frd 4B **28**
King's Dr. BD2: B'frd 1B **28**
King's Ga. BD1: B'frd 6A **28**
Kings Gro. BD16: Bgly 1G **15**
BD17: Bail 4C **16**
Kings Lea HX3: Hal 5B **56**
Kingsley Av. BD2: B'frd 4A **28**
HX6: Hal 4B **54**
Kingsley Cres. BD17: Bail 3G **17**
Kingsley Pl. HX1: Hal 1A **56**
Kingsmark Freeway
BD12: B'frd 6B **44**
King's Rd. BD1: B'frd 5A **28**
BD16: Bgly 5E **9**
Kingston Cl. BD15: B'frd 2C **24**
HX1: Hal 1H **55**
Kingston Ct. HX1: Hal 1H **55**
Kingston Dr. HX1: Hal 1H **55**
Kingston Gro. BD10: B'frd 4D **18**
Kingston Ho. *BD10: B'frd 1E 29*
(off Rowantree Dr.)
Kingston Rd. BD10: B'frd 4D **18**
Kingston St. HX1: Hal 1H **55**
Kingston Ter. HX1: Hal 1H **55**
King St. BD2: B'frd 2E **29**
BD19: Cleck 6G **53**
BD21: Keigh 5D **6**
BD22: Haw 1G **21**
HD6: Brigh 5F **59**
HX1: Hal 6D **48** (3D **62**)
HX5: Ell 3G 61
(off Brook St.)
HX6: Hal 4A **54**
Kings Vw. HX3: Hal 3G **57**
Kingsway BD2: B'frd 6B **18**
BD16: Bgly 2G **15**
BD20: Keigh 2A **8**
Kingswood Grn. HX3: Hal 4F **49**
Kingswood Pl. BD7: B'frd 5E **35**
Kingswood St. BD7: B'frd 5E **35**
Kingswood Ter. BD7: B'frd 5E **35**
Kinnaird Cl. HX5: Ell 1F **61**
Kinross Ho. *BD4: B'frd 1G 45*
(off Muirhead Dr.)
Kinsey M. *BD17: Bail 2F 17*
(off West La.)
Kipling Ct. BD10: B'frd 6F **19**
Kipping La. BD13: B'frd 3D **32**
Kipping Pl. BD13: B'frd 3D **32**
Kirby Leas
HX1: Hal 1C **56** (6B **62**)
Kirby St. BD21: Keigh 3F **7**
Kirkbourne Gro. BD17: Bail . . .3A **18**
Kirkburn Pl. BD7: B'frd 3F **35**
Kirkcroft BD13: B'frd 1F **31**
Kirkdale Ho. *BD10: B'frd 1E 29*
(off Rowantree Dr.)
Kirkdale Way BD4: B'frd 2H **45**
Kirk Dr. BD17: Bail 1H **17**
Kirkfields BD17: Bail 1A **18**
Kirk Ga. BD11: B'frd 4H **45**
Kirkgate BD1: B'frd 2A **36** (4C **4**)
(not continuous)
BD18: Ship 6E **17**
Kirkgate Cen.
BD1: B'frd 2A **36** (4C **4**)
Kirkgate Mall BD1: B'frd 4C **4**
Kirkham Ho. *BD5: B'frd 1B 44*
(off Parkway)
Kirkham Rd. BD7: B'frd 4F **35**
Kirklands Av. BD13: B'frd 3E **33**
BD17: Bail 2A **18**
Kirklands Cl. BD17: Bail 3A **18**
Kirklands Gdns. BD17: Bail . . .2A **18**
Kirklands La. BD17: Bail 2A **18**
Kirklands Rd. BD17: Bail 2H **17**
Kirk La. HX3: Hal 5A **50**
Kirklees Rd. BD15: B'frd 2H **33**
Kirkley Av. BD12: B'frd 4G **51**
Kirkstall Gro. BD8: B'frd 2B **34**
Kirkstone Dr. HX2: Hal 5D **46**
Kirkwall Dr. BD4: B'frd 6G **37**
Kismet Gdns. BD3: B'frd 1E **37**
Kitchener St. BD12: B'frd 6C **44**
Kite M. BD8: B'frd 2A **34**
Kitson La. HX6: Hal 6F **55**
Kitson St. BD18: Ship 1G **27**
Kitten Clough HX2: Hal 4G **47**
Kitwood Cl. BD4: B'frd 1H **45**
Kliffen Pl. HX3: Hal 3D **56**
Knightsbridge Ct.
HD6: Brigh 4E **59**
Knightsbridge Wlk.
BD4: B'frd 4D **44**
Knight's Fold BD7: B'frd 5E **35**
Knight St. HX1: Hal 1H **55**
Knightsway Ct. BD3: B'frd 6H **29**
Knoll Gdns. BD17: Bail 4F **17**
Knoll Pk. Dr. BD17: Bail 4F **17**
Knoll Ter. BD17: Bail 4F **17**
Knoll Vw. BD17: Bail 3F **17**
Knowle La. BD12: B'frd 3H **51**
KNOWLE PARK 6C **6**
Knowles Av. BD4: B'frd 1F **45**
Knowles La. BD4: B'frd 1E **45**
Knowle Spring Rd.
BD21: Keigh 1D **12**
(Foster Rd.)
BD21: Keigh 6D **6**
(Selborne Gro.)
Knowles St. BD4: B'frd 1E **45**
BD13: B'frd 1F **31**
Knowles Vw. BD4: B'frd 1F **45**
Knowle Top HX4: Hal 6A **60**
Knowle Top Dr. HX3: Hal 5C **50**
Knowle Top Rd. HX3: Hal 5C **50**
Knowsley St.
BD3: B'frd 2C **36** (4H **5**)
Knutsford Gro. BD4: B'frd 1G **45**
Komla Cl. BD1: B'frd 3F **5**
Kyffin Pl. BD4: B'frd 4G **37**

L

Laburnum Dr. BD17: Bail 1H **17**
Laburnum Gro. BD22: Haw . . .5A **12**
HX3: Hal 1E **59**
Laburnum Pl. BD8: B'frd 6G **27**
BD10: B'frd 5G **19**
Laburnum Rd. BD18: Ship . . .2H **27**
Laburnum St. BD8: B'frd 6G **27**
Laburnum Ter. *HX3: Hal 3E 51*
(off Village St.)
Laceby Cl. BD10: B'frd 5E **19**
Lacey M. BD4: B'frd 1E **45**
Lacy Way HX5: Ell 1G **61**
Ladbroke Gro. BD4: B'frd 2G **45**
Ladderbanks La.
BD17: Bail 1H **17**
(not continuous)
Ladstone Towers HX6: Hal . . .3D **54**
Lady Fld. *BD13: B'frd 3D 32*
(off West La.)
Lady La. BD16: Bgly 5G **9**
Lady Pk. Av. BD16: Bgly 5G **9**
Ladyroyd Dr. BD4: B'frd 5G **45**
Ladysmith Rd. BD13: B'frd . . .3C **40**
Ladywell Cl. BD5: B'frd 6A **36**
Ladywood Ter. HX1: Hal 5A **48**
LAISERDYKE 2F **37**
Laisterdyke BD4: B'frd 3F **37**
Laisteridge La. BD5: B'frd . . .3G **35**
BD7: B'frd 3G **35** (6A **4**)
Laithe Gro. BD6: B'frd 2E **43**
Laithe Rd. BD6: B'frd 2F **43**
Lake Row BD4: B'frd 4D **36**
Lakeside BD20: Keigh 1E **9**
Lake St. BD4: B'frd 4D **36**
BD21: Keigh 2G **7**
Lake Vw. HX3: Hal . . .5B **48** (1A **62**)
Lambert Cl. HX4: Hal 2D **60**
Lambert Pl. *BD2: B'frd 5D 28*
(off Thirlmere Gdns.)
Lambert St. HX4: Hal 2D **60**
Lambourne Av. BD10: B'frd . . .2F **29**
Lampards Cl. BD15: B'frd 5G **25**
Lancaster Ct. *BD21: Keigh 6D 6*
(off Rutland St.)
Landemere Syke HX3: Hal . . .1G **49**
Landford Ho. *BD5: B'frd 5H 35*
(off Park La.)
Landmark Ho. BD1: B'frd 4D **4**
Landor St. BD21: Keigh 3F **7**
Landscove Av. BD4: B'frd 1G **45**
Lands Head La. HX3: Hal 1F **49**
Landsholme Ct. BD4: B'frd . . .1H **45**
Lands La. BD10: B'frd 2E **29**
Landsmoor Gro. BD16: Bgly . . .6H **9**
Lane Bottom HX6: Hal 5C **54**
Lane Ct. *HD6: Brigh 4F 59*
(off Old La.)
LANE END 5A **34**
Lane End BD13: B'frd 3D **32**
BD14: B'frd 6A 34
(off Station Rd.)
BD16: Bgly 4B 14
(off Spring Row)
BD17: Bail 2G **17**
HX6: Hal 6A **54**
LANE ENDS 3F **11**
Lane Ends HX2: Hal 6C **46**
HX3: Hal 3A **50**
(Denholme Ga. Rd.)
HX3: Hal 5A **50**
(Halifax Rd.)
HX3: Hal 3G **47**
(Long La.)
HX6: Hal 4E **55**
Lane Ends Cl. BD8: B'frd 1D **34**
Lane Ends Grn. HX3: Hal 5H **49**
LANE HEAD 4D **58**
Lane Head La. HX2: Hal 3E **39**
Lane Ho. Gro. HX2: Hal 5A **46**
Lane Side BD12: B'frd 1F **51**
BD13: B'frd 6C **32**
BD15: B'frd 3B **24**
Laneside HX4: Hal 5B **60**
Lane Top BD13: B'frd 5F **23**
Langbar Av. BD9: B'frd 4B **26**
Langdale Av. BD8: B'frd 1C **34**
BD12: Cleck 4A **52**
Langdale Ct. BD16: Bgly 1G **15**
Langdale Cres. HX2: Hal 4G **47**
Langdale Dr. BD13: B'frd 2D **40**
Langdale Rd. BD10: B'frd 3G **29**
Langdales HX6: Hal 3C **54**
Langdale St. HX5: Ell 3F **61**
Langela Ter. HX3: Hal 5A **50**

Langlands Rd.—Ling Bob

Langlands Rd. BD16: Bgly . . .6G 15
Lang La. BD2: B'frd 2H 27
Langley Av. BD4: B'frd 2D 44
BD16: Bgly 1G 15
Langley Cres. BD17: Bail 2A 18
Langley Gro. BD16: Bgly 1G 15
Langley La. BD17: Bail 1A 18
Langley Rd. BD16: Bgly 1G 15
Langport Cl. BD13: B'frd 2F 41
Langton Av. BD4: B'frd 2D 44
Langton St. HX6: Hal 2D 54
Lanrick Ho. *BD4: B'frd 5G 37*
(off Broadstone Way)
Lansdale Ct. BD4: B'frd 1H 45
Lansdowne Cl. BD17: Bail 2B 18
Lansdowne Ho. *BD8: B'frd . . .6G 27*
(off Trenton Dr.)
Lansdowne Pl.
BD5: B'frd 3H 35 (6B 4)
Lapage St. BD3: B'frd 2E 37
Lapage Ter. BD3: B'frd 3E 37
Lapwing Cl. BD8: B'frd 2H 33
Larch Cl. BD22: Keigh 3H 11
Larch Dr. BD6: B'frd 4G 43
Larch Gro. BD16: Bgly 6G 9
BD17: Bail 4C 16
Larch Hill BD6: B'frd 4H 43
Larch Hill Cres. BD6: B'frd . . .3H 43
Larchmont BD14: B'frd 5A 34
Larch St. BD21: Keigh 1D 12
Larkfield BD9: B'frd 4D 26
Larkfield Ter. BD21: Keigh 5G 7
BD22: Keigh 3H 11
(off Keighley Rd.)
Lark Hill Av. BD19: Cleck 6D 52
Lark Hill Cl. BD19: Cleck 6D 52
Lark Hill Dr. BD19: Cleck 6D 52
Lark St. BD16: Bgly 2F 15
BD21: Keigh 4D 6
BD22: Haw 6H 11
BD22: Keigh 3H 11
Lark Va. BD16: Bgly 1A 16
Larne Ho. *BD5: B'frd 5H 35*
(off Roundhill St.)
Larwood Av. BD10: B'frd 3G 29
Lastingham Grn.
BD6: B'frd 2C 42
Latham La. BD19: Cleck 2H 53
Latimer Ho. *BD5: B'frd 5A 36*
(off Manchester Rd.)
Launceston Dr. BD4: B'frd 1G 45
Launton Way BD5: B'frd 5H 35
Laura St. HD6: Brigh 6E 59
HX3: Hal 4C 48 (1B 62)
Laurel Bank BD12: Brigh 5G 51
BD16: Bgly 1A 16
HX2: Hal 4A 40
(Holdsworth Rd.)
HX2: Hal 4A 46
(Stocks La.)
HX6: Hal 6A 54
(off Hollin St.)
Laurel Bank Cl. HX2: Hal 5A 40
Laurel Cl. HX3: Hal 4A 42
HX5: Ell 3E 61
Laurel Cres. BD20: Keigh 3D 6
HX2: Hal 2H 47
Laurel Gro. BD16: Bgly 6E 9
BD21: Keigh 3D 6
Laurel Mt. HX1: Hal 2A 56
HX4: Hal 5C 60
(off Well St.)
HX6: Hal 2D 54
(off Bright St.)
Laurel Pk. BD15: B'frd 3C 24
Laurels, The BD16: Bgly 2H 15
Laurel St. BD3: B'frd 3E 37
HX1: Hal 2A 56
Laurel Ter. HX4: Hal 5A 60
Lavell M. BD2: B'frd 4E 29
Lavender Ct. BD18: Ship 2H 27
Lavender Hill BD10: B'frd 2E 29
Laverack Fld. BD12: B'frd 2G 51
Laverock Cres. HD6: Brigh . . .2D 58
Laverock La. HD6: Brigh 2D 58
Laverock Pl. *HD6: Brigh 2D 58*
(off Huntock Pl.)
Laverton Rd. BD4: B'frd 5D 36
Lavinia Ter. BD14: B'frd 5B 34
Lawcliffe Cres. BD22: Haw . . .5H 11
Lawkholme Cres.
BD21: Keigh 4E 7
Lawkholme La. BD21: Keigh . . .4E 7
Law La. HX3: Hal 2F 57
Lawler Cl. *HX3: Hal 2H 47*
(off Rugby Ter.)
Lawns, The HX3: Hal 4B 56
Lawnswood Rd.
BD21: Keigh 6C 6
Lawrence Dr. BD7: B'frd 1C 42
Lawrence Rd. HX3: Hal 4B 56
Lawrence St. HX3: Hal 4A 48
Lawson Rd. HD6: Brigh 5F 59
Lawson St.
BD3: B'frd 1B 36 (1E 5)
Law St. BD4: B'frd 1E 45
BD19: Cleck 4F 53
Laxton Ho. *BD5: B'frd 5H 35*
(off Launton Wlk.)
Laythorp Ter. BD20: Keigh 2D 8
Layton Ho. *BD5: B'frd 5H 35*
(off Newall St.)
Lea Av. HX3: Hal 4C 56
Leach Cres. BD20: Keigh 1G 7
Leach Ri. BD20: Keigh 1G 7
Leach Rd. BD20: Keigh 1F 7
Leach Way BD20: Keigh 1G 7
Lea Cl. HD6: Brigh 3E 59
Lea Ct. BD7: B'frd 1C 42
Leadenhall St. HX1: Hal 2H 55
Leafield Av. BD2: B'frd 3E 29
Leafield Cres. BD2: B'frd 3D 28
Leafield Dr. BD2: B'frd 3E 29
Leafield Gro. BD2: B'frd 4E 29
Leafield Ho. *BD5: B'frd 5H 35*
(off Newall St.)
Leafield Ter. BD2: B'frd 4E 29
Leafield Way BD2: B'frd 4E 29
Leafland St. HX1: Hal 6A 48
Leaf St. BD22: Haw 5A 12
Leafsway BD6: B'frd 5D 42
Leamington Dr. BD10: B'frd . . .5E 19
Leamington St. BD9: B'frd 5F 27
Leamside Wlk. BD4: B'frd 1G 45
Leaside Dr. BD13: B'frd 2D 32
Leathley Ho. *BD5: B'frd 5H 35*
(off Hutson St.)
Leavens, The BD10: B'frd 5F 19
LEAVENTHORPE 3A 34
Leaventhorpe Av.
BD8: B'frd 2B 34
Leaventhorpe Cl.
BD8: B'frd 2B 34
Leaventhorpe Gro.
BD13: B'frd 3A 34
Leaventhorpe La.
BD8: B'frd 3H 33
BD13: B'frd 3H 33
Leaventhorpe Way
BD8: B'frd 2B 34
Leavington Cl. BD6: B'frd 5F 43
Leconfield Ho. BD10: B'frd . . .6E 19
Ledbury Pl. BD4: B'frd 5D 36
Lee Bank HX3: Hal . . .4B 48 (1A 62)
Lee Bri. HX3: Hal 5B 48 (1A 62)
Lee Bri. Ind. Est.
HX3: Hal 5B 48 (1A 62)
Leech La. BD16: Bgly 5H 13
Lee Cl. BD15: B'frd 1C 24
Lee Ct. BD21: Keigh 5H 7
Leeds Old Rd. BD3: B'frd 1F 37
Leeds Rd.
BD1: B'frd 2B 36 (4E 5)
(not continuous)
BD2: B'frd 3D 28
BD3: B'frd 2F 37 (4G 5)
BD10: B'frd 3D 18
BD18: Ship 5G 17
HX3: Hal 4F 49
(Bradford Rd.)
Leeds Rd. HX3: Hal 5B 50
(Crescent, The)
HX3: Hal 4C 50
(Flowerfields)
LEEDS ROAD HOSPITAL 2D 36
Leeds St. BD21: Keigh 4D 6
Lee La. BD15: B'frd 1B 24
BD16: Bgly 6C 14
BD22: Oxen 4D 20
HX3: Hal 2C 48
LEEMING 6H 21
Leeming St.
BD1: B'frd 1B 36 (2E 5)
LEE MOUNT 4A 48
Lee Mt. Gdns. HX3: Hal 4A 48
Lee Mt. Rd. HX3: Hal 4A 48
LEES .5A 12
Lees Bank Av. BD22: Haw 5A 12
Lees Bank Dr. BD22: Haw 5A 12
Lees Bank Hill
BD22: Haw 5A 12
Lees Bank Rd. BD22: Haw 5A 12
Lees Bldgs. HX3: Hal 5A 50
Lees Cl. BD13: B'frd 1E 23
Lees La. BD22: Haw 6H 11
HX3: Hal 4C 50
Lees Moor Rd. BD13: B'frd . . .1E 23
Lee St. BD1: B'frd 3A 36 (4C 4)
BD13: B'frd 3D 40
HD6: Brigh 3E 59
Lee Ter. BD12: B'frd 6B 44
Legrams Av. BD7: B'frd 4D 34
Legrams La. BD7: B'frd 4E 35
Legrams Mill La.
BD7: B'frd 3E 35
Legrams St. BD7: B'frd 2F 35
Legrams Ter. BD7: B'frd 2G 35
Leicester St. BD4: B'frd 5C 36
Leicester Ter. HX3: Hal 3B 56
Leigh St. HX6: Hal 2E 55
Leisure Exchange, The 5F 5
Leith Ho. *BD4: B'frd 6G 37*
(off Stirling Cres.)
Leith St. BD21: Keigh 3D 6
Le Mar Vw. HX3: Hal 1E 57
Lemington Av. HX1: Hal 1A 56
Lemmingbeck Cl.
BD22: Oxen 4G 21
Lemon St. BD5: B'frd 6G 35
HX1: Hal 6H 47
Lennie St. BD21: Keigh 5D 6
Lennon Dr. BD8: B'frd 1F 35
Lens Dr. BD17: Bail 1G 17
Lentilfield St. HX3: Hal 3A 48
Lentilfield Ter. HX3: Hal 3A 48
Lenton Vs. BD10: B'frd 4D 18
Leonard's Pl. BD16: Bgly 3G 15
Leonard St. BD12: B'frd 2H 51
BD16: Bgly 3G 15
Lesmere Gro. BD7: B'frd 1D 42
Lessarna Ct. BD4: B'frd 4E 37
Lever St. BD6: B'frd 2E 43
Levisham Cl. BD10: B'frd 2F 29
Levita Gro. BD4: B'frd 5F 37
Levita Pl. BD4: B'frd 4G 37
Lewis Cl. BD13: B'frd 2D 40
Lewis St. HX1: Hal . . .6B 48 (3A 62)
Lexington Cl. BD4: B'frd 3D 44
Leyburn Av. HX3: Hal 5C 50
Leyburne St. BD8: B'frd 6G 27
Leyburn Gro. BD16: Bgly 1G 15
BD18: Ship 6E 17
Leyden Ri. BD15: B'frd 1H 33
Leyfield BD17: Bail 2E 17
Ley Fleaks Rd.
BD10: B'frd 6D 18
(not continuous)
Leylands Av. BD9: B'frd 4D 26
Leylands Gro. BD9: B'frd 4D 26
Leylands Ho. BD21: Keigh 5F 7
Leylands La. BD9: B'frd 4D 26
BD21: Keigh 5F 7
Leylands Ter. BD9: B'frd 4D 26
Leys, The BD17: Bail 1G 17
Leys Cl. BD10: B'frd 4C 18
Leyside Dr. BD15: B'frd 5H 25
Leyton Cres. BD10: B'frd 6D 18
Leyton Dr. BD10: B'frd 6D 18
Leyton Gro. BD10: B'frd 6D 18
Leyton Ter. BD10: B'frd 6D 18
Ley Top La. BD15: B'frd 1A 34
Lichen Cl. BD7: B'frd 6E 35
Lichfield Mt. BD2: B'frd 3A 28
LIDGET 3H 11
Lidget Av. BD7: B'frd 4D 34
LIDGET GREEN 3E 35
Lidget Pl. BD7: B'frd 4D 34
Lidget Ter. BD7: B'frd 4D 34
BD14: B'frd 5B 34
LIGHTCLIFFE 6D 50
Lightcliffe Rd. HD6: Brigh 2E 59
Lightowler Cl. HX1: Hal 6A 48
Lightowler Rd. HX1: Hal 6A 48
Lightowler St. BD6: B'frd 2G 43
Lilac Cl. HD6: Brigh 4G 59
Lilac Gro. BD4: B'frd 3F 37
BD18: Ship 2H 27
BD19: Cleck 4H 53
Lilac St. HX3: Hal 4A 48
Lilian St. BD4: B'frd 6E 37
Lillands Av. HD6: Brigh 5D 58
Lillands La. HD6: Brigh 6D 58
Lillands Ter. HD6: Brigh 5D 58
Lilly La. HX1: Hal 1D 56 (5D 62)
(not continuous)
HX3: Hal 5D 62
Lilly St. HX6: Hal 4D 54
Lilycroft BD8: B'frd 6F 27
Lilycroft Pl. BD8: B'frd 5F 27
Lilycroft Rd. BD9: B'frd 6E 27
Lilycroft Wlk. BD9: B'frd 5E 27
(not continuous)
Lily St. BD8: B'frd 5F 27
Lilythorne Av. BD10: B'frd 5E 19
Lime Cl. BD20: Keigh 2C 6
Lime Ct. *BD16: Bgly 5E 9*
(off Aire St.)
Limes Av. HX3: Hal 3C 56
Lime St. BD7: B'frd 5E 35
BD16: Bgly 2F 15
BD21: Keigh 4D 6
BD22: Haw 1G 21
Lime Tree Av. HX5: Ell 3G 61
Lime Tree Sq. BD18: Ship 4B 16
Lime Va. Way BD6: B'frd 2C 42
Lincoln Cl. BD8: B'frd 6G 27
Lincoln Rd. BD8: B'frd 1G 35
Lincoln St. BD15: B'frd 1A 34
Lincoln Way HX3: Hal 4B 48
Linden Av. BD3: B'frd 1G 37
Linden Cl. HD6: Brigh 4G 59
Linden Pl. HX6: Hal 2E 55
Linden Ri. BD21: Keigh 6G 7
Linden Rd. HX3: Hal 3C 56
HX5: Ell 3E 61
Linden Ter. *HX3: Hal 6A 50*
(off Barfield Rd.)
Lindholme Gdns.
BD15: B'frd 1H 33
Lindisfarne Rd.
BD18: Ship 6D 16
Lindley Av. HD3: Hud 6G 61
Lindley Dr. BD7: B'frd 1D 42
Lindley Moor Rd.
HD3: Hud 6F 61
Lindley Rd. BD5: B'frd 6H 35
HX5: Ell 5E 61
Lindon St. BD22: Haw 1G 21
Lindrick Gro. HX2: Hal 4H 39
Lindrick Wlk. HX2: Hal 4H 39
Lindrick Way HX2: Hal 4H 39
LINDWELL 1D 60
Lindwell Av. HX4: Hal 2C 60
Lindwell Gro. HX4: Hal 2C 60
Lindwell Pl. *HX4: Hal 2C 60*
(off Wellgate)
Lingard St.
BD1: B'frd 1B 36 (2E 5)
LINGBOB 3C 24
Ling Bob HX2: Hal 5F 47

88 A-Z Bradford

Ling Bob Cl.—Lowther St.

Ling Bob Cl. HX2: Hal 5F 47
Lingbob Ct. BD15: B'frd 3C 24
Ling Bob Cft. HX2: Hal 4F 47
Lingcroft Grn. BD5: B'frd 1C 44
(off Tristram Av.)
Lingdale Rd. BD6: B'frd 5E 43
Lingfield Cres. BD13: B'frd . . .1A 42
Lingfield Dr. BD22: Haw 4C 12
Lingfield Gro. BD15: B'frd 2D 24
Lingfield Ho. BD10: B'frd 1E 29
(off Savile Av.)
Lingfield Rd. BD15: B'frd 2C 24
Lingfield Ter. BD13: B'frd 1A 42
Lingmell Cres. BD4: B'frd 1H 45
(off Simon Cl.)
Ling Pk. App. BD15: B'frd 3C 24
Ling Pk. Av. BD15: B'frd 3C 24
Ling Royd Av. HX2: Hal 5F 47
Lingwood Av. BD8: B'frd 6D 26
Lingwood Rd. BD8: B'frd 1D 34
Lingwood Ter. BD8: B'frd 1D 34
Links Av. BD19: Cleck 4F 53
Linkway BD16: Bgly 6G 15
Linnet Cl. BD8: B'frd 1A 34
Linnet St. BD21: Keigh 3E 7
Linnhe Av. BD6: B'frd 5D 42
Linton St. BD4: B'frd 5B 36
Lion Chambers BD19: Cleck . . .5F 53
(off Whitcliffe Rd.)
Lismore Rd. BD20: Keigh 3D 6
Lister Av. BD4: B'frd 6D 36
Lister Ct. HX1: Hal 4B 62
Lister Gdns. BD8: B'frd 5H 27
LISTER HILLS 2G 35
Listerhills Ind. Est.
BD1: B'frd 2H 35 (4A 4)
Listerhills Rd.
BD7: B'frd 3G 35 (4A 4)
Listerhills Science Pk.
BD7: B'frd 2G 35
Lister La. BD2: B'frd 5B 28
HX1: Hal 6A 48 (4A 62)
(not continuous)
Lister's Ct. HX1: Hal 6A 48
Listers Rd. HX3: Hal 5E 49
Lister St. BD4: B'frd 1E 45
(Bela Av.)
BD4: B'frd 2G 45
(Edward St.)
BD21: Keigh 5C 6
HD6: Brigh 4E 59
Lister Vw. BD8: B'frd 6G 27
Lister Ville BD15: B'frd 2C 24
Lit. Baines St. HX1: Hal 6A 48
Littlebeck Dr. BD16: Bgly 2A 16
Lit. Bradley HX4: Hal 3C 60
Little Cote BD10: B'frd 4C 18
Lit. Cross St. BD5: B'frd 1A 44
Littlefield Wlk. BD6: B'frd 3F 43
Little Haley BD22: Oxen 4H 21
Lit. Hew Royd BD10: B'frd . . .4B 18
LITTLE HORTON 5G 35
LITTLE HORTON GREEN 4H 35
Lit. Horton Grn. BD5: B'frd . . .4H 35
Lit. Horton La.
BD5: B'frd 4H 35 (6B 4)
(Bk. Trinity Ter., not continuous)
BD5: B'frd 6G 35
(Canterbury Av.)
BD5: B'frd 1F 43
(Carr Bottom Rd.)
Littlelands BD16: Bgly 6G 15
Littlelands Ct. BD16: Bgly 6G 15
Little La. BD9: B'frd 5D 26
BD20: Keigh 2E 9
HX3: Hal 6G 49
LITTLE LONDON 2H 19
Little London HX3: Hal 1F 49
LITTLE MOOR 2G 41
Little Moor BD13: B'frd 2G 41
Littlemoor Gdns. HX2: Hal . . .5G 39
Littlemoor Rd. HX2: Hal 4G 39
Little Pk. BD10: B'frd 4G 19
Little St. BD22: Haw 6G 11
Littlewood Cl. BD6: B'frd 4G 43
Littlewood Dr. BD19: Cleck . . .3F 53
Lit. Woodhouse HD6: Brigh . . .6E 59
Littondale Cl. BD17: Bail 1A 18
Litton Rd. BD22: Keigh 5C 6
Liverpool Row HX2: Hal 1D 54
(off Stock La.)
Liversedge Row BD7: B'frd . . .6E 35
(off Perseverance La.)
Livingstone Cl. BD2: B'frd 1B 28
Livingstone Rd. BD2: B'frd . . .3H 27
(Bolton Hall Rd.)
BD2: B'frd 2B 28
(Cheltenham Rd.)
Livingstone St. HX3: Hal 4A 48
Livingstone St. Nth.
HX2: Hal 6A 40
Livingston Ho. BD10: B'frd . . .1E 29
Lloyds Dr. BD12: B'frd 5A 44
Locarno Av. BD9: B'frd 5C 26
Locherbie Grn. BD15: B'frd . . .6H 25
Lochy Rd. BD6: B'frd 5D 42
Locks, The BD16: Bgly 2G 15
(off Granville Ter.)
BD16: Bgly 1F 15
(Wilson Rd.)
Locksley Rd. HD6: Brigh 6H 59
Lock St. HX3: Hal 1D 56
Lock Vw. BD16: Bgly 1E 15
HX5: Ell 1G 61
Lockwood St. BD6: B'frd 2G 43
BD12: B'frd 6A 44
BD18: Ship 5D 16
Lode Pit La. BD16: Bgly 1B 16
Lodge Av. HX5: Ell 2H 61
Lodge Dr. HX5: Ell 2H 61
Lodge Ga. Cl. BD13: B'frd 6G 23
Lodge Hill BD17: Bail 2D 16
Lodge St. BD13: B'frd 1F 23
BD22: Haw 6F 11
Lodore Av. BD2: B'frd 4C 28
Lodore Pl. BD2: B'frd 4D 28
Lodore Rd. BD2: B'frd 4C 28
Loft St. BD8: B'frd 1D 34
Lombard St. HX1: Hal 2H 55
London Rd. HX6: Hal 4F 55
Longacre La. BD22: Haw 5H 11
Longacres BD22: Haw 5A 12
Longbottom Av. HX6: Hal 4A 54
Longbottom Ter. HX3: Hal 3D 56
Long C'way. BD22: B'frd 6B 22
HX2: Hal 6F 31
Long Cl. BD12: B'frd 1F 51
Longcroft BD21: Keigh 5E 7
Longcroft Link
BD1: B'frd 2H 35 (3B 4)
Longcroft Pl.
BD1: B'frd 2H 35 (3B 4)
Long C'way BD13: B'frd 6B 22
Longfield HX4: Hal 5B 60
Longfield Av. HX3: Hal 4G 49
Longfield Dr. BD4: B'frd 6E 37
Longfield Ter. HX3: Hal 4G 49
(off Longfield Av.)
Longford Ter. BD7: B'frd 4D 34
Long Heys HX4: Hal 3C 60
Longhouse Dr. BD13: B'frd . . .1F 31
Longhouse La. BD13: B'frd . . .1F 31
Long Ho. Rd. HX2: Hal 5E 39
Longlands Dr. BD22: Haw 5H 11
Longlands La. BD13: B'frd 6F 23
Longlands St.
BD1: B'frd 2H 35 (3B 4)
(Baptist Pl.)
BD1: B'frd 2H 35 (3B 4)
(Providence St.)
Long La. BD9: B'frd 2B 26
BD13: B'frd 4D 40
BD15: B'frd 6D 24
BD16: Bgly 4A 14
HX3: Hal 6F 49
(Barrowclough La.)
HX3: Hal 3G 47
(Lane Ends)
HX6: Hal 6C 54
LONG LEE 5G 7
Long Lee La. BD21: Keigh 6F 7
Long Lee Ter. BD21: Keigh 6G 7
Longley La. HX6: Hal 6B 54
Long Lover La. HX2: Hal 5G 47
Long Mdws. BD2: B'frd 3A 28
Long Preston Chase
BD10: B'frd 6F 19
Long Reach HX2: Hal 2C 46
Long Row BD12: B'frd 6H 43
Long Row Ct. BD5: B'frd 6A 36
Longroyd BD10: B'frd 5B 18
Long Royd Cl. BD17: Bail 1H 17
Long Royd Dr. BD17: Bail 1A 18
Longroyde Cl. HD6: Brigh 6D 58
Longroyde Gro. HD6: Brigh . . .6D 58
Longroyde Rd. HD6: Brigh . . .6D 58
Longside Hall BD7: B'frd 3G 35
Longside La.
BD7: B'frd 3G 35 (5A 4)
Long St. BD4: B'frd 4D 36
Long Wall HX4: Hal 2D 60
HX5: Ell 3E 61
Longwood Av. BD16: Bgly 6D 8
Longwood Cl. HX3: Hal 4B 56
Longwood Vw. BD16: Bgly 6E 9
Lonsdale St.
BD3: B'frd 1D 36 (2H 5)
Lord La. BD22: Haw 5F 11
Lordsfield Pl. BD4: B'frd 2F 45
Lord's La. HD6: Brigh 6F 59
Lord St. BD21: Keigh 4E 7
BD22: Haw 6H 11
HX1: Hal 6C 48 (4B 62)
HX6: Hal 2E 55
Loris St. BD4: B'frd 2F 45
Lorne St. BD4: B'frd 6D 36
BD21: Keigh 3G 7
BD22: Haw 5B 12
(off Bingley Rd.)
Lot St. BD22: Haw 6H 11
Loughrigg St. BD5: B'frd 6A 36
Louisa St. BD10: B'frd 5D 18
Louis Av. BD5: B'frd 5G 35
Love La. HX1: Hal 1B 56 (6A 62)
Low Ash Av. BD18: Ship 6H 17
Low Ash Cres. BD18: Ship . . .6H 17
Low Ash Dr. BD18: Ship 6H 17
Low Ash Gro. BD18: Ship 6H 17
Low Ash Rd. BD18: Ship 6A 18
LOW BAILDON 1H 17
LOW BANK 2F 11
Low Bank Dr. BD22: Keigh 2F 11
Low Bank La. BD22: Keigh 2F 11
LOW BANKS 1H 7
Low Banks BD20: Keigh 2H 7
Low Bentley HX3: Hal 6C 42
Low Cl. BD16: Bgly 3H 15
Lowell Av. BD7: B'frd 4D 34
Lwr. Ainley HX2: Hal 5H 39
Lwr. Ashgrove
BD5: B'frd 3H 35 (6B 4)
Lwr. Bentley Royd
HX6: Hal 3C 54
Lwr. Bracken Bank
BD22: Keigh 1C 12
(off Diamond St.)
Lwr. Brea HX3: Hal 5G 49
Lwr. Brockholes HX2: Hal 4F 39
Lwr. Brockwell La.
HX6: Hal 5B 54
Lwr. Brown Hurst HX2: Hal . . .2E 47
Lwr. Clay Pits HX1: Hal 5H 47
Lwr. Clifton St. HX6: Hal 3E 55
Lwr. Clyde St. HX6: Hal 4D 54
Lwr. Copy BD15: B'frd 6H 25
Lwr. Crow Nest Dr.
HX3: Hal 6F 51
LOWER EDGE BOTTOM 2H 61
Lwr. Edge Rd.
HX5: Brigh, Ell 2H 61
Lwr. Ellistones HX4: Hal 2A 60
(off Saddleworth Rd.)
Lwr. Exley HX3: Hal 6D 56
LOWER FAGLEY 4G 29
Lwr. Finkil St. HD6: Brigh 2C 58
Lwr. Fleet BD13: B'frd 2C 40
Lwr. Fold HX1: Hal 4B 62
Lwr. Gaukrodger HX6: Hal 4B 54
Lwr. George St. BD6: B'frd . . .2F 43
Lwr. Globe St. BD8: B'frd 1G 35
LOWER GRANGE 2H 33
Lwr. Grange Cl. BD8: B'frd . . .2A 34
Lwr. Grattan Rd.
BD1: B'frd 2H 35 (4A 4)
Lower Grn. BD17: Bail 3F 17
Lwr. Green Av. BD19: Cleck . . .5B 52
Lwr. Hazelhurst BD13: B'frd . . .4E 41
Lwr. Heights Rd.
BD13: B'frd 1C 32
Lwr. Hollins HX6: Hal 3D 54
Lwr. Holme BD17: Bail 4G 17
Lwr. Horley Grn. HX3: Hal 4E 49
Lwr. House Cl. BD10: B'frd . . .4B 18
Lower Ings HX2: Hal 2E 39
Lwr. Kipping La.
BD13: B'frd 3D 32
Lwr. Kirkgate HX1: Hal 6D 48
Lower La. BD4: B'frd 5D 36
(Fenby La.)
BD4: B'frd 6F 45
(Hunsworth La.)
Lwr. Lark Hill BD19: Cleck . . .6D 52
Lwr. Newlands HD6: Brigh 6F 59
Lwr. Ox Heys HX3: Hal 2D 50
Lwr. Pierce Cl. BD22: Haw . . .4B 12
Lwr. Range HX3: Hal 4C 48
Lwr. Range Ter. HX3: Hal 1C 62
Lwr. Rayleigh St.
BD4: B'frd 5C 36
Lwr. Rushton Rd.
BD3: B'frd 2G 37
Lwr. Saltonstall HX2: Hal 6A 38
Lower Scholes BD22: Keigh . . .5D 10
Lwr. School St.
BD12: B'frd 5G 43
BD18: Ship 5D 16
Lwr. Skircoat Grn.
HX3: Hal 5C 56
(off Cow La.)
Lwr. Slack HX2: Hal 5B 38
LOWER TOWN 5H 21
Lowertown BD22: Oxen 5G 21
Lwr. Wellgate HX4: Hal 2C 60
Lwr. Westfield Rd.
BD9: B'frd 6E 27
Lwr. Whiteshaw M.
BD13: B'frd 5F 23
LOWER WOODLANDS 6D 44
LOWER WYKE 5G 51
Lwr. Wyke Grn.
BD12: Brigh 5F 51
Lwr. Wyke La. BD12: Brigh . . .5F 51
Loweswater Av. BD6: B'frd . . .5D 42
Lowfield Cl. BD12: B'frd 6A 44
Lowfields Bus. Pk. HX5: Ell . . .1H 61
(not continuous)
Lowfields Cl. HX5: Ell 1G 61
Lowfields Way HX5: Ell 1G 61
Low Fold BD2: B'frd 4B 28
BD13: B'frd 1E 41
BD17: Bail 1G 17
(off Moorgate)
BD19: Cleck 5B 52
Low Grn. BD7: B'frd 6E 35
Low Grn. Ter. BD7: B'frd 6F 35
Low Ho. Flats BD19: Cleck . . .6F 53
(off Westgate)
Low Laithes HX6: Hal 4C 54
Low La. BD13: B'frd 6C 32
BD14: B'frd 4F 33
HD6: Brigh 1G 59
Low Mill La. BD21: Keigh 4F 7
LOW MOOR 5G 43
Low Moor St. BD12: B'frd 5H 43
Low Moor Ter. HX2: Hal 1F 55
Lowry Vw. BD21: Keigh 5E 7
Low Spring Rd. BD21: Keigh . . .5G 7
Low St. BD21: Keigh 4E 7
(not continuous)
Lowther St. BD2: B'frd 5D 28

Marston Cl.—Mixenden Grn.

Marston Cl. BD13: B'frd 2F **41**
Marten Rd. BD5: B'frd 6G **35**
Martin Ct. BD6: B'frd 2A **42**
Martindale Cl. BD2: B'frd 4F **29**
Martin Grn. La. HX4: Hal 2A **60**
(not continuous)
Martin St. HD6: Brigh 4F **59**
Martlett Dr. BD5: B'frd 1B **44**
Marton Ct. BD3: B'frd 2F **37**
Marton Hgts. HX6: Hal 3C **54**
Mary St. BD4: B'frd 4E **37**
BD12: B'frd 1G **51**
BD13: B'frd 3D **32**
(George St.)
BD13: B'frd 6F **23**
(Minorca Mt.)
BD18: Ship 5D **16**
BD22: Oxen 5G **21**
HD6: Brigh 3E **59**
Mary St. Cvn. Site
BD4: B'frd 4E **37**
Maryville Av. HD6: Brigh 2C **58**
Masefield Av. BD9: B'frd 4A **26**
Masham Pl. BD9: B'frd 5D **26**
Masino Ter. *BD7: B'frd 5E 35*
(off Paternoster La.)
Masonic St. HX1: Hal 1G **55**
Mason's Grn. HX2: Hal 6G **39**
Mason Sq. *HX2: Hal 2H 47*
(off Keighley Rd.)
Massey Flds. BD22: Haw 5H **11**
Master La. HX2: Hal 3H **55**
Matheson Ho. BD3: B'frd 2F **5**
Matlock St. HX3: Hal 4A **48**
Matthew Cl. BD20: Keigh 2G **7**
Matthews Ct. HX3: Hal 3G **49**
Maude Av. BD17: Bail 3G **17**
Maude Cres. HX6: Hal 4A **54**
Maude St. HX3: Hal 1A **48**
HX4: Hal 2D **60**
Maudsley St.
BD3: B'frd 2C **36** (4H **5**)
Maud St. BD3: B'frd 3D **36**
Maurice Av. HD6: Brigh 3D **58**
Mavis St.
BD3: B'frd 2D **36** (3H **5**)
Mawson Ct. BD1: B'frd 4C **4**
Mawson St. BD18: Ship 5D **16**
Maw St. BD4: B'frd 4B **36**
Maxwell Rd. BD6: B'frd 3D **42**
May Av. BD13: B'frd 3E **33**
Mayfair BD5: B'frd 5H **35**
Mayfair Way BD4: B'frd 4F **37**
Mayfield HX3: Hal 4A **50**
(Northedge La.)
HX3: Hal 3D **50**
(Norwood Grn. Hill)
Mayfield Av. BD12: B'frd 2G **51**
HD6: Brigh 5F **51**
HX1: Hal 1A **56**
Mayfield Dr. BD20: Keigh 3C **8**
HX1: Hal 1A **56**
Mayfield Gdns. HX1: Hal 1A **56**
HX6: Hal 3F 55
(off Park Rd.)
Mayfield Gro. BD15: B'frd 1B **24**
BD17: Bail 2H **17**
HD6: Brigh 5F **51**
HX1: Hal 1A **56**
Mayfield Mt. HX1: Hal 1A **56**
Mayfield Pl. BD12: B'frd 2G **51**
Mayfield Ri. BD12: B'frd 2H **51**
Mayfield Rd. BD20: Keigh 3D **6**
Mayfield St. HX1: Hal 2A **56**
Mayfield Ter. BD12: B'frd 2H **51**
BD14: B'frd 6A **34**
BD19: Cleck 6G 53
(off Neville St.)
HX1: Hal 6H **47**
Mayfield Ter. Sth.
HX1: Hal 2A 56
(off Mayfield St.)
Mayfield Vw. BD12: B'frd 2H **51**
Mayo Av. BD5: B'frd 1H **43**
Mayo Cres. BD5: B'frd 2A **44**
Mayo Dr. BD5: B'frd 2A **44**
Mayo Gro. BD5: B'frd 2A **44**
Mayo Rd. BD5: B'frd 2A **44**
Mayroyde HX3: Hal 6B **50**
May St. BD19: Cleck 5F **53**
BD21: Keigh 3E **7**
BD22: Haw 1H **21**
Maythorne Cres.
BD14: B'frd 5B **34**
Maythorne Dr. BD14: B'frd 5C **34**
May Tree Cl. BD14: B'frd 4B **34**
Mayville Av. BD20: Keigh 3B **8**
Mazebrook Av.
BD19: Cleck 3G **53**
Mazebrook Cres.
BD19: Cleck 3G **53**
Meadowbank Av.
BD15: B'frd 6H **25**
Meadow Cl. BD16: Bgly 4B **14**
HX3: Hal 5B **42**
Meadow Ct. *BD13: B'frd 3D 32*
(off Chapel St.)
BD15: B'frd 3G **25**
Meadow Cres. HX3: Hal 3G **47**
Meadow Cft. BD22: Keigh 5A **6**
Meadowcroft BD5: B'frd 2B **44**
Meadow Cft. Cl.
BD10: B'frd 5B **18**
Meadowcroft Ri.
BD4: B'frd 3E **45**
Meadow Dr. HX3: Hal 3G **47**
Meadow Fold BD15: B'frd 3D **24**
Meadowlands BD19: Cleck . . .4A **52**
Meadow La. HX3: Hal 3G **47**
Meadow Rd. BD10: B'frd 5G **19**
Meadows, The BD6: B'frd 2G **43**
Meadowside Rd.
BD17: Bail 1A **18**
Meadow Vw. BD12: B'frd 4G **51**
BD22: Keigh 3H **11**
Meadow Wlk. *HX3: Hal 3G 47*
(off Meadow La.)
Mead Vw. BD4: B'frd 6G **37**
Meadway BD6: B'frd 5C **42**
Mean La. BD22: Keigh 4A **10**
Mearclough Rd. HX6: Hal 3F **55**
Mecca Bingo
Bradford **6C 4**
Halifax **3B 62**
Medley La. HX3: Hal 1F **49**
Medway BD13: B'frd 3F **41**
Meggison Gro. BD5: B'frd 5G **35**
Megna Way BD5: B'frd 5A **36**
Melba Rd. BD5: B'frd 6F **35**
Melbourne Gro. BD3: B'frd . . .1G **37**
Melbourne Pl.
BD5: B'frd 4H **35** (6B **4**)
Melbourne St. BD18: Ship 5E **17**
HX3: Hal 4A **48**
Melbourne Ter.
BD5: B'frd 4A **36** (6C **4**)
Melcombe Wlk. BD4: B'frd . . .5G **37**
Meldon Way BD6: B'frd 2A **42**
Melford St. BD4: B'frd 1E **45**
Melilot Cl. BD16: Bgly 3H **15**
Mellor Mill La. HX4: Hal 5B **60**
Mellor St. HD6: Brigh 5F **59**
HX1: Hal 2A **56**
Mellor Ter. HX1: Hal 2A **56**
Melrose BD22: Haw 1G **21**
Melrose Ct. HX5: Ell 3E **61**
Melrose Ho. *BD4: B'frd 5G 37*
(off Ned La.)
Melrose St. BD7: B'frd 5E **35**
HX3: Hal 4A **48**
Melrose Ter. HX5: Ell 3F **61**
Melton M. BD22: Haw 5H **11**
Melton Ter. BD10: B'frd 3G **29**
Melville Ho. *BD7: B'frd 2G 35*
(off Preston St.)
Melville St. BD7: B'frd 2G **35**
Mendip Way BD12: B'frd 5F **43**
Menin Dr. BD17: Bail 1G **17**
Menstone St.
BD8: B'frd 1G **35** (2A **4**)
Merchants Ct. BD4: B'frd 4C **36**
Merlin Ct. BD21: Keigh 6D **6**
Merlin Gro. BD8: B'frd 2A **34**
Merlinwood Dr. BD17: Bail . . .1H **17**
Merrion Cres. HX3: Hal 2E **57**
Merrion St. HX3: Hal 2E **57**
Merrivale Rd. BD15: B'frd 1G **33**
Merrydale Rd. BD4: B'frd 5C **44**
Merton Fold BD5: B'frd 5A **36**
Merton Rd.
BD7: B'frd 4H **35** (6A **4**)
Merville Av. BD17: Bail 1G **17**
Metcalfe St. BD4: B'frd 5D **36**
Methuen Oval BD12: B'frd 4G **51**
Mexborough Ho. *HX5: Ell 2F 61*
(off Gog Hill)
Mexborough Rd.
BD2: B'frd 2H **27**
Meynell Ho. BD10: B'frd 1E **29**
Miall St. HX1: Hal 5A **48**
Mickledore Ridge
BD7: B'frd 6C **34**
Micklemoss Dr.
BD13: B'frd 1C **40**
MICKLETHWAITE **4E 9**
Micklethwaite Dr.
BD13: B'frd 3E **41**
Micklethwaite La.
BD16: Bgly 5E **9**
Middlebrook Cl. BD8: B'frd . . .2C **34**
Middlebrook Cres.
BD8: B'frd 3B **34**
Middlebrook Dr. BD8: B'frd . . .2B **34**
Middlebrook Hill
BD8: B'frd 2B **34**
Middlebrook Ri. BD8: B'frd . . .2B **34**
Middlebrook Vw.
BD8: B'frd 2C **34**
Middlebrook Wlk.
BD8: B'frd 2C **34**
Middlebrook Way
BD8: B'frd 3B **34**
Middle Dean St. HX4: Hal 3C **60**
Middle Ellistones *HX4: Hal . . .2A 60*
(off Saddleworth Rd.)
Middlefield Ct. BD20: Keigh . . .2B **8**
Middlegate Ct. BD4: B'frd 3D **44**
Middleham Ct. BD4: B'frd 6H **37**
Middle La. BD14: B'frd 4A **34**
Middle St.
BD1: B'frd 2A **36** (3D **4**)
HX6: Hal 6A **54**
Middleton St. BD8: B'frd 6F **27**
Middle Way BD21: Keigh 4G **7**
Midgeham Gro.
BD16: Bgly 4A **14**
Midgeley Rd. BD17: Bail 4E **17**
Midgley Row BD4: B'frd 2D **44**
Midland Hill BD16: Bgly 2F **15**
Midland Rd.
BD8: B'frd 5H **27** (1C **4**)
BD9: B'frd 2G **27**
BD17: Bail 3H **17**
Midland Ter. BD2: B'frd 4H **27**
BD21: Keigh 3E **7**
Mid Point BD3: Pud 1H **37**
Mid Point Bus. Pk.
BD3: Pud 1H **37**
Midway Av. BD16: Bgly 6G **15**
Mildred St.
BD3: B'frd 6C **28** (1G **5**)
Mile Cross Gdns. HX1: Hal . . .1G **55**
Mile Cross Pl. HX1: Hal 1G **55**
Mile Cross Rd. HX1: Hal 1G **55**
Mile Cross Ter. HX1: Hal 1G **55**
Miles Hill Cres. BD4: B'frd . . .2E **45**
Miles Hill Dr. BD4: B'frd 2E **45**
Mile Thorn St. HX1: Hal 6H **47**
Milford Pl. BD9: B'frd 4E **27**
Millbeck Cl. BD13: B'frd 3A **34**
Millbeck Dr. BD16: Bgly 3A **14**
Mill Carr Hill Rd.
BD4: B'frd 1D **52**
BD12: B'frd 6D **44**
Mill Ct. BD22: Oxen 5G **21**
Miller Cl. BD2: B'frd 2H **27**
Millergate
BD1: B'frd 2A **36** (4C **4**)
Millersdale Cl. BD4: B'frd 4C **44**
Mill Fld. Rd. BD16: Bgly 6H **15**
Millgate BD16: Bgly 2F **15**
HX5: Ell 2F **61**
Mill Gro. HD6: Brigh 3D **58**
Millhaven M. *BD8: B'frd 6H 27*
(off Holywell Ash La.)
Mill Hey BD22: Haw 6H **11**
Mill Hill BD22: Haw 6G **11**
Mill Hill La. HD6: Brigh 3C **58**
Mill Hill Top BD16: Bgly 5B **14**
Mill Ho. La. HX6: Hal 5B **54**
Mill Ho. Ri. BD5: B'frd 2D **44**
Milligan Av. BD2: B'frd 2B **28**
Milligan Ct. BD16: Bgly 4A **14**
Mill La. BD4: B'frd 4A **36**
BD5: B'frd 4A **36**
BD6: B'frd 5C **42**
BD13: B'frd 1C **40**
BD19: Cleck 2F **53**
BD22: Keigh 3F **11**
BD22: Oxen 4G **21**
HD6: Brigh 5F **59**
HX2: Hal 3A **46**
(Brook Ter.)
HX2: Hal 4E **39**
(Hays La.)
HX3: Hal 3B **48**
HX4: Hal 5C **60**
Millmoor Cl. BD9: B'frd 5B **26**
Mill Royd St. HD6: Brigh 5F **59**
Millside Way HX3: Hal 4D **56**
Mill St. BD1: B'frd 1B **36** (2E **5**)
BD6: B'frd 2E **43**
BD13: B'frd 1F **23**
HX3: Hal 6A **56**
Mill Vw. BD18: Ship 5E **17**
Milner Cl. HX4: Hal 2C **60**
Milner Ing BD12: B'frd 1G **51**
Milner La. HX4: Hal 2C **60**
Milner Rd. BD17: Bail 4F **17**
Milner Royd La. HX6: Hal 4G **55**
Milner St. HX1: Hal 6B **48**
Milne St. BD7: B'frd 2G **35**
(not continuous)
Milton Av. HX6: Hal 2D **54**
Milton Pl. HX1: Hal 6B **48**
HX6: Hal 2D 54
(off Milton St.)
Milton St. BD7: B'frd 2G **35**
BD13: B'frd 1G **31**
HX6: Hal 2D **54**
Milton Ter. BD19: Cleck 5E **53**
HX1: Hal 6B **48**
(not continuous)
Minister Dr. BD4: B'frd 4F **37**
Minnie St. BD21: Keigh 5D **6**
BD22: Haw 1G **21**
Minorca Mt. BD13: B'frd 6F **23**
Minster Cl. HX4: Hal 2B **60**
Minstrel Dr. BD13: B'frd 2E **41**
Mint St. BD2: B'frd 5D **28**
Mirfield Av. BD2: B'frd 2C **28**
Mission St. HD6: Brigh 6G **59**
Mistal, The BD10: B'frd 5B **18**
Mistral Cl. BD12: B'frd 3G **51**
Mitcham Dr. BD9: B'frd 5E **27**
Mitchell Cl. BD10: B'frd 4E **19**
Mitchell La. BD10: B'frd 4E **19**
Mitchell Sq. BD5: B'frd 5A **36**
Mitchell St. BD21: Keigh 3F **7**
HD6: Brigh 4E **59**
HX6: Hal 3E **55**
Mitchell Ter. BD16: Bgly 4F **15**
Mitre Ct. BD4: B'frd 6F **37**
Mitton St. BD5: B'frd 6G **35**
BD16: Bgly 1H **25**
MIXENDEN **6E 39**
Mixenden Cl. HX2: Hal 6E **39**
Mixenden Ct. *HX2: Hal 1F 47*
(off Mixenden Rd.)
Mixenden Grn. HX2: Hal 4D **38**

A-Z Bradford 91

Mixenden La.—Myrtle Rd.

Mixenden La. HX2: Hal 5F **39**
Mixenden La. Ends
HX2: Hal 1D **46**
Mixenden Rd. HX2: Hal 5E **39**
Mixenden Stones HX2: Hal 6E **39**
Moat Cres. BD10: B'frd 5E **19**
Moffat Cl. BD6: B'frd 4D **42**
Moffatt Cl. HX3: Hal 2G **47**
Monarch Ga. BD13: B'frd 3G **31**
Monckton Ho. *BD5: B'frd 1B **44***
(off Parkway)
Mond Av. BD3: B'frd 6F **29**
Monk Barn Cl. BD16: Bgly 1G **15**
Monk St. BD7: B'frd 2G **35** (4A **4**)
Montague St. BD5: B'frd 6G **35**
HX6: Hal 4C **54**
Monterey Dr. BD15: B'frd 4F **25**
Montgomery Ho.
*BD8: B'frd 6G **27***
(off Trenton Dr.)
Mont Gro. *BD5: B'frd 6G **35***
(off Montague St.)
Montrose Pl. BD13: B'frd 1C **40**
Montrose St. BD2: B'frd 3H **27**
Montserrat Rd. BD4: B'frd 2H **45**
Moody St. BD4: B'frd 4B **36**
Moor Bank BD4: B'frd 4H **45**
MOORBOTTOM 6D 52
Moor Bottom HX2: Hal 3C **46**
Moorbottom BD19: Cleck 6D **52**
Moor Bottom La.
BD16: Bgly 2G **15**
BD21: Keigh 3D **12**
HX4: Hal 6A **56**
(not continuous)
HX6: Hal 6D **54**
Moor Bottom Rd. HX2: Hal 5H **39**
Moor Cl. Av. BD13: B'frd 3C **40**
Moor Cl. Farm M.
BD13: B'frd 3C **40**
Moor Cl. La. BD13: B'frd 3C **40**
Moor Cl. Pde. BD13: B'frd 2C **40**
Moor Cl. Rd. BD13: B'frd 3C **40**
Moorcroft BD16: Bgly 6H **9**
Moorcroft Av. BD3: B'frd 6F **29**
BD22: Keigh 2A **12**
Moorcroft Dr. BD4: B'frd 2H **45**
Moorcroft Rd. BD4: B'frd 2H **45**
Moorcroft Ter. BD4: B'frd 2H **45**
Moor Dr. BD22: Keigh 2G **11**
Moore Av. BD7: B'frd 6D **34**
MOOR EDGE 3A 14
Moor Edge High Side
BD16: Bgly 3A **14**
Moor Edge Low Side
BD16: Bgly 3A **14**
MOOR END
BD2 1C 28
HX2 1D 46
MOOREND 4F 53
Moor End BD22: Haw 1H **21**
HX6: Hal 5F **55**
Moor End Av. HX2: Hal 4E **47**
Moor End Gdns. HX2: Hal 4F **47**
Moor End La. HX6: Hal 5F **55**
(not continuous)
Moor End Rd. HX2: Hal 6D **38**
Moor End Vw. HX2: Hal 5G **47**
Moore St. BD21: Keigh 5E **7**
Moore Vw. BD7: B'frd 6D **34**
Moorfield Av. BD3: B'frd 6F **29**
BD19: Cleck 6A **52**
Moorfield Dr. BD17: Bail 1G **17**
BD22: Keigh 2H **11**
Moorfield Pl. BD10: B'frd 5D **18**
(not continuous)
Moorfield Rd. BD16: Bgly 6G **15**
Moorfield St. HX1: Hal 2A **56**
Moorfield Way BD19: Cleck 6A **52**
Moorgarth Av. BD3: B'frd 6F **29**
Moorgate BD17: Bail 1G **17**
Moorgate Av. BD3: B'frd 6F **29**
Moorgate St. HX1: Hal 2H **55**
Moorgreen Fold
BD10: B'frd 6C **18**

Moor Gro. HX3: Hal 4A **42**
MOORHEAD 6C 16
Moorhead Cres.
BD18: Ship 6C **16**
Moorhead La. BD18: Ship 6C **16**
Moorhead Ter. BD18: Ship 6C **16**
Moor Hey La. HX5: Ell 4H **61**
Moorhouse BD22: Oxen 3F **21**
Moorhouse Av. BD2: B'frd 2C **28**
Moorhouse Bri.
BD22: Oxen 4G **21**
Moor Ho. Cl. BD22: Oxen 4G **21**
Moorhouse Ct. BD22: Oxen 4G **21**
Moorhouse Dr. BD11: B'frd 4H **45**
Moorhouse La.
BD11: B'frd 4H **45**
BD22: Oxen 3F **21**
Moorhouse Ter. HX3: Hal 4B **48**
Moorings, The BD10: B'frd 5F **19**
Moorland Av. BD16: Bgly 6H **9**
BD17: Bail 1H **17**
Moorland Cl. HX2: Hal 2G **47**
Moorland Cres. BD17: Bail 1H **17**
LS28: Pud 6H **29**
Moorland Mills
BD19: Cleck 4F **53**
Moorland Pl. BD12: B'frd 6A **44**
Moorland Rd. LS28: Pud 6H **29**
Moorlands Av. BD3: B'frd 6F **29**
BD22: Keigh 1B **12**
HX2: Hal 2G **47**
Moorlands Bus. Cen.
*BD19: Cleck 5F **53***
(off Balme Rd.)
Moorlands Ct. HX4: Hal 1B **60**
Moorlands Cres. HX2: Hal 2G **47**
Moorlands Dr. HX2: Hal 3G **47**
Moorlands Pl. HX1: Hal 2B **56**
Moorlands Rd. BD11: B'frd 4H **45**
HX4: Hal 1B **60**
Moorlands Vw. HX1: Hal 2B **56**
Moorland Ter. BD21: Keigh 5H **7**
Moorland Vw. BD12: B'frd 6A **44**
BD15: B'frd 3D **24**
HX6: Hal 4B **54**
Moorland Villa HX6: Hal 6B **54**
Moor La. HX2: Hal 1G **47**
Moorlea Dr. BD17: Bail 2H **17**
Moor Pk. Cl. BD3: B'frd 1E **37**
Moor Pk. Dr. BD3: B'frd 1F **37**
Moor Pk. Rd. BD3: B'frd 1E **37**
Moor Royd HX3: Hal 3A **56**
MOOR SIDE
Bradford 5D **28**
Low Moor 6G **43**
Moorside BD9: B'frd 5C **26**
BD19: Cleck 6D **52**
(not continuous)
Moorside Av. BD2: B'frd 5E **29**
BD11: B'frd 4H **45**
Moorside Cl. BD2: B'frd 4E **29**
Moorside Cft. BD2: B'frd 5E **29**
Moorside Farm
BD22: Oxen 4E **21**
Moorside Gdns. BD2: B'frd 4E **29**
HX3: Hal 1H **47**
Moorside Ho. *BD15: B'frd 3C **24***
(off Crooke La.)
Moor Side La.
BD22: Haw, Oxen 2D **20**
Moorside La. BD3: B'frd 2F **37**
Moorside M. BD2: B'frd 4E **29**
Moorside Pl. BD3: B'frd 2F **37**
Moorside Ri. BD19: Cleck 6D **52**
Moorside Rd. BD2: B'frd 3E **29**
*BD3: B'frd 2F **37***
(off Moorside La.)
BD15: B'frd 3C **24**
Moorside St. BD12: B'frd 5F **43**
Moorside Ter. BD2: B'frd 5F **29**
Moor Smith Copse
HX2: Hal 4G **39**
Moor Stone Pl. HX3: Hal 6A **42**
Moor St. BD13: B'frd 2E **41**
BD22: Keigh 2H **11**

Moor Ter. *BD2: B'frd 6E **29***
(off Glenmore Cl.)
Moorthorpe Av. BD3: B'frd 6F **29**
MOOR TOP 5F 43
Moor Top Gdns. HX2: Hal 3G **39**
Moor Top Rd. BD12: B'frd 5F **43**
HX2: Hal 5D **46**
Moor Vw. BD4: B'frd 4H **45**
Moor Vw. Av. BD18: Ship 5E **17**
Moor Vw. Ct. BD20: Keigh 4C **8**
Moor Vw. Cres. BD16: Bgly 1E **25**
Moorview Dr. BD16: Bgly 1E **25**
BD18: Ship 6B **18**
Moorview Gro. BD21: Keigh 6F **7**
Moor Vw. Ter. BD22: Haw 6B **10**
Moorville Av. BD3: B'frd 6F **29**
Moorville Dr. BD11: B'frd 4H **45**
Moor Way BD22: Keigh 2G **11**
Moorwell Pl. BD2: B'frd 3E **29**
Moravian Ho. *HX3: Hal 6B **50***
(off Wakefield Rd.)
Moravian Pl. BD5: B'frd 5H **35**
Moresby Rd. BD6: B'frd 5C **42**
Moreton Ho. BD3: B'frd 2G **5**
Morley Av. BD3: B'frd 6F **29**
MORLEY CARR 6H 43
Morley Carr Rd.
BD12: B'frd 6H **43**
Morley St.
BD7: B'frd 3H **35** (6B **4**)
Morley Vw. HX3: Hal 4E **57**
Morningside BD8: B'frd 6F **27**
BD13: B'frd 5F **23**
Morning St. BD21: Keigh 1D **12**
Mornington Rd.
BD16: Bgly 2G **15**
Mornington St. BD21: Keigh 3D **6**
Mornington Vs. BD8: B'frd 6H **27**
Morpeth St. BD7: B'frd 2G **35**
BD13: B'frd 2E **41**
Morrell Ct. BD4: B'frd 6F **37**
Mortimer Av. BD3: B'frd 6F **29**
Mortimer Row BD3: B'frd 2F **37**
Mortimer St. BD8: B'frd 1D **34**
BD19: Cleck 6F **53**
Morton Gro. BD20: Keigh 3D **8**
Morton La. BD16: Bgly 3D **8**
BD20: Keigh 3D **8**
Morton Rd. BD4: B'frd 4F **37**
Mortons Cl. HX3: Hal 4E **57**
Moser Av. BD2: B'frd 2C **28**
Moser Cres. BD2: B'frd 2C **28**
Mosley Ho. *BD4: B'frd 4F **37***
(off Parsonage Rd.)
Moss Carr Av. BD21: Keigh 6H **7**
Moss Carr Gro. BD21: Keigh 6H **7**
Moss Carr Rd. BD21: Keigh 6H **7**
Moss Carr Ter. BD21: Keigh 5H **7**
Mossdale Av. BD9: B'frd 4A **26**
Moss Dr. HX2: Hal 5G **39**
Moss La. HX2: Hal 5G **39**
Moss Row BD15: B'frd 1C **24**
Moss Side BD9: B'frd 5C **26**
Moss St. BD13: B'frd 2C **32**
BD22: Haw 5A **12**
Mosstree Cl. BD13: B'frd 1C **40**
Mossy Bank Cl.
BD13: B'frd 1E **41**
Mostyn Gro. BD6: B'frd 3E **43**
Mostyn Mt. HX3: Hal 2A **48**
Mould Greave BD22: Oxen 3F **21**
Moulson Cl. BD6: B'frd 2F **43**
Moulson Ct. BD5: B'frd 6A **36**
Moulson Ter. BD13: B'frd 1F **31**
Mount, The BD17: Bail 3H **17**
MOUNTAIN 1C 40
Mountain Vw. BD18: Ship 1H **27**
HX2: Hal 5A **40**
Mount Av. BD2: B'frd 2D **28**
HX2: Hal 6E **47**
Mountbatten Ct. BD5: B'frd 1A **44**
Mount Cres. BD19: Cleck 5F **53**
HX2: Hal 6E **47**
Mountfields HX3: Hal 5C **50**
Mount Gdns. BD19: Cleck 5F **53**

Mount Gro. BD2: B'frd 2D **28**
Mountleigh Cl. BD4: B'frd 5C **44**
Mt. Pellon HX2: Hal 5H **47**
Mt. Pellon Rd. HX2: Hal 5G **47**
Mount Pl. BD18: Ship 5E **17**
Mount Pleasant BD6: B'frd 4C **42**
BD9: B'frd 5G **27**
BD13: B'frd 1F **31**
BD17: Bail 2G **17**
BD20: Keigh 4C **8**
HX3: Hal 3G **57**
Mt. Pleasant Av.
HX1: Hal 5B **48** (2A **62**)
Mt. Pleasant St.
BD13: B'frd 2E **41**
Mount Rd. BD2: B'frd 2E **29**
BD6: B'frd 2E **43**
Mt. Royd BD8: B'frd 5H **27**
Mount St. BD2: B'frd 2D **28**
BD3: B'frd 3C **36** (5H **5**)
BD4: B'frd 3D **36**
BD19: Cleck 5F **53**
BD21: Keigh 4D **6**
HX1: Hal 6C **48** (4B **62**)
HX6: Hal 3D **54**
Mt. Street W. HX2: Hal 5G **47**
MOUNT TABOR 2C 46
Mt. Tabor Rd. HX2: Hal 6B **38**
Mount Ter. BD2: B'frd 2D **28**
HX2: Hal 5G **47**
Mount Vw. BD13: B'frd 2D **40**
BD16: Bgly 2H **15**
BD22: Keigh 3F **11**
HX2: Hal 2C **46**
Mt. View Dr. BD19: Cleck 5E **53**
Mowbray Cl. BD13: B'frd 2E **23**
Mozeley Dr. HX2: Hal 5H **39**
Mucky La. HX5: Hal 5D **60**
Muff St. BD4: B'frd 4D **36**
Muff Ter. BD6: B'frd 2E **43**
Muirhead Ct. BD4: B'frd 1G **45**
Muirhead Dr. BD4: B'frd 1G **45**
Muirhead Fold BD4: B'frd 1G **45**
Mulberry St. BD21: Keigh 3F **7**
Mulcture Hall Rd.
HX1: Hal 6D **48** (3D **62**)
Mulgrave St.
BD3: B'frd 3D **36** (6H **5**)
Mulhalls Mill HX6: Hal 3E **55**
Mumford St. BD5: B'frd 6A **36**
Munby St. BD8: B'frd 2C **34**
Munster St. BD4: B'frd 6D **36**
Munton Cl. BD6: B'frd 5C **42**
Murdoch St. BD21: Keigh 3H **7**
Murdstone Cl. BD5: B'frd 6A **36**
Murgatroyd St. BD5: B'frd 1A **44**
(not continuous)
BD18: Ship 5F **17**
Murray St. BD5: B'frd 6G **35**
Museum Ct. BD2: B'frd 5E **29**
Musgrave Dr. BD2: B'frd 5E **29**
Musgrave Gro. BD2: B'frd 5E **29**
Musgrave Mt. BD2: B'frd 5E **29**
Musgrave Rd. BD2: B'frd 5E **29**
Musselburgh St.
BD7: B'frd 2G **35**
Mutton Fold *HX3: Hal 3G **49***
(off Towngate)
Mutton La. BD15: B'frd 5D **24**
Myers Av. BD2: B'frd 3C **28**
Myers La. BD2: B'frd 3C **28**
Myrtle Av. BD16: Bgly 3F **15**
HX2: Hal 1G **47**
Myrtle Bank HX3: Hal 3D **56**
Myrtle Ct. BD16: Bgly 3F **15**
Myrtle Dr. BD22: Haw 4B **12**
HX2: Hal 1G **47**
Myrtle Gdns. HX2: Hal 1G **47**
Myrtle Gro. BD13: B'frd 4C **40**
BD16: Bgly 3F **15**
HX2: Hal 1G **47**
Myrtle Pl. BD16: Bgly 2F **15**
BD18: Ship 5D **16**
HX2: Hal 1G **47**
Myrtle Rd. HX5: Ell 4F **61**

92 A-Z Bradford

Myrtle St. BD3: B'frd 3E **37**
BD16: Bgly 2G **15**
Myrtle Ter. BD22: Haw 4B **12**
HX6: Hal 3D **54**
Myrtle Vw. BD22: Keigh 2H **11**
Myrtle Wlk. *BD16: Bgly 2F 15*
(off Ferncliffe Rd.)
MYTHOLMES **5G 11**
Mytholmes BD22: Haw 5G **11**
Mytholmes La. BD22: Haw ...6G **11**
(not continuous)
Mytholmes Ter.
BD22: Haw 5G **11**

N

NAB END **1A 42**
Nab End BD12: B'frd 3H **51**
Nab End Rd. HX4: Hal 2D **60**
Nab La. BD18: Ship 6B **16**
NAB WOOD **6B 16**
Nab Wood Bank
BD18: Ship 6B **16**
Nab Wood Cl. BD18: Ship 6C **16**
Nab Wood Crematorium
BD18: Ship 5B **16**
Nab Wood Cres.
BD18: Ship 6B **16**
Nab Wood Dr. BD18: Ship 1B **26**
Nab Wood Gdns.
BD18: Ship 6C **16**
Nab Wood Gro. BD18: Ship ...6B **16**
Nab Wood Mt. BD18: Ship ...6B **16**
Nab Wood Pl. BD18: Ship 6B **16**
Nab Wood Ri. BD18: Ship 6B **16**
Nab Wood Rd. BD18: Ship ...1B **26**
Nab Wood School Sports Cen.
...................**6A 16**
Nab Wood Ter. BD18: Ship ...6B **16**
Naden Cl. BD6: B'frd 1A **42**
Napier Rd. BD3: B'frd 2F **37**
HX5: Ell 3E **61**
Napier St. BD3: B'frd 2F **37**
BD13: B'frd 2F **41**
BD21: Keigh 5F **7**
Napier Ter. BD3: B'frd 2F **37**
Naples St. BD8: B'frd 6F **27**
Napoleon Bus. Pk.
BD4: B'frd 4D **36**
Nares St. BD21: Keigh 4D **6**
BD22: Haw 5A **12**
Narrow La. BD16: Bgly 4B **14**
Narrows, The BD16: Bgly 4B **14**
Naseby Ho. BD4: B'frd 2H **45**
Naseby Ri. BD13: B'frd 2F **41**
Nashville Rd. BD22: Keigh 5C **6**
Nashville St. BD22: Keigh 5C **6**
Nashville Ter. *BD22: Keigh 5C 6*
(off Nashville Rd.)
Nathaniel Waterhouse Homes
HX1: Hal 5B **62**
National Mus. of Photography, Film & Television, The
.............**3A 36 (5C 4)**
Natty Fields Cl. HX2: Hal 4G **39**
Nature Way BD6: B'frd 5C **42**
Navigation Cl. HX5: Ell 1G **61**
Navigation Rd. HX3: Hal 1D **56**
Naylor's Bldgs.
BD19: Cleck 5B 52
(off Tabbs La.)
Naylor St. HX1: Hal 6H **47**
Neal St. BD5: B'frd 3A **36** (6C **4**)
Nearcliffe Rd. BD9: B'frd 5E **27**
Near Crook BD10: B'frd 4B **18**
Near Highfield
BD22: Keigh 2G **11**
Near Hob Cote BD22: Keigh ...4E **11**
Near Royd HX3: Hal 2A **48**
Necropolis Rd. BD7: B'frd 4D **34**
Ned Hill Rd. HX2: Hal 1G **39**
Ned La. BD4: B'frd 5G **37**
Nelson Pl. BD13: B'frd 2E **41**
HX6: Hal 3F **55**
Nelson St.
BD1: B'frd 3A **36** (6D **4**)
BD13: B'frd 2E **41**
BD15: B'frd 6A **26**
BD22: Haw 5A **12**
(Albion St.)
BD22: Haw 5A **12**
(East Ter.)
HX6: Hal 3E **55**
Nene St. BD5: B'frd 5G **35**
Nesfield St.
BD1: B'frd 1H **35** (1B **4**)
Nessfield Dr. BD22: Keigh 6B **6**
Nessfield Gro. BD22: Keigh 6B **6**
Nessfield Rd. BD22: Keigh 6B **6**
Netherby St. BD3: B'frd 2D **36**
Netherfield Pl. BD19: Cleck ...6G **53**
Netherhall Pk. *BD17: Bail 2H 17*
(off Netherhall Rd.)
Netherhall Rd. BD17: Bail 2H **17**
Netherlands Av. BD6: B'frd ...4G **43**
BD12: B'frd 4G **43**
Netherlands Sq.
BD12: B'frd 4H **43**
Nether Moor Vw.
BD16: Bgly 2G **15**
Netherwood BD13: B'frd 1F **31**
Nettle Gro. HX3: Hal 4G **49**
Neville Av. BD4: B'frd 2D **44**
Neville Ct. BD18: Ship 5D **16**
Neville Rd. BD4: B'frd 5D **36**
Neville St. BD19: Cleck 6G **53**
BD21: Keigh 3F **7**
Nevill Gro. BD9: B'frd 4B **26**
Newall St. BD5: B'frd 5H **35**
Newark Ho. *BD5: B'frd 5H 35*
(off Roundhill St.)
Newark Rd. BD16: Bgly 6F **9**
Newark St. BD4: B'frd 4C **36**
New Augustus St.
BD1: B'frd 3B **36** (6F **5**)
New Bank HX3: Hal ...5D **48** (1D **62**)
New Bank Ri. BD4: B'frd 6F **37**
New Bond St.
HX1: Hal 6B **48** (4A **62**)
Newbridge Ind. Est.
BD21: Keigh 4F **7**
NEW BRIGHTON **1A 26**
New Brighton *BD12: B'frd 6C 44*
(off Dyehouse Rd.)
BD16: Bgly 1A **26**
New Brunswick St.
HX1: Hal 6B **48** (4A **62**)
Newburn Rd. BD7: B'frd 4F **35**
Newbury Cl. BD17: Bail 1H **17**
Newby Ho. *BD2: B'frd 5D 28*
(off Otley Rd.)
Newby St. BD5: B'frd 5A **36**
Newcastle Ho. BD3: B'frd 3F **5**
New Cheapside
BD1: B'frd 2A **36** (4D **4**)
New Clayton Ter.
BD13: B'frd 2F **23**
New Cl. BD13: B'frd 4H **31**
New Cl. Rd. BD18: Ship 6A **16**
New Clough Rd. HX6: Hal 5F **55**
Newcombe St. HX5: Ell 4G **61**
New Cross St. BD5: B'frd 1A **44**
(not continuous)
BD12: B'frd 6D **44**
New Delight HX2: Hal 4E **39**
New England Rd.
BD21: Keigh 6E **7**
New Fold BD6: B'frd 4C **42**
Newforth Gro. BD5: B'frd 1G **43**
New Grange Vw. HX2: Hal ...3H **39**
NEWHALL **2B 44**
Newhall Dr. BD6: B'frd 3B **44**
Newhall Mt. BD6: B'frd 3B **44**
Newhall Rd. BD4: B'frd 2D **44**
New Hey Rd. BD4: B'frd 5C **36**
HD2: Hud 5H **61**
New Holme HX3: Hal 6A **50**
New Holme Cotts.
HX2: Hal 6B **38**
New Holme Rd.
BD22: Haw 1H **21**
New Ho. La. BD13: B'frd 3H **41**
Newill Cl. BD5: B'frd 1C **44**
New John St.
BD1: B'frd 2H **35** (4C **4**)
New Kirkgate BD18: Ship 5F **17**
New Laithe HX2: Hal 6G **39**
New Laithe Rd. BD6: B'frd ...2E **43**
Newlands, The HX6: Hal 5A **54**
Newlands Av. BD3: B'frd 6F **29**
HX3: Hal 1G **49**
HX6: Hal 4A **54**
Newlands Cl. HD6: Brigh 6F **59**
Newlands Cres. HX3: Hal 2G **49**
Newlands Dr. BD16: Bgly 5E **9**
HX3: Hal 2G **49**
Newlands Ga. HX2: Hal 6C **46**
Newlands Gro. HX3: Hal 2G **49**
Newlands Pl. BD3: B'frd 6D **28**
Newlands Rd. HX2: Hal 6C **46**
Newlands Vw. HX3: Hal 2G **49**
New La. BD3: B'frd 3F **37**
BD4: B'frd 3F **37**
HX3: Hal 4A **56**
(Birdcage La.)
HX3: Hal 3D **56**
(Whitegate)
Newlay Cl. BD10: B'frd 6G **19**
New Line BD10: B'frd 6F **19**
New Longley HX6: Hal 6C **54**
New Longley La. HX6: Hal 6C **54**
Newlyn Rd. BD20: Keigh 2A **8**
Newman St. BD4: B'frd 1D **44**
New Mkt. Pl. *BD1: B'frd 4D 4*
(off Hustlergate)
New Marsh HX6: Hal 2D **54**
New Mill HX2: Hal 5A **38**
New Otley Rd.
BD3: B'frd 1C **36** (2G **5**)
New Pk. Rd. BD13: B'frd 1D **40**
New Popplewell La.
BD19: Cleck 5B **52**
Newport Pl. BD8: B'frd 6G **27**
Newport Rd. BD8: B'frd 6G **27**
New Rd. BD13: B'frd 1F **31**
HX1: Hal 1C **56** (5C **62**)
HX2: Hal 4A **46**
HX4: Hal 6C **60**
(Jagger Grn. La.)
HX4: Hal 2A **60**
(Spring La.)
New Rd. E. BD19: Cleck 5B **52**
NEW ROAD SIDE **1H 51**
New Row BD9: B'frd 5C **26**
BD12: B'frd 3H **51**
BD16: Bgly 5H **15**
HX4: Hal 5C **60**
LS28: Pud 4H **29**
Newroyd Rd. BD5: B'frd 1A **44**
NEWSHOLME **1E 11**
Newsholme New Rd.
BD22: Keigh 1E **11**
Newstead Av. HX1: Hal 6G **47**
Newstead Gdns. HX1: Hal 6G **47**
Newstead Gro. HX1: Hal 6G **47**
Newstead Heath HX1: Hal 6G **47**
Newstead Pl. HX1: Hal 6G **47**
Newstead Ri. BD20: Keigh 2B **8**
Newstead Ter. HX1: Hal 6G **47**
Newstead Wlk. BD5: B'frd 5H **35**
New St. BD4: B'frd 3D **44**
BD10: B'frd 5D **18**
BD12: B'frd 6D **44**
BD13: B'frd 1F **31**
BD16: Bgly 4E **9**
BD22: Haw 1G **21**
BD22: Keigh 3H **11**
HD6: Brigh 4H **59**
(Savile Cl.)
HD6: Brigh 6F **51**
(West St.)
HX2: Hal 5G **47**
HX3: Hal 3G **57**
NEW TOFTSHAW **3F 45**
New Toftshaw BD4: B'frd 3F **45**
Newton Pk. HD6: Brigh 1D **58**
Newton Pl. BD5: B'frd 5H **35**
Newton St. BD5: B'frd 5A **36**
(Ripley St.)
BD5: B'frd 6A **36**
(St Stephen's Ter.)
HX6: Hal 3D **54**
Newton Ter. HX6: Hal 4D **54**
Newton Way BD17: Bail 1G **17**
NEW TOWN **5C 6**
New Town Cl. BD21: Keigh 4D **6**
New Town Ct. BD21: Keigh 4D **6**
New Works Rd.
BD12: B'frd 6G **43**
Nialls Ct. BD10: B'frd 3D **18**
Nicholas Cl. BD7: B'frd 2D **34**
Nicholson Cl. BD16: Bgly 5G **9**
Nichols Yd. HX6: Hal 3E **55**
Nidderdale Wlk.
BD17: Bail 1A **18**
Nidd St. BD3: B'frd 3D **36**
Nightingale St. *BD21: Keigh ...3E 7*
(off Linnet St.)
Nightingale Wlk.
BD16: Bgly 1A **16**
Nile Cres. BD22: Keigh 5B **6**
Nile St. BD22: Haw 5A **12**
BD22: Keigh 5B **6**
Nina Rd. BD7: B'frd 6D **34**
Noble St. BD7: B'frd 4F **35**
Nog La. BD9: B'frd 3E **27**
Nook, The BD19: Cleck 5G **53**
HX6: Hal 4D **54**
NOON NICK **3A 26**
Norbreck Dr. BD22: Haw 5A **12**
Norbury Rd. BD10: B'frd 2G **29**
Norcliffe La. HX3: Hal 1G **57**
Norcroft Brow
BD7: B'frd 3H **35** (5A **4**)
Norcroft Ind. Est.
BD7: B'frd 2G **35** (4A **4**)
Norcroft St.
BD7: B'frd 2G **35** (4A **4**)
Norfolk Gdns.
BD1: B'frd 3A **36** (5D **4**)
Norfolk Pl. HX1: Hal 1A **56**
Norfolk St. BD16: Bgly 2G **15**
Norham Gro. BD12: B'frd 3H **51**
Norland Rd. HX4: Hal 6F **55**
HX6: Hal 4D **54**
Norland St. BD7: B'frd 6D **34**
NORLAND TOWN **5F 55**
Norland Town Rd. HX6: Hal ...5F **55**
Norland Vw. *HX2: Hal 3A 56*
(off Delph Hill Rd.)
HX6: Hal 3F **55**
Norman Av. BD2: B'frd 2D **28**
HX5: Ell 3G **61**
Norman Cres. BD2: B'frd 2D **28**
Norman Gro. BD2: B'frd 2D **28**
HX5: Ell 3G **61**
Norman La. BD2: B'frd 2D **28**
Norman Mt. BD2: B'frd 2D **28**
Norman St. BD16: Bgly 2G **15**
BD22: Haw 6H **11**
HX1: Hal 2H **55**
HX5: Ell 3G **61**
Norman Ter. BD2: B'frd 2D **28**
HX5: Ell 3G **61**
NORR **1D 24**
Norr Grn. Ter. BD15: B'frd 1D **24**
Northallerton Rd.
BD3: B'frd 6B **28**
Northampton St.
BD3: B'frd 6B **28**
North Av. BD8: B'frd 4H **27**
Nth. Bank Rd. BD16: Bgly 2G **25**
North Beck Ho. *BD21: Keigh ...5D 6*
(off Aireworth St.)
North Bolton HX2: Hal 4F **39**
North Bri.
HX1: Hal 5C **48** (2C **62**)
North Bridge Leisure Cen.
.............**5C 48 (2C 62)**

North Bri. St.—Old La.

North Bri. St.
HX1: Hal 5C **48** (2C **62**)
Northbrook St.
BD1: B'frd 1B **36** (2E **5**)
Nth. Byland HX2: Hal 4G **39**
North Cliffe HX6: Hal 4D **54**
Nth. Cliffe Av. BD13: B'frd 3F **33**
Nth. Cliffe Cl. BD13: B'frd 2E **33**
Nth. Cliffe Dr. BD13: B'frd 3E **33**
Nth. Cliffe Gro.
BD13: B'frd 2E **33**
Nth. Cliffe La. BD13: B'frd 2F **33**
Northcliffe Rd. BD18: Ship ...1E **27**
Nth. Clough Head
HX2: Hal 5D **46**
Northcote Rd. BD2: B'frd 5D **28**
Northcroft Ri. BD8: B'frd 6C **26**
North Cut HD6: Brigh 5D **58**
Northdale Av. BD5: B'frd 1G **43**
Northdale Cres. BD5: B'frd ...1G **43**
Northdale Mt. BD5: B'frd 1G **43**
Northdale Rd. BD9: B'frd 2F **27**
Nth. Dean Av. BD22: Keigh 4A **6**
Nth. Dean Bus. Pk.
HX4: Hal 6C **56**
Nth. Dean Rd. BD22: Keigh 4A **6**
HX4: Hal 6A **56**
North Edge *HX3: Hal 4A **50***
(off Brighouse & Denholme Ga. Rd.)
Northedge La. HX3: Hal 4A **50**
Northedge Mdw.
BD10: B'frd 1D **28**
Northedge Pk. HX3: Hal 4B **50**
Northern Cl. BD7: B'frd 1D **42**
Northfield Cl. *HX5: Ell 3F **61***
(off Victoria Av.)
Northfield Cres.
BD16: Bgly 6G **15**
Northfield Gdns.
BD6: B'frd 2G **43**
Northfield Gro. BD6: B'frd 2G **43**
Northfield Ho. BD10: B'frd 6E **19**
Northfield Pl. BD8: B'frd 6G **27**
Northfield Rd. BD6: B'frd 2F **43**
Northfield Ter. BD13: B'frd ...2G **41**
North Fold BD10: B'frd 5D **18**
Northgate
BD1: B'frd 2A **36** (3C **4**)
BD17: Bail 1G **17**
BD19: Cleck 6F **53**
HX1: Hal 6C **48** (3C **62**)
HX4: Hal 5B **60**
HX5: Ell 2F **61**
Nth. Hall Av. BD10: B'frd 3C **18**
Nth. Holme St.
BD1: B'frd 1A **36** (2D **4**)
North Ives BD22: Oxen 3G **21**
Nth. John St. BD13: B'frd 2E **41**
North Lea *HX6: Hal 3D **54***
(off Tuel La.)
Northlea Av. BD10: B'frd 4C **18**
North Lodge BD13: B'frd 6G **23**
NORTHOWRAM 2G **49**
Northowram Grn. HX3: Hal ...2G **49**
North Pde.
BD1: B'frd 2A **36** (3C **4**)
BD15: B'frd 5G **25**
HX1: Hal 6C **48** (3C **62**)
Nth. Park Rd. BD9: B'frd 4F **27**
Nth. Park Ter. BD9: B'frd 5G **27**
Nth. Queen St. BD21: Keigh ...4E **7**
North Rd. BD6: B'frd 2F **43**
Northrop Cl. BD8: B'frd 6D **26**
Nth. Royd HX3: Hal 4A **50**
Nth. Selby HX2: Hal 4F **39**
Northside Av. BD7: B'frd 3E **35**
Northside Rd. BD7: B'frd 3D **34**
Northside Ter. BD7: B'frd 3D **34**
North St. BD1: B'frd ...2B **36** (3F **5**)
BD10: B'frd 3D **18**
BD12: B'frd 1C **52**
BD21: Keigh 4E **7**
BD22: Haw 6F **11**
HX4: Hal 5B **60**
(Cross St.)
North St. HX4: Hal 2D **60**
(Green La.)
North Ter. *BD16: Bgly 3G **15***
(off Leonard St.)
Nth. Vale Ct. HD6: Brigh 6F **51**
North Vw. BD13: B'frd 1C **40**
(Glazier Rd.)
BD13: B'frd 2F **23**
(Walker Ter.)
BD15: B'frd 6G **25**
(North Pde.)
BD15: B'frd 2C **24**
(Townfield)
HX3: Hal 5A **50**
HX4: Hal 5B **60**
North Vw. Rd. BD3: B'frd 5B **28**
BD4: B'frd 4H **45**
North Vw. St. BD20: Keigh 2D **6**
North Vw. Ter. *BD20: Keigh 3D **8***
(off Main Rd.)
BD22: Haw 5G **11**
North Wlk. BD16: Bgly 4A **14**
North Wing
BD3: B'frd 1B **36** (2F **5**)
Northwood Cres.
BD10: B'frd 6E **19**
Norton Cl. HX2: Hal 6D **46**
HX5: Ell 4F **61**
Norton Dr. HX2: Hal 6D **46**
Norton St. HX5: Ell 3F **61**
NORTON TOWER 6D **46**
Norton Twr. HX2: Hal 6D **46**
Norwood Av. BD18: Ship 1F **27**
NORWOOD GREEN 3D **50**
Norwood Grn. Hill
HX3: Hal 3D **50**
Norwood Pl. BD18: Ship 1F **27**
Norwood Rd. BD18: Ship 1F **27**
Norwood St. BD5: B'frd 1H **43**
BD18: Ship 1F **27**
Norwood Ter. BD18: Ship 1F **27**
HX3: Hal 3E **51**
Nostell Cl.
BD8: B'frd 1H **35** (1A **4**)
Nottingham St. BD3: B'frd 2G **37**
No. 7 Health Club *4D **6***
(off Devonshire St.)
Nunburnholme Wlk.
BD10: B'frd 1E **29**
Nunlea Royd HX3: Hal 1E **59**
Nunroyd Ho. *BD4: B'frd 3F **37***
(off Sticker La.)
Nurser La. BD5: B'frd 5G **35**
Nurser Pl. BD5: B'frd 5G **35**
Nursery Av. HX3: Hal 2H **47**
Nursery Cl. BD17: Bail 3D **16**
BD20: Keigh 1C **6**
HX3: Hal 3H **47**
Nursery Gdns. BD16: Bgly 5F **15**
Nursery Gro. HX3: Hal 2H **47**
Nursery La. HX3: Hal 2G **47**
Nursery Rd. BD7: B'frd 1D **42**
BD14: B'frd 5H **33**
Nuthatch M. BD6: B'frd 2A **42**
Nuttall Rd.
BD3: B'frd 2C **36** (3G **5**)
Nutter St. BD19: Cleck 6E **53**
Nutwood Wlk. BD6: B'frd 5C **42**

O

Oak Av. BD8: B'frd 5G **27**
BD16: Bgly 4F **15**
HX6: Hal 2D **54**
Oak Bank BD16: Bgly 3G **15**
BD17: Bail 3G **17**
BD18: Ship 2H **27**
Oakbank Av. BD22: Keigh 6B **6**
Oakbank B'way.
BD22: Keigh 1B **12**
Oakbank Ct. BD22: Keigh 1B **12**
Oakbank Cres.
BD22: Keigh 1B **12**
Oakbank Dr. BD22: Keigh 6B **6**
Oakbank Gro. BD22: Keigh 6B **6**
Oakbank La. BD22: Keigh 1B **12**
Oakbank Mt. BD22: Keigh 1B **12**
Oakdale BD16: Bgly 6G **9**
Oakdale Av. BD6: B'frd 2F **43**
BD18: Ship 1H **27**
Oakdale Cl. BD10: B'frd 4G **29**
HX3: Hal 3A **48**
Oakdale Cres. BD6: B'frd 2F **43**
Oakdale Dr. BD10: B'frd 4G **29**
BD18: Ship 1A **28**
Oakdale Gro. BD18: Ship 1A **28**
Oakdale Rd. BD18: Ship 1A **28**
Oakdale Ter. BD6: B'frd 2F **43**
Oakdene Mt. BD14: B'frd 6G **33**
OAKENSHAW 6B **44**
Oakenshaw Ct. BD12: B'frd ...3G **51**
Oakenshaw La.
BD12: B'frd 3C **52**
BD19: B'frd 3C **52**
Oakes Gdns. HX4: Hal 5B **60**
Oakfield Av. BD16: Bgly 3A **16**
Oakfield Cl. HX5: Ell 3E **61**
Oakfield Dr. BD17: Bail 3H **17**
Oakfield Gro. BD9: B'frd 5G **27**
Oakfield Rd. BD21: Keigh 1C **12**
Oakfield Ter. BD18: Ship 6H **17**
Oak Gro. BD20: Keigh 1H **7**
BD21: Keigh 2C **12**
Oakhall Pk. BD13: B'frd 2D **32**
Oakham Wlk. BD4: B'frd 5C **36**
Oak Hill HX6: Hal 6A **54**
Oak Hill Rd. HD6: Brigh 4F **59**
Oakhurst Ct. BD8: B'frd 5H **27**
Oaklands BD10: B'frd 5C **18**
BD18: Ship 6B **16**
HD6: Brigh 6D **58**
Oaklands Av. HX3: Hal 2G **49**
Oak La. BD9: B'frd 5F **27**
HX1: Hal 6A **48**
HX6: Hal 6A **54**
Oakleigh Av. BD14: B'frd 6H **33**
(not continuous)
HX3: Hal 4C **56**
Oakleigh Cl. BD14: B'frd 5H **33**
Oakleigh Gdns.
BD14: B'frd 6H **33**
Oakleigh Gro. BD14: B'frd 6H **33**
(not continuous)
Oakleigh M. BD22: Keigh 3G **11**
Oakleigh Rd. BD14: B'frd 6H **33**
Oakleigh Ter. BD14: B'frd 5H **33**
Oakleigh Vw. BD17: Bail 2F **17**
Oakley Ho. *BD5: B'frd 5H **35***
(off Park La.)
Oak Mt. BD8: B'frd 5H **27**
HX3: Hal 5C **50**
Oak Pl. BD17: Bail 1B **18**
HX1: Hal 6A **48**
HX6: Hal 2D **54**
Oakridge Ct. BD16: Bgly 1G **15**
Oak Ri. BD19: Cleck 3F **53**
Oakroyd Av. BD6: B'frd 2G **43**
Oakroyd Cl. BD11: B'frd 6H **45**
HD6: Brigh 2F **59**
Oak Royd Cotts. HX3: Hal 5B **56**
Oakroyd Dr. BD11: B'frd 1H **53**
HD6: Brigh 2F **59**
Oakroyd Rd. BD6: B'frd 2F **43**
Oakroyd Ter. BD8: B'frd 5H **27**
BD17: Bail 3H **17**
Oakroyd Vs. BD8: B'frd 5H **27**
Oaks, The BD15: B'frd 1B **24**
Oaks Dr. BD15: B'frd 1A **34**
Oaks Fold BD5: B'frd 6A **36**
Oakshaw Ct. BD4: B'frd 5C **36**
Oaks La. BD8: B'frd 2B **34**
BD15: B'frd 1A **34**
Oak St. BD14: B'frd 5H **33**
BD22: Haw 6H **11**
BD22: Oxen 4G **21**
HX5: Ell 3F **61**
HX6: Hal 2D **54**
Oak Ter. *HX1: Hal 6A **48***
(off Acorn St.)
Oak Ter. HX4: Hal 5A **60**
*HX6: Hal 2D **54***
(off Oak Pl.)
Oak Vs. BD8: B'frd 5H **27**
Oakwell Cl. BD7: B'frd 6F **35**
Oakwood Av. BD2: B'frd 3H **27**
Oakwood Cotts. BD16: Bgly ...5G **9**
Oakwood Ct. BD8: B'frd 1G **35**
Oakwood Dr. BD16: Bgly 6F **9**
Oakwood Gro. BD8: B'frd 6E **27**
OAKWORTH 3G **11**
Oakworth Hall BD22: Keigh ...3G **11**
Oakworth Rd. BD21: Keigh 6B **6**
BD22: Keigh 6B **6**
Oakworth Station
Keighley & Worth Valley Railway 4H **11**
Oakworth Ter. *BD22: Keigh ...3G **11***
(off Dockroyd La.)
Oasby Cft. BD4: B'frd 2G **45**
Oastler Pl. BD12: B'frd 5H **43**
Oastler Rd. BD18: Ship 5D **16**
Oastler Shop. Cen.
BD1: B'frd 2A **36** (3C **4**)
Oats St. BD22: Keigh 1C **12**
Occupation La.
BD22: Keigh 1H **11**
HX2: Hal 5G **39**
Octagon Ter. HX2: Hal 3G **55**
Oddfellows Ct.
BD1: B'frd 2A **36** (4C **4**)
Oddfellows St.
BD19: Cleck 5B **52**
HD6: Brigh 4F **59**
Oddy Pl. BD6: B'frd 2F **43**
Oddy St. BD4: B'frd 2G **45**
Odeon Cinema 1H **37**
ODSAL 3H **43**
Odsal Rd. BD6: B'frd 2G **43**
(not continuous)
Odsal Stadium 3A **44**
ODSAL TOP 3A **44**
Office Row BD22: Haw 5G **11**
OGDEN 1F **39**
Ogden Cres. BD13: B'frd 5F **23**
Ogden Ho. BD4: B'frd 6H **37**
Ogden La. BD13: B'frd 5F **23**
HX2: Hal 1F **39**
Ogden St. HX6: Hal 4C **54**
Ogden Vw. Cl. HX2: Hal 4F **39**
Ogden Water Vis. Cen. 1E **39**
Old Allen Rd. BD15: B'frd 4A **24**
Old Arc., The HX1: Hal 4C **62**
Old Bank HX3: Hal 6D **48**
(not continuous)
Old Bell Ct. HX1: Hal 5B **62**
Old Canal Rd.
BD1: B'frd 1A **36** (1D **4**)
Old Cawsey HX6: Hal 3E **55**
Old Cock Yd.
HX1: Hal 6C **48** (4C **62**)
Old Corn Mill, The
BD4: B'frd 6F **37**
Old Corn Mill La.
BD7: B'frd 5E **35**
Old Dalton La.
BD21: Keigh 4F **7**
Old Dan La. HX4: Hal 4C **60**
OLD DOLPHIN 1H **41**
Old Earth HX5: Ell 2H **61**
Old Farm Cres.
BD4: B'frd 6D **36**
OLDFIELD 5A **10**
Oldfield Ga. BD22: Haw 6E **11**
Oldfield La. BD22: Haw 5E **11**
BD22: Keigh 6A **10**
Oldfield St. HX3: Hal 1A **48**
Old Fort BD13: B'frd 3G **31**
Old Godley La. HX3: Hal 5E **49**
Old Guy Rd. BD13: B'frd 1C **40**
Old Hall Cl. BD22: Haw 1G **21**
Oldham St. *HD6: Brigh 6E **59***
(off Bridge End)
Old La. BD13: B'frd 1F **23**
HD6: Brigh 4F **59**

Old La.—Park Vw.

Old La. HX2: Hal 4A **46**
HX3: Hal 2A **48** (1A **62**)
Old Lane Ct. *HD6: Brigh 4F 59*
(off Old La.)
Old Langley La. BD17: Bail . . .1H **17**
Old Lee Bank HX3: Hal 4B **48**
OLD LINDLEY **6C 60**
Old Lindley Rd. HD3: Hal 6E **61**
HX4: Hal 6C **60**
Old Main St. BD16: Bgly 1F **15**
Old Manse Cft.
BD22: Oxen 5G **21**
Old Mkt. HX1: Hal 6C **48** (4C **62**)
Old Marsh *HX6: Hal 2D 54*
(off Burnley Rd.)
Old Mill BD2: B'frd 3E **29**
Old Mill Gro. HX1: Hal 1G **55**
Old Oxenhope La.
BD22: Oxen 2F **21**
Old Pk. Ct.
BD3: B'frd 2C **36** (4G **5**)
Old Park Rd. BD10: B'frd 5E **19**
Old Popplewell La.
BD19: Cleck 5A **52**
Old Power Way HX5: Ell 1G **61**
Old Riding La. HX2: Hal 2B **46**
Old Rd. BD7: B'frd 1C **42**
BD13: B'frd 1F **31**
(New Rd.)
BD13: B'frd 3F **33**
(Watkin Av.)
Old Robin BD19: Cleck 6F **53**
Old School Gdns.
HX3: Hal 4C **48**
Old Side Ct. BD20: Keigh 2E **9**
Old Souls Way BD16: Bgly 5E **9**
Old Tannery *BD16: Bgly 2F 15*
(off Industrial St.)
Old Vicarage Cl.
BD16: Bgly 1H **25**
Old Well Head
HX1: Hal 2C **56** (6B **62**)
Olive Gro. BD8: B'frd 1C **34**
Olive Pl. BD13: B'frd 2E **41**
Oliver Cl. HX6: Hal 3D **54**
Oliver Mdws. HX5: Ell 2H **61**
Oliver St. BD4: B'frd 4C **36**
Olive Ter. BD16: Bgly 2G **15**
Olivia's Ct. BD9: B'frd 5C **26**
Ollerdale Av. BD15: B'frd 4G **25**
(not continuous)
Ollerdale Cl. BD15: B'frd 5G **25**
Olympic Pk. BD12: B'frd 6A **44**
Olympic Way BD12: B'frd 6A **44**
One St. BD1: B'frd 4B **4**
Onslow Cres. BD4: B'frd 1D **44**
Opal St. BD22: Keigh 1C **12**
Orange St. BD3: B'frd 3E **37**
HX1: Hal 6C **48** (3B **62**)
Orchard, The BD21: Keigh 4H **7**
Orchard Cl. HX2: Hal 1F **55**
Orchard Gro. BD10: B'frd 6F **19**
Orchard Ri. HX6: Hal 5B **54**
Orchards, The BD16: Bgly 6G **9**
Orchard Way HD6: Brigh 3E **59**
Orchid Cl. BD18: Ship 2H **27**
Orion Pl. *HX6: Hal 3D 54*
(off Greenups Ter.)
Orleans St. BD6: B'frd 4D **42**
Ormonde Dr. BD15: B'frd 1G **33**
Ormond Rd. BD6: B'frd 2F **43**
Ormondroyd Av. BD6: B'frd . . .3G **43**
Ormond St. BD7: B'frd 5E **35**
Osborne Gro. HX3: Hal 6B **50**
Osborne St. BD5: B'frd 4H **35**
HX1: Hal 5H **47**
Osbourne Dr. BD13: B'frd 2D **40**
Osdal Rd. *BD6: B'frd 3H 43*
(off Glenfield Mt.)
Osmond Ho. *BD5: B'frd 4A 36*
(off Crosscombe Wlk.)
Osprey Ct. BD8: B'frd 2A **34**
Osterley Cres. BD10: B'frd . . .2G **29**
Osterley Gro. BD10: B'frd 2G **29**
Oswald St. BD18: Ship 6H **17**
Oswaldthorpe Av.
BD3: B'frd 6F **29**
Otley Mt. BD20: Keigh 3E **9**
Otley Rd. BD2: B'frd 6C **28**
BD3: B'frd 2B **36** (1G **5**)
BD16: Bgly . . . . . . .2E **9** & 6H **9**
BD18: Ship 1F **27**
BD20: Bgly, Keigh 2E **9**
Otley St. BD21: Keigh 5D **6**
HX1: Hal 6H **47**
Otterburn Cl. BD5: B'frd 5H **35**
Otterburn St. BD21: Keigh 3E **7**
Oulton Ter. BD7: B'frd 4G **35**
Ounsworth St. BD4: B'frd 5D **36**
OUSEL HOLE **1E 9**
Ouse St. BD22: Haw 6H **11**
Outlands Ri. BD10: B'frd 5F **19**
Outside La. BD22: Oxen 5C **20**
Ouzel Dr. BD6: B'frd 2A **42**
Oval, The BD8: B'frd 1C **34**
BD16: Bgly 3H **15**
BD17: Bail 4F **17**
Ovendale Hall *HX3: Hal 3A 48*
(off Gro. Ct.)
OVENDEN **3H 47**
Ovenden Av. HX3: Hal 4A **48**
Ovenden Cl. HX3: Hal 4A **48**
Ovenden Cres. HX3: Hal 3A **48**
Ovenden Grn. HX3: Hal 3H **47**
Ovenden Pk. **1H 47**
Ovenden Rd.
HX1: Hal 2A **48** (1A **62**)
HX3: Hal 2A **48** (1A **62**)
Ovenden Rd. Ter. HX3: Hal . . .3A **48**
Ovenden Ter. HX3: Hal 3A **48**
Ovenden Way HX3: Hal 3G **47**
OVENDEN WOOD **3E 47**
Ovenden Wood Rd.
HX2: Hal 3E **47**
Overdale Dr. BD10: B'frd 4B **18**
Overdale Mt. HX6: Hal 2E **55**
Overdale Ter. BD22: Haw 6G **11**
Overend St. BD6: B'frd 2E **43**
OVERGATE HOSPICE **3D 60**
Overgreen Royd HX2: Hal 1C **46**
Overland Cres. BD10: B'frd . . .5F **19**
Overmoor Fold BD10: B'frd . . .6C **18**
Overton Dr. BD6: B'frd 1B **42**
Overton Ho. *BD5: B'frd 5H 35*
(off Newstead Wlk.)
Ovington Dr. BD4: B'frd 1G **45**
Owen Ct. BD16: Bgly 5G **9**
Owler Ings Rd. HD6: Brigh . . .5E **59**
OWLET **3H 27**
Owlet Grange BD18: Ship 1G **27**
Owlet Rd. BD18: Ship 6G **17**
Owl St. *BD21: Keigh 3F 7*
(off Parson St.)
OXENHOPE **5G 21**
Oxenhope Station
Keighley & Worth Valley
Railway **4G 21**
Oxford Cl. BD13: B'frd 3C **40**
Oxford Cres. BD14: B'frd 5H **33**
HX3: Hal 3D **56**
Oxford La. HX3: Hal 3D **56**
Oxford Pl. BD3: B'frd . . .1B **36** (1F **5**)
BD17: Bail 3A **18**
Oxford Rd. BD2: B'frd 5C **28**
BD13: B'frd 3C **40**
HX1: Hal 1C **56** (6B **62**)
Oxford St. BD14: B'frd 5H **33**
BD21: Keigh 5C **6**
HX6: Hal 3F **55**
Oxford Ter. *BD17: Bail 3A 18*
(off Union St.)
Ox Heys Mdw. BD13: B'frd . . .3G **33**
Oxley Gdns. BD12: B'frd 4G **43**
Oxley St. BD8: B'frd . . .1G **35** (2A **4**)

P

Packington St. BD13: B'frd . . .1C **32**
Padan St. HX3: Hal 3D **56**
Paddock BD9: B'frd 3G **27**
HX3: Hal 6F **41**
Paddock, The BD13: B'frd 1F **23**
BD17: Bail 1B **18**
BD19: Cleck 5B **52**
Paddock Cl. BD12: B'frd 4G **51**
Paddock La. HX2: Hal 5E **47**
Paddock Rd. HX3: Hal 6E **41**
Padgate Ho. *BD5: B'frd 5H 35*
(off Park La.)
Padgum BD17: Bail 1G **17**
Padma Cl. BD7: B'frd 2F **35**
Page Hill HX2: Hal 2G **47**
Paget St. BD21: Keigh 4C **6**
Pagewood Ct. BD10: B'frd 4C **18**
Pakington St. BD5: B'frd 5H **35**
Paley Rd. BD4: B'frd 5C **36**
Paley Ter. BD4: B'frd 5C **36**
Palin Av. BD3: B'frd 6F **29**
Palm Cl. BD6: B'frd 3F **43**
Palmer Rd. BD3: B'frd 1D **36**
Palmerston St. BD2: B'frd 5D **28**
Palm St. HX3: Hal 3B **48**
Pannal St. BD7: B'frd 6E **35**
Paper Hall, The **3F 5**
Parade, The BD4: B'frd 6G **37**
BD16: Bgly 6G **15**
Paradise Fold BD7: B'frd 5C **34**
PARADISE GREEN **5C 34**
Paradise La. HX2: Hal 1D **54**
Paradise Rd. BD9: B'frd 3D **26**
Paradise St.
BD1: B'frd 2H **35** (3A **4**)
(not continuous)
HX1: Hal 1B **56** (5A **62**)
Paradise Vw. BD15: B'frd 1B **24**
Paris Gates *HX3: Hal 2D 56*
(off Boys La.)
PARK **1B 18**
Park, The HX3: Hal 3G **57**
Park Av. BD10: B'frd 3D **18**
BD16: Bgly 3F **15**
BD18: Ship 5E **17**
BD21: Keigh 5D **6**
BD22: Keigh 3H **11**
HX5: Ell 3E **61**
Park Bottom BD12: B'frd 6G **43**
Park Cliffe Rd. BD2: B'frd 5C **28**
Park Cl. BD10: B'frd 2E **29**
BD13: B'frd 2D **40**
BD16: Bgly 1G **15**
BD21: Keigh 6E **7**
HX2: Hal 3D **46**
HX3: Hal 6C **50**
Park Ct. BD9: B'frd 5G **27**
Park Cres. BD3: B'frd 5C **28**
HX3: Hal 4A **48**
HX6: Hal 3F 55
(off Grove St.)
Park Dr. BD9: B'frd 3E **27**
BD16: Bgly 6H **9**
HX1: Hal 1A **56**
HX2: Hal 2F **55**
Park Dr. Rd. BD21: Keigh 6E **7**
Parker's La. BD20: Keigh 1C **6**
Parkfield Av. HX5: Ell 3F **61**
Parkfield Dr. BD13: B'frd 2D **40**
HX6: Hal 5C **54**
Parkfield La. HX6: Hal 4F **55**
Parkfield Rd. BD8: B'frd 5H **27**
BD18: Ship 5C **16**
Park Flds. HX2: Hal 3D **46**
Park Gdns. HX2: Hal 2F **55**
Park Ga. BD1: B'frd 2B **36** (3F **5**)
Park Grn. HX3: Hal 4F **49**
Park Gro. BD9: B'frd 3G **27**
BD13: B'frd 2D **40**
BD18: Ship 5D **16**
BD21: Keigh 3E **7**
Park Gro. Ct. BD9: B'frd 3G **27**
Parkhead Cl. BD6: B'frd 5E **43**
Pk. Hill Cl. BD8: B'frd 6B **26**
Pk. Hill Dr. BD8: B'frd 6B **26**
Pk. Hill Gro. BD16: Bgly 1G **15**
Park Ho. Cl. BD12: B'frd 4A **44**
Park Ho. Cres. BD12: B'frd . . .4A **44**
Park Ho. Gro. BD12: B'frd 4A **44**
Park Ho. Rd. BD12: B'frd 5H **43**
Park Ho. Wlk. BD12: B'frd 4A **44**
Parkin La. BD10: B'frd 5H **19**
Parkinson La. HX1: Hal 1G **55**
Parkinson Rd. BD13: B'frd . . .1G **31**
Parkinson St. BD5: B'frd 5H **35**
Parkland Bus. Cen.
BD10: B'frd 6F **19**
Parkland Dr. BD10: B'frd 6E **19**
Parklands BD16: Bgly 6H **9**
Parklands Dr. HX6: Hal 6A **54**
Park La. BD5: B'frd 5H **35**
BD13: B'frd 2F **41**
BD14: B'frd 5H **33**
BD17: Bail 1B **18**
BD21: Keigh 5E **7**
HX3: Hal 5D **56**
Park La. Ends HX2: Hal 3F **39**
Parklee Ct. BD21: Keigh 5F **7**
Park Lodge BD15: B'frd 2C **24**
Park Mead BD10: B'frd 3D **18**
Parkmere Cl. BD4: B'frd 4D **44**
Park Mt. Av. BD17: Bail 2A **18**
Park Nook HX3: Hal 5F **57**
Park Pl. BD10: B'frd 3D **18**
HX1: Hal 1A 56
(off Warley St.)
Park Pl. E. HX3: Hal 6C **50**
Park Pl. W. HX3: Hal 6C **50**
Park Rd. BD5: B'frd 4A **36**
BD10: B'frd 3D **18**
(Ainsbury Av.)
BD10: B'frd 2E **29**
(Victoria Rd.)
BD12: B'frd 4G **43**
BD16: Bgly 2F **15**
BD18: Ship 6G **17**
HX1: Hal 1B **56** (5A **62**)
HX5: Ell 1F **61**
HX6: Hal 2E **55**
Park Row HD6: Brigh 5F **59**
Park School M. *BD16: Bgly . . .2F 15*
(off Lime St.)
PARKSIDE **1B 44**
Park Side BD14: B'frd 5H **33**
Parkside BD16: Bgly 1G **15**
BD19: Cleck 6G **53**
HX3: Hal 3B **56**
Parkside Av. BD13: B'frd 2D **40**
Parkside Ct. BD22: Haw 5A **12**
Parkside Dr. BD9: B'frd 4E **27**
Parkside Gro. BD9: B'frd 4E **27**
Parkside Rd. BD5: B'frd 1H **43**
Parkside Ter. BD13: B'frd 1F **23**
Park Sq. BD6: B'frd 3D **42**
HX3: Hal 3G 49
(off Hough)
Parkstone Dr. BD10: B'frd 2E **29**
Park Stone Ri. HX3: Hal 5H **41**
Park St. BD18: Ship 5E **17**
BD19: Cleck 6D **52**
BD22: Haw 6H **11**
HD6: Brigh 5F **59**
HX6: Hal 3F **55**
Park Ter. *BD12: B'frd 5G 43*
(off Park Rd.)
BD18: Ship 5E **17**
BD21: Keigh 5H 7
(off Bank Top Way)
BD21: Keigh 4F **7**
(Dalton La.)
HX1: Hal 1A **56**
(not continuous)
HX3: Hal 4G **49**
(Leeds Rd.)
HX3: Hal 6B **50**
(Wakefield Rd.)
Pk. Top Cotts. BD16: Bgly 6H **9**
Pk. Top Row BD22: Haw 6G **11**
Park Vw. BD11: B'frd 6H **45**
BD13: B'frd 1D **40**
BD19: Cleck 5E **53**
HX1: Hal 1A **56**

Park Vw.—Portland Ho.

Park Vw. HX3: Hal 6C 50
HX6: Hal 2D 54
(off Tuel La.)
Park Vw. Av. BD22: Haw 5A 12
HX3: Hal 4G 49
Parkview Ct. BD18: Ship 6E 17
Park Vw. Rd. BD9: B'frd 5F 27
Park Vw. Ter. BD9: B'frd 4F 27
BD16: Bgly 3B 14
Park Vs. *HX6: Hal 3F 55*
(off Grove St.)
Park Way BD17: Bail 4D 16
Parkway BD5: B'frd 1B 44
BD13: B'frd 2D 40
BD21: Keigh 6E 7
PARKWOOD 5E 7
Parkwood Cen. for Young People
. . . . .5F 7
Park Wood Crematorium
HX5: Hal 6F 57
Parkwood Ri. BD21: Keigh 5E 7
Parkwood Rd. BD18: Ship 6D 16
Parkwood St. BD21: Keigh 5E 7
Pk. Wood Top BD21: Keigh 5F 7
Parma St. BD5: B'frd 4A 36
Parratt Row BD3: B'frd 2F 37
Parrott St. BD4: B'frd 2F 45
Parry Cl. BD16: Bgly 4A 14
Parry La. BD4: B'frd 4E 37
Parsonage La. HD6: Brigh 4E 59
(not continuous)
Parsonage Rd. BD4: B'frd 4F 37
BD5: B'frd 6A 36
Parsonage St. HX3: Hal 4D 48
Parsons Rd. BD9: B'frd 3E 27
Parson St. BD21: Keigh 3E 7
Partridge Dr. BD6: B'frd 2A 42
Paslew Ct. BD20: Keigh 2B 8
Pasture Av. BD22: Keigh 4G 11
Pasture Cl. BD14: B'frd 5B 34
Pasture La. BD14: B'frd 5A 34
Pasture Ri. BD14: B'frd 5B 34
Pasture Rd. BD17: Bail 3H 17
Pastureside Ter. E.
BD14: B'frd 5B 34
Pastureside Ter. W.
BD14: B'frd 5A 34
Pasture Wlk. BD14: B'frd 5A 34
Patchett Sq. *BD13: B'frd 2H 41*
(off Highgate Rd.)
Patent St. BD9: B'frd 5F 27
Paternoster La. BD7: B'frd . . .5E 35
Patricia Gdns. HX6: Hal 2C 54
Patterdale Ho. *BD5: B'frd 5H 35*
(off Hutson St.)
Pattie St. BD20: Keigh 2D 6
Pavement La. HX2: Hal 3G 39
Pavement St. *BD19: Cleck . . .6G 53*
(off Bradford Rd.)
Pavilion Ct. BD4: B'frd 3E 45
Paw La. BD13: B'frd 4F 41
Pawson St. BD4: B'frd 3F 37
Peabody St. HX3: Hal 4A 48
Peace Mus., The 4D 4
Peace St. BD4: B'frd 4E 37
Peach Wlk. BD4: B'frd 5D 36
Pearl St. BD22: Keigh 1C 12
Pearson Fold BD12: B'frd 1B 52
Pearson La. BD9: B'frd 6B 26
Pearson Rd. BD6: B'frd 3H 43
Pearson Rd. W. BD6: B'frd . . .3H 43
Pearson Row BD12: B'frd 2H 51
Pearson St. BD3: B'frd 3E 37
BD19: Cleck 6G 53
Pear St. BD21: Keigh 2C 12
BD22: Oxen 5G 21
HX1: Hal 1H 55
Peas Acre BD16: Bgly 3E 9
Peaseland Av. BD19: Cleck . . .6E 53
Peaseland Cl. BD19: Cleck . . .6F 53
Peaseland Rd. BD19: Cleck . . .6F 53
Peaselands BD18: Ship 6E 17
Peckover Dr. LS28: Pud 6H 29
Peckover St.
BD1: B'frd 2B 36 (3F 5)
Peel Cl. BD4: B'frd 3G 37
Peel Ct. BD3: B'frd 5B 28
Peel Ho. BD16: Bgly 3H 15
Peel Pk. Dr. BD2: B'frd 5D 28
Peel Pk. Ter. BD2: B'frd 5D 28
Peel Pk. Vw. BD3: B'frd 6C 28
Peel Row BD7: B'frd 5E 35
Peel Sq. BD8: B'frd . . .1H 35 (2B 4)
Peel St. BD13: B'frd 3D 32
(George St.)
BD13: B'frd 2F 41
(Scarlet Hgts.)
BD15: B'frd 3C 24
BD16: Bgly 2H 15
HX6: Hal 3D 54
Pelham Ct. BD2: B'frd 4D 28
Pelham Rd. BD2: B'frd 4D 28
PELLON 5G 47
Pellon La. HX1: Hal . . .5H 47 (2A 62)
Pellon New Rd. HX2: Hal 5G 47
Pellon Ter. BD10: B'frd 4D 18
Pellon Wlk. BD10: B'frd 4D 18
Pemberton Dr.
BD7: B'frd 3H 35 (6A 4)
Pembroke Ct. *BD8: B'frd 1D 34*
(off St Leonards Rd.)
Pembroke Ho. *BD4: B'frd 1G 45*
(off Launceston Dr.)
Pembroke St. BD5: B'frd 5A 36
Pendle Ct. BD13: B'frd 4E 41
Pendle Rd. BD16: Bgly 2H 15
(not continuous)
Pendragon BD2: B'frd 4C 28
Pendragon La. BD2: B'frd 4D 28
Penfield Gro. BD14: B'frd 5A 34
Pengarth BD16: Bgly 6H 9
Penistone Hill Country Pk. 1E 21
Penistone M. BD22: Haw 6G 11
Pennard Ho. *BD5: B'frd 5H 35*
(off Launton Way)
Penn Cl. BD2: B'frd 3D 28
Pennine Cl. BD13: B'frd 4D 40
Pennington Ter. BD5: B'frd . . .5G 35
Pennithorne Av. BD17: Bail . . .1G 17
Penn St. HX1: Hal 5A 48
Penny Hill Dr. BD14: B'frd 5B 34
Penrose Dr. BD7: B'frd 6D 34
Penrose Pl. HX3: Hal 3G 49
Pentland Av. BD14: B'frd 5A 34
Pentland Cl. BD22: Keigh 5C 6
Penuel Pl. HX3: Hal 4D 56
Penzance Ct. *BD8: B'frd 1F 35*
(off Fearnsides St.)
PEPPER HILL 5G 41
Percival St.
BD3: B'frd 2C 36 (4H 5)
Percy St. BD13: B'frd 1C 40
BD16: Bgly 2G 15
BD21: Keigh 1D 12
Peregrine Way BD6: B'frd 2A 42
Perkin La. *BD10: B'frd 4B 18*
(off Far Crook)
Per La. HX2: Hal 4F 39
Perry Cl. BD22: Keigh 2C 12
Perseverance La.
BD7: B'frd 6E 35
Perseverance Rd.
BD13: B'frd 6A 32
HX2: Hal 6A 32
Perseverance St.
BD12: B'frd 1G 51
BD17: Bail 1H 17
HX1: Hal 2A 56
HX6: Hal 2D 54
Perth Av. BD2: B'frd 4A 28
Perth Ho. *BD4: B'frd 4F 37*
(off Parsonage Rd.)
Peterborough Pl.
BD2: B'frd 4D 28
Peterborough Rd.
BD2: B'frd 5D 28
Peterborough Ter.
BD2: B'frd 4D 28
Peter La. HX2: Hal 6D 46
Petersgarth BD18: Ship 5C 16
Pether Hill HX4: Hal 6A 60
Petrel Cl. BD6: B'frd 2A 42
Petrie Gro. BD3: B'frd 2G 37
Petrie Rd. BD3: B'frd 2G 37
Pevensey Gth. *BD10: B'frd . . .1E 29*
(off Savile Av.)
Peverell Cl. BD4: B'frd 6G 37
Peveril Mt. BD2: B'frd 4E 29
Pheasant St. BD21: Keigh 3F 7
Phoebe La. HX3: Hal 3D 56
Phoebe La. Ind. Est.
HX3: Hal 3D 56
Phoenix Bldgs.
BD7: B'frd 3G 35 (6A 4)
Phoenix St. HD6: Brigh 5F 59
Phoenix Way BD4: Pud 3G 37
Physical Jerks Health &
Fitness Cen. *6G 53*
(off Horncastle St.)
Physiques Health Studio 2E 5
Piccadilly BD1: B'frd . . .2A 36 (3C 4)
Piccadilly Chambers
BD1: B'frd 3C 4
(off Up. Piccadilly)
Pickerings, The
BD13: B'frd 3E 41
PICKLES HILL 1D 42
Pickles Hill BD22: Keigh 4D 10
Pickles La. BD7: B'frd 1D 42
Pickles St. BD21: Keigh 6D 6
Pickwood La. HX6: Hal 5G 55
PICKWOOD SCAR 5G 55
Picton Ho. *BD8: B'frd 6G 27*
(off Green La.)
Picton St. BD8: B'frd 6H 27
Piece Hall HX1: Hal 4D 62
Piece Hall Yd.
BD1: B'frd 2A 36 (4D 4)
Piggott St. HD6: Brigh 4E 59
Pigman La. HX2: Hal 1C 54
Pinebury Dr. BD13: B'frd 2C 40
Pine Cft. BD20: Keigh 2C 6
Pinedale BD16: Bgly 6F 9
Pine St. BD1: B'frd 2B 36 (3F 5)
BD22: Haw 1G 21
HX1: Hal 1C 56 (5B 62)
Pinewood Gdns. HX4: Hal 5B 60
Pinfold BD14: B'frd 5A 34
Pinfold Grn. HX6: Hal 4A 54
Pinfold La. HX6: Hal 3A 54
Pink St. BD22: Haw 2G 21
Pinnar Cft. HX3: Hal 3G 57
Pinnar La. HX3: Hal 2F 57
Pintail Av. BD6: B'frd 2A 42
Pipercroft BD6: B'frd 5C 42
Pirie Cl. BD2: B'frd 4B 28
Pitcliffe Way BD5: B'frd 5B 36
Pit Hill HX3: Hal 1D 56
Pit La. BD6: B'frd 4D 42
BD13: B'frd 1D 30
(Drive, The)
BD13: B'frd 6C 32
(Low La.)
Pits La. BD19: Cleck 6B 52
Pitts St. BD4: B'frd 5F 37
Pitt St. BD21: Keigh 4F 7
Pitt St. Bus. Cen.
BD21: Keigh 4F 7
Plainfield HX6: Hal 2F 55
Plains La. HX5: Hal 6F 57
Plane Tree Nest HX2: Hal 1G 55
Plane Tree Nest La.
HX2: Hal 1G 55
Plane Tree Rd. HX6: Hal 2D 54
Plane Trees HX2: Hal 5F 47
(Ashville Cft.)
HX2: Hal 3B 38
(Spring Mill Fold)
Plane Trees Cl.
BD19: Cleck 2F 53
Planetrees Rd. BD4: B'frd 3E 37
Planetrees St. BD15: B'frd . . .6G 25
Plantation Fold
BD22: Keigh 1B 12
Plantation Pl. BD4: B'frd 5F 37
Plantation Way BD17: Bail . . .2H 17
Platt Sq. *BD19: Cleck 6F 53*
(off Westgate)
Playhouse, The 1B 56 (5A 62)
Pleasant Pl. BD15: B'frd 6G 25
Pleasant Row BD13: B'frd 3C 40
Pleasant St. BD7: B'frd 5E 35
HX6: Hal 3E 55
Pleasant Views
BD13: B'frd 6G 23
Plevna Ter. BD16: Bgly 1F 15
Plimsoll St. BD4: B'frd 5C 36
Ploughcroft La. HX3: Hal 3B 48
Ploughman's Cft.
BD2: B'frd 3A 28
Plover St. BD5: B'frd 6G 35
BD21: Keigh 3E 7
Plumpton Av. BD2: B'frd 1B 28
Plumpton Cl. BD2: B'frd 2C 28
Plumpton Dr. BD2: B'frd 1B 28
Plumpton End BD2: B'frd 1C 28
Plumpton Gdns. BD2: B'frd . . .1A 28
Plumpton Lea BD2: B'frd 1B 28
Plumpton Mead BD2: B'frd . . .1B 28
Plumpton St. BD8: B'frd 1E 35
Plumpton Wlk. BD2: B'frd 1B 28
Plum St. BD21: Keigh 2C 12
HX1: Hal 1H 55
Plymouth Gro. *HX1: Hal 5A 48*
(off Diamond St.)
Pochard Cl. BD6: B'frd 2A 42
Pohlman St. HX1: Hal 2H 55
Pole Position Indoor Karting
. . . . .1F 35
Pollard Av. BD16: Bgly 6H 9
Pollard La. BD2: B'frd 6D 28
Pollard St. BD4: B'frd 4B 36
BD16: Bgly 1H 25
Pollard St. Nth.
HX3: Hal 5D 48 (2C 62)
Pollit Av. HX6: Hal 4A 54
Pond, The HX6: Hal 6A 54
Ponden La. BD22: Haw 6A 10
Pond Farm Dr. HD6: Brigh 2C 58
Pond St. BD21: Keigh 4E 7
Pond Ter. HD6: Brigh 2C 58
Pool Ct. BD3: B'frd 2C 36 (3H 5)
Pool St. BD21: Keigh 2G 7
Pope St. BD21: Keigh 3F 7
Poplar Av. BD7: B'frd 1D 42
BD18: Ship 2G 27
HX6: Hal 2E 55
Poplar Ct. BD7: B'frd 3F 35
Poplar Cres. BD18: Ship 1G 27
HX2: Hal 4H 39
Poplar Dr. BD18: Ship 2G 27
BD20: Keigh 4C 8
Poplar Gro. BD7: B'frd 1C 42
BD16: Bgly 4A 14
BD17: Bail 4C 16
BD18: Ship 2G 27
BD19: Cleck 6D 52
Poplar Rd. BD7: B'frd 1E 43
BD18: Ship 1G 27
Poplars, The HX3: Hal 3E 51
Poplars Pk. Rd. BD2: B'frd . . .3A 28
Poplar St. HX3: Hal . . .5C 48 (1B 62)
Poplar Ter. BD16: Bgly 3G 15
BD20: Keigh 4D 8
BD21: Keigh 4C 6
(off W. Leeds St.)
Poplar Vw. BD7: B'frd 1C 42
HX3: Hal 1E 59
Poplarwood Gdns.
BD10: B'frd 2G 29
Popples HX2: Hal 4H 39
Popples Dr. HX2: Hal 4H 39
Popple Wells La.
HX2: Hal 6B 46
Poppy Ct. BD6: B'frd 5D 42
Porritt St. BD19: Cleck 4F 53
Portland Ho. *BD4: B'frd 3F 37*
(off Fearnville Dr.)
HX5: Ell 2F 61
(off Huddersfield Rd.)

96 A-Z Bradford

Portland Pl. BD16: Bgly 3G **15**
HX1: Hal 1C **56** (5C **62**)
Portland Rd.
HX3: Hal 5D **48** (1D **62**)
Portland St.
BD5: B'frd 3A **36** (6D **4**)
BD22: Haw 6H **11**
HX1: Hal 6C **48** (3C **62**)
Portman Cl. HX4: Hal 5A **60**
Portree Dr. BD6: B'frd 3C **42**
Portslade Ho. *BD8: B'frd 6G 27*
(off Green La.)
Portsmouth Av. BD3: B'frd 6C **28**
Portwood St. BD9: B'frd 5B **26**
Post Office Rd. BD2: B'frd 2E **29**
Pothouse Rd. BD6: B'frd 3F **43**
Potter Cl. BD12: B'frd 6A **44**
Powell Av. BD5: B'frd 5G **35**
Powell Rd. BD16: Bgly 2H **15**
BD18: Ship 2H **27**
Powell St. HX1: Hal . . .6C **48** (4B **62**)
(not continuous)
Pratt La. BD18: Ship 1G **27**
Premier Way HX5: Ell 1G **61**
Prescott Pl. HX4: Hal 5A **60**
Prescott St.
HX1: Hal 1C **56** (6B **62**)
Prescott Ter. BD15: B'frd 6H **25**
Preston Bldgs. *BD19: Cleck . . .4B 52*
(off Tabbs La.)
Preston La. HX2: Hal 4E **47**
(not continuous)
Preston Pl. HX1: Hal 6A **48**
Preston St. BD7: B'frd 2G **35**
Preston Ter. *BD16: Bgly 6F 9*
(off Sleningford Rd.)
Pretoria Rd. BD3: B'frd 2F **37**
Pretoria Ter. HX2: Hal 5F **47**
Priesthorpe Rd. LS28: Pud . . .3H **29**
(not continuous)
Priestley Av. BD6: B'frd 3G **43**
Priestley Cen. for the Arts 4F **5**
PRIESTLEY GREEN 4C **50**
Priestley Hill BD13: B'frd 5C **40**
Priestley Pl. HX6: Hal 4C **54**
Priestley St.
BD1: B'frd 1B **36** (2E **5**)
BD13: B'frd 3D **32**
Priestley Ter. BD6: B'frd 2G **43**
Priestman Cl. BD8: B'frd 6G **27**
Priestman St. BD8: B'frd 6G **27**
PRIESTTHORPE 1G **15**
Priestthorpe Cl.
BD16: Bgly 1G **15**
Priestthorpe La.
BD16: Bgly 1G **15**
Priestthorpe Rd.
BD16: Bgly 2G **15**
Primrose Bank BD16: Bgly . . .3H **15**
Primrose Dr. BD16: Bgly 3H **15**
Primrose Gro. BD21: Keigh 4G **7**
Primrose Hill *BD7: B'frd 4G 35*
(off Gt. Horton Rd.)
BD16: Bgly 4A **16**
Primrose La. BD2: B'frd 3H **27**
BD16: Bgly 4H **15**
Primrose Row BD17: Bail 1B **18**
Primrose St.
BD8: B'frd 1G **35** (1A **4**)
BD21: Keigh 4G **7**
Primrose Way HX3: Hal 4B **42**
Prince Albert Sq.
BD13: B'frd 1H **41**
Princeroyd Way BD8: B'frd . . .2E **35**
Prince's Ct. BD18: Ship 1F **27**
Prince's Cres. BD2: B'frd 4A **28**
Prince's Ga. HX3: Hal 3B **56**
Princess St.
HX1: Hal 6C **48** (3C **62**)
HX4: Hal 2D **60**
HX6: Hal 3E **55**
Prince's St. BD6: B'frd 4C **42**
(Beck Hill)
BD6: B'frd 3F **43**
(Pothouse Rd.)
Prince St. BD4: B'frd 2E **45**
BD22: Haw 6H **11**
Prince's Way
BD1: B'frd 3A **36** (5C **4**)
Princeton Cl. HX2: Hal 4H **47**
PRINCEVILLE 2F **35**
Princeville Rd. BD7: B'frd 2E **35**
Princeville St. BD7: B'frd 2F **35**
Prior St. BD21: Keigh 3G **7**
Priory Cl. BD16: Bgly 1G **15**
Priory Ct.
BD8: B'frd 1H **35** (1A **4**)
BD16: Bgly 1G **15**
Priory Gro. BD16: Bgly 1G **15**
Priory Ho. *BD10: B'frd 6E 19*
(off Cavendish Rd.)
Priory Rd. HD6: Brigh 6G **59**
Privet Dr. BD22: Keigh 3H **11**
Proctor St. BD4: B'frd 1F **45**
Prod La. BD17: Bail 3C **16**
Progress Av. BD16: Bgly 4A **14**
Prospect Av. BD18: Ship 6G **17**
HX2: Hal 3G **55**
Prospect Cl. BD18: Ship 6G **17**
HX2: Hal 3G **55**
Prospect Ct. HX2: Hal 5D **46**
Prospect Cres. BD22: Keigh . . .6A **6**
Prospect Dr. BD22: Keigh 6A **6**
Prospect Gro. BD18: Ship 6G **17**
Prospect Mt. BD18: Ship 6G **17**
BD22: Keigh 6A **6**
Prospect Pl. BD2: B'frd 5E **29**
BD9: B'frd 6D **26**
BD13: B'frd 2E **41**
HD6: Brigh 5E **59**
HX2: Hal 2H **47**
(Prospect Row)
HX2: Hal 2C **46**
(Waindale Cres.)
HX3: Hal 3E 51
(off Village St.)
Prospect Rd.
BD3: B'frd 1B **36** (1F **5**)
(not continuous)
BD16: Bgly 1A **16**
BD19: Cleck 5F **53**
Prospect Row HX2: Hal 2H **47**
(Prospect Pl.)
HX2: Hal 4E **39**
(Spring Row)
Prospect St. BD4: B'frd 4B **36**
BD6: B'frd 4D **42**
BD10: B'frd 2E **29**
BD13: B'frd 3E **33**
BD18: Ship 6G **17**
BD19: Cleck 6F **53**
BD22: Haw 1G **21**
BD22: Keigh 5B **6**
HX3: Hal 5D **48** (1D **62**)
Prospect Ter. BD15: B'frd 6A **26**
BD19: Cleck 5F **53**
BD20: Keigh 1H **7**
HX2: Hal 2A **54**
HX6: Hal 5D **54**
Prospect Vw. BD13: B'frd 4C **40**
Prospect Vs. *BD19: Cleck 5F 53*
(off Prospect St.)
Prospect Wlk. BD18: Ship 6G **17**
Prospect Way HD6: Brigh 1F **59**
Providence Av. BD17: Bail 1G **17**
Providence Bldgs.
HX3: Hal 3G 57
(off New St.)
Providence Ct.
BD22: Keigh 3G **11**
Providence Cres.
BD22: Keigh 3G **11**
Providence La.
BD22: Keigh 3G **11**
Providence Pl. BD12: B'frd . . .1G **51**
HD6: Brigh 6G **59**
HX6: Hal 4B **54**
Providence Row BD2: B'frd . . .4D **28**
BD17: Bail 1G **17**
BD20: Keigh 1E **9**
Providence Row HX2: Hal 2H **47**
(Club Ho's.)
HX2: Hal 4E **39**
(Hebble Brook Bus. Pk.)
Providence St.
BD1: B'frd 2H **35** (4B **4**)
BD19: Cleck 5G **53**
(Coach La.)
BD19: Cleck 4A **52**
(Old Popplewell La.)
HX5: Ell 2F **61**
Providence Ter.
BD13: B'frd 3D **32**
Providence Vs.
BD19: Cleck 4A 52
(off Providence St.)
Prune Pk. La. BD15: B'frd 4E **25**
Puffin Cl. BD6: B'frd 2A **42**
Pule Grn. La. HX3: Hal 2B **48**
PULE HILL 2B **48**
Pullan Av. BD2: B'frd 3D **28**
Pullan Dr. BD2: B'frd 3E **29**
Pullan Gro. BD2: B'frd 3E **29**
Pullan St. BD5: B'frd 4H **35**
Pulmans Pl. *HX3: Hal 5C 56*
(off Skircoat Grn.)
Pulmans Yd. HX3: Hal 5C **56**
Pump La. HX3: Hal 5F **49**
Punch Bowl Yd.
BD19: Cleck 6E **53**
Pundles HX2: Hal 3G **39**
Purbeck Ct. *BD4: B'frd 1G 45*
(off Dorchester Cres.)
Purley Wlk. BD6: B'frd 3F **43**
Pyebank BD15: B'frd 1B **24**
PYE NEST 2H **55**
Pye Nest Av. HX2: Hal 2F **55**
Pye Nest Dr. HX2: Hal 3G **55**
Pye Nest Gdns. HX2: Hal 2G **55**
Pye Nest Gro. HX2: Hal 2G **55**
Pye Nest Ri. HX2: Hal 3G **55**
Pye Nest Rd. HX3: Hal 3F **55**
HX6: Hal 3F **55**
Pye Nook BD12: B'frd 4H **43**
Pyenot Av. BD19: Cleck 6G **53**
Pyenot Gdns. BD19: Cleck 6G **53**
Pyenot Hall La.
BD19: Cleck 6G **53**
Pyrah Fold BD12: B'frd 1G **51**
Pyrah Rd. BD12: B'frd 4H **43**
Pyrah St. BD12: B'frd 1H **51**

Q

Quail Av. BD6: B'frd 2A **42**
Quail St. BD21: Keigh 3F **7**
Quaker La. BD5: B'frd 6F **35**
BD19: Cleck 6F **53**
Quarry Ct. *HD6: Brigh 2C 58*
(off Spout Ho. La.)
HX3: Hal 6E **49**
Quarry Gap Row
BD4: B'frd 3G **37**
Quarry Hill HX6: Hal 4D **54**
Quarry Pl. BD2: B'frd 5D **28**
Quarry Rd. BD19: Cleck 6E **53**
HX3: Hal 3G **47**
Quarry St. BD9: B'frd 3E **27**
BD21: Keigh 4F **7**
Quaver La. BD15: B'frd 6H **25**
Quayside BD18: Ship 5F **17**
Quayside, The BD10: B'frd . . .5G **19**
Quebec BD16: Bgly 1H **25**
Quebec Ho. *BD21: Keigh 5D 6*
(off Aireworth St.)
Quebec St.
BD1: B'frd 3A **36** (5C **4**)
BD21: Keigh 5D **6**
HX5: Ell 2G **61**
Queen's Av. BD2: B'frd 4B **28**
QUEENSBURY 2E **41**
Queensbury Rd. HX3: Hal 1B **48**
Queensbury Sq.
BD13: B'frd 2E **41**
Queensbury Swimming Pool
. . . . .2E **41**
Queens Cl. BD16: Bgly 3H **15**
Queens Ct. BD16: Bgly 2F **15**
BD18: Ship 6D **16**
Queens Dr. HX3: Hal 3G **57**
Queen's Ga. HX3: Hal 3B **56**
Queensgate
BD1: B'frd 2A **36** (4D **4**)
Queen's Gro. BD21: Keigh 6D **6**
Queens Mead HX3: Hal 2G **49**
Queen's Pl. BD18: Ship 5D **16**
Queen's Ri. BD2: B'frd 4B **28**
Queen's Rd. BD2: B'frd 5H **27**
BD8: B'frd 5H **27**
BD16: Bgly 5E **9**
BD18: Ship 5D **16**
BD21: Keigh 1C **12**
HX1: Hal 6H **47**
HX3: Hal 3D **50**
Queens Sports Club 2B **56**
Queen St. BD6: B'frd 4C **42**
BD10: B'frd 6F **19**
BD13: B'frd 1F **23**
BD15: B'frd 3C **24**
BD16: Bgly 2F **15**
BD17: Bail 4G **17**
BD19: Cleck 6G **53**
BD22: Haw 1G **21**
HX4: Hal 3C **60**
HX6: Hal 4A **54**
Queensway BD16: Bgly 2H **15**
BD21: Keigh 4E 7
(off Airedale Shop. Cen.)
HX1: Hal 5H **47**
Queen Victoria Cres.
HX3: Hal 2H **49**
Quincy Cl. BD2: B'frd 3E **29**
Qureshi Vw. BD8: B'frd 6G **27**

R

Race Moor La. BD22: Keigh . . .2F **11**
Racemoor La. BD22: Keigh . . .2H **11**
Radcliffe Av. BD2: B'frd 2C **28**
Radfield Dr. BD6: B'frd 2A **44**
Radfield Rd. BD6: B'frd 2A **44**
Radnor St. BD3: B'frd 2E **37**
Radwell Dr.
BD5: B'frd 4A **36** (6C **4**)
Raeburn Dr. BD6: B'frd 4E **43**
Rae Rd. BD18: Ship 1F **27**
Raglan Av. BD22: Keigh 5B **6**
Raglan Ct. *HX1: Hal 6A 48*
(off Raglan St.)
Raglan Gdns. *HX1: Hal 6A 48*
(off Lister's Cl.)
Raglan St. BD3: B'frd 2F **37**
BD13: B'frd 2F **41**
BD22: Keigh 5B **6**
HX1: Hal 6A **48**
Raglan Ter. BD3: B'frd 2G **37**
Raikes La. BD4: B'frd 1H **45**
(Holme La.)
BD4: B'frd 3G **45**
(Toftshaw La.)
Raikes Wood Dr. BD4: B'frd . . .4G **45**
Railes Cl. HX2: Hal 4A **46**
Railes Cotts. HX2: Hal 4A **46**
Railway Rd. BD10: B'frd 5D **18**
Railway St. BD4: B'frd 1E **45**
BD19: Cleck 6F **53**
BD20: Keigh 2E **7**
HD6: Brigh 6F **59**
Railway Ter. BD12: B'frd 6A **44**
HD6: Brigh 5G 59
(off Clifton Comn.)
HX3: Hal 5A **56**
Rainbow M. BD6: B'frd 5D **42**
Rainton Ho. *BD5: B'frd 5H 35*
(off Park La.)
Raistrick Way BD18: Ship 5H **17**
Rake Bank HX2: Hal 1F **47**
Raleigh St. HX1: Hal 2H **55**

Rooley Av.—St Albans Av.

Rooley Av. BD6: B'frd 3H **43**
Rooley Banks HX6: Hal 4A **54**
Rooley Cl. BD5: B'frd 2A **44**
Rooley Ct. HX6: Hal 4A **54**
Rooley Cres. BD6: B'frd 2A **44**
Rooley Hgts. HX6: Hal 4A **54**
ROOLEY HILL 4A **54**
Rooley La. BD4: B'frd 2B **44**
BD5: B'frd 2H **43**
HX6: Hal 4A **54**
Roper Gdns. HX2: Hal 1F **47**
Roper Grn. HX2: Hal 1F **47**
Roper Ho. HX2: Hal 1F **47**
Roper La. BD13: B'frd 6B **32**
HX2: Hal 3H **39**
Roper St. BD21: Keigh 4D **6**
Rope Wlk. HX2: Hal 4B **38**
Rose Bank *BD8: B'frd 6G **27***
(off E. Squire La.)
BD12: B'frd 1H **51**
HX2: Hal 2H **55**
Rose Bank Pl. BD8: B'frd 2C **34**
Roseberry St. BD22: Keigh 3H **11**
Rosebery Av. BD18: Ship 6G **17**
HX3: Hal 3D **56**
Rosebery Mt. BD18: Ship 6H **17**
Rosebery Rd. BD8: B'frd 5G **27**
Rosebery St. HX5: Ell 3F **61**
Rosebery Ter. HX1: Hal 5A **48**
Rosechapel Cl. BD6: B'frd 5D **42**
Rosedale Av. BD15: B'frd 5F **25**
Rosedale Cl. BD17: Bail 3E **17**
Rosedale Ct. BD4: B'frd 4G **45**
Rosedale Ho. BD10: B'frd 1F **29**
*HX6: Hal 4D **54***
(off Sowerby St.)
Rose Gro. HX2: Hal 2A **46**
HX6: Hal 2C **54**
Rose Gro. La. HX2: Hal 2B **54**
HX6: Hal 2B **54**
Rose Heath HX2: Hal 4F **39**
Rose Hill *HX6: Hal 3E **55***
(off Beech Rd.)
Rose Hill Cres.
BD12: B'frd 1G **51**
Rosehip Ri. BD14: B'frd 6H **33**
Roselee Cl. HX3: Hal 4E **57**
Rose Lynn Ter. *BD6: B'frd 4D **42***
(off Halifax Rd.)
Rosemary Cl. HD6: Brigh 6E **59**
Rosemary Gdns.
BD15: B'frd 6G **25**
Rosemary Gro. HX3: Hal 4E **57**
(not continuous)
Rosemary Hill HX3: Hal 5E **57**
Rosemary La. HD6: Brigh 6E **59**
HX3: Hal 4E **57**
Rosemary Pl. *HD6: Brigh 6E **59***
(off Rosemary La.)
Rosemary Ter. HX3: Hal 4E **57**
Rose Mdws. BD22: Keigh 6A **6**
Rosemont La. BD17: Bail 3A **18**
ROSEMOUNT 3G **61**
Rose Mt. BD2: B'frd 4C **28**
BD4: B'frd 3H **45**
HX2: Hal 3A **56**
Rosemount Av. HX5: Ell 3G **61**
Rosemount Cl. *BD21: Keigh 4D **6***
(off Well St.)
Rosemount Ter. HX5: Ell 3G **61**
Rosemount Wlk.
*BD21: Keigh 4D **6***
(off Well St.)
Rose Pl. HX2: Hal 2A **54**
Rose St. BD8: B'frd 6F **27**
BD21: Keigh 4H **7**
BD22: Haw 1G **21**
HX1: Hal 1H **55**
Rose Ter. *HX1: Hal 6A **48***
(off West St.)
HX2: Hal 3A **56**
Rosetta Dr. BD8: B'frd 1D **34**
Rosewood Av. BD20: Keigh 2H **7**
Rosewood Gro. BD4: B'frd 4F **37**
Rosley Mt. BD6: B'frd 5D **42**
Roslyn Pl. BD7: B'frd 3F **35**
Rosse Fld. Pk. BD9: B'frd 3F **27**
Rossefield Rd. BD9: B'frd 3E **27**
Rossendale Pl. BD18: Ship 6E **17**
Rosse St. BD8: B'frd 2E **35**
BD18: Ship 5F **17**
Rossett Ho. BD3: B'frd 2F **5**
Rosslyn Gro. BD22: Haw 1G **21**
Rossmore Dr. BD15: B'frd 6A **26**
Rothery Ct. *HX1: Hal 5A **48***
(off Crossley Gdns.)
Rothesay Ter. BD7: B'frd 3G **35**
Rothwell Dr. HX1: Hal 2B **56**
Rothwell Mt. HX1: Hal 2B **56**
Rothwell Rd.
HX1: Hal 2B **56** (6A **62**)
Rough Hall La. HX2: Hal 6B **38**
Rough Hey Wood HX6: Hal 6B **54**
Roundell Av. BD4: B'frd 3D **44**
Roundfield Pl. *BD13: B'frd 2D **32***
(off West La.)
Roundhead Fold
BD10: B'frd 5G **19**
Round Hill *BD13: B'frd 3C **40***
(off Rope La.)
HX2: Hal 5H **39**
Roundhill Av. BD16: Bgly 5H **15**
Round Hill Cl. BD13: B'frd 1H **41**
HX2: Hal 5H **39**
Roundhill Mt. BD16: Bgly 6H **15**
Round Hill Pl. BD13: B'frd 1H **41**
Roundhill Pl.
BD1: B'frd 2H **35** (4B **4**)
Roundhill St. BD5: B'frd 5H **35**
Round St. BD5: B'frd 6A **36**
(not continuous)
Round Thorn Pl. BD8: B'frd 1E **35**
Roundwood BD18: Ship 6C **16**
Roundwood Av.
BD10: B'frd 2G **29**
BD17: Bail 2B **18**
Roundwood Glen
BD10: B'frd 6G **19**
Roundwood Rd. BD17: Bail 2A **18**
Roundwood Vw.
BD10: B'frd 1G **29**
Rouse Fold
BD4: B'frd 4B **36** (6F **5**)
Rowan Av. BD3: B'frd 2G **37**
Rowanberry Cl. BD2: B'frd 3D **28**
Rowan Ct. BD2: B'frd 6E **29**
Rowan Dr. HD6: Brigh 4G **59**
Rowans, The BD17: Bail 2D **16**
Rowan St. BD20: Keigh 1C **6**
Rowantree Av. BD17: Bail 1F **17**
Rowantree Dr. BD10: B'frd 1D **28**
Rowanwood Gdns.
BD10: B'frd 2G **29**
Row Bottom Ter. HX6: Hal 3A **54**
Row La. HX6: Hal 4A **54**
Rowlestone Ri.
BD10: B'frd 1G **29**
Rowsley St. BD21: Keigh 4F **7**
Rowton Thorpe BD10: B'frd 1G **29**
Roxburgh Gro. BD15: B'frd 1H **33**
Roxby St. BD5: B'frd 6H **35**
Roxholme Ho. *BD4: B'frd 1E **45***
(off Prince St.)
Royal Arc. BD21: Keigh 4E **7**
Royal Cl. BD7: B'frd 6D **34**
Royal Ind. Pk.
HX1: Hal 6B **48** (4A **62**)
Royal Lofts, The *HX6: Hal 4D **54***
(off Sowerby St.)
Royd HX6: Hal 4A **54**
Royd Av. BD16: Bgly 2A **16**
HD3: Hud 6G **61**
Royd Cres. HX1: Hal 5G **47**
Royd End BD15: B'frd 2C **24**
Royden Gro. BD9: B'frd 5E **27**
Royd Farm *HX2: Hal 4G **39***
(off Causeway Foot)
Royd Ho. Gro. BD21: Keigh 6G **7**
Royd Ho. Rd. BD21: Keigh 6G **7**
Royd Ho. Wlk. BD21: Keigh 6G **7**
Royd Ho. Way BD21: Keigh 6G **7**
Royd Ings Av. BD21: Keigh 2E **7**
Roydlands St. HX3: Hal 6B **50**
Roydlands Ter. HX3: Hal 6B **50**
Royd La. BD20: Keigh 2D **6**
HX2: Hal 4G **39**
HX3: Hal 1A **48**
Royd Mill Bus. Pk.
HD6: Brigh 6G **59**
Royd Moor Rd. BD4: B'frd 2H **45**
Royd Mt. HX3: Hal 3C **48**
Royd Pl. HX3: Hal 3C **48**
Royds, The HX3: Hal 4B **56**
Royds Av. HD6: Brigh 5F **51**
Roydscliffe Dr. BD9: B'frd 3D **26**
Roydscliffe Rd. BD9: B'frd 4D **26**
Royds Cres. HD6: Brigh 6F **51**
Roydsdale Way BD4: B'frd 5C **44**
Royds Hall Av. BD6: B'frd 3G **43**
Royds Hall La. BD6: B'frd 5E **43**
(Alderholt Dr.)
BD6: B'frd 6E **43**
(Lingdale Rd.)
BD12: B'frd 2E **51**
Royds Pk. Cres.
BD12: B'frd 1H **51**
Roydstone Rd. BD3: B'frd 1F **37**
Roydstone Ter. BD3: B'frd 1F **37**
Royd St. BD12: B'frd 1G **51**
BD13: B'frd 3C **32**
BD15: B'frd 3C **24**
BD20: Keigh 1D **6**
(not continuous)
Royds Wood BD18: Ship 2E **27**
Royd Way BD21: Keigh 2E **7**
Royd Wood BD19: Cleck 6F **53**
BD22: Oxen 3H **21**
Roydwood Ter. BD13: B'frd 1F **23**
Roy Rd. BD6: B'frd 2B **42**
Ruby St. BD22: Keigh 1C **12**
Rudding Av. BD15: B'frd 6G **25**
Rudding Cres. BD15: B'frd 6G **25**
Rudd St. BD7: B'frd 5E **35**
Ruffield Side BD12: B'frd 6G **43**
Rufford Pl. HX3: Hal 3B **56**
Rufford Rd. HX3: Hal 3B **56**
HX5: Ell 3F **61**
Rufford St. BD3: B'frd 2E **37**
Rufford Vs. HX3: Hal 3B **56**
Rufforth Ho. *BD10: B'frd 1E **29***
(off Rowantree Dr.)
Rufus St. BD5: B'frd 6F **35**
BD21: Keigh 3E **7**
Rugby Av. HX3: Hal 2H **47**
Rugby Dr. HX3: Hal 2H **47**
Rugby Gdns. HX3: Hal 2H **47**
Rugby Mt. HX3: Hal 2H **47**
Rugby Pl. BD7: B'frd 3F **35**
Rugby Ter. HX3: Hal 2H **47**
Runnymede Ct. *BD10: B'frd 6D **18***
(off Cobden St.)
Runswick Gro. BD5: B'frd 2H **43**
Runswick St. BD5: B'frd 2H **43**
Runswick Ter. BD5: B'frd 2H **43**
Rupert St. BD21: Keigh 3E **7**
BD22: Haw 5B **12**
Rush Cft. BD10: B'frd 4B **18**
Rushcroft Ter. BD17: Bail 2G **17**
Rushdene Ct. BD12: B'frd 4G **51**
Rushmoor Rd. BD4: B'frd 1F **45**
Rushton Av. BD3: B'frd 1G **37**
Rushton Hill HX2: Hal 4E **47**
Rushton Hill Cl. HX2: Hal 4E **47**
Rushton Rd. BD3: B'frd 1F **37**
Rushton St. HX1: Hal 5H **47**
Rushton Ter. BD3: B'frd 2G **37**
Rushworth St. HX3: Hal 4A **48**
Ruskin Av. BD9: B'frd 4B **26**
Ruskin Ter. HX3: Hal 4A **48**
Russel Ho. *BD10: B'frd 1E **29***
(off Yewdall Way)
Russell Av. BD13: B'frd 3E **41**
Russell Hall La.
BD13: B'frd 2E **41**
Russell Rd. BD13: B'frd 3D **40**
Russell St. BD5: B'frd 4H **35**
BD13: B'frd 2E **41**
BD18: Ship 2G **27**
BD21: Keigh 4D **6**
HX1: Hal 6C **48** (4C **62**)
Russell Way HD6: Brigh 3F **59**
Russetts, The HX3: Hal 5E **49**
Rustic Av. HX3: Hal 3G **57**
Ruswarp Cres. BD10: B'frd 1F **29**
Ruth Ho. *BD3: B'frd 3G **5***
(off Otley Rd.)
Ruth St. BD22: Haw 5A **12**
Rutland Ho. *BD16: Bgly 2G **15***
(off Lyndon Ter.)
Rutland St. BD4: B'frd 5C **36**
BD21: Keigh 6D **6**
Ryan Gro. BD22: Keigh 3A **6**
Ryan St. BD5: B'frd 6H **35**
Ryburn Bldgs. *HX6: Hal 4D **54***
(off Town Hall St.)
Ryburn Ct. *HX1: Hal 6H **47***
(off Hanson La.)
Ryburn Ho. *HX1: Hal 6H **47***
(off Clay St.)
Ryburn St. HX6: Hal 4D **54**
Ryburn Ter. HX1: Hal 6H **47**
Ryburn Vw. HX2: Hal 2G **55**
Rycroft Av. BD16: Bgly 1G **25**
Rycroft St. BD18: Ship 2H **27**
Rydal Av. BD9: B'frd 3G **27**
BD17: Bail 4C **16**
Rydale Ho. HX6: Hal 4D **54**
Rydal St. BD21: Keigh 5C **6**
Rydings, The *HD6: Brigh 4E **59***
(off Halifax Rd.)
Rydings Av. HD6: Brigh 4E **59**
Rydings Cl. HD6: Brigh 4D **58**
Rydings Dr. HD6: Brigh 4D **58**
Rydings Wlk. HD6: Brigh 4D **58**
Rye Cft. HX2: Hal 5H **39**
Ryecroft BD16: Bgly 4H **13**
Ryecroft Cres. HX2: Hal 4F **47**
Ryecroft La. HX2: Hal 5F **47**
Ryecroft Rd. BD16: B'frd 3F **13**
Ryecroft Ter. HX2: Hal 4F **47**
Ryedale Way BD15: B'frd 5G **25**
Ryefield Av. BD14: B'frd 4H **33**
Ryelands Gro. BD9: B'frd 3B **26**
Rye La. HX2: Hal 4D **46**
Rye St. BD21: Keigh 1D **12**
Rylands Av. BD16: Bgly 2H **15**
Rylands Mdw. BD22: Haw 5A **12**
Rylstone Gdns. BD3: B'frd 6C **28**
Rylstone Rd. BD17: Bail 3D **16**
Rylstone St. BD21: Keigh 3F **7**
Rylston Gdns. HX3: Hal 4B **56**
Ryshworth Av. BD16: Bgly 4D **8**
Ryshworth Bri. BD16: Bgly 5D **8**
Ryshworth Cres. BD16: Bgly 4D **8**
Ryton Dale BD10: B'frd 1G **29**

S

Sable Crest BD2: B'frd 3B **28**
Sackville St.
BD1: B'frd 2A **36** (4C **4**)
Saddleworth Rd. HX4: Hal 3A **60**
HX5: Ell 2D **60**
Sadler St. BD12: B'frd 1G **51**
Saffron Dr. BD15: B'frd 6H **25**
Sage St. BD5: B'frd 5G **35**
Sahara Ct. BD8: B'frd 5H **27**
St Abbs Cl. BD6: B'frd 4G **43**
St Abbs Dr. BD6: B'frd 4G **43**
St Abbs Fold BD6: B'frd 4G **43**
St Abbs Ga. BD6: B'frd 4G **43**
St Abbs Wlk. BD6: B'frd 4G **43**
St Abbs Way BD6: B'frd 4G **43**
St Aidan's Rd. BD17: Bail 3H **17**
St Aidans Sq. *BD16: Bgly 5E **9***
(off Micklethwaite La.)
St Albans Av. HD3: Hud 6G **61**
HX3: Hal 4C **56**
(not continuous)

St Albans Cft. HX3: Hal 3D 56
St Albans Rd. HX3: Hal 4C 56
St Andrew's Cl. HX2: Hal 6A 40
St Andrews Ct. HD6: Brigh . . .3E 59
    (off Mary St.)
St Andrews Cres.
  BD12: B'frd 1C 52
St Andrews Dr. HD6: Brigh . . .3E 59
St Andrews Pl. BD7: B'frd 3G 35
St Andrew's Sq. BD16: Bgly . .5E 9
    (off Micklethwaite La.)
St Anne's Av. HD3: Hud 6G 61
St Anne's Rd. HX3: Hal 5C 56
St Annes Ter. BD17: Bail 3H 17
St Ann's Pl. HX1: Hal 5A 48
    (off Pellon La.)
St Anns Sq. HX6: Hal 3E 55
St Anthonys Gdns.
  BD18: Ship 1H 27
    (off Snowden Rd.)
St Augustine's Ter.
  BD3: B'frd 6C 28 (1G 5)
  HX1: Hal 6A 48
St Bevan's Rd. HX3: Hal 4C 56
St Blaise Ct.
  BD5: B'frd 4A 36 (6D 4)
St Blaise Sq.
  BD1: B'frd 2A 36 (3D 4)
St Blaise Way
  BD1: B'frd 2A 36 (3D 4)
ST CATHERINES HOSPITAL
  . . . . .5G 27
St Chad's Av. HD6: Brigh 2C 58
St Chad's Rd. BD8: B'frd 6F 27
St Clare's Av. BD2: B'frd 5F 29
St Davids Ct. HX3: Hal 4B 48
St Elmo BD13: B'frd 4C 40
St Eloi Av. BD17: Bail 1G 17
St Enoch's Rd. BD6: B'frd . . .2F 43
St George's Concert Hall 5E 5
St Georges Cres.
  HX3: Hal 4B 48
St George's Pl. BD4: B'frd . . .5D 36
  BD5: B'frd 4A 36
St George's Rd. HX3: Hal 4A 48
St George's Sq. HX3: Hal 4B 48
St George's St.
  BD3: B'frd 3D 36 (5H 5)
St George's Ter. HX3: Hal 4B 48
St Giles Cl. HD6: Brigh 2C 58
St Giles Ct. HX3: Hal 6C 50
  HX3: Hal 6C 50
St Giles Rd. HD6: Brigh 1C 58
  HX3: Hal 6C 50
St Helena BD13: B'frd 6G 23
St Helena Rd. BD6: B'frd 2F 43
St Helens Sq. HX4: Hal 5C 60
    (off Station Rd.)
St Helier Gro. BD17: Bail 1H 17
St Hilda's Ter. BD3: B'frd 1G 37
St Ives Est. BD16: Bgly 3C 14
St Ives Gdns. HX3: Hal 4C 56
St Ives Gro. BD16: Bgly 3C 14
St Ives Pl. BD16: Bgly 3C 14
St Ives Rd. BD16: Bgly 2D 14
    (Cross Gates La.)
  BD16: Bgly 3C 14
    (St Ives Pl.)
  HX3: Hal 4C 56
St James Bus. Pk.
  BD1: B'frd 3C 36 (5G 5)
St James Ct. HD6: Brigh 4F 59
  HX1: Hal 3B 62
St James Pl. BD17: Bail 1B 18
    (off Otley Rd.)
St James Rd. BD17: Bail 1B 18
  HX1: Hal 6C 48 (3B 62)
St James's Mkt.
  BD4: B'frd 3C 36 (6G 5)
St James Sq. HX3: Hal 3G 49
St James's Sq. BD5: B'frd . . .4A 36
St James St.
  HX1: Hal 6C 48 (3B 62)
St John's Cl. BD19: Cleck 6G 53

St John's Ct. BD17: Bail 3A 18
  BD20: Keigh 1C 6
    (off St John's Rd.)
St Johns Cres. BD8: B'frd 1C 34
St John's Cross HX2: Hal 3A 40
St John's La.
  HX1: Hal 1C 56 (6B 62)
St Johns M. BD13: B'frd 1F 23
    (off Station Rd.)
St John's Pl. BD19: Cleck 6G 53
St John's Rd. BD20: Keigh 1C 6
St John St. HD6: Brigh 6E 59
St Johns Way BD22: Keigh . . .5B 6
St Jude's Pl.
  BD1: B'frd 1H 35 (1B 4)
St Jude's St.
  BD8: B'frd 1H 35 (1A 4)
  HX1: Hal 2B 56
St Laurence's Cl.
St Leonards Ct. BD8: B'frd . . .6D 26
St Leonard's Gro.
  BD8: B'frd 6D 26
St Leonard's Rd.
  BD8: B'frd 6D 26
St Lukes Cl. BD5: B'frd 4H 35
  BD19: Cleck 6D 52
ST LUKE'S HOSPITAL (BRADFORD)
  . . . . .5H 35
St Luke's Ter. BD19: Cleck . . .6D 52
  BD20: Keigh 3D 8
St Margaret's Av.
  BD4: B'frd 1F 45
St Margaret's Pl.
  BD7: B'frd 4F 35
St Margaret's Rd.
  BD7: B'frd 3F 35
St Margaret's Ter.
  BD7: B'frd 4F 35
St Mark's Av. BD12: B'frd . . .6G 43
St Mark's Pl. BD12: B'frd 6G 43
St Mark's Ter. BD12: B'frd . . .6G 43
St Martins Av. BD7: B'frd 2G 35
St Martin's Vw. HD6: Brigh . . .4E 59
St Mary Magdalenes Cl.
  BD8: B'frd 1H 35 (1A 4)
St Mary's Av. BD12: B'frd . . .3G 51
St Mary's Cl. BD12: B'frd 3F 51
St Mary's Ct. HX2: Hal 6F 39
St Mary's Cres. BD12: B'frd . .4F 51
St Mary's Dr. BD12: B'frd 3G 51
St Mary's Gdns.
  BD12: B'frd 3G 51
St Mary's Ga. HX5: Ell 2F 61
St Mary's Hgts. HX2: Hal 6F 39
St Mary's Mt. BD12: B'frd 3F 51
St Mary's Rd. BD4: B'frd 4F 37
  BD9: B'frd 5G 27
  BD20: Keigh 1H 7
St Mary's Sq. BD12: B'frd . . .3G 51
St Mary St.
  HX1: Hal 1B 56 (5A 62)
St Matthews Cl.
  BD15: B'frd 3B 24
St Matthew's Dr. HX3: Hal . . .2G 49
St Matthews Gro.
  BD15: B'frd 3C 24
St Matthews Rd.
  BD5: B'frd 2H 43
St Michaels Cl. BD16: Bgly . . .1H 25
St Michael's Rd.
  BD8: B'frd 1G 35
St Paul's Av. BD6: B'frd 3F 43
St Paul's Bldgs HX5: Ell 3F 61
    (off Langdale St.)
St Paul's Cl. BD8: B'frd 6G 27
    (off Church St.)
St Paul's Gro. BD6: B'frd 3F 43
St Paul's Rd. BD6: B'frd 3F 43
  BD8: B'frd 5G 27
    (not continuous)
  BD18: Ship 6E 17
  BD21: Keigh 5F 7
  HX1: Hal 2H 55
St Peg Cl. BD19: Cleck 5G 53

St Peg La. BD19: Cleck 6G 53
St Peter's Av. HX6: Hal 4A 54
St Peters Sq. HX6: Hal 4A 54
St Philips Ct. HD3: Hud 6H 61
St Phillips Ct. BD8: B'frd 6E 27
    (off Thorn St.)
St Stephen's Ct. HX3: Hal . . .5A 56
St Stephen's Rd.
  BD5: B'frd 6H 35
  LS28: Pud 6H 19
St Stephen's St. HX3: Hal . . .5A 56
St Stephen's Ter.
  BD5: B'frd 6A 36
  HX3: Hal 5B 56
Saint St. BD7: B'frd 5E 35
St Thomas's Rd.
  BD1: B'frd 2H 35 (3B 4)
St Wilfrid's Cl. BD7: B'frd 4D 34
St Wilfrid's Cres.
  BD7: B'frd 4D 34
St Wilfrid's Rd. BD7: B'frd 4D 34
St Winifred's Cl. HX2: Hal 6F 39
Salcombe Pl. BD4: B'frd 1G 45
Salem St. BD1: B'frd . . .1A 36 (2C 4)
  BD13: B'frd 2D 40
Salisbury Av. BD17: Bail 2G 17
Salisbury Pl. HX3: Hal 4B 48
Salisbury Rd. BD9: B'frd 2G 27
  BD12: B'frd 5G 43
  BD19: Cleck 5B 52
  BD22: Keigh 5C 6
Salisbury St. HX6: Hal 4C 54
Salisbury Ter. HX3: Hal 4B 48
Sal Nook Cl. BD12: B'frd 4H 43
Sal Royd Rd. BD12: B'frd 6A 44
Saltaire 5D 16
Saltaire BD22: Haw 5B 12
Saltaire Rd. BD16: Bgly 1B 16
  BD18: Ship 5D 16
Saltaire Station (Rail) 4D 16
Saltburn Pl. BD9: B'frd 5D 26
Saltburn St. HX1: Hal 6H 47
SALTERHEBBLE 4D 56
Salterhebble Hill HX3: Hal . . .5D 56
Salterhebble Ter. HX3: Hal . . .4D 56
    (off Huddersfield Rd.)
Salterlee HX3: Hal 3E 49
Salt Horn Cl. BD12: B'frd 6B 44
Saltonstall La. HX2: Hal 6A 38
Salts Mill BD18: Ship 4E 17
Salts Mill Rd. BD18: Ship 5E 17
Salt St. BD8: B'frd 6G 27
  HX1: Hal 5A 48
Samuel St. BD21: Keigh 4D 6
Sandacre Cl. BD10: B'frd 4G 29
Sandale Wlk. BD6: B'frd 4D 42
Sandal Magna HX3: Hal 4C 42
Sandals Rd. BD17: Bail 2G 17
Sandal Ter. HX6: Hal 4E 55
Sand Beds BD13: B'frd 2E 41
Sandbeds Cres. HX2: Hal 4G 47
Sandbeds Rd. HX2: Hal 5F 47
Sandbeds Ter. HX2: Hal 4G 47
Sanderling Ct. BD8: B'frd 2A 34
Sanderson Av. BD6: B'frd 2G 43
Sandfield Rd. BD10: B'frd 1D 28
Sandford Rd. BD3: B'frd 2E 37
    (not continuous)
Sandforth Av. HX3: Hal 3C 48
Sandgate Wlk. BD4: B'frd 1H 45
Sandhall Av. HX2: Hal 6F 47
Sandhall Cres. HX2: Hal 5F 47
    (off Sandhall Grn.)
Sandhall Dr. HX2: Hal 6F 47
Sandhall Grn. HX2: Hal 5F 47
    (not continuous)
Sandhall La. HX2: Hal 6F 47
Sandhill Fold BD10: B'frd 6C 18
Sandhill Mt. BD10: B'frd 1D 28
Sandholme Cres. HX3: Hal . . .6B 50
Sandholme Dr. BD10: B'frd . . .1D 28
Sandholme Fold HX3: Hal 6B 50
Sandmead Cl. BD4: B'frd 6G 37
Sandmoor Cl. BD13: B'frd 3E 33
Sandmoor Gdns. HX3: Hal . . .6H 41

Sandmoor Gth. BD10: B'frd . . .4D 18
Sandown Av. HX2: Hal 1G 47
Sandown Rd. HX2: Hal 1G 47
Sandpiper M. BD8: B'frd 2A 34
Sandringham Cl.
  BD14: B'frd 4B 34
Sandringham Ct.
  BD14: B'frd 4B 34
Sandringham Rd.
  BD14: B'frd 4B 34
Sandsend Cl. BD9: B'frd 4B 26
Sandside Cl. BD5: B'frd 1B 44
Sand St. BD21: Keigh 4E 7
  BD22: Haw 1G 21
Sandy Banks BD16: Bgly 5B 14
Sandy Beck BD15: B'frd 4G 25
Sandy Dyke La. HX6: Hal 6A 54
Sandy Fore HX2: Hal 1B 46
Sandy Ga. BD20: Keigh 3C 6
Sandygate Ter. BD4: B'frd 4F 37
SANDY LANE 3G 25
Sandymoor BD15: B'frd 3G 25
Sandywood St. BD21: Keigh . .3E 7
Sangster Way BD5: B'frd 2C 44
Santa Monica Cres.
  BD10: B'frd 6C 18
Santa Monica Gro.
  BD10: B'frd 6C 18
Santa Monica Rd.
  BD10: B'frd 6C 18
Santon Ho. BD5: B'frd 5A 36
    (off Manchester Rd.)
Sapgate La. BD13: B'frd 3E 33
Sapling Gro. Cotts.
  HX1: Hal 3H 55
Saplin St. BD8: B'frd 6F 27
Savile Av. BD10: B'frd 1E 29
Savile Cl. HD6: Brigh 4H 59
Savile Cres.
  HX1: Hal 1B 56 (6A 62)
Savile Dr. HX1: Hal . . .2B 56 (6A 62)
Savile Glen
  HX1: Hal 1B 56 (6A 62)
Savile Grn.
  HX1: Hal 1C 56 (6B 62)
Savile La. HD6: Brigh 4H 59
Savile Lea
  HX1: Hal 1B 56 (6A 62)
Savile M. HX1: Hal 2B 56
Savile Mt.
  HX1: Hal 2B 56 (6A 62)
Savile Pde. HX1: Hal 2B 56
SAVILE PARK 2A 56
Savile Pk. HX1: Hal 2A 56
  HX3: Hal 3B 56
Savile Pk. Gdns. HX1: Hal . . .2B 56
Savile Pk. Mills HX1: Hal 2A 56
    (off Moorfield St.)
Savile Pk. Rd. BD19: Cleck . . .2F 53
  HX1: Hal 2B 56 (6A 62)
Savile Pk. St. HX1: Hal 2A 56
Savile Pk. Ter. HX1: Hal 2A 56
    (off Moorfield St.)
Savile Rd.
  HX1: Hal 1B 56 (6A 62)
  HX5: Ell 3F 61
Savile Row
  HX1: Hal 1B 56 (6A 62)
Savile Royd
  HX1: Hal 2B 56 (6A 62)
Savile St. BD19: Cleck 4F 53
Savile Ter. HX1: Hal 2B 56
    (off Savile Pk. Rd.)
Savile Way HX5: Ell 1G 61
Saville Pk. HX1: Hal 2H 55
Sawley St. BD21: Keigh 5D 6
SAWOOD 6B 22
Sawood La. BD22: Oxen 6B 22
Sawrey Pl.
  BD5: B'frd 3H 35 (6B 4)
Saxilby Rd. BD20: Keigh 2B 8
Saxon Ct. BD12: B'frd 2F 51
Saxon St. BD8: B'frd 1G 35
  HX1: Hal 6H 47
Saxton Av. BD6: B'frd 2C 42

Silverhill Rd.—Spinney Ri.

Silverhill Rd. BD3: B'frd . . . 6E 29
Silver St. BD8: B'frd . . . 6F 27
HX1: Hal . . . 6C 48 (4B 62)
Silverwood HX2: Hal . . . 4E 47
(not continuous)
Silverwood Av. HX2: Hal . . . 4E 47
(not continuous)
Silwood Dr. BD2: B'frd . . . 4E 29
Simes St.
BD1: B'frd . . . 2H 35 (3B 4)
Simm Carr HX3: Hal . . . 1D 48
Simm Carr La. HX3: Hal . . . 1D 48
Simmonds La. HX1: Hal . . . 2D 56
Simms Dene BD15: B'frd . . . 3G 25
Simon Cl. BD4: B'frd . . . 1H 45
Simon Fold BD12: B'frd . . . 3G 51
SIMPSON GREEN . . . 4E 19
Simpson Gro. BD10: B'frd . . . 4E 19
Simpson St. BD21: Keigh . . . 4C 6
HX3: Hal . . . 3B 48
Sinclair Rd. BD2: B'frd . . . 2B 28
Sinden M. BD10: B'frd . . . 3D 18
Singleton St.
BD1: B'frd . . . 1A 36 (1D 4)
Sion Hill HX3: Hal . . . 4E 57
Sir Francis Crossley's Almshouses
HX1: Hal . . . 6B 48
(off Margaret St.)
Sir Isaac Holden Pl.
BD7: B'frd . . . 2F 35
Sir Wilfred Pl. BD10: B'frd . . . 5D 18
Siskin Dr. BD6: B'frd . . . 2A 42
Sixth Av. BD3: B'frd . . . 6E 29
Skellow Dr. BD4: B'frd . . . 2H 45
Skelton Wlk. BD10: B'frd . . . 6F 19
Skinner La. BD8: B'frd . . . 5G 27
Skipton Rd. BD20: Keigh . . . 1B 6
BD21: Keigh . . . 3E 7
SKIRCOAT GREEN . . . 5B 56
Skircoat Grn. HX3: Hal . . . 5C 56
Skircoat Grn. Rd. HX3: Hal . . . 4C 56
Skircoat Lodge HX3: Hal . . . 4B 56
Skircoat Moor Cl. HX3: Hal . . . 3A 56
Skircoat Moor Rd.
HX1: Hal . . . 2H 55
Skircoat Rd.
HX1: Hal . . . 1C 56 (6C 62)
Skirrow St. BD16: Bgly . . . 1H 25
Skylark Av. BD6: B'frd . . . 2A 42
Slack Bottom Rd.
BD6: B'frd . . . 3E 43
Slack End BD6: B'frd . . . 4D 42
Slack La. BD22: Keigh . . . 2E 11
SLACK SIDE . . . 2D 42
Sladdin Row BD13: B'frd . . . 3C 40
Slade Ho. BD2: B'frd . . . 5F 29
(off St Clares Av.)
Slade La. BD20: Keigh . . . 1G 7
Sladen Bri. BD22: Haw . . . 6D 10
Sladen St. BD21: Keigh . . . 4C 6
Slate Quarry La.
BD16: Bgly . . . 1H 15
Slaymaker La. BD22: Keigh . . . 2F 11
Slead Av. HD6: Brigh . . . 3D 58
Slead Ct. HD6: Brigh . . . 3D 58
Slead Cres. HD6: Brigh . . . 3D 58
Slead Gro. HD6: Brigh . . . 3D 58
Slead Royd HD6: Brigh . . . 3D 58
SLEAD SYKE . . . 3C 58
Slead Syke Sports Cen. . . . 2D 58
Slead Vw. HD6: Brigh . . . 3D 58
Sleningford Gro.
BD18: Ship . . . 5C 16
Sleningford Ri. BD16: Bgly . . . 6F 9
Sleningford Rd. BD16: Bgly . . . 6E 9
BD18: Ship . . . 5C 16
Sleningford Ter. BD16: Bgly . . . 6F 9
(off Sleningford Rd.)
Slicer's Yd. BD16: Bgly . . . 2F 15
(off Busfield St.)
Slingsby Cl. BD10: B'frd . . . 5F 19
Slippy La. HX2: Hal . . . 6E 39
(not continuous)
Small Page BD13: B'frd . . . 2E 41
(off Albert Rd.)
Small Page Fold
BD13: B'frd . . . 2E 41
Smiddles La. BD5: B'frd . . . 1H 43
Smith Art Gallery . . . 4E 59
Smith Av. BD6: B'frd . . . 2G 43
Smitherd's St. BD21: Keigh . . . 5D 6
Smithfield Av. HX3: Hal . . . 5A 50
Smith Ho. Av. HD6: Brigh . . . 2E 59
Smith Ho. Cl. HD6: Brigh . . . 1E 59
Smith Ho. Cres. HD6: Brigh . . . 2E 59
(not continuous)
Smith Ho. Dr. HD6: Brigh . . . 1E 59
Smith Ho. Gro. HD6: Brigh . . . 2E 59
Smith Ho. La. HD6: Brigh . . . 2E 59
Smith La. BD9: B'frd . . . 5C 26
Smith Rd. BD7: B'frd . . . 6E 35
Smith's Ter. HX3: Hal . . . 2A 48
Smith St. BD4: B'frd . . . 3D 44
BD7: B'frd . . . 2H 35 (4A 4)
BD16: Bgly . . . 1H 25
BD21: Keigh . . . 3C 6
Smithville BD20: Keigh . . . 2H 7
Smithy Carr La.
HD6: Brigh . . . 3E 59
Smithy Ct. BD19: Cleck . . . 4B 52
Smithy Fold BD13: B'frd . . . 1A 42
Smithy Hill BD6: B'frd . . . 2G 43
BD13: B'frd . . . 2G 31
BD22: Keigh . . . 1B 12
(off Keighley Rd.)
Smithy La. BD15: B'frd . . . 1C 24
Smithy St.
HX1: Hal . . . 6D 48 (3D 62)
Snake Hill BD12: B'frd . . . 6C 44
Snape Dr. BD7: B'frd . . . 1B 42
Snape St. BD21: Keigh . . . 1E 13
Snelsins La. BD19: Cleck . . . 4E 53
Snelsins Rd. BD19: Cleck . . . 4E 53
Snowden Rd. BD18: Ship . . . 1H 27
(not continuous)
Snowden St.
BD1: B'frd . . . 1A 36 (2C 4)
Snowdens Wlk.
BD14: B'frd . . . 5B 34
Snowdrop M. BD15: B'frd . . . 1H 33
Soaper Ho. La. HX3: Hal . . . 3A 50
Soaper La. BD6: B'frd . . . 4A 42
HX3: Hal . . . 4A 42
Sod Ho. Grn. HX3: Hal . . . 2A 48
Soho Mills BD1: B'frd . . . 4B 4
Soho St. BD1: B'frd . . . 2H 35 (4B 4)
HX1: Hal . . . 6H 47
SOIL HILL . . . 6G 31
Solomon Hill HX2: Hal . . . 4A 46
Somerset Av. BD17: Bail . . . 1F 17
Somerton Dr. BD4: B'frd . . . 1F 45
Somerville Av. BD6: B'frd . . . 4F 43
Somerville Pk. BD6: B'frd . . . 4F 43
Sonning Rd. BD15: B'frd . . . 1H 33
Sorrel Way BD17: Bail . . . 1B 18
Sorrin Cl. BD10: B'frd . . . 5C 18
Soureby Cross Way
BD4: B'frd . . . 4H 45
(off Green, The)
BD4: B'frd . . . 4H 45
(Hunsworth La.)
Southampton St.
BD3: B'frd . . . 6B 28 (1F 5)
South Bank BD13: B'frd . . . 2F 41
South Bolton HX2: Hal . . . 4F 39
Southbrook Ter.
BD7: B'frd . . . 3H 35 (5B 4)
South Carr HX2: Hal . . . 4A 46
South Cliffe BD13: B'frd . . . 3E 33
HX2: Hal . . . 6A 40
Southcliffe HX3: Hal . . . 2E 57
(off Bank Top)
Southcliffe Dr. BD17: Bail . . . 4F 17
Southcliffe Way BD17: Bail . . . 4G 17
Sth. Clough Head HX2: Hal . . . 6C 46
Southcote Pl. BD10: B'frd . . . 5D 18
Southdown Cl. BD9: B'frd . . . 5C 26
Southdown Ct. BD9: B'frd . . . 5C 26
(off Southdown Cl.)
Southdown Rd. BD17: Bail . . . 4F 17
South Edge BD18: Ship . . . 6C 16
BD20: Keigh . . . 3C 6
HX3: Hal . . . 6B 50
Southedge Cl. HX3: Hal . . . 6A 50
Southedge Ter. HX3: Hal . . . 6B 50
Southfield Av. BD6: B'frd . . . 3G 43
BD20: Keigh . . . 1H 7
Southfield Dr. BD20: Keigh . . . 1A 8
Southfield La. BD5: B'frd . . . 6F 35
BD7: B'frd . . . 5E 35
Southfield Mt. BD20: Keigh . . . 1H 7
Southfield Rd. BD5: B'frd . . . 6G 35
BD16: Bgly . . . 4G 15
Southfield Sq. BD8: B'frd . . . 6G 27
Southfield Ter. HX3: Hal . . . 4A 50
Southfield Way BD20: Keigh . . . 1A 8
Southgate BD1: B'frd . . . 2A 36 (4C 4)
(not continuous)
HX1: Hal . . . 6C 48 (4C 62)
HX4: Hal . . . 6C 60
HX5: Ell . . . 2F 61
South Gro. BD18: Ship . . . 6B 16
HD6: Brigh . . . 2C 58
Sth. Hill Dr. BD16: Bgly . . . 3A 16
Sth. Holme La. HD6: Brigh . . . 3C 58
Southlands BD17: Bail . . . 4F 17
HX2: Hal . . . 2H 39
Southlands Av. BD13: B'frd . . . 3A 34
BD16: Bgly . . . 4G 15
BD20: Keigh . . . 2A 8
Southlands Dr. BD20: Keigh . . . 2A 8
Southlands Gro BD13: B'frd . . . 3H 33
BD16: Bgly . . . 4F 15
BD20: Keigh . . . 2A 8
Southlands Gro. W.
BD20: Keigh . . . 1A 8
Southlands Mt. BD20: Keigh . . . 2A 8
Southlands Rd. BD20: Keigh . . . 1A 8
South La. HX3: Hal . . . 4H 41
HX5: Ell . . . 5F 61
South La. Gdns. HX5: Ell . . . 4F 61
Southlea BD12: B'frd . . . 6C 44
Southlea Av. BD22: Keigh . . . 3A 12
Southmere Av. BD7: B'frd . . . 6E 35
Southmere Cres. BD7: B'frd . . . 6E 35
Southmere Dr. BD7: B'frd . . . 6D 34
(Bartle Pl.)
BD7: B'frd . . . 6E 35
(Southmere Rd.)
Southmere Gro. BD7: B'frd . . . 6E 35
Southmere Oval BD7: B'frd . . . 1D 42
Southmere Rd. BD7: B'frd . . . 6E 35
Southmere Ter. BD7: B'frd . . . 6E 35
SOUTHOWRAM . . . 3G 57
Southowram Bank
HX3: Hal . . . 6D 48
South Pde. BD8: B'frd . . . 6H 27
BD19: Cleck . . . 5E 53
HX1: Hal . . . 1D 56 (6D 62)
HX5: Ell . . . 4F 61
South Rd. BD9: B'frd . . . 3G 27
BD13: B'frd . . . 2F 23
Sth. Royd Av. HX3: Hal . . . 3C 56
South Selby HX2: Hal . . . 5F 39
South Sq. BD13: B'frd . . . 3D 32
Sth. Square Cen.
BD13: B'frd . . . 3D 32
(off South Sq.)
South St. BD5: B'frd . . . 6G 35
BD12: B'frd . . . 1C 52
BD13: B'frd . . . 1F 31
(Main Rd.)
BD13: B'frd . . . 2D 32
(West La.)
BD20: Keigh . . . 3D 8
BD21: Keigh . . . 6D 6
HD6: Brigh . . . 4E 59
HX1: Hal . . . 1B 56 (5A 62)
HX4: Hal . . . 5B 60
South Ter. HX3: Hal . . . 2G 49
South Vw. BD6: B'frd . . . 5C 42
BD9: B'frd . . . 3G 27
BD10: B'frd . . . 6F 19
BD13: B'frd . . . 1C 40
BD15: B'frd . . . 2C 24
South Vw. BD19: Cleck . . . 6B 52
BD20: Keigh . . . 2B 8
BD22: Haw . . . 6G 11
HX2: Hal . . . 6A 40
(off Blackmires)
HX2: Hal . . . 2B 54
(Warley Wood Av.)
HX3: Hal . . . 3G 57
(Towngate)
HX3: Hal . . . 3E 57
(Whitegate Top)
South Vw. Cl. BD4: B'frd . . . 4G 45
South Vw. Ct. HX3: Hal . . . 1B 58
South Vw. Dr. BD4: B'frd . . . 4H 45
South Vw. Rd. BD4: B'frd . . . 4H 45
South Vw. Ter. BD17: Bail . . . 2G 17
HX1: Hal . . . 5H 47
(off Queen's Rd.)
South Wlk. BD16: Bgly . . . 4A 14
South Way BD4: B'frd . . . 4G 45
BD18: Ship . . . 6B 16
Southway BD16: Bgly . . . 6H 9
Sovereign Pk. BD17: Bail . . . 1A 18
Sovereign St.
HX1: Hal . . . 6B 48 (4A 62)
Sowden Bldgs. BD2: B'frd . . . 5D 28
Sowden Grange
BD13: B'frd . . . 3D 32
(James St.)
BD13: B'frd . . . 3D 32
(Lane End)
Sowden La. BD12: B'frd . . . 2E 51
HX3: Hal . . . 2D 50
(not continuous)
Sowden Rd. BD9: B'frd . . . 4B 26
Sowden St. BD7: B'frd . . . 6F 35
SOWERBY . . . 4A 54
SOWERBY BRIDGE . . . 3E 55
Sowerby Bridge Pool . . . 3D 54
Sowerby Bridge Station (Rail)
. . . 4E 55
Sowerby Cft. HX6: Hal . . . 5E 55
Sowerby Cft. La. HX6: Hal . . . 4D 54
Sowerby Grn. HX6: Hal . . . 4A 54
Sowerby New Rd. HX6: Hal . . . 4A 54
Sowerby St. HX6: Hal . . . 4D 54
Sowerby Town HX6: Hal . . . 4A 54
Spa La. BD16: Bgly . . . 6G 9
Spandola Ct. BD21: Keigh . . . 3B 6
Spanfield La. HX2: Hal . . . 1B 46
Sparable La. BD16: Bgly . . . 2A 16
Spark Ho. La. HX6: Hal . . . 4E 55
Spartan Rd. BD12: B'frd . . . 6H 43
Spearhead Way BD21: Keigh . . . 3E 7
Speeton Av. BD7: B'frd . . . 1C 42
Speeton Gro. BD7: B'frd . . . 1B 42
Speights Pl. BD4: B'frd . . . 1E 45
(off Dawson La.)
Spen Bank BD19: Cleck . . . 6H 53
Spencer Av. BD7: B'frd . . . 4E 35
Spencer Rd. BD7: B'frd . . . 4D 34
(not continuous)
Spencer St. BD21: Keigh . . . 4C 6
(not continuous)
Spen Cl. BD4: B'frd . . . 4D 44
Spen La. BD19: Cleck . . . 5H 53
SPEN LOWER . . . 6H 53
Spen Trad. Est.
BD19: Cleck . . . 5H 53
Spen Vw. La. BD4: B'frd . . . 4D 44
Spicer St. BD5: B'frd . . . 6G 35
Spiers Gth. BD6: B'frd . . . 2H 43
Spiggs HX3: Hal . . . 2F 49
Spindle Point HX3: Hal . . . 6A 40
Spindle St. HX2: Hal . . . 6A 40
Spink Pl. BD8: B'frd . . . 1H 35 (2A 4)
Spink St. BD8: B'frd . . . 1H 35 (2A 4)
Spinkwell Cl.
BD3: B'frd . . . 6B 28 (1E 5)
Spinners Way BD19: Cleck . . . 5B 52
BD22: Haw . . . 1G 21
Spinney, The BD20: Keigh . . . 3D 8
HD6: Brigh . . . 2E 59
LS19: Yead . . . 3H 19
Spinney Ri. BD4: B'frd . . . 2H 45

Stone Cliffe—Tabbs La.

Stone Cliffe *HX3: Hal* 3A 56
(off Wakefield Ga.)
Stone Ct. BD20: Keigh 3D 8
Stonecroft BD2: B'frd 3E 29
Stonecroft Mt. HX6: Hal 1E 55
Stonefield Cl. BD2: B'frd 2D 28
Stone Fold BD17: Bail 3E 17
Stonegate BD16: Bgly 6G 9
Stonegate Rd. BD10: B'frd 1D 28
Stone Hall M. BD2: B'frd 3E 29
Stone Hall Rd. BD2: B'frd 3D 28
Stonehaven Ct. BD21: Keigh 6G 7
Stone Hill BD16: Bgly 1H 15
Stone Ho. Dr. BD13: B'frd 3C 40
Stone Ho. Fold BD22: Keigh 3F 11
Stone La. BD22: Oxen 5E 21
Stonelea BD4: B'frd 3H 45
Stoneleigh BD13: B'frd 2F 41
Stoneleigh Ct. BD19: Cleck 4A 52
Stone St. BD1: B'frd 2A 36 (3D 4)
BD13: B'frd 1C 40
(off South Vw.)
BD15: B'frd 4G 25
BD17: Bail 3A 18
BD19: Cleck 6E 53
BD22: Haw 1G 21
(off Sun St.)
Stone Ter. BD16: Bgly 3B 14
Stoney Battery
HX3: Hal 5C 48 (1C 62)
Stoney Brow HX3: Hal 3E 57
Stoneycroft La. BD20: Keigh 1D 6
Stoney Hill HD6: Brigh 5E 59
Stoneyhurst Sq. BD4: B'frd 6G 37
Stoneyhurst Way BD4: B'frd 6G 37
Stoney La. HX2: Hal 2H 55
HX3: Hal 2A 48
(Ovenden Rd.)
HX3: Hal 2A 58
(Walter Clough La.)
HX3: Hal 6E 51
(West Av.)
Stoney Ridge Av.
BD9: B'frd 3H 25
STONEY RIDGE HOSPITAL 2A 26
Stoney Ridge Rd.
BD16: Bgly 3H 25
STONEY ROYD 2D 56
Stoney Royd Ter. HX3: Hal 3D 56
Stoneys Fold BD15: B'frd 1B 24
Stoney St. BD20: Keigh 1D 6
Stony La. BD2: B'frd 2E 29
BD15: B'frd 5F 25
HX4: Hal 1A 60
Stoodley Ter. HX2: Hal 1G 55
Stormer Hill HX6: Hal 5F 55
Stormer Hill La. HX6: Hal 5F 55
Storr Hill BD12: B'frd 1G 51
Storr Hill Ter. BD12: B'frd 1G 51
Storth Lea HX5: Ell 4H 61
Storth Vw. HX5: Ell 4H 61
Stott Gap BD13: B'frd 2D 32
Stott Hill BD1: B'frd 2B 36 (3E 5)
Stott Ter. BD2: B'frd 3F 29
Stowell Mill St. BD5: B'frd 5H 35
Stradmore Rd. BD13: B'frd 1G 31
Strafford Way BD10: B'frd 5G 19
Straight Acres La.
BD10: B'frd 2F 29
Straight La. HX2: Hal 6F 39
Straits BD17: Bail 1G 17
Strand BD16: Bgly 1H 25
Strangford Ct. BD10: B'frd 5F 19
Stratford Rd. BD7: B'frd 4F 35
Strathallan Dr. BD17: Bail 2H 17
Strathmore Cl. BD2: B'frd 4D 28
Strathmore Dr. BD17: Bail 1F 17
Stratton Cl. HD6: Brigh 6F 59
Stratton Pk. HD6: Brigh 6F 59
Stratton Rd. HD6: Brigh 6F 59
Stratton Vw. BD4: B'frd 5G 37
Stratton Wlk. BD15: B'frd 1G 33
Strawberry Flds.
BD21: Keigh 3E 7
Strawberry St. BD21: Keigh 3E 7
Straw Vw. BD10: B'frd 5B 18
Stray, The BD10: B'frd 1C 28
Stream Cl. BD20: Keigh 2B 8
Stream Head BD13: B'frd 6B 24
Stream Head Rd.
BD13: B'frd 5B 24
Street Head La.
BD22: Keigh 5C 10
Street La. BD20: Keigh 1B 8
Strensall Grn. BD6: B'frd 3C 42
Stretchgate La. HX2: Hal 5G 47
Stringer Cl. BD4: B'frd 3E 45
Strone, The BD10: B'frd 4H 19
STRONG CLOSE 4G 7
Strong Cl. Gro. BD21: Keigh 4G 7
Strong Cl. Rd. BD21: Keigh 4G 7
Strong Cl. Way *BD21: Keigh* 4G 7
(off Strong Cl. Rd.)
Stuart Ct. *BD5: B'frd* 5A 36
(off Swarland Gro.)
Stubbings Rd. BD17: Bail 3D 16
Stubbing Way BD18: Ship 1G 27
(not continuous)
Stubs Beck La. BD19: Cleck 3F 53
Stub Thorn La. HX3: Hal 1F 57
Studdards Fold BD7: B'frd 5E 35
Studdley Cres. BD16: Bgly 2H 15
Studleigh Ter. *HD6: Brigh* 2C 58
(off Brooklyn Ter.)
Studley Av. BD6: B'frd 4F 43
Studley Cl. BD20: Keigh 2D 8
Studley Rd. BD3: B'frd 5B 28
STUMP CROSS 4F 49
Stumps, The BD18: Ship 4A 18
Stunsteads Rd. BD19: Cleck 5F 53
Sturges Gro. BD2: B'frd 6D 28
Sturton Gro. HX2: Hal 4G 39
Sturton La. HX2: Hal 4G 39
Styes La. HX2: Hal 3A 54
HX6: Hal 3A 54
Sty La. BD16: Bgly 5E 9
Suffolk Pl. BD2: B'frd 3B 28
Sugden Bank *HX6: Hal* 3E 55
(off Sunny Bank St.)
Sugden Cl. HD6: Brigh 6E 59
Sugden End BD22: Haw 6B 12
Sugden Ho. Farm
BD21: Haw 6D 12
Sugden Pl. *BD6: B'frd* 4C 42
(off Beck Hill)
Sugden's Almshouses
BD22: Keigh 2H 11
Sugden St.
BD1: B'frd 2G 35 (3A 4)
BD12: B'frd 1B 52
Sulby Gro. BD10: B'frd 6G 19
Summerbridge Cres.
BD10: B'frd 2F 29
Summerbridge Dr.
BD10: B'frd 2F 29
Summerfield Av.
HD6: Brigh 1F 59
Summerfield Cl. BD17: Bail 2E 17
Summerfield Ct. HX2: Hal 6A 40
Summerfield Dr. BD17: Bail 2F 17
Summerfield Grn.
BD17: Bail 2F 17
Summerfield Gro.
BD17: Bail 2E 17
Summerfield Pk.
BD17: Bail 2F 17
Summerfield Rd.
BD10: B'frd 1E 29
Summergate Pl. HX1: Hal 1H 55
Summergate St. HX1: Hal 1H 55
Summer Hall Ing
BD12: B'frd 1F 51
Summer Hill St. BD7: B'frd 4E 35
Summerlands Gro.
BD5: B'frd 1C 44
Summerland Ter. HX6: Hal 3F 55
Summer Lea BD10: B'frd 5C 18
Summerley Ct. BD10: B'frd 6D 18
Summerscale St. HX1: Hal 5A 48
Summerseat Pl. BD7: B'frd 4G 35
Summerset Pl. *BD2: B'frd* 5D 28
(off Green Pl.)
Summer St. HX1: Hal 2H 55
Summerville Rd.
BD7: B'frd 3G 35
Summit St. BD21: Keigh 3D 6
Sunbridge Rd.
BD1: B'frd 2H 35 (2A 4)
Sun Bldgs. HX2: Hal 6B 38
Sunderland Cl. *HD6: Brigh* 4E 59
(off Thornhill Bri. La.)
Sunderland Rd. BD9: B'frd 5F 27
Sunderland St. BD21: Keigh 5D 6
BD22: Haw 5B 12
HX1: Hal 6B 48 (4A 62)
Sundown Av. BD7: B'frd 5C 34
Sunfield Ter. *BD19: Cleck* 6G 53
(off Neville St.)
Sun Fold HX1: Hal 1D 56 (6D 62)
Sunhill Dr. BD17: Bail 3C 16
Sunhurst Cl. BD22: Keigh 3G 11
Sunhurst Dr. BD22: Keigh 3G 11
Sun La. BD22: Haw 6C 10
Sunningdale BD8: B'frd 1B 34
Sunningdale Cres.
BD13: B'frd 2G 23
SUNNYBANK 2B 60
Sunny Bank BD12: B'frd 1A 52
BD13: B'frd 2F 41
BD18: Ship 6F 17
HX3: Hal 3D 50
Sunnybank Av. BD3: Pud 6H 29
BD5: B'frd 2H 43
Sunnybank Cl. BD19: Cleck 6B 52
Sunnybank Cres. HX4: Hal 2B 60
Sunny Bank Dr. HX6: Hal 3E 55
Sunnybank Dr. HX4: Hal 2B 60
Sunnybank Grange
HD6: Brigh 5E 59
Sunnybank Gro. BD3: Pud 6H 29
Sunny Bank La. HX3: Hal 2H 57
Sunnybank La. BD3: Pud 6H 29
HX4: Hal 2B 60
Sunny Bank Rd. BD5: B'frd 2H 43
HD6: Brigh 5E 59
HX2: Hal 6D 38
Sunnybank Rd. HX4: Hal 2A 60
Sunny Bank St. HX6: Hal 3E 55
Sunny Bank Ter. HX3: Hal 4C 48
Sunnybank Ter. HD6: Brigh 4E 59
Sunny Brae Cres.
BD16: Bgly 3H 15
Sunny Brow La. BD9: B'frd 5B 26
Sunny Cliffe HX3: Hal 6C 50
Sunnycliffe BD20: Keigh 3D 8
Sunny Dale BD13: B'frd 5F 23
Sunnydale Gro. BD21: Keigh 5H 7
Sunnydale Pk. BD20: Keigh 2E 9
Sunnyhill Av. BD21: Keigh 6B 6
Sunnyhill Gro. BD21: Keigh 6B 6
Sunny Mt. BD16: Bgly 4B 14
BD20: Keigh 4C 8
BD21: Keigh 3D 6
BD22: Keigh 3A 6
HX3: Hal 6A 50
Sunny Side HX3: Hal 6C 50
Sunnyside HD6: Brigh 6H 59
Sunnyside La. BD3: B'frd 6B 28
Sunny Side St.
HX3: Hal 4C 48 (1C 62)
Sunny Vw. Ter. BD13: B'frd 3C 40
Sunset Cres. HX3: Hal 2E 57
Sunshine Ct. BD6: B'frd 4D 42
Sun St. BD1: B'frd 1B 36 (2F 5)
BD21: Keigh 5E 7
BD22: Haw 1G 21
Sun Way HX3: Hal 2F 57
Sun Wood Av. HX3: Hal 1H 49
Sun Wood Ter. HX3: Hal 1H 49
Suresnes Rd. BD21: Keigh 4D 6
Surgery St. BD22: Haw 1H 21
Surrey Gro. BD5: B'frd 5A 36
Surrey St. BD21: Keigh 3G 7
HX1: Hal 1G 55
Sussex St. BD21: Keigh 3G 7
Sutcliffe Ct. *HX3: Hal* 2E 57
(off Bank Top)
Sutcliffe Fold BD13: B'frd 2G 41
Sutcliffe Pl. BD6: B'frd 3H 43
Sutcliffe Rd. HX3: Hal 6A 50
Sutcliffe St. HX2: Hal 5G 47
Sutcliffe Ter. *HX3: Hal* 4C 48
(off Amblers Ter.)
Sutcliffe Wood La.
HD6: Hal 6A 50
HX3: Brigh, Hal 6A 50
Sutherland Rd. HX3: Hal 5C 50
Sutton Av. BD2: B'frd 2B 28
Sutton Ct. BD16: Bgly 3F 15
Sutton Cres. BD4: B'frd 5G 37
Sutton Dr. BD13: B'frd 2F 23
Sutton Gro. BD4: B'frd 4G 37
Sutton Ho. BD4: B'frd 4G 37
Sutton Rd. BD4: B'frd 4G 37
SWAIN GREEN 4F 37
SWAIN HOUSE 2B 28
Swain Ho. Cres. BD2: B'frd 2C 28
Swain Ho. Rd. BD2: B'frd 2C 28
Swain Mt. BD2: B'frd 2C 28
SWAIN ROYD LANE BOTTOM
4E 25
Swaledale Ho. *HX6: Hal* 4D 54
(off Sowerby St.)
Swales Moor Rd. HX3: Hal 6B 40
Swallow Fold BD8: B'frd 2A 34
Swallow St. BD21: Keigh 3F 7
Swan Av. BD16: Bgly 2A 16
Swan Bank La. HX3: Hal 2D 56
Swan Hill BD9: B'frd 3G 27
Swan St. BD5: B'frd 4A 36 (6C 4)
Swarland Gro. BD5: B'frd 5A 36
Sweet Oak HX6: Hal 6A 54
Swift Dr. BD6: B'frd 2A 42
SWINCLIFFE 1H 53
Swine La. BD20: Keigh 3B 8
Swine Mkt. HX1: Hal 4B 62
Swinton Pl. BD7: B'frd 4F 35
Swinton Ter. HX1: Hal 2H 55
Swires Rd. BD2: B'frd 6E 29
HX1: Hal 1B 56 (6A 62)
Swires Ter.
HX1: Hal 1B 56 (6A 62)
Sycamore Av. BD7: B'frd 2D 34
BD16: Bgly 3F 15
Sycamore Cl.
BD3: B'frd 1C 36 (1G 5)
Sycamore Ct.
BD3: B'frd 1C 36 (1G 5)
Sycamore Dr. BD19: Cleck 6D 52
HX3: Hal 1E 59
HX5: Ell 3D 60
Sycamore Vw. BD22: Keigh 5B 6
HD6: Brigh 4D 58
Sydenham Pl. BD3: B'frd 5C 28
Sydney St. BD16: Bgly 2G 15
Syke Fold BD19: Cleck 6F 53
Syke Fold Grange
BD19: Cleck 6F 53
Syke La. BD13: B'frd 4E 41
HX2: Hal 1G 39
HX3: Hal 4C 50
HX6: Hal 4D 54
Syke Rd. BD9: B'frd 4E 27
Sykes Bottom BD22: Keigh 3H 11
Sykes Head BD22: Keigh 2H 11
Syke Side BD20: Keigh 1D 6
Sykes La. BD12: B'frd 1C 52
BD22: Keigh 2H 11
Sykes St. BD19: Cleck 6F 53
Sykes Yd. *HX1: Hal* 2H 55
(off King Cross Rd.)
Sylhet Cl. BD1: B'frd 1H 35 (2B 4)
Sylvan Av. BD13: B'frd 3D 40
Syringa Av. BD15: B'frd 3G 25

T

Tabbs Ct. BD19: Cleck 4B 52
Tabbs La. BD19: Cleck 4A 52

TOFTSHAW 3F 45
Toftshaw Fold BD4: B'frd 3F 45
Toftshaw La. BD4: B'frd 3G 45
Toftshaw New Rd.
BD4: B'frd 3F 45
Tofts Rd. BD19: Cleck 6F 53
Toller Dr. BD9: B'frd 4C 26
Toller Gro. BD9: B'frd 4D 26
Toller La. BD8: B'frd 5D 26
BD9: B'frd 4C 26
Toller Pk. BD9: B'frd 4D 26
Tollgate Ct. BD8: B'frd 6E 27
Tolworth Fold BD15: B'frd 1H 33
Tomlinson Bldgs.
BD10: B'frd 4C 18
Tonbridge Cl. BD6: B'frd 3D 42
TONG PARK 1B 18
Tong Pk. BD17: Bail 1B 18
Tong Sports College 3H 45
TONG STREET 2G 45
Tong St. BD4: B'frd 1E 45
Tonson Ct. BD21: Keigh 3E 7
Tony Miller App.
BD17: Ship 5G 17
Tor Av. BD12: B'frd 4G 51
Tordoff Av. BD7: B'frd 4C 34
Tordoff Grn. BD6: B'frd 3F 43
Tordoff Rd. BD12: B'frd 5A 44
Tornwood Cl. BD22: Keigh . . .3G 11
Torre Cres. BD6: B'frd 2B 42
Torre Gro. BD6: B'frd 2B 42
Torre Rd. BD6: B'frd 2B 42
Torridon Cres. BD6: B'frd 5C 42
Tourist Info. Cen.
Bradford 3A 36 (5D 4)
Halifax 6D 48 (4D 62)
Haworth 6F 11
Tower Gdns. HX2: Hal 3H 55
Tower Hill HX6: Hal 3D 54
Tower Rd. BD18: Ship 5C 16
Tower St. BD2: B'frd 5D 28
Tower Vw. *HX2: Hal 2G 55*
(off Plane Tree Nest La.)
TOWN END 5G 33
Town End BD7: B'frd 5E 35
Town End Rd. BD14: B'frd 4H 33
Townfield BD15: B'frd 2C 24
Town Flds. Rd. HX5: Ell 3E 61
Town Ga. BD10: B'frd 5D 18
BD12: B'frd 3G 51
BD19: Cleck 5B 52
HX6: Hal 4A 54
Towngate *BD17: Bail 1H 17*
(off Northgate)
BD18: Ship 6H 17
BD21: Keigh 4E 7
HD6: Brigh 4H 59
HX3: Hal 5A 50
(Kirk La.)
HX3: Hal 3G 57
(Law La.)
HX3: Hal 3G 49
(Tetley La.)
Towngate Av. HD6: Brigh 4H 59
Towngate Ho. HX5: Ell 3F 61
Town Hall Bldgs. *HX5: Ell 3F 61*
(off Southgate)
Town Hall Ct. HX6: Hal 3D 54
Town Hall St. BD21: Keigh 4E 7
HX5: Ell 3F 61
HX6: Hal 4D 54
Town Hall St. E.
HX1: Hal 6C 48 (3C 62)
Town Hill St. BD16: Bgly 1H 25
Town Ing Mills HX4: Hal 6A 60
Town Ing Way HX4: Hal 6A 60
Town La. BD10: B'frd 4D 18
Townley Av. HX3: Hal 3G 57
Trackside BD12: B'frd 6B 44
Trafalgar Sq. HX1: Hal 2A 56
Trafalgar St.
BD1: B'frd 1A 36 (2C 4)
HX1: Hal 2A 56
Tramways BD12: B'frd 6B 44
Tranter Gro. BD4: B'frd 4G 37
Tree La. HX2: Hal 6B 38
Trees St. BD8: B'frd 6G 27
Tree Top Vw. BD13: B'frd 1C 40
Trenam Pk. Dr. BD10: B'frd . . .3C 18
Trenance Dr. BD18: Ship 6D 16
Trenance Gdns. HX4: Hal 2A 60
Trenholme Av. BD6: B'frd 5F 43
Trenton Dr. BD8: B'frd 6G 27
Trevelyan St. HD6: Brigh 2E 59
Trevor Foster Way
BD5: B'frd 1B 44
TRIANGLE 6A 54
Trimmingham La. HX2: Hal . . .1F 55
Trimmingham Rd. HX2: Hal . . .1F 55
Trimmingham Vs. HX2: Hal . . .1G 55
Trim 'n' Shape 4B 4
Trinity Bus. Cen. HX1: Hal 6C 62
Trinity Cl. HX2: Hal 5A 40
Trinity Fold HX1: Hal 5B 62
Trinity Pl. BD16: Bgly 3G 15
HX1: Hal 1C 56 (5B 62)
Trinity Rd. BD5: B'frd 4H 35
HX1: Hal 1C 56 (5B 62)
Trinity Row
HX1: Hal 1C 56 (5B 62)
(not continuous)
Trinity St. *BD21: Keigh 3E 7*
(off East Av.)
HX1: Hal 1C 56 (5B 62)
Trinity Vw. BD12: B'frd 4A 44
HX3: Hal 1D 56
Trinity Wlk. BD12: B'frd 4A 44
Tristram Av. BD5: B'frd 1C 44
Trooper La. HX3: Hal 2D 56
Trooper Ter. HX3: Hal 2D 56
Trough La. BD13: B'frd 4D 22
BD22: B'frd 6B 22
Troutbeck Av. BD17: Bail 4C 16
(not continuous)
Trueman Ct. BD12: B'frd 5A 44
TRUNCLIFFE 2H 43
Truncliffe BD5: B'frd 2H 43
Truncliffe Ho. *BD5: B'frd 2H 43*
(off Truncliffe)
Tudor Barn Ct. BD18: Ship 6H 17
Tudor Ct. *BD5: B'frd 4A 36*
(off Swarland Gro.)
Tudor St. BD5: B'frd 5H 35
Tuel La. HX6: Hal 2D 54
Tulip St. BD22: Haw 2G 21
Tumbling Hill St.
BD7: B'frd 3H 35 (5A 4)
Tunnel St. BD13: B'frd 1F 31
Tunstall Grn. BD4: B'frd 6G 37
Tunwell La. BD2: B'frd 3E 29
Tunwell St. BD2: B'frd 3E 29
Turbury La. HX4: Hal 6G 55
Turf Ct. BD13: B'frd 2E 23
Turf La. BD13: B'frd 1E 23
Turnberry Ct. BD20: Keigh 1C 6
Turner Av. BD7: B'frd 4D 34
Turner Av. Nth. HX2: Hal 6F 39
Turner Av. Sth. HX2: Hal 6G 39
Turner Farm *HX2: Hal 4G 39*
(off Causeway Foot)
Turner La.
HX3: Hal 4D 48 (1D 62)
(not continuous)
Turner Pl. BD7: B'frd 4F 35
HX2: Hal 1G 47
Turners Ct. HX3: Hal 3B 48
Turner Vw. *HX2: Hal 1G 47*
(off Bank Edge Rd.)
Turney St. HX3: Hal 3A 48
(not continuous)
Turnpike St. HX5: Ell 2G 61
Turnshaw Rd. BD22: Keigh . . .3D 10
Turnsteads Av. BD19: Cleck . . .5D 52
Turnsteads Cl. BD19: Cleck . . .5E 53
Turnsteads Cres.
BD19: Cleck 5E 53
Turnsteads Dr. BD19: Cleck . . .5E 53
Turnsteads Mt. BD19: Cleck . . .5E 53
Tweedy St. BD15: B'frd 2C 24
Twickenham Ct. BD8: B'frd . . .5H 27
Twinge La. HX3: Hal 1F 57
TYERSAL 3G 37
Tyersal Av. BD4: Pud 2H 37
Tyersal Cl. BD4: Pud 3H 37
Tyersal Ct. BD4: Pud 3G 37
Tyersal Cres. BD4: Pud 3H 37
Tyersal Dr. BD4: Pud 3H 37
Tyersal Gth. BD4: Pud 3H 37
TYERSAL GATE 5G 37
Tyersal Grn. BD4: Pud 3H 37
Tyersal Gro. BD4: Pud 3H 37
Tyersal La. BD4: B'frd 5G 37
(not continuous)
BD4: B'frd, Pud 5H 37
Tyersal Pk. BD4: Pud 3H 37
Tyersal Rd. BD4: Pud 3G 37
Tyersal Ter. BD4: Pud 3G 37
Tyersal Vw. BD4: Pud 3G 37
Tyersal Wlk. BD4: Pud 3H 37
Tyler Ct. BD10: B'frd 5E 19
Tyne St. BD3: B'frd 1B 36 (2F 5)
BD21: Keigh 4F 7
BD22: Haw 6H 11
Tyrls, The BD1: B'frd . . .3A 36 (5C 4)
Tyrrel St. BD1: B'frd . . .2A 36 (4D 4)
(not continuous)
Tyson St. BD1: B'frd . . .1H 35 (2B 4)
HX1: Hal 1G 55

U

Ullswater Cl. HX5: Ell 2H 61
Ullswater Dr. BD6: B'frd 5D 42
UNDERCLIFFE 5C 28
Undercliffe La. BD3: B'frd 6C 28
Undercliffe Old Rd.
BD2: B'frd 6D 28
Undercliffe Rd. BD2: B'frd . . .4D 28
Undercliffe St.
BD3: B'frd 6D 28 (1H 5)
Undercliffe Ter. *HX2: Hal 3H 55*
(off Scarr Bottom Rd.)
Underwood Ho. BD3: B'frd 2F 5
Union Cross Yd.
HX1: Hal 6C 48 (3C 62)
Union Ho. BD13: B'frd 1A 42
Union Ho. Ct. BD13: B'frd 1A 42
Union Ho. La. BD13: B'frd 1A 42
Union La. HX2: Hal 3F 39
Union Rd. BD7: B'frd 4F 35
BD12: B'frd 4G 43
Union St. BD13: B'frd 2E 41
BD16: Bgly 4E 9
BD17: Bail 3A 18
HX1: Hal 6C 48 (4C 62)
HX4: Hal 2D 60
HX6: Hal 6A 54
(Hollin St.)
HX6: Hal 2E 55
(Victoria Av.)
Union Yd. BD10: B'frd 5D 18
Unity St. BD20: Keigh 1H 7
Unity St. Nth. BD16: Bgly 3F 15
Unity St. Sth. BD16: Bgly 3F 15
Unity Ter. HX1: Hal 1G 55
University of Bradford
Dennis Bellamy Hall . . .4G 35
Laisteridge Lane Campus
. . . . .4G 35
Revis Barber Hall 4G 35
School of Health Studies
. . . . .4H 35
School of Management
. . . . .3F 27
Shearbridge Grn.
. . . . .3G 35 (5A 4)
Sports Cen. 3G 35 (6A 4)
Trinity Hall 4G 35
Unwin Pl. BD9: B'frd 5C 26
Upcroft Ct. BD13: B'frd 1C 40
Uplands BD20: Keigh 2C 6
Uplands Av. BD13: B'frd 1H 41
Uplands Cl. BD13: B'frd 1H 41
Uplands Cres. BD13: B'frd 1H 41
Uplands Gro. BD13: B'frd 1H 41
Up. Ada St. BD18: Ship 5D 16
Up. Addison St.
BD4: B'frd 4B 36 (6F 5)
Up. Allerton La. BD15: B'frd . . .1E 33
Up. Ashley La. BD17: Ship . . .5F 17
Up. Bell Cft. HX3: Hal 3G 57
Up. Bell Hall HX1: Hal 2A 56
Up. Bentley Royd HX6: Hal . . .4C 54
(not continuous)
Up. Bolton Brow HX6: Hal 2F 55
Up. Bonegate HD6: Brigh 4F 59
UPPER BROCKHOLES 3F 39
Upper Butts BD19: Cleck 6F 53
Up. Calton St. BD21: Keigh 6D 6
Up. Carr La. LS28: Pud 1H 29
Up. Castle St. BD5: B'frd 5A 36
Up. Chelsea St. BD21: Keigh . . .6D 6
UPPER COMMON 1H 51
Up. Ellistones *HX4: Hal 2A 60*
(off Martin Grn. La.)
Up. Ellistones Ct. HX4: Hal . . .2A 60
UPPER EXLEY 6E 57
UPPER FAGLEY 5F 29
Up. Ferndown Grn.
BD15: B'frd 6G 25
Up. Field Ho. La. HX6: Hal . . .5A 54
Upper Forge
HX1: Hal 6C 48 (4B 62)
Up. Fountain St. HX6: Hal . . .3D 54
Up. Fyfe La. BD17: Bail 2A 18
Up. Gaukroger HX6: Hal 4B 54
Up. George St. BD6: B'frd 2F 43
Up. Grange Av. BD15: B'frd . . .1H 33
UPPER GREEN 5C 34
Upper Grn. BD7: B'frd 6D 34
BD17: Bail 3F 17
Up. Green Av. BD19: Cleck . . .5B 52
Up. Green La. HD6: Brigh 2C 58
Up. Grn. Royd HX2: Hal 1C 46
Upper Haley BD22: Oxen 4H 21
Up. Hall Vw. HX3: Hal 2G 49
Up. Haugh Shaw HX1: Hal 2A 56
Up. Headley BD13: B'frd 4D 32
Up. Heights Rd.
BD13: B'frd 1C 32
Up. Hird St. BD21: Keigh 6C 6
Up. House Cotts.
BD13: B'frd 1G 41
Up. House St. BD4: B'frd 4D 36
Up. Hoyle Ing BD13: B'frd 2F 33
Up. Jackroyd HX3: Hal 4H 47
Up. Kell HX2: Hal 5B 38
Up. Kingston HX1: Hal 1G 55
Up. Kirkgate
HX1: Hal 6D 48 (4D 62)
Upper La. HX3: Hal 1F 49
UPPER MARSH 2E 21
Upper Marsh HX3: Hal 2F 57
Up. Marsh La. BD22: Oxen . . .2D 20
Up. Martin Grn. HX4: Hal 2A 60
Up. Mary St. BD18: Ship 5D 16
Upper Mdws. BD13: B'frd 3E 41
Up. Mill Cotts. BD17: B'frd . . .1D 18
Up. Millergate BD1: B'frd 4C 4
Up. Mill Row BD20: Keigh 1E 9
Up. Mosscar St.
BD3: B'frd 2C 36 (4H 5)
Up. Nidd St. BD3: B'frd 3D 36
Up. Park Ga.
BD1: B'frd 2B 36 (3F 5)
Up. Piccadilly
BD1: B'frd 2A 36 (3C 4)
Up. Pierce Cl. BD22: Haw 4B 12
Upper Pikeley BD15: B'frd . . .1D 32
Up. Range *HX3: Hal 4C 48*
(off Woodlands Gro.)
Up. Reap Hurst HX2: Hal 1C 46
Up. Rushton Rd. BD3: B'frd . . .6F 29
Up. Seymour St.
BD3: B'frd 3D 36 (5H 5)
Up. Slack HX2: Hal 5B 38
Up. Sutherland Rd.
HX3: Hal 5C 50
Up. Tewit HX2: Hal 4H 39

Warley Town—Westfield M.

WARLEY TOWN 1D 54
Warley Town La. HX2: Hal . . .6C **46**
Warley Vw. HX2: Hal 6F **47**
Warley Wood HX2: Hal 2B **54**
Warley Wood Av. HX2: Hal . . .2B **54**
Warley Wood La. HX2: Hal . . .2A **54**
Warmleigh Pk. BD13: B'frd . . .2B **40**
Warneford Sq. *HX1: Hal 2H **55***
(off King Cross Rd.)
Warnford Gro. BD4: B'frd 6F **37**
Warren Av. BD16: Bgly 6H **9**
Warren Dr. BD16: Bgly 1H **15**
Warren Ho. La. HD3: Hud 6G **61**
Warren La. BD16: Bgly 6H **9**
Warren Pk. HD6: Brigh 2C **58**
Warren Pk. Cl. HD6: Brigh 2C **58**
Warren Ter. BD16: Bgly 2A **16**
Warrenton Pl. BD7: B'frd 4E **35**
Warton Av. BD4: B'frd 2D **44**
Warwick Cl. BD4: B'frd 5D **36**
*HX3: Hal 3B **56***
(off Free School La.)
Warwick Dr. BD4: B'frd 5D **36**
Warwick Rd. BD4: B'frd 5D **36**
Waryn Ho. *BD10: B'frd 6E **19***
(off Fairhaven Grn.)
Washer La. HX2: Hal 3G **55**
Washer La. Ind. Est.
HX2: Hal 3H **55**
Washington St. BD8: B'frd . . .6D **26**
HX3: Hal 4A **48**
Wastwater Dr. BD6: B'frd 5D **42**
Watercock St. BD4: B'frd 4C **36**
Waterfront M. BD10: B'frd . . .5G **19**
Watergate HX3: Hal 6A **50**
Water Hill HX6: Hal 2C **54**
Water Hill La. HX2: Hal 2C **54**
HX6: Hal 2C **54**
Waterhouse St. BD21: Keigh . . .4C **6**
HX1: Hal 6C **48** (4B **62**)
Water La.
BD1: B'frd 2G **35** (3A **4**)
(not continuous)
BD21: Keigh 5D **6**
HX1: Hal 1D **56** (6D **62**)
HX3: Hal 1D **56** (6D **62**)
Waterloo Cres. BD10: B'frd . . .5H **19**
Waterloo Fold BD12: B'frd 3H **51**
Waterloo Rd. BD16: Bgly 2F **15**
HD6: Brigh 4E **59**
Waterloo Ter. HX6: Hal 1E **55**
Waterside BD16: Bgly 6D **8**
BD22: Oxen 5G **21**
HX3: Hal 1D **56**
Waterside Rd. BD8: B'frd 1E **35**
Water St. HD6: Brigh 4F **59**
HX6: Hal 4D **54**
Watford Av. HX3: Hal 2D **50**
Watkin Av. BD13: B'frd 3F **33**
Watkinson Av. HX2: Hal 6H **39**
Watkinson Bungs. *HX2: Hal . . .1G **47***
(off Cumberland Cl.)
Watkinson Dr. HX2: Hal 1H **47**
Watkinson Rd. HX2: Hal 1H **47**
Watmough St. BD7: B'frd 6E **35**
Watson Cl. BD22: Oxen 5G **21**
Watson Mill La. HX6: Hal 5D **54**
Watts St. BD14: B'frd 5H **33**
Watt St. BD4: B'frd 4F **37**
Watty Hall Av. BD6: B'frd 1E **43**
Watty Hall La. BD6: B'frd 1F **43**
Watty Hall Rd. BD6: B'frd 1E **43**
Wauds Gates *BD17: Bail 4G **17***
(off Baildon Rd.)
Waverley Av. BD7: B'frd 4F **35**
BD20: Keigh 3B **8**
Waverley Cres. HX3: Hal 6A **50**
Waverley Pl. BD7: B'frd 4F **35**
Waverley Rd. BD7: B'frd 4F **35**
HX5: Ell 4F **61**
Waverley Ter. BD7: B'frd 4F **35**
HX3: Hal 6A **50**
Waverton Grn. BD6: B'frd 4D **42**
Wavertree Pk. Gdns.
BD12: B'frd 1G **51**
Wayside Ct. BD20: Keigh 1C **6**
Wayside Cres. BD2: B'frd 2D **28**
Weardale Cl. BD4: B'frd 2E **45**
Weatherhill Cres.
HD3: Hud 6G **61**
Weatherhill Rd. HD3: Hud . . .6G **61**
Weatherhouse Ter.
HX2: Hal 4F **47**
Weaver Ct. *BD10: B'frd 5D **18***
(off Moorfield Pl.)
Weavers Cotts.
*BD22: Oxen 5G **21***
(off Waterside)
Weavers Cft. BD10: B'frd 3C **18**
BD19: Cleck 6H **53**
HX2: Hal 1E **55**
Weavers Hill BD22: Haw 1G **21**
Weavers La. BD13: B'frd 1F **23**
Weaverthorpe Retail Pk.
BD4: B'frd 2G **45**
Weaverthorpe Rd.
BD4: B'frd 2G **45**
Weaving Shed, The
*HX6: Hal 3E **55***
(off Old Cawsey)
Webb Dr. BD2: B'frd 5C **28**
Webb's Ter. HX3: Hal 5D **48**
Weber Ct. *BD3: B'frd 2E **37***
(off Amberley St.)
Webster Pl.
BD3: B'frd 2D **36** (3H **5**)
Webster St. BD3: B'frd 2D **36**
Wedgemoor Cl.
BD12: B'frd 1G **51**
Weetwood Rd. BD8: B'frd 1E **35**
Welbeck Dr. BD7: B'frd 5C **34**
Welbeck Ri. BD7: B'frd 5C **34**
Welburn Av. HX3: Hal 6B **50**
Welburn Mt. BD6: B'frd 3C **42**
Welbury Dr. BD8: B'frd 5G **27**
Weldon Ct. BD4: B'frd 5G **37**
Welham Wlk.
BD3: B'frd 1C **36** (1G **5**)
Wellands Grn. BD19: Cleck . . .6D **52**
Wellands La. BD19: Cleck 5B **52**
Wellands Ter. BD3: B'frd 2E **37**
Well Bank Rd. BD4: B'frd 6F **37**
Well Cl. Pl. HD6: Brigh 4E **59**
Well Cl. St. HD6: Brigh 4F **59**
Well Cft. BD18: Ship 6F **17**
Weller Cl. *BD5: B'frd 6A **36***
(off Boynton St.)
Wellesley Ho. *BD4: B'frd 3F **37***
(off Wellington St.)
Wellesley St.
BD1: B'frd 2B **36** (3F **5**)
Wellfield Gdns. BD13: B'frd . . .6D **32**
Well Fold BD10: B'frd 5D **18**
Wellgarth BD6: B'frd 4D **42**
HX1: Hal 2C **56**
Wellgate HX4: Hal 1C **60**
Well Grn. Ct. BD4: B'frd 4G **45**
Well Grn. La. HD6: Brigh 2D **58**
Well Gro. HD6: Brigh 2D **58**
Well Head Dr.
HX1: Hal 1C **56** (6B **62**)
Well Head Ho. *HX1: Hal 6C **62***
(off Well Head Dr.)
Well Head La.
HX1: Hal 1C **56** (6B **62**)
HX6: Hal 4A **54**
Well Head Ri. HX1: Hal 2C **56**
WELL HEADS 2A 32
Well Heads BD13: B'frd 3H **31**
Wellholme HD6: Brigh 4F **59**
Wellington Arc. *HD6: Brigh 5F **59***
(off Briggate)
Wellington Bus. Cen.
HX5: Ell 2G **61**
Wellington Ct. HX2: Hal 5G **47**
Wellington Cres.
BD18: Ship 6E **17**
Wellington Gro. BD2: B'frd . . .5D **28**
Wellington Pl. BD2: B'frd 4E **29**
HX1: Hal 1C **56** (5D **62**)
Wellington Rd. BD2: B'frd 4D **28**
BD15: B'frd 3B **24**
BD21: Keigh 5E **7**
Wellington St.
BD1: B'frd 2B **36** (3E **5**)
BD2: B'frd 4D **28**
BD4: B'frd 3F **37**
BD10: B'frd 6D **18**
BD13: B'frd 2F **41**
BD15: B'frd 6A **26**
(Nelson St.)
BD15: B'frd 3C **24**
(Peel St.)
BD16: Bgly 2F **15**
Wellington St. Sth.
HX1: Hal 1D **56** (5D **62**)
Wellington St. W. *HX1: Hal . . .6A **62***
Well La. BD19: Cleck 4B **52**
HX1: Hal 6D **48** (3D **62**)
Well Royd Av. HX2: Hal 6E **47**
Well Royd Cl. HX2: Hal 6F **47**
(not continuous)
Wells, The HX2: Hal 6E **47**
(Roils Head Rd.)
HX2: Hal 2G **55**
(Willowfield Ter.)
Wells Ct. HX3: Hal 4B **48**
Wells Ho. *HX6: Hal 3E **55***
(off Church Vw.)
Wells Ter. *HX3: Hal 3E **51***
(off Village St.)
Well St. BD1: B'frd 2B **36** (4E **5**)
BD13: B'frd 1F **31**
BD15: B'frd 2C **24**
BD21: Keigh 4D **6**
HX4: Hal 5B **60**
Welwyn Av. BD18: Ship 6B **18**
Welwyn Dr. BD17: Bail 3G **17**
BD18: Ship 6B **18**
Wembley Av. BD13: B'frd 3F **33**
Wenborough La.
BD4: B'frd 6H **37**
Wendron Way BD10: B'frd . . .6D **18**
Wenlock St.
BD3: B'frd 3C **36** (5G **5**)
Wenning St. BD21: Keigh 3G **7**
Wensley Av. BD18: Ship 6E **17**
Wensley Bank BD13: B'frd 3C **32**
Wensley Bank Ter.
BD13: B'frd 3C **32**
Wensley Bank W.
BD13: B'frd 3C **32**
Wensleydale Ri.
BD17: Bail 1A **18**
Wensleydale Rd.
BD3: B'frd 2G **37**
Wensley Ho. BD10: B'frd 1F **29**
Wentworth Dr. HX2: Hal 4H **39**
Wentworth Gro. HX2: Hal 4H **39**
Wesleyan St. BD4: B'frd 6E **37**
Wesley Av. BD12: B'frd 4A **44**
Wesley Av. Sth. BD12: B'frd . . .5A **44**
Wesley Ct.
HX1: Hal 6C **48** (3C **62**)
Wesley Dr. BD12: B'frd 4A **44**
Wesley Gro. BD10: B'frd 4E **19**
WESLEY PLACE 5H 43
Wesley Pl. *BD12: B'frd 5A **44***
(off Main St.)
BD21: Keigh 2C **12**
HX6: Hal 4A **54**
Wesley St. BD19: Cleck 5F **53**
West 26 Ind. Est.
BD19: Cleck 3E **53**
West Av. BD15: B'frd 4F **25**
BD17: Bail 2G **17**
HX3: Hal 3B **56**
(Queen's Ga.)
HX3: Hal 6E **51**
(Stoney La.)
West Bank BD9: B'frd 3D **26**
*BD22: Keigh 3B **6***
(off W. Bank Ri.)
HX2: Hal 1F **47**
(not continuous)
W. Bank Cl. BD22: Keigh 3B **6**
W. Bank Gro. BD20: Keigh 1G **7**
W. Bank Ri. BD22: Keigh 3B **6**
W. Bank Rd. BD20: Keigh 1F **7**
West Bolton HX2: Hal 4F **39**
Westborough Dr. HX2: Hal 6F **47**
W. Bottom HX6: Hal 5D **54**
Westbourne Cres. HX3: Hal . . .4D **56**
Westbourne Gro. HX3: Hal . . .4D **56**
Westbourne Rd. BD8: B'frd . . .5F **27**
Westbourne Ter.
*BD13: B'frd 2E **41***
(off Albert Rd.)
HX3: Hal 4D **56**
WEST BOWLING 6A 36
Westbrook Ct. HX1: Hal 2A **62**
Westburn Av. BD22: Keigh 5B **6**
Westburn Cres. BD22: Keigh . . .6B **6**
Westburn Gro. BD22: Keigh . . .6B **6**
Westburn Pl. BD19: Cleck 6E **53**
Westburn Way BD22: Keigh . . .6B **6**
Westbury Cl. BD4: B'frd 4F **37**
Westbury Ct. HX1: Hal 1G **55**
Westbury Pl. HX1: Hal 1G **55**
Westbury Rd. BD6: B'frd 2B **42**
Westbury St. BD4: B'frd 4F **37**
HX5: Ell 2G **61**
Westbury Ter. HX1: Hal 1G **55**
W. Byland HX2: Hal 4G **39**
Westcliffe Av. BD17: Bail 1F **17**
Westcliffe Dr. HX2: Hal 6F **47**
Westcliffe M. *BD18: Ship 6F **17***
(off Westcliffe Rd.)
Westcliffe Ri. BD19: Cleck . . .6E **53**
Westcliffe Rd. BD18: Ship 6E **17**
BD19: Cleck 5E **53**
Westcombe Ct. BD12: B'frd . . .1G **51**
W. Cote Dr. BD10: B'frd 4B **18**
Westcott Ho. BD8: B'frd 1A **4**
West Cft. BD12: B'frd 3G **51**
Westcroft Av. HX3: Hal 1H **49**
Westcroft Rd. BD7: B'frd 5E **35**
West Dr. BD22: Oxen 4G **21**
WEST END
Bradford 3D 40
Cleckheaton 5E 53
West End BD13: B'frd 3D **40**
BD19: Cleck 5E **53**
HX1: Hal 1G **55**
W. End Dr. BD19: Cleck 6D **52**
Westend La. BD1: B'frd 3B **4**
West End Rd. HX1: Hal 1G **55**
W. End St.
BD1: B'frd 2H **35** (4B **4**)
West End Ter. BD2: B'frd 2D **28**
BD18: Ship 5E **17**
Westercroft HX3: Hal 2H **49**
Westercroft La. HX3: Hal 2G **49**
Westercroft Vw. HX3: Hal 2H **49**
Western Av. BD20: Keigh 1F **7**
Western Pl. BD13: B'frd 2H **41**
Western Way BD6: B'frd 4E **43**
Westerton Ct. BD12: B'frd 6D **44**
Westfell Cl. BD22: Keigh 5B **6**
Westfell Rd. BD22: Keigh 5B **6**
Westfell Way BD22: Keigh 5B **6**
West Fld. HX6: Hal 5E **55**
Westfield BD13: B'frd 3G **33**
HX3: Hal 4F **57**
Westfield Av. HX3: Hal 6B **50**
Westfield Cres. BD2: B'frd . . .6D **28**
BD18: Ship 1A **28**
BD20: Keigh 1H **7**
Westfield Dr. BD20: Keigh 2H **7**
HX3: Hal 6B **50**
Westfield Gdns. HX3: Hal 6B **50**
Westfield Gro. BD10: B'frd . . .5C **18**
BD18: Ship 1A **28**
Westfield Ho. *BD10: B'frd 6D **18***
(off Buckfast Ct.)
Westfield La. BD10: B'frd 5B **18**
BD12: B'frd 3G **51**
BD18: Ship 1A **28**
BD19: Cleck 3G **51**
Westfield M. BD13: B'frd 3G **33**

108 A-Z Bradford

Whitwell St.—Wood Mt.

Whitwell St. BD4: B'frd 4C 36
Whitwood La. HD6: Brigh 6G 51
(not continuous)
Whytecote End BD12: B'frd 1G 51
WIBSEY 2F 43
Wibsey Bank BD6: B'frd 2H 43
Wibsey Pk. Av. BD6: B'frd 3D 42
Wicken Cl. BD10: B'frd 1E 29
Wicken La. BD13: B'frd 2D 32
Wickets, The BD2: B'frd 5E 29
Wickets Cl. BD6: B'frd 3H 43
Wickham Av. BD6: B'frd 3G 43
Wickham St. BD19: Cleck 5B 52
Wide La. BD22: Keigh 2E 11
Wigan St.
BD1: B'frd 2H 35 (4A 4)
(not continuous)
Wightman St. BD3: B'frd 6C 28
Wignall St. BD20: Keigh 1D 6
Wilby St. BD19: Cleck 6F 53
Wilday Cl. BD16: Bgly 5E 9
Wild Gro. LS28: Pud 2H 37
Wilfred St. BD14: B'frd 5B 34
Wilkinson Fold BD12: B'frd 2G 51
Wilkinson Ter. BD7: B'frd 3D 34
Wilkin St. BD21: Keigh 4D 6
Willgutter La. BD22: Keigh 3D 10
William Henry St.
BD18: Ship 4D 16
HD6: Brigh 4E 59
Williamson St. HX1: Hal 5A 48
William St. BD4: B'frd 2F 45
BD5: B'frd 3A 36 (6C 4)
BD6: B'frd 4D 42
BD13: B'frd 6F 23
HD6: Brigh 6E 59
HX4: Hal 3D 60
Willow Av. BD2: B'frd 1C 28
Willow Bank HX1: Hal 2A 56
Willow Cl. BD6: B'frd 4G 43
HX2: Hal 1F 55
Willow Cres. BD2: B'frd 1C 28
HX6: Hal 2E 55
Willowcroft BD19: Cleck 6E 53
Willow Dene Av. HX2: Hal 2F 55
Willow Dr. BD6: B'frd 4G 43
HX2: Hal 1F 55
WILLOW FIELD 2E 55
Willowfield Av. HX2: Hal 2F 55
Willowfield Cl. HX2: Hal 1F 55
Willowfield Cres.
BD2: B'frd 1C 28
HX2: Hal 1F 55
Willowfield Dr. HX2: Hal 2F 55
Willowfield Rd. HX2: Hal 1F 55
Willowfield St. BD7: B'frd 2F 35
Willowfield Ter. HX2: Hal 2G 55
Willowfield Vw. HX2: Hal 1F 55
Willow Gdns. BD2: B'frd 1C 28
HX2: Hal 2G 55
Willow Gro. BD2: B'frd 1C 28
BD21: Keigh 2C 12
Willow Hall Dr. HX6: Hal 2F 55
Willow Hall Fold *HX6: Hal 2F 55*
(off Bairstow La.)
Willow Hall La. HX6: Hal 2F 55
Willow Ho's. *HX6: Hal 2F 55*
(off Rochdale Rd.)
Willow Ind. Complex
HX6: Hal 5D 54
Willow Mt. *HX3: Hal 5B 42*
(off Witchfield Hill)
HX6: Hal 2E 55
(off Overdale Mt.)
Willow Pk. Dr. HX3: Hal 5B 42
Willow Ri. HX2: Hal 1F 55
Willows, The BD16: Bgly 4B 14
BD17: Bail 3C 16
HX2: Hal 4G 39
Willow St. BD8: B'frd 1D 34
BD19: Cleck 4F 53
HX1: Hal 1A 56
HX6: Hal 3F 55
Willow Ter. HX6: Hal 2E 55
Willow Tree Cl. BD21: Keigh 6F 7
Willow Tree Gdns.
BD16: Bgly 6H 9
Willow Vw. *HX6: Hal 2F 55*
(off Bairstow Mt.)
Willow Vs. BD2: B'frd 1C 28
Will St. BD4: B'frd 5F 37
Wilman Hill BD6: B'frd 2F 43
(not continuous)
Wilmer Dr. BD9: B'frd 3E 27
BD18: Ship 2E 27
Wilmer Rd. BD9: B'frd 4E 27
Wilmur Mt. HX2: Hal 1A 54
WILSDEN 2C 24
Wilsden Hill Rd.
BD15: B'frd 2B 24
Wilsden Old Rd.
BD16: Bgly 4B 14
Wilsden Rd. BD15: B'frd 3E 25
BD16: Bgly 4B 14
Wilson Fold BD12: B'frd 6H 43
Wilson Rd. BD12: B'frd 1H 51
BD16: Bgly 1F 15
HX1: Hal 2H 55
Wilson St. BD8: B'frd 6G 27
Wilton St.
BD5: B'frd 3H 35 (6B 4)
HD6: Brigh 4D 58
Wilton Ter. BD19: Cleck 6F 53
Wimborne Dr. BD15: B'frd 6A 26
BD21: Keigh 3B 6
Winbrooke Ter. BD6: B'frd 2E 43
Winburg Rd. BD7: B'frd 4E 35
Winburn Ter. HX2: Hal 1D 54
Winchester Gdns.
BD4: B'frd 4F 37
Winchester Ho. *HX6: Hal 3E 55*
(off Church Vw.)
Windermere Ri. HD6: Brigh 1F 59
Windermere Rd. BD7: B'frd 6C 34
BD17: Bail 4D 16
(not continuous)
Windermere Ter.
BD7: B'frd 6C 34
WINDHILL 6G 17
Windhill Old Rd.
BD10: B'frd 4B 18
Winding Rd.
HX1: Hal 6C 48 (3C 62)
Windle Royd La.
HX2: Hal 6E 47
Windmill Cres. HX3: Hal 3G 49
Windmill Dr. HX3: Hal 3G 49
Windmill Hill BD6: B'frd 2E 43
HX3: Hal 4G 49
Windmill La. BD6: B'frd 2G 43
HX3: Hal 3G 49
Windsor Ct. *BD5: B'frd 4A 36*
(off Swarland Gro.)
BD18: Ship 6F 17
(off Manor La.)
Windsor Cres. BD22: Keigh 3F 11
HX2: Hal 4G 47
Windsor Gro. BD13: B'frd 3D 32
BD22: Keigh 3F 11
Windsor Rd. BD18: Ship 6F 17
BD22: Keigh 3F 11
Windsor St. BD4: B'frd 4C 36
HX1: Hal 1C 56 (6B 62)
Windsor Ter. HX6: Hal 5D 54
Windsor Vs. HX3: Hal 3D 50
Windsor Wlk. HX3: Hal 1E 59
Windy Bank La.
BD13: B'frd 5B 40
Windy Gro. BD15: B'frd 3D 24
Winfield Dr. BD4: B'frd 5G 45
Wingate Av. BD22: Keigh 5B 6
Wingate Way BD22: Keigh 5B 6
Wingfield Ct. BD16: Bgly 1G 15
Wingfield Mt. BD3: B'frd 1D 36
Wingfield St. BD3: B'frd 1D 36
Winnard Row BD5: B'frd 1B 44
Winrose Cl. BD12: B'frd 1G 51
Winscar Av. BD6: B'frd 2A 42
Winslow Rd. BD10: B'frd 3G 29
Winston Ter. BD7: B'frd 4E 35
Winterburn Hill HX2: Hal 1C 54
Winterburn La. HX2: Hal 6C 46
Winterburn St. BD21: Keigh 3E 7
Winter Ct. BD15: B'frd 4G 25
Winter Hill HX3: Hal 4G 57
Winterneb HX2: Hal 2A 54
Winter St. HX1: Hal 2H 55
Winterton Dr. BD12: B'frd 6G 43
Winton Grn. BD6: B'frd 5F 43
Winton Ho. *BD5: B'frd 5H 35*
(off Hutson St.)
Winton Mill HX6: Hal 3E 55
Wistons La. HX5: Ell 2G 61
(Elland Riorges Link)
HX5: Ell 1G 61
(Old Power Way)
WITCHFIELD 5B 42
Witchfield Ct. *HX3: Hal 5B 42*
(off Shelf Moor Rd.)
Witchfield Grange
HX3: Hal 5A 42
Witchfield Hill HX3: Hal 5B 42
Withens Hill Cft. HX2: Hal 4F 39
Withens New Rd. HX2: Hal 1B 38
(not continuous)
Withens Rd. HX2: Hal 1B 38
Withinfield Ct. HX3: Hal 3G 57
Within Flds. HX3: Hal 3G 57
Withins Cl. BD5: B'frd 1F 43
Woburn Ho. *BD5: B'frd 5H 35*
(off Park La.)
Woburn Ter. BD14: B'frd 5H 33
Wold Cl. BD13: B'frd 3D 32
Wolseley St. BD14: B'frd 4A 34
Wolston Cl. BD4: B'frd 1G 45
Womersley St. HX1: Hal 6H 47
Woodale Av. BD9: B'frd 4B 26
Woodbine Gro.
BD10: B'frd 6D 18
Woodbine St.
BD3: B'frd 2C 36 (3G 5)
HX1: Hal 2A 56
Woodbine Ter. BD10: B'frd 6D 18
HX1: Hal 2A 56
(off Woodbine St.)
Wood Bottom La.
HD6: Brigh 2B 58
Woodbrook Av. HX2: Hal 6E 39
Woodbrook Cl. HX2: Hal 6E 39
Woodbrook Pl. HX2: Hal 6E 39
Woodbrook Rd. HX2: Hal 6E 39
Wood Cl. BD17: Bail 3F 17
Woodcot Av. BD17: Bail 3H 17
Wood Cft. HD6: Brigh 6D 58
HX6: Hal 4A 54
WOODEND 6H 17
Wood End Cl. HX3: Hal 4B 56
Woodend Ct. BD5: B'frd 1B 44
Wood End Cres.
BD18: Ship 5H 17
Woodfield Av. HX4: Hal 2B 60
Woodfield Cl. BD10: B'frd 5E 19
Woodfield Dr. HX4: Hal 3B 60
Woodfield Rd. BD13: B'frd 6G 13
Woodford Av. HX3: Hal 3D 56
Woodford Cl. BD15: B'frd 1G 33
Woodgarth Gdns.
BD4: B'frd 6H 37
WOODHALL 5H 29
Woodhall Av. BD3: B'frd 6G 29
Woodhall Cres. HX3: Hal 4A 56
WOODHALL HILLS 4H 29
Woodhall Hills LS28: Pud 4H 29
Woodhall La. LS28: Pud 4H 29
Woodhall Pl. BD3: B'frd 6G 29
Woodhall Retail Cen., The
BD3: B'frd 6G 29
Woodhall Rd. BD3: B'frd 1G 37
BD3: Pud 6G 29
LS28: Pud 3H 29
Woodhall Ter. BD3: B'frd 6G 29
Woodhall Vw. BD3: B'frd 6H 29
Woodhead Rd. BD7: B'frd 4F 35
Woodhead St. BD19: Cleck 6G 53
HX2: Hal 5G 47
Woodhill Ri. BD10: B'frd 5G 19
WOODHOUSE
Brighouse 6G 59
Keighley 6E 7
Woodhouse BD16: Bgly 3G 15
Woodhouse Av. BD21: Keigh 6E 7
Woodhouse Cl. BD21: Keigh 6E 7
Woodhouse Dr. BD21: Keigh 6E 7
Woodhouse Gdns.
HD6: Brigh 6G 59
Woodhouse Gro.
BD15: B'frd 3G 25
BD21: Keigh 6E 7
Woodhouse La. HD6: Brigh 6G 59
HX3: Hal 4A 56
Woodhouse Rd.
BD21: Keigh 6E 7
Woodhouse Ter. BD6: B'frd 3A 44
Woodhouse Wlk.
BD21: Keigh 6E 7
Woodhouse Way
BD21: Keigh 6E 7
Woodkirk Gro. BD12: B'frd 4G 51
Woodland Cl. BD9: B'frd 3A 26
Woodland Cres. BD9: B'frd 3H 25
Woodland Dr. HD6: Brigh 4D 58
HX2: Hal 2F 55
Woodland Gro. BD9: B'frd 2A 26
Woodland Ho. *BD10: B'frd 6E 19*
(off Garsdale Av.)
Woodlands BD12: B'frd 6C 44
BD17: Bail 1A 18
BD22: Keigh 3G 11
HX6: Hal 5B 54
Woodlands Av. BD13: B'frd 2H 41
BD19: Cleck 4H 53
HX3: Hal 4C 48
Woodlands Cl. BD10: Pud 4H 19
Woodlands Ct. BD8: B'frd 2A 4
BD16: Bgly 6E 9
Woodlands Cres.
BD19: Cleck 4H 53
Woodlands Dr. BD10: Pud 4H 19
BD19: Cleck 4H 53
LS19: Yead 3H 19
Woodlands Gro.
BD13: B'frd 2G 41
BD16: Bgly 6H 15
BD17: Bail 3D 16
HX3: Hal 4C 48
Woodlands Mt. HX3: Hal 3C 48
(not continuous)
Woodlands Pk. BD19: B'frd 2D 52
Woodland Sq. HD6: Brigh 6G 59
Woodlands Ri. BD22: Haw 1G 21
Woodlands Rd. BD8: B'frd 1E 35
BD13: B'frd 2G 41
BD16: Bgly 1A 16
HX3: Hal 4C 48
HX5: Hal 1F 61
Woodlands St. BD8: B'frd 1G 35
Woodlands Ter. BD8: B'frd 6E 27
BD12: B'frd 6D 44
Woodlands Vw. *HX3: Hal 4C 48*
(off Range St.)
Woodland Ter. HX3: Hal 4C 48
Wood La. BD2: B'frd 3A 28
(not continuous)
BD16: Bgly 4F 9
HD6: Hal 5B 58
HX2: Hal 4F 47
HX3: Hal 4H 49
(Bird Holme La.)
HX3: Hal 4H 57
(Dark La.)
HX6: Hal 4A 54
Woodlark Cl. BD6: B'frd 2B 42
Woodleigh Av. BD5: B'frd 2A 44
Woodlesford HX2: Hal 4E 47
Woodlesford Cres.
HX2: Hal 3D 46
Woodman Av. HX5: Ell 4F 61
Woodman Ct. BD6: B'frd 5C 42
Woodman Works HX5: Ell 4F 61
Wood Mt. HX2: Hal 3H 55

Wood Nook HX6: Hal 6C **54**
Wood Nook La. HX6: Hal 2E **55**
Woodpecker Cl.
BD15: B'frd 2H **33**
Wood Pl. BD8: B'frd . . .1G **35** (1A **4**)
BD9: B'frd 3G **27**
Wood Rd. BD5: B'frd 5A **36**
BD9: B'frd 3G **27**
Woodrow Dr. BD12: B'frd 5A **44**
Woodroyd HX2: Hal 2B **54**
Woodroyd Av. BD5: B'frd 1B **44**
Woodroyd Cres. HX6: Hal 2C **54**
Woodroyd Dr. HX3: Hal 3H **47**
Woodroyd Gdns. HX2: Hal 2B **54**
Woodroyd Rd. BD5: B'frd 6A **36**
(not continuous)
Woodroyd Ter. BD5: B'frd 1B **44**
WOODSIDE
Bradford 4E 43
Halifax 5C 48 (1B 62)
Woodside BD18: Ship 5H **17**
BD20: Keigh 2C **6**
Woodside Av. BD16: Bgly 6F **15**
BD18: Ship 5C **16**
Woodside Ct. BD13: B'frd 1F **23**
Woodside Cres.
BD16: Bgly 6F **15**
HX3: Hal 4B **48** (1A **62**)
Woodside Dr. BD16: Bgly 6F **15**
Woodside Gro. HX3: Hal 4C **48**
HX4: Hal 3C **60**
Woodside Mt.
HX3: Hal 5B **48** (1A **62**)
Woodside Pl.
HX3: Hal 4B **48** (1A **62**)
Woodside Rd. BD12: B'frd . . .2G **51**
HX3: Hal 5B **48** (1A **62**)
Woodside Ter. HX3: Hal 4C **48**
HX4: Hal 3D **60**
Woodside Vw. BD16: Bgly 6F **15**
HX3: Hal 4B **48** (1A **62**)
HX4: Hal 3D ***60***
(off Woodside Ter.)
Woodsley Rd. BD10: B'frd 1C **28**
Woodstock Wlk. *BD5: B'frd . . .4A* ***36***
(off Park Rd.)
Wood St. BD8: B'frd . . .1G **35** (1A **4**)
BD12: B'frd 5H **43**
BD15: B'frd 6A **26**
BD16: Bgly 5E **9**
BD17: Bail 4G **17**
BD19: Cleck 6E **53**
BD22: Haw 1G **21**
HD6: Brigh 5F **59**
HX5: Ell 3G **61**
Woodthorpe BD13: B'frd 1F **31**
Wood Top BD18: Ship 5H **17**
Woodtop HD6: Brigh 2C **58**
Woodvale Cl. BD4: B'frd 4G **37**
Woodvale Cres.
BD16: Bgly 6G **9**
Woodvale Gro. BD7: B'frd 4C **34**
Woodvale Office Pk.
HD6: Brigh 3F **59**
Woodvale Rd. HD6: Brigh 4F **59**
Woodvale Way BD7: B'frd 4C **34**
Wood Vw. BD8: B'frd 4H **27**
BD12: B'frd 1C **52**
BD17: Bail 4E **17**
HX3: Hal 3A **56**
Woodview BD13: B'frd 4E **23**
BD22: Keigh 1A **12**
Woodview Av. BD17: Bail 1B **18**
Wood Vw. Dr. BD2: B'frd 5E **29**
Wood Vw. Gro. HD6: Brigh . . .3D **58**
Woodview Rd.
BD22: Keigh 1B **12**
Woodview Ter. BD8: B'frd 4H **27**
BD21: Keigh 1D ***12***
(off Haincliffe Pl.)
Woodville Gro. BD22: Haw . . .5B **12**
Woodville Pl. BD9: B'frd 3D **26**
Woodville Rd. BD20: Keigh 3D **6**
Woodville St. BD18: Ship 5H **17**
HX3: Hal 4A **48**
Woodville Ter. BD5: B'frd 4H **35**
BD18: Ship 5H **17**
BD22: Haw 5B ***12***
(off Vernon St.)
Woodway BD16: Bgly 6F **15**
Woodworth Gro.
BD21: Keigh 2D **12**
Woolcomb Ct. BD9: B'frd 5F **27**
Wool Exchange, The
BD1: B'frd 4D ***4***
(off Market St.)
Wool Ga. BD16: Bgly 6H **15**
Wooller Rd. BD12: B'frd 6H **43**
Woolpack HX1: Hal . . .6C **48** (3C **62**)
(not continuous)
Woolrow La. HD6: Brigh 1G **59**
Woolshops
HX1: Hal 6C **48** (4C **62**)
Wootton St. BD5: B'frd 5A **36**
Worcester Pl. BD4: B'frd 5C **36**
Worden Gro. BD7: B'frd 5C **34**
Wordsworth Way
BD16: Bgly 6G **9**
Workhouse La. HX2: Hal 6C **46**
HX4: Hal 3D **60**
(not continuous)
Workouts Health & Fitness Cen.
. . . . .5C 6
(off Oakworth Rd.)
Wormald Lea *BD4: B'frd 6G* ***37***
(off Stirling Cres.)
Worsnop Bldgs.
BD12: B'frd 1G **51**
Worsnop St. BD12: B'frd 5H **43**
Worstead Rd. BD22: Haw 4B **12**
Worth Av. BD21: Keigh 2G **7**
Worth Bri. Rd. BD21: Keigh . . .4G **7**
Worthing Head Cl.
BD12: B'frd 2H **51**
Worthing Head Rd.
BD12: B'frd 2G **51**
Worthing St. BD12: B'frd 2H **51**
Worthington Ct. BD8: B'frd 2A **4**
Worthington St.
BD8: B'frd 1G **35** (2A **4**)
Worth Valley Vw.
BD22: Keigh 3H **11**
Worth Vw. BD22: Keigh 2A **12**
WORTH VILLAGE 3G 7
Worthville Cl. BD21: Keigh 6E **7**
Worth Way BD21: Keigh 5E **7**
Wortley St. BD16: Bgly 2H **15**
Wren Av. BD7: B'frd 4C **34**
Wren St. BD21: Keigh 3E **7**
BD22: Haw 6H **11**
Wright Av. BD22: Keigh 2H **11**
Wright St. BD22: Keigh 3H **11**
Wrigley HX2: Hal 5G **39**
Wrigley Av. BD4: B'frd 2D **44**
Wrigley Hill HX2: Hal 6G **39**
Wroe Cres. BD12: B'frd 2G **51**
Wroe Pl. BD12: B'frd 2G **51**
Wroe Ter. BD12: B'frd 2G **51**
WROSE 1H 27
Wrose Av. BD2: B'frd 2C **28**
BD18: Ship 1H **27**
Wrose Brow Rd.
BD18: Ship 5H **17**
Wrosecliffe Gro.
BD10: B'frd 5B **18**
Wrose Dr. BD18: Ship 1H **27**
Wrose Gro. BD2: B'frd 1B **28**
BD18: Ship 1H **27**
Wrose Hill Pl. BD2: B'frd 2H **27**
Wrose Mt. BD18: Ship 1A **28**
Wrose Rd. BD2: B'frd 1H **27**
BD18: Ship 1H **27**
Wrose Vw. BD17: Bail 1G **17**
BD18: Ship 1H **27**
Wycliffe Gdns. BD18: Ship . . .5E **17**
Wycliffe Rd. BD18: Ship 5E **17**
Wycoller Rd. BD12: B'frd 1G **51**
Wycombe Grn. BD4: B'frd 6G **37**
WYKE 2G 51
Wyke Bottoms BD12: B'frd . . .1B **52**
WYKE COMMON 3H 51
Wyke Cres. BD12: B'frd 3H **51**
Wyke La. BD12: B'frd 3G **51**
Wykelea Cl. BD12: B'frd 2H **51**
Wyke Old La. HD6: Brigh 6F **51**
Wyncroft Ri. BD18: Ship 2H **27**
Wyndham Av. BD2: B'frd 4B **28**
Wyndy Ridge BD13: B'frd 2C **32**
Wynford Way BD12: B'frd 3A **44**
Wynne St.
BD1: B'frd 1H **35** (2A **4**)
Wyre Cl. BD6: B'frd 2C **42**
Wyvern Cl. BD7: B'frd 4D **34**
Wyvern Pl. HX2: Hal 5G **47**
Wyvern Ter. HX2: Hal 5G **47**

Y

Yarborough Cft. HX3: Hal 1G **49**
Yardley Way BD12: B'frd 5A **44**
Yarwood Gro. BD7: B'frd 6C **34**
Yateholm Dr. BD6: B'frd 2A **42**
Yate La. BD22: Oxen 5G **21**
Yates Flat BD18: Ship 1H **27**
Yeadon Dr. HX3: Hal 3G **57**
Ye Farre Cl. HD6: Brigh 3E **59**
Yeoman Ct. BD6: B'frd 1A **42**
Yewdall Way BD10: B'frd 1E **29**
Yew Pk. HD6: Brigh 2C **58**
YEWS GREEN 6E 33
Yew Tree Av. BD8: B'frd 6B **26**
Yew Tree Cl. BD18: Ship 1H **27**
Yew Tree Cres. BD8: B'frd 6C **26**
Yew Tree Gro. BD8: B'frd 6C **26**
Yew Tree La. BD15: B'frd 1D **32**
Yew Tree Rd. HD2: Hud 6G **61**
HD3: Hud 6G **61**
Yew Trees HX3: Hal 3G **57**
Yew Trees Av. HX3: Hal 2G **49**
York Cres. BD16: Bgly 3G **15**
York Ho. BD10: B'frd 6E **19**
(Billing Vw.)
BD10: B'frd 6E ***19***
(off Fairhaven Grn.)
HX5: Ell 2F ***61***
(off Gog Hill)
HX6: Hal 3E ***55***
(off Beech Rd.)
York Pl. BD19: Cleck 5F **53**
Yorkshire Academy of Cricket, The
. . . . .5G 35
YORKSHIRE CLINIC, THE 6A 16
Yorkshire Dr. BD5: B'frd 2C **44**
Yorkshire Way BD7: B'frd 6F **35**
York St. BD8: B'frd 2C **34**
BD13: B'frd 2D **40**
BD16: Bgly 3G **15**
HD6: Brigh 6E **59**
(Capel St.)
HD6: Brigh 6E ***59***
(off Thomas St.)
HX1: Hal 1B **56** (5A **62**)
York Ter. HX3: Hal 4B **48**
Young St. BD8: B'frd 1D **34**
Young St. Ind. Est.
BD8: B'frd 1D **34**

Z

Zealand St. BD4: B'frd 5F **37**